The LITERATURE *of* American Legal History

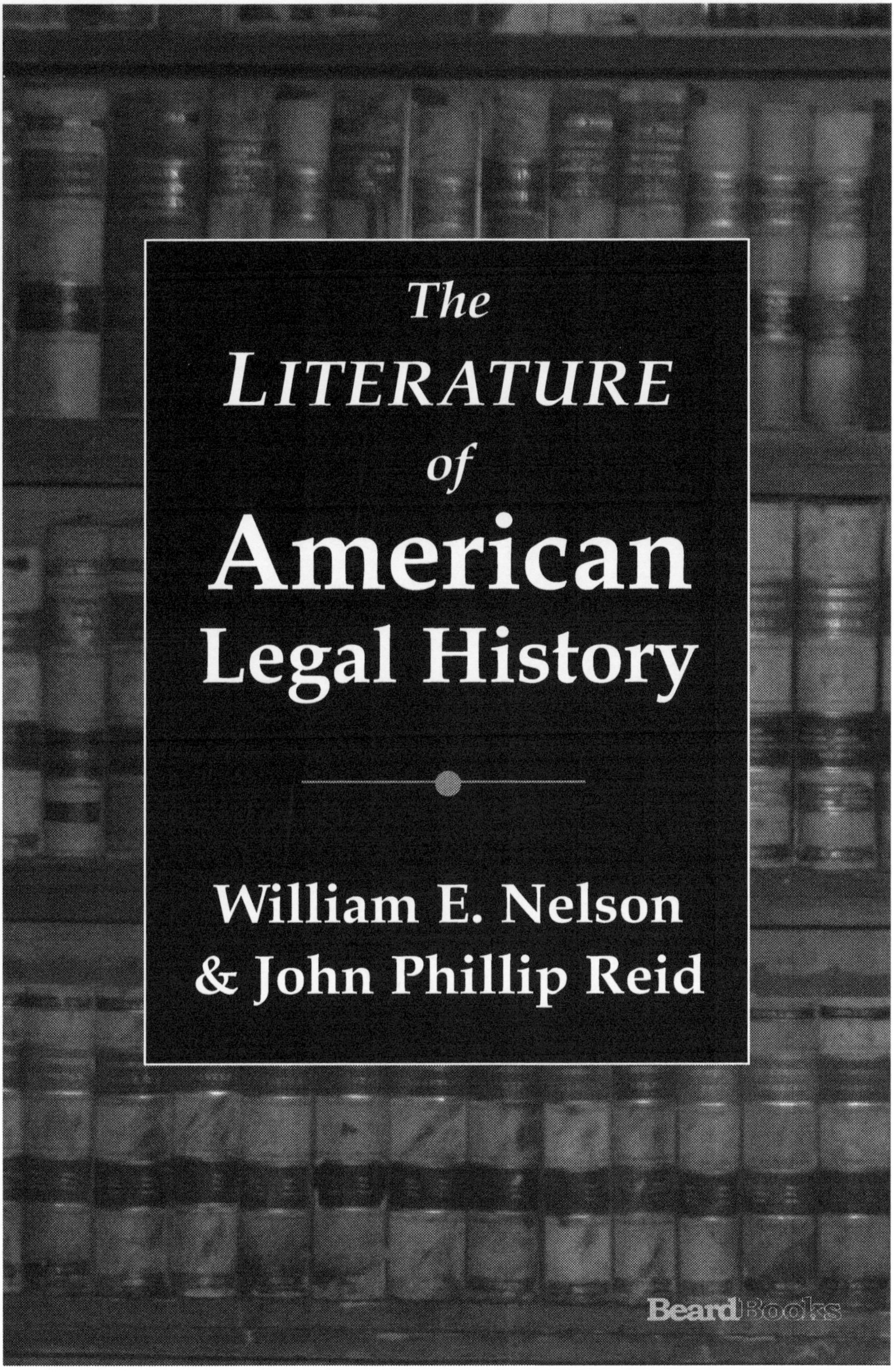

The LITERATURE of American Legal History

William E. Nelson
& John Phillip Reid

BeardBooks

Originally published by Oceana Publications, Inc.
Reprinted 2006 by Beard Books, Washington, D.C.

ISBN - 13: 978-1-58798-280-3
ISBN - 10: 1-58798-280-3

Printed in the United States of America

To George Lee Haskins and
James Willard Hurst,
Whose efforts created the discipline
of American legal history.

TABLE OF CONTENTS

FOREWORD

Norman Redlich*

Since 1942 New York University School of Law has published the *Annual Survey of American Law.* A publication for lawyers, the *Annual Survey* reports on events during the year in articles on a variety of legal categories such as "conflict of law," "constitutional law," "civil rights," "labor law," "contracts," "torts," and others covering all areas of American law. Beginning with the second volume, the *Annual Survey* has included articles on legal history. These *Annual Survey* volumes reflect the importance of legal history in the academic life of our Law School, and the role of Professors John Phillip Reid and William E. Nelson in the development of our legal history program.

The article for 1962 was the first assigned to Professor Reid, then commencing his career as a legal historian on the New York University School of Law faculty. He continued to write the legal-history article until 1966 when he was joined by William E. Nelson, then a member of the New York Bar, and now professor of law in New York University. The subject that year was divided into two articles, "Legal History" and "Constitutional History." Mr. Nelson was responsible for the articles in 1967 and 1968. The article for 1969/70 was co-authored, and from then until 1980, "Legal History" in the *Annual Survey of American Law* has been written by Professor Nelson.

This book reprints the two decades of *Annual Survey* "Legal History" articles by Reid and Nelson. In addition, Professor Nelson has contributed three new pieces, an introductory survey of the legal-and constitutional-history literature prior to 1962, a survey of the literature published between 1980 and 1984, and a concluding essay that discusses current standards of legal-history scholarship.

The *Annual Survey* articles reprinted in this book have not been altered. Except for bracketed updates in the footnotes, they appear as originally published. The only significant change is that the legal method of citation has been adapted to conform more closely to that employed by historical journals. The purpose of the *Annual Survey* is to report on

*Norman Redlich is Dean and Judge Edward Weinfeld Professor of Law, New York University School of Law.

the leading events in law during the survey year. The "Legal History" articles adhere to the *Annual Survey's* format. They are surveys of the year's legal-history literature and do not attempt to be a bibliography of every publication concerned with legal or constitutional history.

There is one change in the content of the articles that deserves notice. The *Annual Survey* articles of the 1940's and 1950's reported on English legal history as well as American. It is not without interest that the first article reprinted in this book (1962) laments the paucity of legal-history scholarship. Yet it is the last *Survey* year to contain a section reporting on developments in English legal history. In 1963 there was enough material published to devote that year's article exclusively to American legal and constitutional history. This change in content may be indicative of the remarkable growth in American legal-history literature that occurred during the two decades covered by the *Survey* articles reprinted in this book. That growth owed much to the work of George Lee Haskins and James Willard Hurst. It is not only that during these decades Professor Haskins of the University of Pennsylvania wrote the leading studies in colonial legal history, and Professor Hurst of the University of Wisconsin dominated nineteenth-century legal-history scholarship. Even more significant is the inspiration that they have provided for young men and woman to follow in their footsteps. It is fitting that this volume is dedicated to them. For American legal history these two decades were the decades of George Haskins and Willard Hurst.

PREFACE

This book is designed to collect and supplement articles surveying the literature of American legal history which its two authors have published since 1962 in the *Annual Survey of American Law*. We hope that this supplement to the *Annual Survey,* with its index, can serve as a guide to major legal history literature both for subscribers and for others, for whom it is being made available as a separate volume.

Over the years, many people assisted us with the book. We wish to thank the publishers who provided review copies of books mentioned in the following pages, the librarians who helped search for other material, and the various faculty colleagues and student editors who worked on our draft articles. As we assembled the articles into this book, we were assisted by Richard B. Bernstein, who cite-checked the footnotes, and by Barbara W. Kern and Thomas Mackey, who helped with the proofreading. We are especially indebted to Dean Norman Redlich who, in addition to his usual generous support for legal history at New York University School of Law, has provided a grant to fund distribution of a limited number of copies to individual legal historians.

Chapters Two through Sixteen originally appeared as articles in the *Annual Survey* between 1962 and 1985 and are reprinted with the permission of the *Annual Survey*. Portions of Chapters One and Seventeen were originally published under the title, "Standards of Criticism," in 60 *Texas L. Rev.* 477 (1982), copyright © by the *Texas Law Review* and reprinted by permission.

Finally we wish to express our gratitude to the Filomen D'Agostino Greenberg and Max E. Greenberg Faculty Research Fund at the Law School for the research support it has provided over the years for the preparation both of the original articles and of the book as a whole.

WEN

New York JPR

May, 1985

Chapter One

LEGAL HISTORY BEFORE THE 1960s

William E. Nelson

Today it would be presumptuous to attempt to define the boundaries of the discipline of legal history or to specify the sorts of scholarship upon which practitioners within the field should work. Those who now label themselves legal historians share no consensus about what it means to labor as an historian of American law. There was, however, a time —perhaps little more than two decades ago — when widely accepted traditions existed among those who assumed the label of legal historian concerning the function of legal history scholarship and the criteria by which to evaluate work within the field.

A. *The Early Professional Tradition*

The impetus underlying the traditions existing prior to the 1960s was, at bottom, a legal professional one. "Lawyers," observed Max Radin, were "necessarily historians," for "they derive[d] their law from precedent, which is pure history, and they . . . [sought] to interpret statutes by considering the conditions under which the statute arose and was framed, which is also pure history." Radin accordingly urged lawyers to take "their obligations as historians seriously and consider carefully their legal ideas in the historical setting in which they were developed." He warned that if lawyers "do not take this task seriously, they will not cease to be historians. They merely will be bad historians."[1]

In view of the fact that "history" had such "direct and specific utility" within the common law system, research in legal sources from the past was commonly thought to have "possible practical uses." As Julius Goebel, Jr., wrote with his usual precision, "Traditionally it is by an inquiry into what the law was or has been that the solution of present perplexities is sought."[2] "'History,'" observed Francis S. Philbrick, "'sets us free and enables us to make up our mind dispassionately'"; "[i]n fact,

---

[1] Max Radin, *The Law and You* (1950), quoted in Frank W. Grinnell, "The Legal History of Massachusetts 1620-1953," 37 *Mass. L.Q.* 1, 5-6 (1953).

[2] Julius Goebel, Jr. and T. Raymond Naughton, *Law Enforcement in Colonial New York: A Study in Criminal Procedure (1664-1776),* at xiii, xxxiii (1944).

it seem[ed] likely that it is *only* with reference to a past time . . . that we can hope to *agree* . . . in approving or disapproving the value-judgments . . . embodied in the law."[3] Roscoe Pound likewise believed that legal history was a practical discipline in which researchers could find "principles tried by experience" to "give stability to the legal order" and "principles of legal growth" to "help us chart the orbit of legal change."[4] Historians, Pound added, could also learn "of the origin and shaping of the legal materials which we are to reshape to the ends of today and tomorrow."[5] The understanding of the profession, in short, was that legal historians undertook research in order to obtain data that would provide answers to or at least insight into legal questions that had or were likely to come before the courts.

This understanding made it possible, among other things, to differentiate the work of legal historians from that of historians studying the constitutional structure or policy-making processes of the nation's governmental system. The professional character of legal historical research rested upon a quite traditional view of the legal process as different from the political process. Determinations of whether government should subsidize industry through such a device as a protective tariff or whether power to regulate a particular industry should be lodged in Congress or the state legislatures were understood to depend ultimately upon the will of those possessing political power. Questions, on the other hand, such as whether the English Statute of Frauds of 1676 had been received by 1775 as part of the law of colonial New York were thought to depend upon scholarly research and analysis of the records and practices of the past.[6]

The abiding faith, then, of early legal historians was that modern law should not respond directly and immediately to the will of those holding political power. Legal historians of the first half of the twentieth century believed that the scholarly research in which they engaged would uncover facts that would serve to restrain judges from simplistically transforming their personal value preferences into law. Early legal historians never believed, however, in the total autonomy of law from political, social and economic forces: they knew that the law had responded to such forces in the past and that it would respond to them again in the future. Consider, for example, the writings of Joseph H. Beale, a leading law professor and a not insubstantial legal historian during the first third of the twentieth

---

[3] Francis S. Philbrick, "Possibilities of American Legal History," 27 *Law Lib. J.* 191, 203, 205 (1934).

[4] Roscoe Pound, "New Possibilities of Old Materials of American Legal History," 40 *W. Va. L.Q.* 205, 206 (1934).

[5] Id. at 206.

[6] See *Beers v. Hotchkiss*, 256 N.Y. 41 (1931).

century. Beale, who was one of the most extreme legal formalists of his generation, was the principal draftsman of the First Restatement of Conflicts of Law — a Restatement that advocated judicial resolution of conflicts questions in accordance with principles unrelated to the actual social interests at stake in multistate litigation.[7] He believed that people could "learn from scientific observation and from historical discovery" and felt himself to be "living in an age of scientific scholarship" that had "at last made possible the intelligent statement of the principles of law."[8] At the same time, however, Beale wrote of legal history as "the social calculus of law"[9] and spoke approvingly of "the emergence of a distinctly sociological jurisprudence in the decisions of the Supreme Court."[10] He argued that judges should in reaching decisions take account of the fact "that society requires the final distribution of all costs, including those of accidents, so that they will come into the cost of production or of use and be shared among the ultimate consumers."[11] He continued:[12]

> Occupational injury is a necessary part of industry; and the cost of insuring against such injury is as much part of the cost of a yard of cloth as the cost of the labor of the weaver or of the night watchman, and must be reflected in the price — although this enhancement of price must slightly lower the standard of living of everybody. This is better than greatly lowering the standard of the injured party. In the other case, part of the cost of running an automobile is the danger of injuring someone by it; the owner of an automobile should therefore insure against such injury, even though the cost of such insurance may require him to relinquish the pleasure he would have gained from running his car. It is unjust and anti-social that he should gain that pleasure at the expense of uncompensated injury to his fellow man.

On another occasion, Beale maintained that "the real purpose of a study of legal history" was to "examine the progress of law in each state" and to identify "change" in the law "caused by . . . social, economic and political changes."[13]

---

[7] See Robert A. Leflar, *The Law of Conflict of Laws* 2-5 (1959).

[8] Joseph H. Beale, "The Development of Jurisprudence during the Nineteenth Century," in 1 Association of American Law Schools ed., *Select Essays in Anglo-American Legal History* 558, 572-73 (1907).

[9] Joseph H. Beale, "Social Justice and Business Costs — A Study in the Legal History of Today," 49 *Harv. L. Rev.* 593, 609 (1936).

[10] Id. at 608.

[11] Ibid.

[12] Ibid.

[13] Joseph H. Beale, "The Study of American Legal History," 39 *W. Va. L. Rev.* 95, 99 (1933).

Some readers no doubt will find a curious tension in Beale's scholarship, which sought to control the capacity of judges to respond to political, economic and social forces while at the same time describing how law had developed in the past in response to those forces. This tension can also be found in the writing of other scholars of Beale's time. For example, Simeon E. Baldwin, the arch-formalist judge and law professor who believed law to be a "science which rests on reason" also thought that law "must reflect the political and economic views of the State for which it speaks" and "must answer the needs of the people who are subject to it."[14] Similarly, in the classic article, "King's Law and Local Custom in Seventeenth Century New England,"[15] which was written to correct that "fallacy" commonly held by judges "that the sum of the law of England" in force in the United States pursuant to reception statutes was "the law of the King's Courts — the common law,"[16] Julius Goebel rested his conclusion that local custom rather than common law was the basis of the Plymouth Colony's legal system on the premise that the colonists availed themselves of their "cultural heritage whether this ha[d] to do with religion, with law, or with methods of farming" — a premise whose validity had been established "by lay historians in fields other than the law."[17] Like Beale and Baldwin, Goebel was writing to persuade judges to ground their decisions on historically documented facts while simultaneously recognizing that law had developed in the past in response to more basic cultural forces.

The tension between a scholarly program of encouraging judges to make reason the basis of adjudication and a scholarly awareness that the common law had often grown in response to deeper political, economic and social forces was most acute in the work of Roscoe Pound. Pound spoke often of "the common legal heritage of English-speaking peoples,"[18] at the root of which he perceived "a deep-seated urge in human nature not to be subject to the arbitrary will of a fellow man."[19] He had "faith that this tradition will have continued strength to . . . secure to the English-speaking world the liberty which it has always claimed as its birthright,"[20] and he maintained that law professors and law schools,

---

[14] Simeon E. Baldwin, "History of the Law of Private Corporations in the Colonies and States," in 3 Association of American Law Schools ed., *supra* note 8, at 236, 250-51.

[15] 31 *Col. L. Rev.* 416 (1931).

[16] Ibid.

[17] Id. at 418.

[18] Roscoe Pound, *The Formative Era of American Law* 83 (1938).

[19] Roscoe Pound, "The Development of American Law and its Deviation from English Law," 67 *L.Q.R.* 49, 66 (1951).

[20] Ibid.

through teaching and scholarship, did much to uphold the common law's heritage and traditions against the "many forces of disintegration."[21] Like Beale, Baldwin and Goebel, Pound hoped that his historical researches would limit the capacity of judges to substitute their will for what was truly law. But, at the same time, he was aware that "[e]conomic and political conditions of time and place"[22] had altered the course of the common law's development — that judges in the past had permitted considerations other than what was truly law to influence their decisions.

To show how prevalent the tension I have been describing was in early writing in the field of legal history I must turn to yet one more author. Like Pound, this eminent legal historian "believe[d] that there are opportunities to apply informed, humane reason to influence the course of events." He continued that "[t]he hope of a decent and reasonably secure community rests partly in the chance that there will be in key positions at the right moment a leadership based on values for which the university stands; and partly in the preparation in the state of a body of intelligent opinion ready and capable of supporting that leadership against unreason." He thought "this carrie[d] a particular challenge to legal education" and to legal history. In particular, he wrote that "the call for directed intelligence in community affairs" warranted the planning of "a research program in 'legal history.'"[23] Also like Roscoe Pound, this most eminent of American legal historians — J. Willard Hurst — recognized that the "pressure of politics, the strands of class, religious, racial and national attitudes," and "the clash of interests" often impacted upon the course of the law.[24]

In short, a long line of American legal historians — the legal formalists Simeon E. Baldwin and Joseph H. Beale, the legal realist Julius Goebel, the sociological jurisprude Roscoe Pound, and today's dean of legal historians Willard Hurst — all wrote legal history in the hope that the facts they discovered and the intelligence with which they assembled those facts would limit the effect on the law of those basic political, economic and social forces that had always shaped the law in the past. What I find characteristic of legal history scholarship prior to the 1960s is not a belief in the autonomy of law or any set of specially conservative social attitudes on the part of scholars in the field. Rather the quality that linked together the work of the diverse scholars who called themselves historians of American law was a faith that trained

---

[21] Roscoe Pound, *supra* note 18, at 83.

[22] Ibid.

[23] Willard Hurst, "Legal History: A Research Program," [1942] *Wis. L. Rev.* 323 (1942).

[24] J. Willard Hurst, *The Growth of American Law: The Law Makers* 266 (1950).

intelligence could affect the course of legal development — a faith that was sometimes explicitly and always at least implicitly in tension with the awareness that deeper political, social and economic forces ultimately determined the law's direction. Most legal history prior to the 1960s — indeed, I suspect, most legal scholarship prior to that decade — was at the same time both realist and formalist in character, recognizing the power of elemental human drives over the law and yet seeking to control those drives by recourse to higher ideals elaborated by the legal profession.

Some tension between a formalist appeal to ideals and a realist recognition of the force of elemental human drives is probably inherent in any effort by professional legal thinkers, historians or otherwise, to control those drives. Of course, the tension can be worked out in different ways. Roscoe Pound, for example, emphasized idealism at the expense of realism, writing that "[t]enacity of a taught legal tradition is much more significant in our legal history than the economic conditions of time and place."[25] Pound believed that professionally elaborated ideals rather than elemental human drives had determined and should continue to determine, as much as possible, the course of legal development. At the opposite pole, Willard Hurst argued that "group interest was" and by implication would continue to be "the most dynamic force that played on our law."[26] Hurst, unlike Pound, wanted legal history scholarship to illustrate the emptiness of received legal ideas, thereby relieving judges from the tyranny of those ideas and enabling courts to respond to genuine social needs. Hurst, of course, knew that ideas had force in the law, just as Pound knew that they were not the only force affecting the law's shape. Thus, despite their different emphases, the scholarly researches of Hurst and Pound were tied together by their common effort to develop a synthesis that would explain how legal ideas and elemental human drives contributed jointly to the law's development. Indeed, nearly every other legal historian who wrote prior to the 1960s joined in this effort to elaborate an historical synthesis of the formalist and realist impulses — a synthesis that historians and other scholars perceived would facilitate control of the course of legal change in the future.

The one book prior to the 1960s that surveyed the whole field of American legal history reflected this presentist, professional orientation. Francis R. Aumann's *The Changing American Legal System: Some Selected Phases*[27] in large part simply and quite usefully summarized the

---

[25] Roscoe Pound, *supra* note 18, at 82.

[26] J. Willard Hurst, *supra* note 24, at 439.

[27] Francis R. Aumann, *The Changing American Legal System: Some Selected Phases* (1940).

scholarship in the field that was extant in 1940. But the theme that was central to pre-1960s legal history also surfaced in *The Changing American Legal System* as Aumann in his concluding chapter surveyed the jurisprudential literature of the 1930's debating whether legal professionals should regard the preservation of traditional legal principles and values or the adjustment of law to changing social conditions as their primary professional task.

B. *The Primary Issue in Early Research: The Reception of the Common Law*

Most legal history scholarship prior to the 1960s did not, of course, attempt to synthesize knowledge in the entire field or analyze theoretically the issues that such a synthesis should address. Most legal historians, then as now, engaged in narrow research leading to the publication of scholarly articles and monographs. But even as they addressed narrower topics, the professional orientation of most scholars in the discipline pointed toward the investigation and analysis of subjects of concern to their contemporaries in the law.

The issue of when the common law of England was received as the basis of American law was an important question facing courts in several states in the first half of the twentieth century. The earliest important historical scholarship on the subject was Paul S. Reinsch's *English Common Law in the Early American Colonies.*[28] The central thesis of Reinsch's book was that the early American colonies "had a period of rude, untechnical popular law, followed, as lawyers became numerous and the study of law prominent, by the gradual reception of most of the rules of the English common law."[29] Even after the common law had been generally received, "still the marks of the old popular law remain[ed] strong," according to Reinsch, and indeed, Reinsch traced "most of the original departures in American jurisprudence . . . back to the earliest times."[30] One "general trait of early colonial law" that also appeared in later American law was "codification."[31] Another early trait was "informality in judicial proceedings."[32] Reinsch continues:[33]

> The original elements in the early colonial laws are great in number and import. They foreshadow and anticipate some of the most far-

---

28 (1899).
29 Id. at 8.
30 Id. at 9.
31 Id. at 53.
32 Id. at 54.
33 Id. at 55.

> reaching American law reforms. Pleading is simplified, and the intention is in many places expressed that it shall be possible for any man of ordinary intelligence to plead his own cause before the courts. This innovation supports the same conclusions that we have reached from the facts of the institution of popular courts and the absence of trained jurists. Evidence was in many colonies given in writing, or at least taken down by the clerk and made a part of the record in the action; a practice utterly abhorrent to common law ideas, not so to the popular mind to whom the evidence is the most important part of the case. Various modifications of the jury system have been noted, but in general this venerable and highly popular institution was finally adopted in the colonies in its English form at an early date. The period of prescription was in many of the colonies lowered to five or seven years, a change that was of course eminently consistent with the conditions of an infant colony on a new continent. Executions on land were permitted, and in many cases the fundamental distinction between real and personal property in the English law was obliterated or ignored. The laws of inheritance and of tenure were, as we have seen, very materially modified, very often leading to the adoption of a system totally unlike the common law at that period.

Other legal historians agreed with Reinsch that the process of reception was a gradual one and that much early colonial law survived the adoption of the common law. In *The Spirit of the Common Law,*[34] for instance, Roscoe Pound wrote that "the colonies began with all manner of experiments in administering justice without law and it was not till the middle of the eighteenth century that the setting up of a system of courts and the rise of a custom of studying law in England began to make for a general administration of justice according to English law."[35] "[A]s late as 1791," Pound continued, "the law was so completely at large in New York" — the state which Reinsch thought to have been the first to adopt the common law[36] — "that the genius of a Kent was needed to make the common law the law of that state."[37] Leon P. Lewis also agreed that the common law system came late to America, arguing that in Connecticut, which he thought to be "[t]he first state to establish a system of common law,"[38] the common law system was not fully in place until about 1800.[39]

---

[34] (1921).

[35] Id. at 115.

[36] Paul S. Reinsch, *supra* note 28, at 30.

[37] Roscoe Pound, *The Spirit of the Common Law* 116 (1912).

[38] Leon P. Lewis, "The Development of a Common Law System in Connecticut," 27 *Conn. B.J.* 419 (1953).

[39] See id. at 427.

The notion that early colonial law was rude, popular and untechnical — what became known as the frontier theory of American jurisprudence — was attacked by Julius Goebel, who with his usual sarcasm labelled it the "*pons asinorum* of American historiography."[40] Goebel agreed with Pound and Reinsch that the initial settlers of the colonies, particularly of the New England colonies, brought little of the law of the King's courts to America with them. "To suppose that they would introduce a system as complex and esoteric as that which prevailed in the King's Courts is as absurd as to expect that they would establish a religious system on the principles of the Anglican church."[41] But Goebel further argued that, while they abandoned the royal, common law, the early colonists did bring English law to America with them — namely the customary law that had been administered by the local institutions in England with which the early colonists had often had daily familiarity.[42]

Goebel also disagreed with Reinsch and especially with Pound when he argued that the common law replaced customary law as the basis of American jurisprudence not at the end but by the beginning of the eighteenth century. At least in New York, according to Goebel, reception of the common law began in 1683-84, when "an elected assembly enacted a new judicature law," "the whole procedural apparatus . . . [was] renovated, the practices and forms of the English central courts c[a]me into use," and "on all sides the magistrates and attorneys set about to cut a substantive law to fit what they had to use as due process."[43] Goebel concludes that "the forms and rules of Westminster Hall itself had secured a firm footing in the superior courts by the year 1691; and if it be conceded that our General Sessions must be compared not with the King's Bench but with English Quarter Sessions, and that reception can be tested by Dalton's manuals as well as by Coke's *Institutes*, the last of any reasonable doubt must vanish."[44]

Powerful reinforcement was lent to Goebel's thesis that the common law took root in the American colonies in the late seventeenth and early eighteenth centuries by Joseph H. Smith's monumental study of *Appeals to the Privy Council from the American Plantations.*[45] In a book that has greater enduring value, perhaps, than any other book in American legal history written prior to the 1960s, Smith traces the development and operation of the mechanisms by which the Privy Council, which had a

---

40 Julius Goebel, Jr., *supra* note 15, at 420.
41 Ibid.
42 Ibid.
43 Julius Goebel, Jr. and T. Raymond Naughton, *supra* note 2, at xxiii-xxiv.
44 Id. at 760.
45 (1950).

policy of requiring colonial adherence to the common law, heard judicial appeals from the American colonies. Smith shows that the Council's appellate processes were put into place in the late seventeenth century and were fully operable in the early eighteenth. These facts are important because they show when a royal policy of imposing the common law on the colonies was put into operation and further suggest that, unless that royal policy was a total failure, significant reception of the common law probably took place at about the time Goebel claimed it did.

Connected with the reception of the common law was the appearance in America of the ideal of the rule of law. Several early legal historians described how colonial Americans became committed to preservation of the "rights of men against the tyranny either of majorities or minorities"[46] and to the "effort to curb, by written law, the discretionary power of magistrates."[47] Some early writers argued that colonial legal systems operated "in accordance with the conception of legal justice that . . . [the colonists] had been born into, lived under and absorbed as part of their lives in England" even before the common law was received in America,[48] but Julius Goebel believed that the reception of the common law and the emergence of the ideal of the rule of law had been interconnected. According to Goebel, the history of reception was ultimately the history of that "freedom we have sought to protect by law." Goebel argued that lawyers of his generation could "not suffer the deeds of colonial lawyers and judges to sleep in death," since "the dry phrases in which . . . protections [of rights] are cast will succumb to the compulsion of logic unless their meaning as the distillation of past happening is kept clear." Nor could they "speak in generalities of reception" until they had first determined the "prosy particulars of practice."[49] It was in an effort to determine the particulars of criminal practice in colonial New York and thus to study how the reception of the common law in New York contributed to the protection of individual rights that Goebel undertook his massive study, *Law Enforcement in Colonial New York*.[50]

Other scholars studied the particulars of the common law's reception not by examining the legal history of the thirteen colonies, but by turning to the newer states of the West and South. William Wirt Blume, for

---

[46] R.A. Humphreys, "The Rule of Law and the American Revolution," 53 *L.Q.R.* 80, 98 (1937).

[47] Thorpe L. Wolford, "The Laws and Liberties of 1648: The First Code of Laws Enacted and Printed in English America," 28 *B.U.L. Rev.* 426, 430 (1948).

[48] Henry H. Townshend, "Judicial Administration in New Haven Colony before the Charter of 1662," 24 *Conn. B.J.* 210, 234 (1950).

[49] Julius Goebel, Jr., and T. Raymond Naughton, *supra* note 2, at xxxviii-xxxix.

[50] (1944).

example, looked at "Civil Procedure on the American Frontier"[51] and concluded, consistently with Goebel's view, that common law forms quickly came to dominate the legal system of the newly settled West. Blume wrote that "one will find little if anything to suggest that the law of the Northwest Territory . . . was a product of the frontier or that the spirit of the law was 'sensibly affected by the spirit of the pioneer.'" "To suggest that . . . [judges] felt free to decide cases according to their own notions of right and justice would be absurd." On the contrary, they felt bound by the Northwest Ordinance's "guarantee of judicial proceedings according to the course of the common law" and were primarily "concerned with the broad problem of adapting the law . . . to the needs of the new republic."[52] James M. Carson and Edward L. Markham, Jr., studying the legal history of Florida and Texas respectively, similarly found that the common law followed rapidly in the wake of American settlement and quickly became the basis of the legal system of the two states.[53]

The only state that never received the common law as the basis of its jurisprudence was, of course, Louisiana. But even there, according to Mitchell Franklin, the assumption of political power by the United States in 1803 led within five years to the replacement of a feudal, medieval legal system with a new code that reflected "the most liberal aspirations of all humanity."[54] Elizabeth G. Brown has shown how "French law, in effect in Louisiana at the time of the Spanish occupation in 1769, was entirely and deliberately supplanted by Spanish law between 1769 and 1803," with the result that except for a French slave code put into force four days before Louisiana was ceded to the United States, "the 'laws in force' in the Louisiana Purchase at the dates of transfer to the United States were the laws of Spain."[55] Professor Franklin notes that the territorial legislature of what is now the state of Louisiana attempted in 1806 to codify this "Spanish medieval system" and that the

---

[51] William Wirt Blume, "Civil Procedure on the American Frontier: A Study of the Records of a Court of Common Pleas of the Northwest and Indiana Territories (1796-1805)," 56 *Mich. L. Rev.* 161 (1957).

[52] Id. at 206, 209.

[53] See James Milton Carson, "Historical Background of Florida Law," 3 *Miami L.Q.* 254 (1949): Edward Lee Markham, "The Reception of the Common Law of England in Texas and the Judicial Attitude toward that Reception, 1840-1859," 29 *Tex. L. Rev.* 904 (1951).

[54] Mitchell Franklin, "The Eighteenth *Brumaire* in Louisiana: Talleyrand and the Spanish Medieval Legal System of 1806," 16 *Tulane L. Rev.* 514,. 560 (1942).

[55] Elizabeth Gaspar Brown, "Law and Government in the 'Louisiana Purchase': 1803-1804," 2 *Wayne L. Rev.* 169, 186, 189 (1956).

attempt failed only when the territorial governor vetoed it "because he desired to receive the Anglo-American judge-made common law into Louisiana."[56] Franklin thus implies that, in turning to the Code Napoleon rather than medieval Spanish law as the basis for the Louisiana code of 1808, the codifiers adopted a more democratic, egalitarian and libertarian — ultimately a more American system of jurisprudence.

Most historians who studied the reception of the common law and the related emergence of what they viewed as an American system of jurisprudence based on ideals of liberty, equality and the rule of law looked sympathetically at those developments. Occasional writers, however, were more critical. Judicial obeisance to the rule of law was, in particular, criticized in three of the most important early works of legal history written by three of the most important scholars who have ever worked in the field — Felix Frankfurter, J. Willard Hurst, and Mark DeWolfe Howe.

In *The Commerce Clause under Marshall, Taney and Waite,*[57] Frankfurter sought to show that the reliance on precedent which was central to the common law system of adjudication and implicit in the ideal of the rule of law was misplaced, at least in constitutional adjudication. Frankfurter warned that in studying constitutional doctrine "[w]e must be on our guard against over-sophistication, and not find luminous, deeply conceived, rational processes where there is only tentative, groping, obscure empiricism, or the instinctive and only half conscious response of habituation to a concrete controversy."[58] Recognizing that "[c]onstitutional law . . . is history" and that "the Constitution of the United States is most significantly not a document but a stream of history," Frankfurter was concerned that "[u]nless we know this history, we may unwittingly . . . be imprisoned by it. Law necessarily expresses the pressures of the past, and the basic inquiry of any self-conscious jurisprudence is the extent to which it should do so."[59] Writing at a time when he believed that the Supreme Court was adhering too rigidly to "wooden doctrine,"[60] Frankfurter strove to free the Court from its rigid subservience to the rule of law and precedent so that it could decide cases, as the great courts of the nineteenth century had, in response to the needs and pressures of the times.

Like Frankfurter, Hurst attacked the "prevailing legal philosophy" which "divorced the law and its agents from the grubby conflict of

---

[56] Mitchell Franklin, "The Place of Thomas Jefferson in the Expulsion of Spanish Medieval Law from Louisiana," 16 *Tulane L. Rev.* 319, 322 (1942).

[57] (1937).

[58] Felix Frankfurter, *supra* note 57, at 9.

[59] Id. at 2.

[60] Id. at 9.

interests" and conceived of "law as a self-sufficient system, its premises lawyer-made, its growth requiring only the logical development of what could be found in the Reports and the treatises."[61] Hurst wrote his 1950 masterpiece, *The Growth of American Law: The Law Makers,*[62] to demonstrate how much more was encompassed by the legal system than mere elaboration by appellate courts of existing rules of law. Hurst broke new ground in his book about the makers of law when he discussed not only judicial institutions, but also the legislature, the executive, the legal profession and the organs of constitution making. Hurst's main point was that "[o]nly the legislature — with its control of the purse, its powers of investigation, and its varied array of benefits and sanctions — could begin to cope with the demands made on government after the 1870s." As a result, "[b]etween about 1880 and 1920 legislation again became, as it once had been, the main growing point of the law in the United States." Hurst also observed that by the 1920s administrative lawmaking was gaining increased importance. "In either case," he concluded, "after 1880 the leadership in making general policy had passed from the courts; their creative opportunity had become the subordinate . . . task of imaginative, firm implementation of legislative policy."[63]

As an illustration of the declining importance of the courts, Hurst looked at office dockets of law firms in a moderate-sized Illinois city. He reported that the 1874 firm whose dockets he examined "had dealt solely with the local courts." The firm Hurst studied for 1904 "had its only dealings with government outside the courts in procedures to obtain two corporation charters." The 1934 firm, on the other hand, "made only 30 per cent of its appearances before government agencies in the courts; 70 per cent of its appearances were before agencies that had not existed a generation earlier."[64] At bottom, Hurst's entire book made the argument that courts could no longer establish effective social policies through elaboration of the rules of law, but must instead accept and apply the policies made by executive and legislative institutions.

In his leading article, "Juries as Judges of Criminal Law,"[65] Mark DeWolfe Howe, like Frankfurter and Hurst, also analyzed "the conflict between the people's aspiration for democratic government, and the judiciary's desire for the orderly supervision of public affairs by judges."[66] Howe's article shows how juries, which in the early nineteenth century

---

[61] J. Willard Hurst, *supra* note 24, at 185.

[62] Id.

[63] Id. at 187.

[64] Id. at 300-01.

[65] 52 *Harv. L. Rev.* 582 (1939).

[66] Id. at 615.

had possessed the right to determine law as well as fact in criminal cases, slowly lost that power through a series of judicial decisions made despite the existence of statutory and constitutional provisions designed to protect the jury's right. Howe approved the result at which the courts arrived, for he knew that in every case in which courts had cut back on the prerogative of the jury they had acted to "preserve the legislative enactment" of "an increasingly democratic government" from "the condemnation of irresponsible jurors" who were "prejudiced perhaps by interest or political affiliation."[67] Although he approved the end result, Howe nonetheless argued that his story about the end of jury power over the law in criminal cases could teach two lessons to those jurists who were troubled by the excessive claims often put forth on behalf of the ideal of the rule of law. First, he thought it could

> be doubted . . . whether the faith of judges in their own purity of constitutional thought has always been warranted. What seems discreditable to the judiciary in the story which I have related is the fierce resolution and deceptive ingenuity with which the courts have refused to carry out the unqualified mandate of statutes and constitutions. It is possible to feel that the final solution of the problem has been wise without approving the frequently arrogant methods which courts have used in reaching that result.[68]

Second, Howe implied that his essay proved that courts had power to overrule precedents and ignore statutes and even constitutional provisions in order to attain correct results. "[A] reversal of opinion, if it were isolated, might have little significance," but that would not be true "when many . . . courts throughout the country . . . [were] found to be making the same shift and to be doing so despite the provisions of statutes and constitutions."[69] Then, jurists would have to wonder whether courts did not at times bend the rule of law to respond to real needs and felt pressures from society.[70]

C. *Research in the History of Property*

When we turn away from studies of the reception of the common law and the related emergence of the rule of law to analysis of other

---

67 Id. at 616.

68 Ibid.

69 Id. at 615.

70 For another article questioning whether continued strict adherence to the rule of law was consistent with the nation's social and economic needs, see Francis R. Aumann, "Some Problems of American Legal Development during the Period of Industrial Growth, 1865-1900," 12 *U. Cinn. L. Rev.* 519 (1938).

developments in American legal history, such as the history of property, we find a similar pattern of frequent scholarly approval of the changes in American law wrought in the past and occasional scholarly dissent.

One subject on which several legal historians wrote was the substitution of partible inheritance for primogeniture as the rule of descent in cases of intestacy. Early legal historians tended to look upon this development with favor: George L. Haskins, for one, called partible inheritance "a wise method of distribution which produced on the whole fair results."[71] The rule of partibility did not, however, completely carry the day; primogeniture occasionally remained the rule of descent, especially in regard to entailed estates. Agreeing with Haskins that the abolition of primogeniture "was evidence of a liberal trend in property law,"[72] Richard B. Morris sought to explain why primogeniture remained the rule in many states in cases of entails. His conclusion was that, when courts in the nineteenth century determined the rule for the descent of entails, they lacked the knowledge of legal history that would have led them to adopt the rule of partibility and instead adopted the wrong rule — primogeniture.[73] Observing that primogeniture serves as a bulwark of conservatism that was favored by such thinkers, among others, as "the philosophers of the Cotton Kingdom," Morris' final point was that courts which adopted it had "not realized in which direction they have travelled."[74]

Another subject in the area of property law on which much was written prior to the 1960s was the development of the system of recording deeds. This body of literature was concerned almost entirely with locating the origins of the practice of recordation,[75] as to which "the colonists were ahead of their English contemporaries."[76] No writer on the subject of recording criticized the practice as it developed.

---

[71] George L. Haskins, "The Beginnings of Partible Inheritance in the American Colonies," 51 *Yale L.J.* 1280, 1315 (1942). For another article approving the substitution of partible inheritance for primogeniture, see Thorpe L. Wolford, *supra* note 47, at 462-63.

[72] Richard B. Morris, "Primogeniture and Entailed Estates in America," 27 *Col. L. Rev.* 24, 51 (1924).

[73] Id. at 47.

[74] Id. at 51.

[75] See Joseph H. Beale, "The Origin of the System of Recording Deeds in America," 19 *Green Bag* 335 (1907); George L. Haskins, "The Beginnings of the Recording System in Massachusetts," 21 *B.U.L. Rev.* 281 (1941); Mark DeWolfe Howe, "The Recording of Deeds in the Colony of Massachusetts Bay," 28 *B.U.L. Rev.* 1 (1948).

[76] Thorpe L. Wolford, *supra* note 47, at 453.

D. *The Study of Equity*

Equity was another area of the law to which pre-1960s legal historians devoted substantial attention. Those who studied the history of equity uniformly favored the grant of strong equity powers to the courts. Indeed, in the best of the articles on the subject, William J. Curran observed that "[i]t is perhaps difficult for us in the present day to grasp the depth and vigor of the opposition to a system generally regarded today as not only an essential part of our jurisprudence, but as that part which most perfectly conforms to natural justice."[77] He therefore hoped that "a realization of the history of Massachusetts equity jurisdiction in its proper perspective would do much to achieve a more catholic exercise of the Commonwealth's equity powers."[78] Sidney G. Fisher spoke equally approvingly of Pennsylvania's system, which had developed during the colonial period when equity was administered through common law forms.[79] Historical research was undertaken even for the narrow purpose of showing that the office of master in chancery was a useful one: as James R. Bryant wrote, "an understanding of the historical development of the office" would demonstrate "that the office has served the administration of justice . . . so well and has in it qualities so advantageous . . . that a careful consideration of this office would be well worth while before any casual determination should be made to abolish it."[80]

E. *Law and the Economy: The History of Regulation*

A final broad area of early legal history scholarship that remains to be discussed is that of legal regulation of the economy. Those who did research in this area prior to the 1960s generally favored the early American practice of governmental exercise of "a large degree of control over individual commercial enterprise." Scholars of the early period found that "[g]overnment regulation of wages, prices and trade practices" was "not unreasonable."[81] They were correspondingly critical of late nineteenth and early twentieth century laissez-faire attitudes.

---

[77] William J. Curran, "The Struggle for Equity Jurisdiction in Massachusetts," 31 *B.U.L. Rev.* 269 (1951).

[78] Id. at 296.

[79] Sidney G. Fisher, "The Administration of Equity Through Common Law Forms in Pennsylvania," in 2 Association of American Law Schools ed., *supra* note 8, at 810. See also James R. Wilson, "Courts of Chancery in the American Colonies," in 2 id. at 779.

[80] James R. Bryant, "The Office of Master in Chancery — Development and Use in Illinois," 49 *Nw. U.L. Rev.* 458 (1954).

[81] Thorpe L. Wolford, *supra* note 47, at 459-60.

For example, in *Government and Labor in Early America,*[82] Richard B. Morris found that "a great many contemporary labor problems were not really new at all" but had analogs "in the colonial and Revolutionary period."[83] Morris continued that "[c]olonial experience, rooted in medieval and Tudor labor legislation, provides us with an enlarged historical perspective,"[84] and, in particular, he praised the "Fair Labor Standards Act of 1938 [a]s evidence that the government is once more concerned with the regulation of the wages and hours of labor."[85]

In their classic monograph on *The Labor Injunction*, Felix Frankfurter and Nathan Greene took a similar view that "a full understanding of a legal institution . . . is necessary to wise reform" of "the abuses to which" it has "given rise."[86] In the end they catalogued a whole series of abuses to which labor injunctions had led,[87] but they also learned from their sojourn into history that reform of labor law was no simple task. They therefore concluded that "the remedies [so far] proposed ha[d] heeded too little the intricacies of our legal system and the psychologic forces that determine the judicial process."[88] Not surprisingly, they perceived a need for "[w]ise statesmanship" — something which they thought was "[p]rimarily . . . the task of legislatures," since "[o]nly within very narrow limits . . . [was] it the function of courts to apply their own notions of policy."[89]

A final study whose general tenor is consistent with those just mentioned is E. Merrick Dodd's *American Business Corporations until 1860, with Special Reference to Massachusetts.*[90] Although he died before his massively detailed book was completed and so left no explicit statement about its objective, Dodd appears to have been studying the history of corporation law in order to understand better how to reform it. This, at least, is the inference that may be drawn from arguments which he makes throughout the book, such as the one that "a system of factory production may live and grow" even in the absence of the doctrine of limited liability for shareholders.[91]

Another book on a business law subject that was not without concern for the presentist policy implications of historical study was

---

[82] (1946).
[83] Id. at 513.
[84] Id. at 519.
[85] Id. at 521-22.
[86] Felix Frankfurter and Nathan Greene, *The Labor Injunction* 1 (1930).
[87] See id. at 200-03.
[88] Id. at 199.
[89] Id. at 205.
[90] (1954).
[91] Id. at 436. See also id. at 390.

Charles Warren's 1935 monograph, *Bankruptcy in United States History.* Warren wrote that his "sketch of the great depressions of the past, and . . . [his] description of the relations of debtor and creditor . . . have a bearing upon present conditions and upon future developments of a National economic life."[92]In particular, Warren was convinced that the history of bankruptcy legislation showed that over time Congress, in response to ever broader popular demands for relief from nationwide economic disasters, had given an increasingly expansive meaning to the Constitution's bankruptcy clause; Warren hoped that this, in turn, would encourage those "inclined to despond . . . to believe in the adequacy . . . of the Federal Constitution to meet the conditions of the day."[93]

In writing upon topics ranging from the reception of the common law and the ideal of the rule of law to the growth of equity, the law of property, labor law and business law, early legal historians could sensibly strive to influence the course of judicial decisions because the judiciary did, in fact, pay heed to historical findings. The importance of legal history to judicial decisionmaking was prominently illustrated in *Erie R.R. v. Tompkins,*[94] where in overruling *Swift v. Tyson*, Justice Brandeis placed significant emphasis on Charles Warren's historical analysis of the purposes of the Judiciary Act of 1789.[95] *In Swift,* it will be recalled, the Court had construed section 34 of the act, which provides that the laws of the states shall be the rules of decision in diversity cases in federal courts, to comprehend only state statutory law and not state common law. After examining primary source material in the National Archives which previous researchers had never studied, Warren concluded in his 1923 article "that the word 'laws' in this Section 34 was not intended to be confined to 'statute laws,' as Judge Story held in the famous case of *Swift v. Tyson,* but was intended to include the common law of a State as well as the statute law." Warren added that, if Justice Story had known of the source materials which he, Warren, had examined, "it is almost certain that his decision would have been the reverse of what it was."[96] *In Erie,* Justice Brandeis accepted the conclusions set forth in Warren's article, which he labelled "recent research of a competent scholar, who examined the original document." According to Brandeis, Warren's research "established that the construction given to it [section 34] by the Court [in *Swift*] was erroneous; and that the purpose of the

---

92 Charles Warren, *Bankruptcy in United States History* vi (1935).

93 Id. at vi. See also id. at 92, 159.

94 304 U.S. 64 (1938).

95 16 Pet. 1 (1842).

96 Charles Warren, "New Light on the History of the Federal Judiciary Act of 1789," 37 *Harv. L. Rev.* 49, 52 (1923).

section was merely to make certain that, in all matters except those in which some federal law is controlling, the federal courts exercising jurisdiction in diversity of citizenship cases would apply as their rules of decision the law of the State, unwritten as well as written."[97]

I know of no other work of historical scholarship that had the same impact on the courts as Charles Warren's "New Light on the History of the Federal Judiciary Act of 1789."[98] But the work of other early legal historians plainly was of significance to judges. Joseph H. Smith told me, for example, that Julius Goebel, Jr. provided information about the history of reception to Chief Judge Cardozo while the New York Court of Appeals was struggling with a series of reception cases[99] that culminated in *Beers v. Hotchkiss.*[100] Likewise, the historical writings of Felix Frankfurter, before he was appointed to the Supreme Court, must have been of substantial significance to his professional intimates then on the bench, Louis D. Brandeis and Oliver Wendell Holmes, Jr.

F. *Beyond the Professional Tradition: The Study of Law in Constitutional, Economic, and Social History*

In view of the practical impact that historical writing could have on the course of judicial decision, it is not surprising that most early legal historians addressed their work to a professional legal audience in hopes of having that impact. But not all work that scholars of today might classify as legal history strove to influence the courts. Some scholars addressed other audiences.

One extensive body of scholarly writing that focused upon legal developments in the past but was addressed to an audience beyond the bench and bar was constitutional, as distinguished from legal history. Although Charles A. Beard surely hoped to alter the direction of American constitutional development with his *An Economic Interpretation of the Constitution of the United States,*[101] he did not make legal arguments addressed to judges. Instead, Beard advanced a kind of polemical argument addressed to the public at large. Beard could not have expected the Supreme Court to alter its course of constitutional

---

[97] 304 U.S. at 72-73.

[98] 37 *Harv. L. Rev.* 49 (1923).

[99] Conversation between Joseph H. Smith and the author, July 6, 1981.

[100] 256 N.Y. 41 (1931).

[101] (1913). On Beard, see Robert E. Brown, *Charles Beard and the Constitution* (1955), Lee Benson, *Turner and Beard* (1960), and Richard Hofstadter, *The Progressive Historians: Turner, Beard, Parrington* (1968); Robert A. Skothum, *American Intellectual Histories and Historians* (1966).

adjudication in response to his polemical position, but rather must have hoped to influence public opinion and ultimately to bring about a judicial response to the pressure of that opinion.

Other great constitutional historians of the pre-1960s period also sought to influence public opinion generally instead of making legal arguments to the courts. This was certainly true of the work of the greatest historian of the Supreme Court, the Princeton political scientist Edward S. Corwin, who authored several widely read books as well as numerous articles.[102] What characterized Corwin's work and placed it outside what leading legal historians like Julius Goebel saw as the bounds of the discipline was its lack of narrow doctrinal analysis and its emphasis on seeing constitutional development in a broader context of political and social change. Like Corwin, Albert J. Beveridge addressed *The Life of John Marshall*[103] to the general reading public. Even Charles Warren in *The Supreme Court in United States History*[104] reached out for a broad audience by emphasizing the reaction of politicians and newspapers to the Court's decisions rather than the doctrinal logic of the opinions themselves. What is true of the writing of Beard, Corwin, Beveridge, and Warren is equally true of the scholarship of numerous other leading constitutional historians of the pre-1960s era, such as

---

[102] See, e.g., Edward S. Corwin, *The Constitution and What It Means Today* (1920); Edward S. Corwin, *Court Over Constitution: A Study of Judicial Review as an Instrument of Popular Government* (1938); Edward S. Corwin, *The Doctrine of Judicial Review: Its Legal and Historical Basis* (1914); Edward S. Corwin, *John Marshall and the Constitution: A Chronicle of the Supreme Court* (1919); Edward S. Corwin, *The Twilight of the Supreme Court: A History of Our Constitutional Theory* (1934); Edward S. Corwin, "The Basic Doctrine of American Constitutional Law," 12 *Mich. L. Rev.* 247 (1914); Edward S. Corwin, "The Doctrine of Due Process of Law Before the Civil War," 24 *Harv. L. Rev.* 366, 460 (1911); Edward S. Corwin, "The Establishment of Judicial Review," 9 *Mich. L. Rev.* 283 (1911); Edward S. Corwin, "The Extension of Judicial Review in New York," 15 *Mich. L. Rev.* 281 (1917); Edward S. Corwin, "National Power and State Interposition," 10 *Mich. L. Rev.* 535 (1912); Edward S. Corwin, "The Higher Law Background of American Constitutional Law," 42 Harv. L. Rev. 149, 365 (1928-29) (republished 1955); Edward S. Corwin, *Corwin on the Constitution* (Richard Loss ed. 1981). *See* Alfred S. Konefsky, "Men of Great and Little Faith: Generations of Constitutional Scholars," 30 Buffalo L. Rev. 365 (1981).

[103] (1919).

[104] (rev. ed. 1926).

Charles G. Haines,[105] Robert G. McCloskey,[106] and Benjamin F. Wright.[107]

Another extensive body of scholarship that often examined and analyzed legal materials was in the area of economic and social history. Books such as John R. Commons' *History of Labour in the United States,*[108] John Hope Franklin's *The Free Negro in North Carolina,*[109] Lawrence A. Harper's *The English Navigation Laws,*[110] Shaw Livermore's *Early American Land Companies,*[111] and Charles Warren's *Bankruptcy in United States History*[112] were not studies solely in the history of law. But they were books about subjects on which the law did bear significantly. Hence these books, and hundreds of other scholarly works like them, examined legal materials from the past. But the examination occurred and the legal materials were placed in a broad economic and social context, the function of which was not to persuade current legal decisionmakers to alter their policies but rather to learn about the past. The effort that I am undertaking in this chapter to describe the field of legal history prior to the 1960s as legal historians of that time would have perceived it, together with limitations of space, preclude further mention of the vast amount of law buried in scholarly studies of American economic and social history.

---

[105] See, e.g., Charles G. Haines, *The American Doctrine of Judicial Supremacy* (1914; 2d ed., 1932); Charles G. Haines, "Judicial Review of Legislation in the United States and the Doctrine of Vested Rights and of Implied Limitations on Legislatures," 2 *Tex. L. Rev.* 257, 387 (1924), and 3 *Tex. L. Rev.* 1 (1924); Charles Grove Haines, *The Role of the Supreme Court in American Government and Politics 1789-1835* (1944); Charles Grove Haines and Foster G. Sherwood, *The Role of the Supreme Court in American Government and Politics, 1835-1864* (1957). See Alfred S. Konefsky, supra note 102.

[106] See, e.g., Robert G. McCloskey, *The American Supreme Court* (1960); Robert G. McCloskey, *Essays in Constitutional Law* (1957); Robert G. McCloskey, *The Modern Supreme Court* (Martin Shapiro ed. 1968).

[107] See, e.g., Benjamin F. Wright, *American Interpretations of Natural Law: A Study in the History of Political Thought* (1931); Benjamin F. Wright, *The Contract Clause of the Constitution* (1938); Benjamin F. Wright, *The Growth of American Constitutional Law* (1942); *The Federalist* (Benjamin F. Wright ed. 1961); Benjamin F. Wright, *Consensus and Continuity: 1776-1787* (1958).

[108] (1918-1935).

[109] (1943).

[110] (1939).

[111] (1939).

[112] (1935).

G. *The Birth of a Counter - Tradition: Legal History as the Study of Law and Social Change*

A third body of scholarship that examined the American legal past also differed from most legal history written prior to the 1960s in that its writers' objective was to shed light on the past, not to influence current decisionmaking by judges. But, unlike the work in constitutional, economic and social history that has just been examined, this third body of scholarship can only be labelled legal history since the study of how law functioned in the past was virtually the sole theme of work in the area.

Three articles written to broaden understanding of the past had as their topic the problem most studied by legal historians striving to influence judicial decisionmaking. That topic was the reception of English law in America. Thus, St. George L. Sioussat in a brief essay set forth various theories propounded by seventeenth and eighteenth century lawyers about the circumstances under which acts of Parliament possessed binding legal force in the colonies[113] — a matter of overriding concern to Americans of the Revolutionary generation. Charles F. Mullett studied the attitudes of Revolutionary Americans toward medieval common law. He explained how American legal thinkers strove, contrary to the bulk of medieval precedent, to develop a common-law based justification for opposing parliamentary legislation over the colonies and that Americans began to rely on natural law justifications only after their effort to build a common-law case failed.[114] Francis R. Aumann, in turn, explained how post-Revolutionary Americans, despite their knowledge of civil law and their antipathy toward most things English, continued to accept the common law as the basis of their legal system.[115]

A fourth article, which has become a classic in the literature of American legal history, also dealt with the general problem of reception. The article, "The Influence of Colonial Conditions as Illustrated in the Connecticut Intestacy Law,[116] focused on the case of *Winthrop v. Lech-*

---

[113] St. George L. Sioussat, "The Theory of the Extension of English Statutes to the Plantations," in 1 Association of American Law Schools ed., *supra* note 8, at 416.

[114] Charles F. Mullett, "Medieval English Law and the American Revolution," 20 *Va. L. Rev.* 523 (1934).

[115] Francis R. Aumann, "The Influence of English and Civil Law Principles upon the American Legal System during the Critical Post-Revolutionary Period," 12 *Cinn. L. Rev.* 289 (1938).

[116] Charles M. Andrews, "The Influence of Colonial Conditions as Illustrated in the Connecticut Intestacy Law," in 1 Association of American Law Schools ed., *supra* note 8, at 431. On Andrews see note 139 *infra* and accompanying text.

mere, a 1728 decision by the Privy Council reversing an earlier judgment of the highest court of Connecticut. The author of the article, Charles M. Andrews, explained how economic conditions and social attitudes in Connecticut led that colony to abandon primogeniture as its rule of inheritance and to put in its place a rule of partibility, with a double portion going to the eldest son. The case that utimately went to the Privy Council arose when a scion of the Winthrop family sought to obtain all of his father's inheritance by claiming that Connecticut's intestacy law was contrary to the provision of its charter requiring that none of its laws be contrary to the laws of England. After reporting both on proceedings in Connecticut in which the Connecticut rule was sustained and proceedings before the Privy Council in which Connecticut law was invalidated, Andrews next reports upon subsequent litigation through which Connecticut and the other New England colonies managed despite the Privy Council's holding in *Winthrop v. Lechmere* to preserve their scheme of partible inheritance.

Another work that has stood the test of time and become a classic work of American legal history is Richard B. Morris' book, *Studies in the History of American Law, with Special Reference to the Seventeenth and Eighteenth Centuries.*[117] The most interesting part of the book identified four general influences on early American law: (1) "[t]he rugged independence . . . born of the frontier [which] brought about the scrapping of important common-law practices incompatible with life in the new agrarian communities";[118] (2) "[t]heological-political [c]oncepts," especially those associated with Puritanism,[119] (3) "[a]dverse [c]riticism of the [c]ommon [l]aw in England" which was parallel to "the most radical experiments in the American colonies,"[120] and (4) the absence of lawyers and law books which accounted "for the liberation of American law from many of the shackles of English medievalism" during the seventeenth century,[121] until what Morris calls "[t]he [n]ew [i]mperial [d]iscipline" introduced at the end of the century ultimately led in the eighteenth century to "[t]he [r]ise of the American [b]ar" and thereby to a more complete reception of the common law.[122] The rest of the book, with extensive citations to cases culled from manuscript sources in several colonies, traced the impact of these influences on the law of procedure,

---

[117] (1930).

[118] Id. at 20.

[119] Id. at 21. For an early article tracing the impact of Puritanism, see Richard B. Morris, "Massachusetts and the Common Law: The Declaration of 1646," 31 *Am. Hist. Rev.* 443 (1926).

[120] Richard B. Morris, *supra* note 117, at 45-46.

[121] Id. at 42.

[122] Id. at 62, 65.

the law of property, the law of tort, and the law of women's rights. All this was done to illustrate the relationship between "changing mores" and "changing law,"[123] not to induce twentieth century courts to alter specific rules of law.

Another book addressed to historians rather than to judges and lawyers was *Commonwealth: A Study of the Role of Government in the American Economy, Massachusetts, 1774-1861,* by Oscar Handlin and Mary F. Handlin.[124] *Commonwealth* was, in large part, an effort to examine the role of state government in the promotion and regulation of the economy by focusing on public and private acts adopted by the state legislature. But the Handlins also devoted substantial attention to case law, especially in a series of chapters tracing the emergence of modern business corporation law in early nineteenth century Massachusetts. With no objective other than to understand the historical interplay of law and economic development, the Handlins showed how the eighteenth-century rule that members of a corporation were responsible to creditors for its debts was transformed in the first third of the nineteenth century into a rule that corporate shareholders can be held to no greater liability for the corporation's debts than the amount they had subscribed upon purchase of their shares — a rule designed to encourage investment in corporate enterprise.

These efforts by four leading members of the historical profession — Charles M. Andrews, Richard B. Morris, Oscar Handlin, and Mary F. Handlin — to understand particular legal developments in their larger historical context were not, in general, well received by lawyers. Morris' book, in particular, was the target of one of the nastiest reviews I have ever read.[125] It is worth examining this review at some length because it reveals a great deal about the intellectual objectives and methodological assumptions of early legal historians.

The reviewer whose name was signed to the most vehement of the attacks on *Studies in the History of American Law* was Karl N. Llewellyn, although I suspect that Llewellyn's colleague at the Columbia Law School, Julius Goebel, Jr., played some part in Llewellyn's reaction to the book. Llewellyn found Morris' monograph "depressing and grotesque."[126] Its "grotesquerie" lay "in over-ambition of scope, compared to achievement" — in "the profusion of statements which gallop beyond facts cited or even known."[127] What makes Llewellyn's criticism odd is

---

[123] Id. at 11.
[124] (1947).
[125] "Book Review," 31 *Col. L. Rev.* 729 (1931).
[126] Ibid.
[127] Ibid.

the extraordinary thoroughness of Morris' research and the depth of his citation: it may be that no one in the past fifty years has examined as many colonial legal records as Richard B. Morris had examined in the several years of research that culminated in *Studies in the History of American Law*. Thus, Llewellyn could not fairly criticize Morris for failing to do his homework, nor do I think that Llewellyn intended to accuse Morris of laziness or incompetence. Indeed, Llewellyn found *Studies* "depressing because the author has ability — more than the book would indicate; and because he knows better than he does."[128] Llewellyn continued:[129]

> If Dr. Morris were a dilettante, or a beginning scholar of poor schooling, one might well be gentle in reviewing, and welcome the wheat grains in the chaff pile. But Dr. Morris proclaims his contact with the careful and patient scholarship of craftsmen of the first rank. His book requires, for their justification, to be judged by the standard they set. He has turned his back on them. Goebel has gently but firmly repudiated any responsibility for Dr. Morris' methods or conclusions. . . . I admire his moderation. The third chapter of Dr. Morris' book began as a seminar paper under me. Its author was then impervious to criticism of flaws in his method. The paper now appears, still a botched treatment of a promising subject.

What troubled Llewellyn was not Morris' carefulness and competence, but his method and approach — the fact that he was examining legal records from the point of view of an historian rather than a lawyer.

Llewellyn wanted the American legal past to be examined in a series of narrow and precise studies, like Julius Goebel's "King's Law and Local Custom in Seventeenth Century New England,"[130] which Llewellyn found to be "a workmanlike job on similar material."[131] Whereas Goebel had studied only one issue — the source of colonial law, for a single jurisdiction — what ultimately became the county of Plymouth, over a brief time span — merely three decades, Morris wrote about American law in all thirteen colonies over a span of two centuries. Whereas Goebel had taken the lawyer's approach of dissecting a narrow problem precisely, Morris had written from an historian's perspective, attempting to synthesize a broad panorama and to examine how it changed over a substantial period of time. It was the very breadth of Morris' scholarship that disturbed Llewellyn most. He wrote:[132]

---

[128] Id. at 730.
[129] Id. at 729 n. 1.
[130] 31 *Col. L. Rev.* 416 (1931).
[131] "Book Review," *supra* note 125, at 729 n. 1.
[132] Id. at 731 (italics in orignial).

> No historian of law today has any business *presupposing, without demonstrating point for point*, that there was any one "colonial" view on anything. . . . Each culture must be examined for itself and in itself before any trait of one can be attributed even to its neighbor, much less to all. And within a single colony matters changed fast enough — as Dr. Morris at times indicates — to vitally shorten the time-scope of evidence. Two decades are a gap, three an impasse, unless a provable bridge spans them, or like evidence is found on both ends *together with* an *a priori* case for continuity. . . . In his worst moods Dr. Morris ranges lightly over time as well as space.

Other lawyers joined in Karl Llewellyn's criticism of *Studies in the History of American Law*. Not surprisingly, Julius Goebel accused Morris of "commit[ting] the impropriety of leaping from one colony to another as if the civilization in each were identical" and "ignor[ing] the element of time in grouping cases separated by decades."[133] Joseph H. Beale agreed, taking note of "the impossibility of the author's [Morris'] aim and method."[134] He concluded that Morris had not accomplished what he had set out to do,[135]

> because the history of American law before 1930 is the history of thirteen distinct systems, each with its own development, its own peculiarities, its own literature (mostly in manuscript, and accessible with difficulty), and its own small circle of students. Until these thirteen histories are thoroughly studied and mastered, it is idle to attempt even such modest studies as this.

Eldon R. James likewise found Morris' "attempt at generalization, founded too frequently on single instances, . . . confusing and unsatisfactory"[136] and wrote that, until source materials for each jurisdiction in the United States had been collected and analyzed, "a general history of American law, or even studies in particular topics, is not to be expected, and any attempts in that direction are bound to be unsatisfactory."[137] Only John H. Wigmore gave unqualified praise to Morris' *Studies*, observing that Morris'[138]

> mode of treatment accepts the broadest standards of historical writing. He does not limit himself to the exact terms of the legal rule found in the records, but brings into view the background of social

---

[133] Julius Goebel, Jr., *supra* note 130, at 417 n.3.
[134] "Book Review," 35 *Am. Hist. Rev.* 921-22 (1930).
[135] Id. at 922.
[136] "Book Review," 19 *Calif. L. Rev.* 563, 564 (1931).
[137] Id. at 563-64.
[138] "Book Review," 16 *Iowa L. Rev.* 452 (1931).

> and economic conditions and of the controlling philosophies of life of the colonists. He does not merely announce the various rules in his own words, but intersperses quotations from contemporary writers which admit us to a more realistic understanding of the spirit of the rule. This is the kind of historical writing which we like best.

It should be noted, however, that even in praising *Studies*, Wigmore merely commented, quite correctly, that Richard B. Morris was an outstanding, promising young historian, but that Wigmore never suggested that lawyers would find Morris' variety of legal history useful in their professional activities.

Richard B. Morris, as I have already noted, was not the only historian to feel the critical sting of lawyers when he wrote upon a legal topic. The always critical Julius Goebel, for example, charged Charles M. Andrews with the same failing he found in Morris. In the fourth volume of his *Colonial Period of American History,*[139] Andrews had, according to Goebel, made unwarranted "generalizations about colonial law at large on the basis of matter plucked here and there from various jurisdictions."[140] Although Goebel conceded that Andrews had researched manuscript sources more carefully than he, Goebel, had, Goebel nonetheless commented that Andrews had "failed to grasp" the thrust of his "objection" — "that the mere viewing of a mass of material [does not] entitle . . . one to speak with not-to-be disputed authority on a technical subject";[141] after all, both the technical competence of a researcher and the completeness of his research were open to challenge on cross-examination or its equivalent in a court of law.

A third book to be challenged by a lawyer for overstating conclusions which touched upon the law was *Commonwealth*, by Oscar Handlin and Mary F. Handlin.[142] E. Merrick Dodd, himself the author of a history of corporation law,[143] believed that the Handlins had erred in "their contention that many of the early Massachusetts decisions in the field of business corporations were radical departures from earlier views. . . ."[144] He attributed their error to the fact that they conceptualized their scholarly task as historians rather than as lawyers. Dodd wrote:[145]

---

[139] Charles M. Andrews, *The Colonial Period of American History* (4 vols., 1934).

[140] Julius Goebel, Jr., and T. Raymond Naughton, *supra* note 2 at xxxiii n. 27.

[141] Ibid.

[142] Oscar Handlin and Mary F. Handlin, *supra* note 124.

[143] See E. Merrick Dodd, *American Business Corporations until 1860, with Special Reference to Massachusetts* (1954).

[144] "Book Review," 61 *Harv. L. Rev.* 555, 558 (1948).

[145] Id. at 560.

> By reason of their decision to organize their book in such a way as to give major emphasis to changes in the conception of the role of government in the economy, and to organize that part of it which relates to the business corporation in such a way as to give major emphasis to changes in the concept of the corporation, they have given rather more attention to certain statutes and judicial decisions and rather less attention to others than might have been the case if their object had been to write a history of early Massachusetts business law rather than a history of early Massachusetts political thought.

In particular, Dodd thought that what the Handlins had found to be important legal innovations requiring historical explanation had merely been normal legal developments, squarely grounded in preexisting precedents and in the unchanging analytical principles of the common law. Proper historical analysis by a lawyer would have uncovered the common law's continuities, whereas the historian, searching for change, found judges to have been influenced by social policies and political ideas outside the proper bounds of the judicial reasoning process.

Despite the fact that lawyers often criticized early efforts to write legal history from a genuine historical perspective, several scholars continued during the 1940s and 1950s to write legal history that did not address narrow issues of current concern to the legal profession. The most prolific of these scholars was George L. Haskins, who published a series of articles on the history of Massachusetts law. His first two articles, both appearing in 1942, traced "The Beginnings of Partible Inheritance in the American Colonies,"[146] notably in Massachusetts, and "The Beginnings of the Recording System in Massachusetts."[147] In both articles, Haskins considered a number of sources in which partible inheritance and the recording system might have originated, concluding that "[n]o single 'source' can be pointed to without distorting the facts as they were."[148] Haskins thought it likely, nonetheless, that the most important influence on early Massachusetts law was local custom in England. He argued that there was "much reason to suppose that the colonists availed themselves of their cultural heritage in law, just as they did in religion and farming" and he noted that "[t]he social system of colonial New England was first and last English."[149] Since Massachusetts was settled "[i]n the days before the common law had acquired universal dominion" in England,[150] Haskins concluded that local custom was the

---

146 51 *Yale L.J.* 1280 (1942).
147 21 *B.U.L. Rev.* 281 (1942).
148 51 *Yale L.J.* at 1314.
149 Ibid. Accord, 21 *B.U.L. Rev.* at 303.
150 21 *B.U.L. Rev.* at 303.

most likely source to which a colonist seeking to replicate his cultural heritage in law would turn. Recognizing that religious ideology may also have played a role in the adoption of partibility and recording, Haskins concluded that "[w]haveter the reasons for . . . [their] original adoption, . . . [their] suitability to colonial conditions is why in the long run . . . [they] survived" and developed into "roots of . . . modern law."[151] In his first two articles, Haskins deemphasized the importance of the common law as one of the early sources of Massachusetts law, but his third article, "A Problem in the Reception of the Common Law in the Colonial Period,"[152] did not. There he noted that the Massachusetts Dower Act of 1647 "was based upon the rules of common law dower in England."[153] He also noted, however, that the act "was interpreted by the courts in a manner which was in many instances at variance with the common law rules" and that ultimately "the influence of the common law seems to have been less significant than other elements" in seventeenth-century Massachusetts law.[154]

Haskins had suggested in all three of his articles that "the background of colonial law . . . [was] significant from a sociological point of view as a study in survival and adaptation of patterns of thought and habits of life."[155] He returned to this theme in his fourth article, "The Spread of Massachusetts Law in the Seventeenth Century,"[156] which examined how provisions of the Massachusetts Code of 1648 were adopted in other colonies, notably Connecticut and New Haven. Haskins found "that the Connecticut and New Haven Codes drew primarily on the earlier Massachusetts legislation," and that "the influence of the latter code did not end in New England" but spread south into New York and even New Jersey and Pennsylvania.[157] He found this spread of Massachusetts law to be part of a process by which "patterns of life and thought were carried from colony to colony."[158]

Haskins's two decades of research into seventeenth-century Massachusetts law culminated in 1960 with the publication of *Law and Authority in Early Massachusetts: A Study in Tradition and Design.*[159] Haskins made it clear that he was writing from a broad historical

---

[151] 51 *Yale L.J.* at 1315.

[152] 97 *U. Pa. L. Rev.* 842 (1949).

[153] Id. at 852.

[154] Id. at 852-53.

[155] Id. at 842.

[156] George L. Haskins and Samuel E. Ewing 3d, "The Spread of Massachusetts Law in the Seventeenth Century," 106 *U. Pa. L. Rev.* 413 (1958).

[157] Id. at 417.

[158] Id. at 413.

[159] (1960).

perspective with his statement that "the evolution of legal rules and doctrines" must "be related to the political and social environments of particular times and places." "Broadly conceived," he continued, "legal history is concerned with determining how certain types of rules, which we call law, grew out of past social, economic, and psychological conditions, and how they accorded with or accomodated themselves thereto."[160] Haskins, in fact, wrote *Law and Authority* as he promised, devoting the first half of the book to political, social and ideological developments in early Massachusetts. His view differed somewhat from what it had been two decades earlier, for in *Law and Authority* he placed greater emphasis on Puritanism as a source of legal ideas than he had in his 1942 articles. In any event, however, it was only after he had fully portrayed the impact of Puritanism and other nonlegal developments on Massachusetts that Haskins turned to law, concluding as he had in his earlier work that colonial law was a complex product of many forces. As Haskins himself wrote:[161]

> Massachusetts law in the colonial period was a syncretization of biblical precedent and a complex English heritage which included not only the common law and the statutes, but practices of the church courts, of the justices of the peace, and of the local courts of manors and towns from which the colonists came. Parts of that heritage were deliberately incorporated into the colony's legal system, but other parts were rejected or adapted as Puritan ideals and the conditions of settlement might require.

George L. Haskins was not alone in conceiving of legal history as the study of how law and political, economic, and intellectual developments were interrelated. Another scholar who believed that "[t]he ultimate question of legal history is, how does the law of a given time and place meaningfully connect with the society of which it is part,"[162] was Leonard W. Levy. In *The Law of the Commonwealth and Chief Justice Shaw,*[163] which was published in 1957, Levy's working premise was that "[a] society reveals itself in its law"[164] and hence that a scholar who, like himself, studied the law of a past society would better understand that society and its values. Levy accordingly studied Massachusetts law as it was elaborated by the Shaw Court and then, in a concluding chapter entitled "Three Decades of Law and Society,"[165] traced the impact of the

---

[160] Id. at viii.

[161] Id. at xi.

[162] Leonard W. Levy, *The Law of the Commonwealth and Chief Justice Shaw* 303 (1957).

[163] Ibid.

[164] Ibid.

[165] Id. at 303-36.

Commonwealth idea, as it had been developed by the Handlins,[166] on the growth of the police power, praised Shaw and his contemporaries for their concern for individual rights, and condemned them for their insensitivity to racial and especially religious minorities.[167] In focusing on the growth of the police power, the emphasis on individual rights and the lack of concern for minorities, Levy painted a fair portrait not only of Shaw but of many antebellum Americans.

Even more important to the discipline of legal history as it would develop during the 1960s and 1970s was the 1956 publication of Willard Hurst's *Law and the Conditions of Freedom in the Nineteenth-Century United States.*[168] Unlike Hurst's first book, *The Growth of American Law,*[169] *Law and the Conditions of Freedom* did not examine legal issues of current concern to practicing lawyers. On the contrary, *Law and the Conditions of Freedom* sought to identify some of the basic social forces underlying the historical development of nineteenth-century America. Hurst's method was to analyze cases on disparate legal issues in conjunction with each other in an effort to identify common threads running either explicitly or by implication through all the opinions. He found two such threads. First, he found that courts often decided cases in a way that "promote[d] the release of individual creative energy" that could be harnessed in the building of a new nation. Second, he found that the "legal order" often strove to "mobilize the resources of the community to help shape an environment which would give men more liberty by increasing the practical range of choices open to them and minimizing the limiting force of circumstances."[170] These two threads, of course, were far more useful as expressions of the "vision" possessed by nineteenth-century Americans of "a new kind of society"[171] than they could ever be as principles for courts to use in deciding twentieth-century cases.

The scholarship of Haskins, Hurst and Levy published in the closing years of this century's sixth decade foretold the directions that scholarship in the field of American legal history would take during the seventh decade, the eighth decade and the opening years of the ninth decade. After *Law and Authority, Law and the Conditions of Freedom*, and *The Law of the Commonwealth*, leading scholars in the field would no longer have a unitary conception of what it meant to write legal history — a conception that they would enforce by nasty reviews of work done by

---

[166] See Oscar Handlin and Mary F. Handlin, *supra* note 124.
[167] See Leonard W. Levy, *supra* note 163, at 306-12, 315-21, 327-30.
[168] (1956).
[169] J. Willard Hurst, *supra* note 24.
[170] J. Willard Hurst, *supra* note 168, at 6.
[171] Id. at 6-7.

others who did not accept their conception. Legal history would no longer be the handmaiden of the law, devoted to providing research for legal questions of current concern to the profession. Beginning in the late 1950s most legal history would be written largely for the purpose of illuminating the past. As we shall see in the forthcoming chapters that survey the literature of the 1960s, 1970s and early 1980s, most legal history today is genuinely historical rather than legalistic in character.

The fact that most legal history during the past quarter century has been genuinely historical in character does not mean, however, that a new unitary conception of the discipline has emerged. This can be seen even from a superficial examination of the books of Haskins, Hurst and Levy. While all three of them brought a genuinely historical approach to bear upon the study of the American legal past, their historical approaches were quite different. Just as general American historians of today bring very different questions and very different values to bear upon their studies of the past, so too do legal historians. George Haskins, like many who have labored in the discipline after him, is at heart an intellectual historian who examines how ideas are transplanted across geographic, temporal and disciplinary bounds. In comparison, Willard Hurst is less interested in ideas; he is not an intellectual but a social historian who studies how legal institutions and social structures interact, grow and change in response to each other. It is worth noting that both Haskins and Hurst write history without reference to their personal political, jurisprudential or ideological values: one cannot discover from *Law and Authority* or from *Law and the Conditions of Freedom* how either author feels about any pending issue of the day. The same is not true of the work of Leonard Levy. Levy is a typical mid-twentieth century American liberal who used his liberal values to provide structure and insight for his biographical study of Lemuel Shaw.

As forthcoming chapters will show, scholars of many different sorts continue to study American legal history. Proteges of Willard Hurst, for example, continue to focus upon the historical relationship between law and society. Other writers continue to study American legal history as a form of intellectual history. Still other scholars use political and ideological values as a tool for obtaining insight into and evaluating developments in the American legal past. In addition, lawyers continue to search in the past for answers to current legal questions. There are still other American legal historians whose work fits into none of these categories.

The forthcoming chapters will show that the discipline of American legal history, in contrast to the unitary character that it possessed into the 1950s, is marked by immense diversity today.

Chapter Two

1962

John Phillip Reid

In a recent address Columbia's Julius Goebel, Jr. lamented for the legal historian forced to labor among the bread and butter subjects of the law. The historian, he says, is tuned to a past which "calls out that we should cherish writing as the exercise of an art"[1] and the prospect of facing a stack of advance sheets "resembles confronting a bowl of peanuts or potato chips."[2] For those who must face the tear sheets harvested from this survey year's crop in legal history, there is also much to lament.

I

LEGAL HISTORIOGRAPHY

If legal history is the foster child of legal studies, then legal historiography is truly the foster child of legal history. This became evident once again during the past year by the almost unanimous refusal of legal periodicals to review the decade's most important book on law and the art of history — James Willard Hurst's *Law and Social Process in United States History*.[3] The disinterest was further demonstrated when the American Society for Legal History undertook to honor the dean of legal historians, Roscoe Pound. It not only turned its back on legal historiography but also on the very subject which it is supposed to be promoting. Instead of presenting him with a volume of essays in legal history, the Society presented him with essays in jurisprudence.[4] Its official publication, *The American Journal of Legal History,* reflected

[1] Julius Goebel, "Learning and Style in the Law — An Historian's Lament," 61 *Colum. L. Rev.* 1393, 1400 (1961).

[2] Id. at 1393.

[3] James Willard Hurst, *Law and Social Process in United States History* (1960).

[4] *Essays in Jurisprudence in Honor of Roscoe Pound* (Ralph A. Newman ed. 1962).

much the same attitude. During 1962 its contribution to legal historiography was contained in, at best, one article and in the book reviews of Earl Finbar Murphy.[5] Indeed, as during years past, the bulk of historiological writing is to be found in book reviews. They are our chief barometer. The number of books reviewed roughly reflects the amount of research being conducted; the number of reviews published measures the interest which the legal profession has in the research; and the comments by the reviewers upon this research mirror present attitudes and fashions concerning legal history.

Since lawyers were downgrading the importance of legal history this past year, it remained for a non-legal historian, Robert H. White, to balance the picture by claiming for it a role it cannot perform:

> In all probability, there is no subject more profitable than a study of the history of jurisprudence. Since the beginning of time, each unit of the human race has struggled along its allotted path through joys and griefs, triumphs and failures, all fashioned and grooved for the most part by a somewhat invisible network of habits, customs, mores, and statutes which surround society on every side and silently guide its daily life. And so, the history of jurisprudence becomes the history of man. . . .[6]

Legal historians have long ceased to confuse legal history with history. The "relationships between law and history," may be, as Frederick Wiener says, the "most hardy of perennial topics,"[7] but the debate now turns on whether legal history should serve law or serve history. Representative of the current trend is A.W.B. Simpson who, in the preface to one of the most valuable of the recent legal histories, expressed the intention to keep his historical discussions distinct from current law and advised students "to read history as history, and law as law."[8] While this is now a familiar argument, it was given fresh dimension by Roscoe Pound when he pointed to "the dangers of reasoning from analogies supplied by history to which judges and legislators and jurists turn in providing for new conditions and situations which continually arise in a

---

[5] Norbert C. Brockman, "The History of the American Bar Association: A Bibliographic Essay," 6 *Am. J. Legal Hist.* 269 (1962). See also Note, "Virginia Court Records Program," 6 *Am. J. Legal Hist.* 309 (1962); "Current Literature: Legal History in American History Journals," 6 *Am. J. Legal Hist.* 310 (1962) (list of 14 articles dealing with legal history in American historical periodicals).

[6] Robert H. White, "Origin and Development of Trial by Jury," 29 *Tenn. L. Rev.* 8 (1961).

[7] Frederick Wiener, *Uses and Abuses of Legal History: A Practitioner's View* 3 (1962).

[8] A.W.B.Simpson, *An Introduction to the History of Land Law* vii (1961).

changing world."[9] Pound believes that since reasoning from analogies is a "process" which is little understood, it may represent a hidden danger in any effort to make legal history serve the needs of contemporary law:

> The jurist historian may think he finds a solution to a new problem of the law of today in what he takes to be a reasoned solution of a problem of the past, when he may in reality, be interpreting the law of the past by what he assumes to be the rationale of the problem of the present and so endeavor to make the latter solve itself.[10]

There are other dangers to making legal history serve law that are more familiar and less subtle than the misapplication of analogies. Pointed out during the current year was the tendency to read the present into the past:

> (It has been far too easy for historians and dabblers in history, including those with legal training, to succumb to the enchanting vision of a mythical ancient English common law containing all of the guaranties of right and privilege which protect the American citizen today. . . .);[11]

to interpret legal history in the light of a judicial application of legal history or legal theory;[12] and to use the history of a legal institution to define the scope of its present day functions.[13] Another familiar criticism against legal history having to do with its purpose, was raised by Charles Wright when he complained that "most historians have become hopelessly lost in the Domesday Book." He wants them to concern themselves "with those aspects of legal history which deepen and illuminate our approach to contemporary legal problems."[14] While many answers have been offered to this in the past a new one may have been added during the survey year by Franklin Russell, when he suggested that Anglo-Saxon law would be profitable reading for Americans

---

[9] Roscoe Pound, "What Do We Ask of Legal History?," 11 *Am. U. L. Rev.* 117, 120 (1962).

[10] Id. at 121.

[11] Richard H. Jones, "Book Review," 40 *Ore. L. Rev.* 375 (1961). The opposite danger was demonstrated by Leonard Levy who is praised for arguing "that modern libertarian ideas have been read back into the past," but criticized for putting too much stress upon the letter of the law while paying "little attention to practice" and for forgetting that law can be a tool in political battles while not being the guiding force. Merrill Jensen, "Book Review," 75 *Harv. L. Rev.* 456, 457 (1961).

[12] William F. Swindler, "Book Review," 11 *J. Pub. L.* 433, 437 (1962).

[13] John Van Voorhis, "Note on the History in New York State of the Powers of Grand Juries," 26 *Albany L. Rev.* 1, 11-12 (1962).

[14] Charles Wright, "Book Review," 40 *Texas L. Rev.* 737 (1962).

> stationed in some under-developed country for some reason, such as missionaries, armed forces personnel, Foreign Service officers, and representatives of business firms. A surprising similarity between the rules of Anglo-Saxon law and those of modern customary law can readily be seen.[15]

Opposed to those who would keep law and history separated, and to those who would have legal history serve the purposes of law, are those who would have legal history serve the cause and interests of general history. "Legal history, expertly interwoven with constitutional and political history," Russell writes, "is much more attractive than taken by itself."[16] George Haskins gave this approach a boost in a recent article when he discussed the theory that the 1636 Code of Plymouth is important as a historical document because "it reveals much of the social organization of the colony."[17] Colonial law, and indeed all law, Haskins suggests, is a sociological study.[18] Rejecting this in part while accepting it in part is the school led by Wisconsin's Hurst. This school, which writes legal history to suit neither law nor history exclusively (unless those words are broadly defined) was summed up during the year by Professor Murphy:

> The historical research which comes out of Madison is not history-*qua*-history. It is, instead, history as part of Law-in-Action, the motto of the Madison circle. Nineteenth century America is part and parcel of America today, so far as the Madison circle is concerned; and American bias today can only be theoretically explicated if its sources have been discovered and mapped. Law is a dynamic event in time that has no single beginning, or any easily discernible difference from other institutions in society. Hence it is essential that the approach to law be total; and that the student come as close to first occurrence as possible. . . .[19]

One of the new books which Murphy feels "has been heavily influenced by the ideas and forms of expression of Hurst," is *Law and Mineral Wealth* by James A. Lake.[20] In his preface, Lake states the Madison

---

[15] Franklin Russell, "Book Review," 28 *Brooklyn L. Rev*. 372, 373 (1962).

[16] Ibid.

[17] George Lee Haskins, "The Legal Heritage of Plymouth Colony," 110 *U. Pa. L. Rev*. 847, 849 (1962).

[18] Id. at 850-53.

[19] Earl Finbar Murphy, "Book Review," 6 *Am. J. Legal Hist*. 408, 409-10 (1962).

[20] For another recent Wisconsin-school book describing the operation of a group of land-use laws in a forest-stripped county, see Erling Day Solberg, *New Laws for New Forests: Wisconsin's Forest-Fire, Tax, Zoning, and County-Forest Laws in Operation* (1961).

creed when he writes: "The discussion avoids technical legal doctrine. This is not a handbook to help a lawyer brief a case. . . ."

> Law is a product of men's efforts — and of their failings. Especially within the frame of values developed in the growth of the United States, law has formed an important part of general history. Over a century ago, De Tocqueville observed that the nature of the United States Constitution turned almost every political question into a judicial question. . . . Justice Felix Frankfurter has characterized Supreme Court opinions as a "good mirror" of our civilization but, as he also pointed out, a mirror of which historians have "little availed themselves. . . ." Of like relevance to our general history, and as little used, are the records of state trial and appellate courts, state legislatures, boards of county supervisors, administrative bodies, and other agencies of legal order.[21]

This economic approach has its compensations as well as its drawbacks. At least H.G. Richardson, when reviewing a book by an author who wrote as "an economist," felt that he could "not criticise him as one would criticise a legal historian, who cannot allow himself either the latitude of language or the amount of conjecture permissible in a field where the discipline seems somewhat lax."[22] This underlines the basic difficulty of those working within the area of legal history. When they address their efforts to historians rather than to lawyers they know reviewers for legal periodicals will be disappointed if they fail to offer new discoveries concerning substantive law. The best they can expect is a warning such as F.A. Mann issued this year when he told his readers not to treat "a historian's masterpiece as a source of legal research."[23]

One non-legal historian suggested that even if legal history has not much to offer history, the common law of evidence does. Observing that "much of what passes for the 'facts' in histories would be thrown out in a court. . . .,"[24] Robert E. Brown asked whether the historian should "perform the expected function of the judge and jury in the courtroom in sifting the facts and arriving at an objective verdict, certainly the philosophy of our legal system, or should the historian assume the role of prosecuting or defense attorney?"[25] One writer of dynastic history put the defense-attorney technique to good use in a popular work this year when

[21] James A. Lake, *Law and Mineral Wealth: The Legal Profile of the Wisconsin Mining Industry* v-vi (1962).

[22] H.G. Richardson, "Book Review," 78 *L.Q. Rev.* 428, 430 (1962).

[23] F.A. Mann, "Book Review," 78 *L.Q. Rev.* 596, 597 (1962).

[24] Robert E. Brown, "Reinterpretation of the Formation of the American Constitution," 42 *B.U.L. Rev.* 412, 474 (1962).

[25] Id. at 473.

he brought the art of cross examination, the principle of burden of proof, and the demand for reliable evidence to bear on the case constructed by Tudor historians against Richard III for the deaths of the princes in the tower.[26] This, however, can be risky business as Professor Prosser demonstrated when reviewing Edward Radin's book about Lizzie Borden and the Fall River "forty whacks" murder.[27] Radin first adopted the "function of judge and jury" and convincingly established a case of not-proven on behalf of Lizzie, just as her lawyer did in a Massachusetts court over a half a century ago. Then he switched to the role of prosecuting attorney and presented an indictment against the Borden's maid. Prosser demonstrated that the technique cuts both ways by using the same arguments Radin has employed against the state's case to destroy his case against the maid.[28] Law may have tricks to teach history but they require skill to perform. This adds an off-beat footnote to the growing list of the problems encountered by any blending of law and history.

The conflict between lawyers and historians is a familiar theme. G.D. Ramsay believes, however, that during the heyday of the Whig interpretation of English history they "lived for the most part in harmony."[29] That epoch has long since passed and during the current year legal historians joined in the reappraisal by restoring to grace some of the institutions the Whig historians have bespattered.[30] A notable instance of this was an article by Richard Noble on the Stuart judges who decided the ship-money controversy in favor of Charles I in *Rex v. Hampden.* [31] They have been traditionally dismissed by Whig historians as a "prostituted crew" and Noble reexamines the question of their integrity by asking whether their chief failing may not have been that "their judgment of law did not anticipate the judgment of history."[32] To answer this he follows an approach which could serve as a model for any writer attempting a reinterpretation of an accepted chapter in legal history.

---

[26] Thomas B. Costain, *The Last Plantagenets* (1962).

[27] Edward Radin, *Lizzie Borden: The Untold Story* (1961).

[28] William L. Prosser, "Book Review," 49 *Calif. L. Rev.* 786-91 (1961), 40 *N.C.L. Rev.* 363-70 (1962).

[29] G.D. Ramsay, "Book Review," 77 *L.Q. Rev.* 582, 583 (1961).

[30] For a study which bucks this trend, gives the Whig or traditionalist school its due by documenting the case against chancery during the Commonwealth, finds the evil was corruption — not prerogativism — and shows Cromwell to have been an ineffective reformer of judicial institutions, see Stuart Prall, "Chancery Reform and the Puritan Revolution," 6 *Am. J. Legal Hist.* 28 (1962).

[31] 3 *How. St. Tr.* 826 (Eng. Exch. 1637).

[32] Richard Noble, "Lions or Jackals? The Independence of the Judges in Rex v. Hampden," 14 *Stan. L. Rev.* 711, 712 (1962).

> First, it is necessary to consider what effect the judge's tenure and appointment, and Charles's policy toward the courts, may have had upon their independence.[33] Next, we shall ask whether the view taken by the majority in *Hampden* could logically have been taken by judges of learning and integrity.[34] Then, we shall consider what we know of the character, conviction, and ability of the individual judges, bearing in mind that our knowledge of several is quite limited and that much can be learned from their *Hampden* opinions. Finally, remembering the debater's maxim that "he who asserts must prove," we will turn to the formal charges brought against them in 1640-41 to determine whether any convincing evidence was brought forward. . . .[35]

A less convincing but significantly more important reappraisal is currently being conducted by Thomas G. Barnes in the history of the favorite legal bugbear of the Whigs — the Star Chamber.[36] This is a definite adventure in historiography; he has set out with the deliberate purpose of proving the Whig historians wrong as demonstrated by the title of his opening attack — *Star Chamber Mythology*.

> I must apoligize [sic] if at times I sounded like counsel retained by Star Chamber against Whig historians! My intent has been to cut away some of the myths surrounding a court which I suspect can stand on its own merits when judged by the only satisfactory standard of historical criticism [sic], did it do substantial justice by the lights of justice in its day. During the next two or three decades of my scholarly life which will be devoted to the court of Star Chamber from its inception to its abolition this will be my criterion of criticism. . . . Star Chamber, whatever its shortcomings were, deserves an assessment befitting what was *prima facie* a court of justice.[37]

---

[33] Conclusion: "The views of both Croke and Hutton were certainly known before Hampden, yet no apparent effort was made to remove them, nor did they suffer for their opinions. While not underrating the importance of the removal power, it should be remembered that Charles did not make the fullest possible use of it. It would indeed be wrong to assume that because he had removed two judges and suspended one during a twelve-year period all those on the bench in 1638 were ipso facto servile." Id. at 721.

[34] Conclusion: yes. "[T]he case in support of ship money was far from being a weak one. . . ." Id. at 760.

[35] Id. at 713. Conclusion on the last point: "[A]s too often happens, legislators in their anger at a judicial decision or series of decisions reacted violently against judges whose greatest fault was a not abnormal human bias on a doubtful point of law." Id. at 759.

[36] Thomas G. Barnes, "Due Process and Slow Process in the Late Elizabethan—Early Stuart Star Chamber (Pts. 1, 2)," 6 *Am. J. Legal Hist.* 221, 315 (1962).

[37] Thomas G. Barnes, "Star Chamber Mythology," 5 *Am. J. Legal Hist.* 1, 11 (1961).

No one can quarrel with the historical method, but it seems likely that during the "next two or three decades" much controversy will be generated as Barnes, who has set out to prove a point, unavoidably overstates his case as he reacts to the old "myths."

Another school of historians which received some hard knocks from legal writers this survey year were those espousing an economic interpretation.[38] Of particular interest was the reappraisal of a term which was a major tool in the work kit of the economic interpreters — "laissez-faire." Leonard Levy presented the traditional view when he argued that a study of Lemuel Shaw demonstrates that the Massachusetts theory of government was unique since it "precluded the laissez-faire state whose function was simply to keep peace and order, and then, like a little child, not be heard. . . ."[39] While Levy's view of Shaw's legal philosophy is generally accepted, the historical significance which he attaches to it seems questionable, in view of studies by men such as Hurst who, in 1956, showed that during the nineteenth century law was used for positive social purposes and that the historical theory that laissez-faire dominated legal thinking is a myth.[40] Now comes a new study by Calvin Woodward which reinterprets the meaning of laissez-faire. In a review of Hurst's work Woodward asserted that "nineteenth century writers advocated 'hands off' only as a general rule and not as a literal absolute . . ." and that some of "the most influential and dogmatic champions of laissez-faire sanctioned many (if not all) of the uses of the law to which Professor Hurst has referred."[41] This year, in a 42-page article, he elaborated on this theme, seeking to prove that champions of laissez-faire never advocated a complete wall between government and economics as Hurst and Levy assume, and that, therefore, judges such as Shaw were not apostates from their age.[42] It is a remarkable study, not so much as it bears on our understanding of law, as it bears on our interpretation of legal history.

---

[38] Robert E. Brown, *supra* note 24; William F. Swindler, *supra* note 12, at 436.

[39] Leonard W. Levy, "Lemuel Shaw: America's 'Greatest Magistrate,'" 7 *Vill. L. Rev.* 389, 390 (1962).

[40] James Willard Hurst, *Law and the Conditions of Freedom in the Nineteenth-Century United States* (1956).

[41] Calvin Woodward, "Book Review," 19 *La. L. Rev.* 560, 563 (1959).

[42] Calvin Woodward, "Reality and Social Reform: The Transition from Laissez-Faire to the Welfare State," 72 *Yale L. J.* 286 (1962).

II

BIOGRAPHY

The most notable aspect of 1962 in this area was the fact that legal and judicial biography was relegated to a back seat by the editors of multi-volume collections of private papers which are, at the moment, monopolizing so much scholarly manpower.[43] Attempts to give these projects a "legal" as well as a "historical" pertinence received a "serious setback" when the organized bar refused to become identified with publication of the Marshall papers because "it was not interested in legal history as such."[44]

The value of current fashions in legal and judicial biography has recently been questioned, usually with a good deal of justification centering on repetition and scholarly significance. Spencer Kimball's complaint that what little work is done seems concentrated on the same familiar figures[45] took new meaning this year. Judge Elijah Adlow, ignoring the many significant Massachusetts jurists of whom no modern studies have been made, published a book on Lemuel Shaw[46] just five years after Levy's notable, *The Law of the Commonwealth and Chief Justice Shaw.*[47] When the Levy book first came out, A.L. Goodhart offered an observation, almost a stereotype of the lawyer's impatience with non-legal historians who dabble in law:

> The fact that the author is not a lawyer may account for some of the minor defects in the book. There are too many quotations from the popular press and not enough citations from Chief Justice Shaw's judgments. As a general rule it is best to leave a judge to speak for himself both inside and out of court.[48]

Adlow is a lawyer and his book should please Goodhart. It is, for the most part, a disconnected recital of cases grouped under traditional

---

[43] For a valuable discussion, see Gerald Gunther, "Book Review," 75 *Harv. L. Rev.* 1669, 1670-71 (1962). The papers of the following lawyers are now being edited: John Adams, Jay, Hamilton, Jefferson, Madison, John Quincy Adams, Marshall, Clay, Calhoun, Webster, and Lincoln.

[44] William F. Swindler, "Legal History — Unhappy Hybrid," 55 *L. Library J.* 98, 105-06 (1962).

[45] Spencer Kimball, "Book Review," 7 *Utah L. Rev.* 285 (1960).

[46] Elijah Adlow, *The Genius of Lemuel Shaw: Expounder of the Common Law* (1962).

[47] Leonard W. Levy, *The Law of the Commonwealth and Chief Justice Shaw* (1957).

[48] A.L. Goodhart, "Book Review," 74 *L.Q. Rev.* 140, 142 (1958).

headings, without much effort at historical evaluation. A comparison of his approach with that of Levy is revealing as to the divergent attitudes and interests of the lawyer and the non-lawyer in the area of legal biography.[49] A tentative conclusion may be that Adlow's study would have been more valuable had it come before Levy's and hence served as a professional guide for the work of the historian.

The American jurist of whom the most has been written, Oliver Wendell Holmes, continued to be the main object of attention. He has passed through many stages, one of which, the debunking stage, seems to be in for a revival.[50] Another stage, which might be called the "literary" stage for want of a better term, got a boost not only from Edmund Wilson,[51] but also from the republication of Justice Frankfurter's sensitive appraisal of Holmes's place in American intellectual history which originally appeared in the *Dictionary of American Biography*.[52]

III

CONSTITUTIONAL HISTORY

Since history is the lock and key of constitutional law, the determinants of constitutional history have usually been more judicial than historical. Premises have been accepted for argumentative utility rather

[49] Consider their chapter titles. Levy's include: "The Unitarian Controversey"; "Satan's Apostle and Freedom of Conscience"; "The Law of Freedom"; "The Fugitive Slave Law"; "Segregation"; "The Formative Period of Railroad Law"; "Constitutional Limitations"; and "Three Decades of Law and Society." Adlow's include: "The Common Law"; "The Federal Power"; "The Legislative Power"; "The Judicial Power"; "Procedural Due Process"; "Negligence"; "Contracts"; "Municipal Corporations"; and "Railroads." For an extended comparison see "Irresponsible and Unimaginative: The Lawyer and Historian as Judicial Biographer," 57 *L. Library J.* 128-39 (1964).

[50] Consider these opening words of a 41-page article: "This Article is one of a series which will attempt to prove that Mr. Justice Holmes was not, as is widely believed, uniquely responsive to claims of civil liberties; that he was, in fact, quite often indifferent to them." Yosal Rogat, "Mr. Justice Holmes: A Dissenting Opinion," 15 *Stan. L. Rev.* 3 (1962).

[51] Edmund Wilson, *Patriotic Gore: Studies in the Literature of the American Civil War* (1962).

[52] Felix Frankfurter, *Mr. Justice Holmes and the Supreme Court* (2d ed. 1961). Also republished was *The Holmes-Pollock Letters: The Correspondence of Mr. Justice Holmes and Sir Frederick Pollock* (Mark De Wolfe Howe 2d ed. 1961). And see *The Occasional Speeches of Justice Wendell Holmes* (Mark De Wolfe Howe ed. 1962).

than historical validity, while underlying theories have often been assumed. Some of the most basic of these theories were re-examined this year by Professor Brown who contends that, as background for the Constitution, "it matters a great deal" whether it was produced by an aristocratic and class-ridden or a democratic and middle-class society. In an important article (which is more than just another attack on the "Beard school" since it questions Beard's basic economic assumptions and not merely his historical method) he sums up recent findings by scholars which may force our concepts regarding the origins of the Constitution to undergo "some rather drastic revisions."

> Some of us no longer believe that colonial America was an aristocratic, class-ridden America, with limited opportunities for the common man and sharp class conflict between upper and lower classes. Instead, we are coming to an interpretation of colonial society as predominantly middle-class, with much economic opportunity, a broad franchise, representation that favored the agricultural areas, educational facilities for the common man, and much religious freedom. Colonial America, so some of us think was much more liberal than we have previously believed.[53]

Another important event during this survey year was the conclusion of William P. Murphy's eleven-article study on "State Sovereignty and the Ratification of the Constitution."[54] Bypassing the currently fashionable method of appealing to later writings of the founding fathers, such as Madison,[55] he went to what Madison himself said was the only valid source — the state ratifying conventions — to determine the true meaning of the Constitution. The compact theory of the Constitution, and the state sovereignty doctrines which flowed from it, he believes, are based on erroneous historical assumptions which were introduced into political theory by the Anti-Federalists and their heirs. Among both supporters and opponents of the Constitution, he says,

> there was no expectation that any strict construction in favor of state power would be followed. Although national powers were enumerated, state power was not expected to be a constitutional limitation on the scope or extent of any enumerated national power.[56]

---

[53] Robert E. Brown, *supra* note 24, at 430.

[54] William P. Murphy, "State Sovereignty and the Ratification of the Constitution — III: Ratification in Virginia," 33 *Miss. L. J.* 292 (1962).

[55] For an example of this approach to Constitutional history see Edmond Cahn, "Jurisprudence," 1961 *Ann. Survey Am. Law* 571.

[56] William P. Murphy, *supra* note 54, at 354.

IV

ENGLISH LEGAL HISTORY

In the last edition of his standard textbook, Theodore Plucknett complained that nothing was known of the Tudor financial courts.[57] In subsequent editions he should complain no more for along with H.E. Bell's *History of the Court of Wards & Liveries,*[58] he can now cite the first published history of the Court of Augmentations.[59] In fact, the chief need for a new edition will be to take advantage of recent researches into the history of various English legal institutions, some of which have never been investigated before.[60] This seems to be something of a trend. The latest work in the "Cambridge Studies of English Legal History," for example, deals with the medieval coroner.[61] As usual, however, there was some reworking of old fields. Charles R. Young, plowing furrows laid bare by Stubbs, Maitland, Round, Gross and Bateson, re-examined the English borough,[62] while R. Wellborn Finn, following Eyton, Round, Maitland, Ballard, *et al.,* reworked the Domesday inquest.[63]

In articles Bruce Peterson demonstrated how military history can be used in writing legal history which in turn contributed to social history;[64]

---

[57] Theodore F.T. Plucknett, *A Concise History of the Common Law* 174 (5th ed. 1956).

[58] H. E. Bell, *An Introduction to the History and Records of the Court of Wards & Liveries* (1953).

[59] Walter Cecil Richardson, *History of the Court of Argumentations 1536-54* (1961).

[60] See, e.g., George Drewry Squibb, *The High Court of Chivalry: A Study of the Civil Law in England* (1959).

[61] R.F. Hunnisett, *The Medieval Coroner* (1961).

[62] Charles R. Young, *The English Borough and Royal Administration, 1130-1307* (1961). Young's justification is that earlier studies tended to concentrate "upon the internal functioning of the borough," usually treating it "in isolation from other parts of the realm." Id. at 3.

[63] R. Wellborn Finn, *The Domesday Inquest and the Making of Domesday Book* (1961). Finn insists that even now much research remains to be uncovered. "The products of the Inquest have received a wealth of labour, but little attention has been devoted to considering just why it was held, with what aims, in what manner, and with what results. Very little work has so far been done upon the problems presented by the actual construction of the surviving documents, and it is largely the palaeographer who should be able to tell us how these were put together, and perhaps when and where. For there is by no means unanimity of opinion about the date at which the Exchequer Domesday was compiled." Id. at 5.

[64] Bruce Peterson, "The Danegeld and Its Effect on the Development of Property Law," 66 *Dick. L. Rev.* 443 (1962).

Geoffrey O. Hazard, Jr., presented the argument that the common law's tradition of technicality, its compartmentalization of substantive law, and its theory that due process is slow process, can all be traced back to the evolution of writs from William I to Henry II;[65] Paul R. Teetor published the first translation of the earliest English treatise on the law merchant, the *Lex Mercatoria* from "The Little Red Book of Bristol";[66] and H.G. Hansbury added legal substance to the rekindling of Richard III's reputation by examining his legislation and concluding that Richard was superior to Richmond in every respect.[67]

V

AMERICAN LEGAL HISTORY

Colonial. — The colonial period continues to belong primarily to Joseph H. Smith and George L. Haskins. Both returned this year to re-explore the areas in which they made their reputations — Smith to the problem of the English legal controls on the colonies;[68] Haskins to the Pilgrims in Plymouth.[69] It is Haskins' belief that legal history can offer much to general history if only general historians would not ignore it. A case in point is Samuel Eliot Morison. Despite the writings of Goebel and of Haskins, Morison insists that Plymouth made few permanent contributions to American heritage, even though he concedes that it instituted civil marriage, a registry of deeds, the Congregational Church, and the first bill of rights. Now Haskins adds to these the equality of descent among children, provision for widows, and beginning of the American principle of the rule of law. This may be too legal a list to impress an old sea dog like Morison, and it seems likely that general historians will continue to attach less significance to Plymouth than Haskins does.

---

[65] Geoffrey O. Hazard, "The Early Evolution of the Common Law Writs: A Sketch," 6 *Am. J. Legal Hist.* 114 (1962).

[66] Paul R. Teetor, "England's Earliest Treatise on the Law Merchant," 6 *Am. J. Legal Hist.* 178 (1962).

[67] He says that Shakespeare's villain was really "a singularly thoughtful and enlightened legislator, who brought to his task a profound knowledge of the nature of contemporary problems, and an enthusiastic determination to solve them in the best possible way, in the interests of every class of his subjects. . . ." H.G. Hansbury, "The Legislation of Richard III, 6 *Am. J. Legal Hist.* 95, 113 (1962).

[68] Joseph H. Smith, "Administrative Control of the Courts of the American Plantations," 61 *Colum. L. Rev.* 1210 (1961).

[69] George Lee Haskins, *supra* note 17.

In the same spirit with which Warren investigated Story's historical assumptions behind *Swift v. Tyson,*[70] L. Kinvin Wroth this year[71] considered Story's famous statement that "the vice admiralty court of Massachusetts, before the Revolution, exercised a jurisdiction far more extensive, than that of the admiralty in England. . . ."[72] He finds as much to question in Story's use of history as Warren did.[73] Story exercised a great influence on the development of admiralty jurisdiction through his assertion that the framers of the Constitution intended to dispense with English limitations. Wroth says that this depends "on contemporary understanding of the meaning of the terms 'admiralty and maritime jurisdiction . . . ,'"[74] and subjects Story's theory to the scrutiny of history. "The Massachusetts records," he concludes, "show only the Vice Admiralty practice in that colony does not offer much support to the theory that the drafters intended a broad jurisdiction."[75]

Western Frontier. — The important book of the year in this area was the excellent study of American Indian policy during its formative period by Francis Paul Prucha.[76] Without neglecting immediate problems, it concentrates on the evolution of the Intercourse Act of 1834; the subsequent application of which is probably the single most important aspect of western legal history which awaits scholarly treatment. The important event of the year was the appearance of William Wirt Blume's last article in his series dealing with law on the American frontier. Having earlier dealt with civil procedure,[77] criminal procedure,[78] probate

---

[70] Charles Warren, "New Light on the History of the Federal Judiciary Act of 1789," 37 *Harv. L. Rev.* 49 (1923).

[71] L. Kinvin Wroth, "The Massachusetts Vice Admiralty Court and the Federal Admiralty Jurisdiction" (Pts. 1, 2), 6 *Am. J. Legal Hist.* 250, 347 (1962).

[72] *De Lovio v. Boit,* 7 Fed. Cas. 418, 422 n. (No. 3776) (C.C.D. Mass. 1815).

[73] An important step toward a long-needed, modern biography of Story was taken in Gerald T.Dunne, "Joseph Story: The Germinal Years," 75 *Harv. L. Rev.* 707 (1962).

[74] L. Kinvin Wroth, supra note 71, at 364.

[75] Id at 365. For a similar use of historical materials arguing that congressional power over appellate jurisdiction is limited to treatment of fact issues, see Henry J. Merry, "Scope of the Supreme Court's Appellate Jurisdiction: Historical Basis," 47 *Minn. L. Rev.* 53 (1962).

[76] Francis Paul Prucha, *American Indian Policy in the Formative Years: The Indian Trade and Intercourse Acts, 1790-1834* (1962).

[77] William Wirt Blume, "Civil Procedure on the American Frontier," 56 *Mich. L. Rev.* 161 (1957).

[78] William Wirt Blume, "Criminal Procedure on the American Frontier," 57 *Mich. L. Rev.* 195 (1958).

and administration,[79] and chancery practice,[80] he has now brought his study to a close by examining *Legislation on the American Frontier.*[81] He began by questioning the assertions put forth by Paxson and Pound, based on broad generalities and doubtful assumptions, concerning the influence of the frontier upon law.[82] Whether he has proved his point, and has forced legal historians to rethink some of the theories underlying American law, may well depend upon whether others agree with him that Wayne County, during the days of Woodward and Cass, was really (notwithstanding the census-line argument of Frederick Jackson Turner) a frontier area.

> In the course of his research and writing, Professor Blume has formed some tentative conclusions as to how American legal history may be approached. He has concluded that, following separate studies of the original colonies, a study of the laws and legal institutions of the territories as a group will serve to provide and be indicative of the feasibility of a unified approach to legal developments west of the original states.[83]

To demonstrate this approach, he is collaborating with Elizabeth Gasper Brown on a two-part article under the general title of *Territorial Courts and Law*, the first part of which, *Establishment of a Standardized Judicial System*, also appeared this year.[84] This approach is not entirely unique. As Murphy has suggested, the "Hurst school" intends to follow a somewhat similar pattern; at least as its first two steps.

> In American legal history for the Midwest, there are certain givens which must be initially understood: the English and eastern seaboard heritage. Then the territorial period must be studied, when every Midwestern state stood in tutelage to the Congress and the confining rule of the Northwest Ordinance that limited law-making to the existing laws of the original states. After that comes the development of law in the sovereign state; and in that must be included the

---

79 William Wirt Blume, "Probate and Administration on the American Frontier," 58 *Mich. L. Rev.* 209 (1959).

80 William Wirt Blume, "Chancery Practice on the American Frontier," 59 *Mich. L. Rev.* 49 (1960).

81 William Wirt Blume, "Legislation on the American Frontier," 60 *Mich. L. Rev.* 317 (1962).

82 William Wirt Blume, "Civil Procedure on the American Frontier," 56 *Mich. L. Rev.* 161, 203-09 (1957).

83 61 *Mich. L. Rev.* 39 (1962).

84 William Wirt Blume & Elizabeth Gaspar Brown, "Territorial Courts and Law: Unifying Factors in the Development of American Legal Institutions (Pt. 1)," 56 *Mich. L. Rev.* 39 (1962).

> interaction between states upon special problems and the contributions of scholars, pressure groups, and the general cultural conditions of times studied. In all this, isolation is hard to find; and the Madison Circle eschews it. . . .[85]

Of course Blume's history, being more tightly disciplined and using conventional materials, would be quite different from that of the "Hurst school." What is significant, however, is that despite this both seem to have adopted the same general approach or pattern. If it proves feasible it could help to solve the problem of manageability which now appears to be the chief obstacle in the way of any unified history of American law. If it can be used by the writer of that history, by the American Holdsworth, then its formulation may prove to be the major event of 1962.

---

[85] Earl Finbar Murphy, "Book Review," 6 *Am. J. Legal Hist.* 408, 410 (1962).

Chapter Three

1963

John Phillip Reid

This has been a year for optimism in legal history. No matter how one might evaluate the wine, none could gainsay the fact that there were laborers in the vineyard. One writer, who dared find fault with such giants as Maitland and Holdsworth, excused their shortcomings on the ground that adequate primary sources were not available in their day and concluded with the happy thought: "Over the last decade, however, a great amount of work has been done by scholars and one of the most exciting prospects for the future lies in the continued publication of their conclusions."[1] He was speaking of research being conducted into "the day to day operations of Tudor and Stuart courts," but he might as easily have included the entire panorama of English and American legal history.

I

LEGAL HISTORIOGRAPHY

Studies devoted to legal historiography continue to be scarce, but the few which appeared during this survey year were both scholarly[2] and thought-provoking.[3] William F. Swindler once more focused attention on the multi-volume collections of private papers now being published.

[1] W.J. Jones, "An Introduction to Petty Bag Proceedings in the Reign of Elizabeth I," 51 *Calif. L. Rev.* 882, 883 (1963).

[2] Most notably, L.J. Downer, "Legal History — Is It Human?," 4 *Melbourne U.L. Rev.* 1 (1963). The year's best historiographical works pertained to continental law and lawyers during the Renaissance. Myron Piper Gilmore, *Humanists and Jurists — Six Studies in the Renaissance* (1963); Julian H. Franklin, *Jean Bodin and the 16th - Century Revolution in The Methodology of Law and History* (1963); Donald R. Kelley, *"Historia Integra:* Francois Baudouin and His Conception of History," 25 *J. History of Ideas* 35 (1964). See also Franklin J. Peques, *The Lawyers of the Last Capetians* (1962).

[3] Edward D. Re, "Legal History Courses in American Law Schools," 13 *Am. U.L. Rev.* 45 (1963).

Last year he noted their neglect of "law";[4] this year he considered the impact which they will have upon legal history in general and legal biography in particular.[5] *The American Journal of Legal History* demonstrated the service which it can perform when it published a ten-year bibliography of legal history articles appearing in "scholarly non-law journals."[6] This is the first step in a project undertaken by Doyce B. Nunis to compile a complete list of printed material relating to American legal history from 1603 to 1960. When completed it will be a milestone, for if studies made by general historians on the fringe areas of law are to be integrated into the work of law-trained legal historians, those studies must be called to their attention.

As 1963's literature makes clear, there are too few appraisals published of the aims, techniques, and requirements of legal history scholarship. They usually appear in the form of book reviews. Yet most book reviews prove worthless as critical evaluations of work accomplished or as thoughtful appraisals of what research remains to be done. The main exceptions are reviews written by Temple's Earl Finbar Murphy.[7] This gap in scholarly criticism can best be filled by *The American Journal of Legal History*. It is hoped that when publication of "The Minutes of the Supreme Court — 1789-1806" is completed, the editors of the *Journal* will allocate to historiography and criticism the pages now drained by the section called "Documents."

"Revisionism" is the chief historiographic theme to emerge from this survey year. Knocking Whig historians remains good sport on both sides of the Atlantic.[8] An especially fine reappraisal has been turned in by Warren S. Howard, historian at Vandenberg Air Force Base.[9] He challenges the traditional assumption that the debacle in enforcement of the anti-slave trade laws was engineered by Southern slaveowners who paralyzed effective police action through their control of the national administration. Familiar villains such as Buchanan are exonerated, and blame is shifted to legal technicalities and to disinterested minor officials — particularly judges in the Southern District of New York. His evidence

---

[4] See chapter 2, at 41.

[5] William F. Swindler, "Book Review," 7 *Am. J. Legal Hist.* 178 (1963).

[6] Doyce B. Nunis, Jr., "Historical Studies in United States Legal History, 1950-1959: A Bibliography of Articles Published in Scholarly Non-Law Journals," 7 *Am. J. Legal Hist.* 1 (1963).

[7] See, e.g., Earl Finbar Murphy, "Book Review," 37 *Tul. L. Rev.* 341 (1963).

[8] W.J. Jones, supra note 1; Loren P. Beth, "The Slaughter House Cases —Revisited," 23 *La. L. Rev.* 487 (1963); Francis Xavier Curran, *Catholics in Colonial Law* 5-6 (1963).

[9] Warren S. Howard, *American Slaves and the Federal Law, 1837-1864* (1963).

is convincing,[10] and should call for major revision in this area of legal history. But "revision" is something more easily proved than accepted. Whiggish legal historians die hard, especially those who cling to emotional causes.[11] Worse, they go right along inventing new historical theories to fit current political fashions. Thus the idea is being advanced — as "history" — that the civil rights struggles of 1963 are the fulfillment of intentions deliberately set in motion by such events as the Emancipation Proclamation; that the social order demanded by today's pressure groups is the one originally formulated; and that history teaches us that we must "catch up."[12] The revisionists of the future should be as busy as those of today.

It is hoped that none of today's historians encounter such brutal revisionist treatment as that suffered this year by Bishop William Stubbs at the hands of H.G. Richardson and G.O. Sayles. In a brilliant, witty, and biting study they carried to extremes the revisionist's art by their polemical scrutiny of Stubb's constitutional histories.[13] Their condemnation is bitter, unqualified, and far too personal. Their very technique raises the question whether the work of a legal historian can be evaluated by cataloging his prejudices and provincialisms. For American readers the picture was balanced by the appearance in book form of Helen Cam's recent essay, "Stubbs Seventy Years After."[14] To compare Cam's tribute to the attack written by Richardson and Sayles is the best exercise in applied legal historiography since Professors Fairman and Crosskey concluded their argument.

Historical figures, as well as historians, had to face revisionists during 1963 — most notably Holmes and Jefferson. Here, however, the attackers seem to be raising up straw men to prove their points. At least Yosal Rogat does so in his exhaustive study which, he explains, seeks "to prove that Mr. Justice Holmes was not, as is widely believed, uniquely

---

[10] One question Howard does not explore is the backgound of the Northern judges who defeated the efforts of Congress and the Navy to end the trade. Were they appointed as "safe men"? Judge Betts, Howard's chief target, relentlessly enforced the Fugitive Slave Act.

[11] See, e.g., Justice Michael A. Musmanno, "The Sacco-Vanzetti Case," 11 *Kan. L. Rev.* 481 (1963).

[12] Irving Dilliard, "The Emancipation Proclamation in the Perspective of Time," 23 *Law in Transition* 95, 105 (1963). See also William Orville Douglas, *Mr. Lincoln & the Negroes — The Long Road to Equality* (1963).

[13] Henry Richardson & George Sayles, *The Governance of Mediaeval England from the Conquest to Magna Carta* 1-21 (1963).

[14] "[T]here is no nineteenth century historian towards whom it is less possible to be condescending without condemning oneself as unfit to study history." Helen Maud Cam, *Law-finders and Law-makers in Medieval England* 188 (1963).

responsive to claims of civil liberties."[15] Whether many still believe Holmes was a prophet for today's liberal is doubtful; H.L. Mencken (to name just one) laid that ghost to rest long ago.[16] Since the technique of relying on a straw man to create initial interest pertains to theme rather than substance, its use does not distract from scholarly worth. But it puts the writer in the position of claiming for his study greater originality than it deserves.

Somewhat in the same manner is Dean Leonard W. Levy's new book enumerating Jefferson's shortcomings as a civil libertarian.[17] His assertion that historians "have fixed a libertarian halo around the brow" of Jefferson and that this halo is his "target,"[18] also seems to set up a straw man. Historians have, for many years, acknowledged the many sides of Jefferson.[19] Levy is much less an offender than Rogat, however, because in popular (as opposed to "professional") history this straw man has often been accepted as the real Jefferson. The attempt by many lawyers, judges, and orators to attribute to Jefferson the prejudices and standards which they favor, has been one of the most conspicuous abuses of the historical method in our times. Yet one cannot escape feeling that Levy reacted too strongly to the popular image; that he is too eager to prove his case and thus distorts the "darker side" of Jefferson by failing to place some of his harsher judgments within the perspective of historical evidence.[20] As Professor Wallace Mendelson pointed out this survey year, too much revisionist doctrine is formulated by liberal attitudes in response to institutions as they exist today. Laying bare his Jeffersonian

[15] Yosal Rogat, "Mr. Justice Holmes: A Dissenting Opinion," 15 *Stan. L. Rev.* 254 (1963).

[16] *The Vintage Mencken* 189-97 (Alistair Cooke ed. 1955). See also the sources gathered in Francis Lucey, "Holmes-Liberal-Humanitarian-Believer in Democracy?," 39 *Geo. L.J.* 523 (1951).

[17] It is interesting to note that while Jefferson's reputation is undergoing revision, Hamilton's reputation, "so tarnished during the grim years of the Great Depression," is being refurbished — even his law career. Raymond Walters, Jr., "Book Review," 345 *The Annals* 165 (1963) (reviewing 2 Broadus Mitchell, *Alexander Hamilton—The National Adventure, 1788-1804* (1962)). See also Clinton Rossiter, *Alexander Hamilton and the Constitution* (1964).

[18] Leonard W. Levy, *Jefferson & Civil Liberties—The Darker Side* ix (1963).

[19] See discussion in Dumas Malone, "Book Review," 69 *Am. Hist. Rev.* 787-89 (1964).

[20] E.g., Levy may be right in suggesting that the "aged Jefferson had soured" when he wrote to Madison to make sure the University of Virginia selected a man of safe, Whig principles as law professor. But Levy might have balanced this by considering the degree of justification when only *one* professor was being selected. Even a conservative will admit that where there is no chance to obtain a variety of philosophies, it is fair game to guarantee that your own will hold the field.

interpretation of history by noting that, "Judicial review was born of Federalist distrust of democracy," Mendelson writes: "Whatever Jefferson may have thought at first, he ultimately repudiated judicial review. And as recently as thirty years ago, few if any liberals could be found to argue in favor of 'the democratic character' of that institution. Obviously there are fashions in liberalism; what only yesterday it found untenable is now a major article of its faith."[21] Today the danger that legal history may become the tool of political theory is greater than Maitland's old worry that history might be made the handmaiden of law.

Finally we should note the strangest historiographic notion to be expressed in some time. Seeking to explain, in part, the conservativism of Butler, McReynolds, Sutherland, and Van Devanter, a professor of political science surmised that they did not acknowledge any creative forces in history. To them, he says,

> History progressed in a series of cause-and-effect sequences. Such a settled philosophy of history may help to explain the Conservatives' habit of repeating themselves in their opinions; they seem to have had a relatively limited number of ideas which recurred in almost the same form over and over again. . . . The Conservatives wanted to retain the old ways and were crusaders for the old. This kind of philosophy of history, couched in neat cause-and-effect formulas, does not permit "accident" or the operation of an extensive free will in history.[22]

II

CONSTITUTIONAL HISTORY

Robert J. Steamer has attempted to place the United States Supreme Court within the evolution of history by saying it is both a "captive" and a "maker" of history.[23] It seems that historians and political scientists really think it is a "captive." At least Dean Levy appears to have undertaken his extensive researches into constitutional beginnings because

---

[21] Wallace Mendelson, "Book Review," 57 *Am. Pol. Sci. Rev.* 161 (1963) (reviewing Eugene Victor Rostow, *The Sovereign Prerogrative: The Supreme Court and the Quest for Law* (1962)).

[22] Ronald F. Howell, "The Judicial Conservatives Three Decades Ago: Aristocratic Guardians of the Prerogatives of Property and the Judiciary," 49 *Va. L. Rev.* 1447, 1473-74 (1963).

[23] Robert J. Steamer, "The Legal and Political Genesis of the Supreme Court," 77 *Pol. Sci. Q.* 546 (1962).

he takes the judges at their word when they say that our understanding of certain freedoms (such as the freedom against self-incrimination) "is quite dependent upon history."[24] During recent months similar studies, based perhaps on the same premise, have been published, dealing especially with the origins of the Bill of Rights.[25] Lawyers, on the other hand, tend to stress the Supreme Court's role as "maker" of history. In one of the most convincing appraisals published this year, F. William O'Brien added solid evidence (if more evidence be needed) supporting studies which prove the "incorporation" doctrine of the fourteenth amendment to be an example of judicial legislation rather than a judicial use of history. O'Brien, however, belongs to the school of thought which holds that the meaning of a constitutional provision depends on the intent of its drafters and enacters, and that intent is to be established by history.[26] Historians should realize that today's Supreme Court is interested only in "history" which substantiates the particular dogmas it wishes to enunciate. The origin of many of these dogmas has recently been probed in an impressively documented article by Dean Levy. He presents the thesis that American libertarianism, triggered by the Sedition Act, erupted in 1798 "like an underwater volcano." Here, he says, we can find the beginnings of the absolutist interpretation of the first amendment — an interpretation which did not exist when the amendment was adopted.[27] In the same spirit, Paul S. Boyer has contributed a footnote to the

---

[24] Leonard W. Levy & Lawrence H. Leder, "'Exotic Fruit': The Right Against Compulsory Self-Incrimination in Colonial New York," 20 *William & Mary Q.* (3d Ser.) 3 (1963).

[25] Irving Brant, "Seditious Libel: Myth and Reality," 39 *N.Y.U.L. Rev.* 1 (1964); Jay Sigler, "A History of Double Jeopardy," 7 *Am. J. Legal Hist.* 283 (1963). For articles examining the *development* of civil liberties see Barton J. Bernstein, "Case Law in Plessy v. Ferguson," 47 *J. Negro Hist.* 192 (1962) (arguing that Plessy was perverted case law); W. Howard Mann, "The Marshall Court: Nationalization of Private Rights and Personal Liberty From the Authority of the Commerce Clause," 38 *Ind. L.J.* 117 (1963); Webster Myers, "Cardozo and Personal Rights," 67 *Dick. L. Rev.* 337 (1963).

[26] Thus he suggests, the "incorporation" doctrine is not law unless it was so intended by "the 39th Congress which proposed and the states which ratified the fourteenth amendment." "This is a question for historians. In 1947, Justice Black judged that he found confirmation for his 'incorporation' thesis in a few isolated statements from a very few members of the 39th Congress. Subsequently, more qualified scholars have produced overwhelming evidence to prove that those responsible for the fourteenth amendment never intended to bind the states by the Bill of Rights. The study of the Blaine Amendment confirms this conclusion." F. William O'Brien, "The Blaine Amendment 1875-1876," 41 *Det. L.J.* 137, 198 (1963).

[27] Leonard W. Levy, "Liberty and the First Amendment: 1790-1800," 68 *Am. Hist. Rev.* 22 (1962).

history of a currently sensitive constitutional issue by exploring the social background of Boston censorship during the Twenties. He concludes that by the end of the decade, the emergence of the Irish as supporters of official government censorship caused a reaction among the intelligentsia and the Establishment. Censorship became "a kind of 'right' which the newer and less affluent groups sought to maintain in the face of the anticensorship 'encroachments' by the wealthy and educated!" Perhaps so, but just as plausible an argument could be made, from the evidence he has compiled, that modern, libertarian insistence on the "right" not to be censored originated in the anti-Irish attacks which pictured the champions of censorship as "immigrant morons" who "spread everywhere, multiplying like rabbits."[28]

A favorite use of history is that employed by many writers to test the present strength of constitutional institutions by comparing them to their historical counterparts. Louis L. Jaffe is one who does this in 1963. He traces English backgrounds to the doctrine of sovereign immunity and concludes that, when the United States became independent, Americans lost "half of the rights against the government which as Englishmen they had previously enjoyed."[29] Leon T. David carries the technique one step further by comparing today's attorney general with the concept of the attorney generalship in colonial times. Then, the attorney general was more than the chief legal officer of the state; he was also the protector of the people's liberties against official usurpation of authority. History, David contends, urges the importance of the colonial pattern, and he asks that the attorney general get back his "full power."[30] Richard D. Younger presents a similar case for the grand jury.[31] His book is the first full-dressed study of the grand jury in America. His discovery of original source material is truly remarkable, but despite his skill Younger has difficulty handling the vast territorial scope of his subject and is forced to string topics together in digest form. He concentrates on the grand jury's administrative, investigatory, and propagandizing functions, and it is these he wants restored as a check on governmental power.

Among the non-law periodicals, the bulk of legal history articles not only concentrates on constitutional subjects, but quite often reflects

---

[28] Paul S. Boyer, "Boston Book Censorship in the Twenties," 15 *Am. Q.* 3, 23-24 (1963).

[29] Louis L. Jaffe, "Suits Against Governments and Officers: Sovereign Immunity," 77 *Harv. L. Rev.* 1, 19 (1963).

[30] Leon T. David, "Councillors and the Law Officers in the Colonies in America," 12 *Am. U.L. Rev.* 23, 50 (1963).

[31] Richard D. Younger, *The People's Panel: The Grand Jury in the United States, 1634-1941* (1963).

current controversies.[32] The contention of Robert E. Brown, noted in last year's *Survey*,[33] that democracy did exist in colonial America, was seriously questioned during 1963 by John Cary.[34] Brown's own defense seems quite convincing.[35] This debate holds meaning for legal institutional history since it relates to the pressures which gave shape to the constitution, and it is upon theories explaining the origin and meaning of these pressures that much constitutional interpretation has turned. Perhaps the most impressive of the constitutional history studies to be published by a non-law periodical, however, dealt with medieval English, rather than modern American, constitutional law and was authored by Amherst's Frederic L. Cheyette. By way of a detailed and challenging analysis of "custom," he casts doubt on the "common view" that custom placed limits on princely or judicial power to make new law for new problems — that there was no place within the scheme of feudal law for direct legislation.[36]

Among new books we should note the project to update the ten volume series, *The Colonial Records of North Carolina* [37] and a study of the drafting of the two constitutions of the Confederate States.[38] The last presents an unusual approach to constitutional history, for the author organizes his discussion in terms of personalities rather than issues. Bernard Schwartz does the opposite. His new book is more law-oriented than most constitutional histories intended for popular consumption. As he views it, "Human history . . . is in essence a history of ideas," and thus he projects Anglo-American constitutional history largely in terms of "a history of the development of the idea of law as a check upon governmental power."[39]

---

[32] E.g., on reapportionment see A. Clark Hagensick, "Revolution or Reform in 1836: Maryland's Preface to the Dorr Rebellion," 57 *Md. Hist. Mag.* 346 (1962).

[33] Brown says that to interpret the constitution "it matters a great deal" whether it was produced by a class-ridden or middle-class society. See chapter 2, at 43.

[34] John Cary, "Statistical Method and the Brown Thesis on Colonial Democracy," 20 *William & Mary Q.* (3d Ser.) 251 (1963).

[35] Id. at 265.

[36] Frederic L. Cheyette, "Custom, Case Law, and Medieval 'Constitutionalism': A Re-examination," 78 *Pol. Sci. Q.* 362 (1963).

[37] *North Carolina Charters and Constitutions, 1578-1698* (Mattie Erma Edwards Parker ed. 1963).

[38] Charles Robert Lee, *The Confederate Constitutions* (1963).

[39] Bernard Schwartz, *The Reins of Power — A Constitutional History of the United States 2* (1963).

III

AMERICAN LEGAL HISTORY

Commenting on a collection of essays dealing with public-land history, Elmo R. Richardson recently wrote: "All of the selections . . . attest to the fact that the writing of public land history calls for competence both in economics and the political and natural sciences."[40] Like most historians he could not be expected to feel that knowledge of legal issues is necessary for a topic such as this. But Paul W. Gates's study of the movement from the common-law doctrine of real property rights to the rule of occupancy established by improvements, demonstrates the central role which law played in the history of American public lands.[41] In what may be the year's most interesting legal history article, Gates examines the evolution of legal theory in terms of economic and social pressures prior to the Homestead Act. If Gates proves to historians that they must not overlook law when writing meaningful histories of public lands, then it must be acknowledged that Sumner Chilton Powell's new book on the early New England village[42] proves to lawyers that the history of American law cannot be written until they integrate studies conducted by historians and economists on land history.[43] The accomplishments of 1963 show that much of the ground work for a history of American land law has been laid. The Hurst school at Wisconsin is showing us how the integration can be effected.[44]

---

[40] Elmo R. Richardson, "Book Note," 68 *Am. Hist. Rev.* 1146 (1963) (reviewing *The Public Lands: Studies in the History of the Public Domain* (Vernon Rosco Carstensen ed. 1963)).

[41] Paul W. Gates, "Tenants of the Log Cabin," 49 *Miss. Valley Hist. Rev.* 3 (1962). See also Gates's article on the Homestead Act between 1862 and 1915 in *Land Use Policy and Problems in the United States* (Howard W. Ottoson ed. 1963).

[42] Sumner Chilton Powell, *Puritan Village: The Formation of a New England Town* (1963).

[43] Compare William Haller, Jr., "Book Review," 350 *Annals* 185 (1963) with James Duane Squires, "Book Review," 21 *William & Mary Q.* (3d Ser.) 143 (1964). The Powell book does not dwell on legal aspects, but contains the rawstuff from which legal historians of towns-as-institutions may draw.

[44] J. Willard Hurst, *Law and Economic Growth: The Legal History of the Lumber Industry in Wisconsin 1836-1915* (1964); James A. Lake, *Law and Mineral Wealth: The Legal Profile of the Wisconsin Mining Industry* (1962); Erling Day Solberg, *New Laws for New Forests: Wisconsin's Forest-Fire, Tax, Zoning, and County-Forest Laws in Operation* (1961). See also chapter 2, at 36-37.

IV

LEGAL BIOGRAPHY

The big event of 1963 occurred in the area of legal and judicial biography. Biographies were published in all shapes and sizes, ranging from a comprehensive life of John Adams[45] and a new study of Morrison R. Waite,[46] down to an encomiastic portrayal of Samuel Seabury.[47] Especially noteworthy is the fact that Gerald T. Dunne continues his excellent articles on Joseph Story,[48] maintaining the high standards previously set. He is retelling, through Story's eyes, the legal aspect of the Federalist-Republican battles, framing it in terms of national sovereignty versus states' rights while avoiding economic interpretation.[49] When Mr. Dunne's work is completed we may expect a first-rate biography.[50]

The highlight of the survey year, however, was the publication of the second volume of Mark DeWolfe Howe's definitive life of Oliver Wendell Holmes. Howe takes Holmes from age twenty-nine to his appointment to the Massachusetts bench; years when Holmes was a practicing attorney, editor of Kent's *Commentaries*, co-editor of the *American Law Review*, Lecturer and Professor of Law, and author of *The Common Law*. He treats these years in terms of Holmes's philosophical growth. Indeed, as far as Holmes is concerned, Howe was able to surmount the difficult problem of "legal" as distinguished from "judicial" biography; *i.e.*, Holmes's career at the bar. He discusses the litigations in which Holmes participated as counsel as they relate to his general intellectual development. Most interesting is his reappraisal of Holmes as a legal historian. As summarized by Professor Willard Hurst:

---

[45] Page Smith, *John Adams,* (1963) (two volumes, not much on law practice).

[46] C. Peter Magrath, *Morrison R. Waite — The Triumph of Character* (1963).

[47] Herbert Mitgang, *The Man Who Rode the Tiger: The Life and Times of Judge Samuel Seabury* (1963).

[48] Story has been attracting much attention of late. For a valuable study appraising Story's influence on the beginnings of American legal literature see, Andrew Johnson, "The Influences of Nathan Dane on Legal Literature," 7 *Am. J. Legal Hist.* 28 (1963).

[49] Gerald T. Dunne, "The American Blackstone," 1963 *Wash. U.L.Q. 321;* Gerald T. Dunne, "Joseph Story: 1812 Overture," *77 Harv. L. Rev.* 240 (1963).

[50] Others who are working on biographies are Professor Daniel J. Meador and Professor Philip B. Kurland. See Daniel J. Meador, "Lamar and the Law at the University of Mississippi," 34 *Miss. L.J.* 227 (1963) and Philip B. Kurland, "Personal Thoughts about Problems of Judicial Biography," 38 *Notre Dame Law.* 490 (1963).

> Mark Howe puts matters in illuminating perspective when he urges that we should view Holmes, in his role as scholar, primarily as a legal philosopher rather than as an historian. *The Common Law* is conventionally taken as a pioneer work in legal history, and of course it does tell a good deal of history. But the features of the book which have made it live — and those which, it is plain, Holmes viewed as most significant — were its epigirammatic hypotheses and fresh concepts concerning the processes by which law grows and finds its roles in the development of social organization. Holmes was interested in history not so much to explain the past as to furnish materials for the development of a more acute jurisprudence.[51]

"Holmes," Hurst goes on, "gave an institutional cast to legal history and to the jurisprudence based on legal history."[52]

It is indicative of the greatness of Howe's biography that it has given rise to several critical studies as well as to many reviews.[53] Regrettably they follow Howe's theme and ignore Holmes, the historian, in favor of Holmes, the philosopher. But Professor Howe himself paid close attention to the beginnings of legal history scholarship in America, particularly evaluating the roles of Henry Adams and Horace Gray.[54] Moreover, he had something to say about how legal history will be written in the future. Speaking of the fact that Holmes's generation felt the need for a philosophic order to the law of torts, Howe postulated an historical theory which no historian dealing with the evolution of legal doctrine during the latter half of the nineteenth century can afford to ignore:

> Bentham's energy had set in motion two separate yet related endeavors. The one was essentially practical seeking drastic reform of procedure in the courts of common law and equity. The other was philosophical and asked for a system of law designed by reason for the achieving of defined ends. The first movement towards practical reform had achieved notable successes . . . by the 1870's. . . . The elimination of artificiality meant, however, the casting aside of the one element which had provided a degree of order in the English legal system. While the forms of action prevailed it was possible for

---

[51] Willard Hurst, "Book Review," 77 *Harv. L. Rev.* 382, 385 (1963).

[52] Id. at 386.

[53] See, e.g., Yosal Rogat, Francis A. Allen, Harry Kalven Jr., & Malcolm P. Sharp, "Mr. Justice Holmes: Some Modern Views," 31 *U. Chi. L. Rev.* 213 (1964) (a symposium); Saul Touster, "Holmes: The Years of *The Common Law,*" 64 *Colum. L. Rev.* 230 (1964); Harry Cohen, "Book Review," 16 *Ala. L. Rev.* 266 (1963); Shale D. Stiller, "Book Review" 23 *Md. L. Rev.* 378 (1963).

[54] For another look at the formative era of American legal history scholarship see Helen Maud Cam,"The Study of English Medieval History Today," in Helen Maud Cam, *supra* note 14, at 176.

lawyers, though doubtless impossible for philosophers, to see structure in the English legal system. The common-law practitioner saw no need for a theory of liability in tort when he knew the scope of the action on the case and the reach of an action of trespass. . . . As the reformers pulled down the scaffolding, the need for carrying forward Bentham's second endeavor — the philosophical — became imperative. By mid-century the time had come for English and American lawyers to offer an arrangement of the law possessing a rational and philosophic strength wholly lacking in the dissolving procedural order of the earlier day.[55]

[55] Mark De Wolfe Howe, *Justice Oliver Wendell Holmes — The Proving Years 1870-1882,* at 65-66 (1963). See also Howe's discussion in O. W. Holmes, Jr., *The Common Law* xiv-xv (Mark DeWolfe Howe ed. 1963).

Chapter Four

1964

John Phillip Reid

Roscoe Pound died this survey year. The cause of American legal history owes Dean Pound as great a debt as that owed by jurisprudence.[1] He was its spokesman for many years, and what popularity it has obtained has been due largely to his devotion. Yet it would be less than truthful to suggest that his mark upon legal history will prove as indelible as his contributions to most other areas of the law. He wrote history in the grand manner, using the sweeping generality and the broad supposition to gloss over what were then unexplored areas of knowledge. Contemporary historians cannot ignore his theories, but all too often research proves them to be insupportable and his writings are usually cited in terms of conceptual references which must be denied. The fact remains, however, that Roscoe Pound was the giant who left the footprints which a generation of more pedestrian historians will spend years covering over.

I

LEGAL HISTORIOGRAPHY

When the debt owed by legal history to Roscoe Pound is totaled up, it seems likely that he will be honored not so much for individual works as for his service in convincing the teachers and scholars of American law that history cannot be ignored even by the most professional and practical of disciplines. Thus Robert F. Fries struck an appropriate note during this, the year of Pound's death, when he noted the changing attitudes toward the usefulness of legal history which, we feel, occurred during a period roughly corresponding to Pound's lifetime.

> Although legal history was once an important subject of study in professional schools of law, it was designed traditionally to explain the genetic background of modern technicalities of the law, especially

[1] Dean Pound was also praised by the 1964 *Survey* in articles entitled "Criminal Law," "The Legal Profession," and "Jurisprudence".

> in the area of procedure. Because many anachronisms have been removed in recent decades through procedural reform, much of the practical reason for the teaching of legal history to prospective lawyers was removed, and the subject lost ground among legal scholars. At the same time the interest of professional historians in legal history was confined almost entirely to the constitutional field. The resulting lacuna in general legal history has produced a deepening sense of loss among scholarly members of law faculties, who feel that a legal system rooted in the past cannot be understood if the past is ignored. The growth of this conviction has led to a renaissance of interest in the subject, which happily takes a broader view of the processes of historical development than the old legal history, and which shows a greater interest in American legal history than in its English antecedents.[2]

There is much truth in what Fries says. Academic interest in legal history is broader than it once was, but this may reflect the fact that the study of law itself is now broader, having moved out from beyond the confines of judicial precedents and statutes into the wider range of social and economic considerations. At the same time American legal history as a distinct area of scholarship has come into its own; a development recounted by William F. Swindler who briefly surveyed nonconstitutional historical writing since the *Lectures* of James Barr Ames.[3] Ames, of course, was interested in English legal history as were such of his fellow countrymen as Gray, Thayer, Holmes, Bigelow, Charles Gross, and George Adams. These seven Americans are among the forty-two correspondents included in C.H.S. Fifoot's collection of Maitland's letters (volume one of the Selden's Society's "supplementary series"). It is revealing how much Maitland depended upon the research of some Americans and how he wished he had them closer at hand for consultation.[4] They in turn pioneered the study of English legal history over here, and these letters to an Englishman help us to appreciate what little thought they gave to the legal past of their own country. Their attitude surprised Maitland. He had a lively curiosity about American legal history and believed its study would have been of value to English legal

---

[2] Robert F. Fries, "Book Review," 51 *J. Am. Hist.* 507, 508 (1964).

[3] William F. Swindler, "Book Review," 63 *Mich. L. Rev.* 952 (1965). Interestingly, Swindler does not mention Pound. Instead he sees Morris as the starting point of the movement.

[4] "I can't tell why it is, but certainly you seem to care a deal more for legal history on your bank of the Atlantic then we do here. It is a mal-arrangement of the universe which puts the records in one continent and those who would care to read them in another." Letter From F.W. Maitland to M.M. Bigelow, 31 July 1888, in *The Letters of Frederic William Maitland* 45 (C.H.S. Fifoot ed. 1965).

historians.[5] As for Maitland himself, we see by his letters that he had to devote time to problems which Fries optimistically suggests may no longer hamper legal-history scholarship. When planning the first Selden Society publication, Maitland took into account the demands of the profession for materials currently of "use," as he explained to the Society's Secretary:

> I venture to suggest that the Society might begin its labours by publishing a few volumes of select Pleas of the Crown illustrating the development of the criminal law throughout the middle ages. Of course, were it certain that the Society's books would find many purchasers, there would be much to be said for working through the plea rolls in their chronological order and taking thence all cases of interest no matter what their subject matter. I doubt however whether at the present time the first volumes of a series made on this principle would prove attractive. The extracts in any volume would be very miscellaneous and some years would elapse before there would be a sufficient mass of matter about any one topic to make any inductions safe or profitable. Subscribers will naturally demand results of which they can at once take advantage.

Besides, he added, real actions would be thought "dull" by some while criminal cases "are very interesting and even entertaining and, at least when translated, would be found readable by many who would not care to study the effects of warranty, discontinuance and so forth."[6]

The scholar who best exemplifies Fries's suggestion that legal history today "takes a broader view of the processes of historical development than the old legal history" is James Willard Hurst of the University of Wisconsin. In many respects, 1964 was Willard Hurst's year. Not only did he publish two books, but his work, influence, and philosophy were made the subject of a forty-four page appraisal by Earl Finbar Murphy.[7] The theme of Murphy's study is Hurst's "jurisprudence of legal history"; a jurisprudence which Hurst restated this survey year in a literary style less complicated than usual:[8]

---

[5] See, e.g., Letter From F.W. Maitland to J.B. Thayer, 20 April 1887, id. at 27; Letter From F.W. Maitland to J.B. Thayer, 21 September 1890, id. at 83; Letter From F.W. Maitland to M.M. Bigelow, 1 February 1891, id. at 88.

[6] Letter from F.W. Maitland to P.E. Dove, 27 April 1887, id. at 27-28. While working on the second volume Maitland told Thayer: "Dove evidently is afraid that the book will be very dull and writes me many letters adjuring me to be lively." Letter From F.W. Maitland to J.B. Thayer, 16 December 1888, id. at 52.

[7] Earl Finbar Murphy, "The Jurisprudence of Legal History: Willard Hurst as a Legal Historian," 39 *N.Y.U.L. Rev.* 900 (1964).

[8] "One may wish that Professor Hurst's prose were less dense and more engaging." Francis A. Allen, "Book Review," 358 *The Annals* 251, 252 (1965).

> The study of United States legal history will come of age when its practitioners give as much effort to framing questions as to assembling answers. A vital philosophy of law needs to work upon the full-dimensioned stuff of experience which legal historians can supply; if there is little reason to be satisfied with the contributions which jurisprudence has been making to the understanding of legal order in the past generation, the deficiencies reflect in part the thin flow of historical studies useful to philosophy. Because the historian's job preoccupies him with concrete particularities, he incurs occupational hazards which may rob his work of meaning. Immersed in detail, he may be diverted into the collector's mania, and wind up an antiquarian. The passing days make him painfully aware of how time-costly it is to uncover the full dimension of events. Harassed by the calendar, he begrudges the time taken from collecting data in order to shape and test the theoretical framework of his inquiries. So he is tempted into a naive empiricism — using his research simply to document the unexamined assumptions and prejudices of common sense or tradition, or behaving as if he believed that meaning could be squeezed out of data by the sheer weight of their accumulation.[9]

In other words, Professor Hurst is warning that American legal history has been narrow in its focus. This, he suggests, is due not only to conceptual schemes on the part of legal historians concerning the scope of their discipline, but also to what Hurst disciples can readily recognize as "inertia" and "drift." Historians can inert and drift as much as institutions. In one of his new books (which might well have been entitled, *Willard Hurst on Legal History*) he quotes Holmes's statement that Maitland gave English legal history an almost deceptive charm. Holmes felt that our "only interest in the past is for the light it throws upon the present" and Hurst agrees. "To insist," he argues, "that legal history be written to show what relevance events bore to meaningful questions was to insist that it be written to enlarge theoretical knowledge of the content and processes of social experience."[10] Whether Holmes meant this is beside the point. Hurst does mean it. It is the central theme of his historiography; that legal history is legitimately concerned with "the whole sweep" of social and economic change and is the "study of the particular performance of law in the context of particular times and situations."[11] He has said this before — in the abstract. What gives it new meaning and makes this survey year significant for Willard Hurst is that now he says it in the particular; he puts his "jurisprudence of legal

[9] J. Willard Hurst, "Themes in United States Legal History", in *Felix Frankfurter — A Tribute* 199-200 (Wallace Mendelson ed. 1964).

[10] James Willard Hurst, *Justice Holmes on Legal History* 6 (1964).

[11] James Willard Hurst, *supra* note 9, at 213.

history" to the test by bringing it to bear, in all its details, on one isolated and laconic topic, the legal history of the lumber industry in Wisconsin. Seeking, as he says, "more meaningful and more useful concepts of the subject matter of legal history,"[12] Hurst "uses the story of lumbering in Wisconsin to show that the broad stream of small-scale events was as important in the development of American law as the roar of the cataracts of famous cases and great constitutional events."[13] As a pioneer work which seeks to examine the drift of law as the only form of control over an unplanned economy, and which also tries to demonstrate the influence of social and economic factors on the law as well as the counter problem of the law's effect on society and economics, the book is over long and bogs down in a mass of details. For this Hurst offers no apology, but blames it on the current state of American legal historiography.

> Labor has no virtue in itself. Nor is there magic in counting items merely to construct tables of figures. More time cost was invested in this project than would be warranted at a more developed stage of legal history research, when more knowledge should make it safe to cut corners. However, given the present relative lack of studies in the relation of law to social process, it seems useful that some work should err on the side of overinvestment.[14]

Among the new recruits to the Hurst school of legal history, the most prolific is Lawrence M. Friedman, also of Wisconsin.[15] He is a convinced Hurstian who, objecting to the "excessive attention" accorded decisional law by historians, asks that legal history be rescued "from its narrowness" and related "to a more general phenomenon (social change)."[16] Of special interest is his criticism of the traditional "perspective" from which legal historians have been accustomed to view events:

> History books are usually written from a near-sighted perspective, i.e., they are very dim about what happened in the early stages of

---

[12] James Willard Hurst, *Law and Economic Growth: The Legal History of the Lumber Industry in Wisconsin 1836-1915* viii (1964).

[13] Rodney C. Loehr, "Book Review," 70 *Am. Hist. Rev.* 269 (1964).

[14] James Willard Hurst, *supra* note 12, at x-xi.

[15] See, e.g., Lawrence M. Friedman & Michael J. Spector, "Tenement House Legislation in Wisconsin: Reform and Reaction," 9 *Am. J. Legal Hist.* 41 (1965); Lawrence M. Friedman, "The Dynastic Trust," 73 *Yale L.J.* 547 (1964).

[16] "The legal historian runs a particular risk of falling into antiquarianism. The danger is greatest when he traces 'concepts,' since this invites him to trace his data the way a lawyer traces precedents, hopping backward from case to case until he can hop no more; and then, at this earliest point, beginning to write his brief." Lawrence M. Friedman, "Book Review," 74 *Yale L.J.* 593, 597 (1965).

> their subject, and devote most of their pages and effort to the more recent past. As many years elapsed from Jamestown to the American Revolution as from the Revolution to the depression of the '30's; but the standard American history text spends two, three, or four times as much space on the latter as on the former period. . . .
>
> Anglo-American legal history has quite the opposite tendency. Its perspective is distinctly far-sighted (in the nasty sense of the word). There is a fuzzy period (up to 1066), but the historians devote most of their attention to the span of time between William the Conqueror and the Statute of Uses. The 400-odd years from then till now are as much the dark ages of legal history as the period of Ine, King of the West Saxons. . . .
>
> . . . .
>
> It can be argued that the study of the living law pays adequate attention to the immediate past, so that legal history, as a discrete field, should concern itself with more remote antecedents. Of course, what passes for "history" in most law courses is usually only a crude counterfeit. Nor do the particular courses deal with patterns of change throughout the legal system. That is a task for the legal historian. It is certainly odd to ignore the study of those patterns at precisely the point in time when they become most relevant to an understanding of our legal system and its place in our social order.[17]

The gulf which separates legal historians from general historians continues to be an historiographic theme.[18] Kathryn Turner complains that legal scholars examining the Judiciary Act of 1801 have commented on jurisdiction without placing the story in adequate historical context. Historians, focusing on organization, have ignored jurisdiction. She blends the two in a splendid study of jurisdictional power employed to effect economic interests.[19] On the other hand, Paul C. Nagel, in a 328-page study of American nationalism as encompassed by the word "Union," draws from hundreds of quotations — "most liberally of all, from Presidents and congressmen." But, as James Rabun points out, Nagel ignores the judiciary. "Such men as John Marshall and Roger Taney, even though they had much to say about the Union, never enter

---

[17] Id. at 594-95.

[18] One aspect of the problem discussed this year is the difficulty which the lawyer-biographer has in reaching a general audience and which the general historian has when he attempts to write the life of a judge which will prove acceptable to lawyers. See the special issue on "Law and Biography" in 57 *L. Library J.* 128-75 (1964).

[19] Kathryn Turner, "Federalist Policy and the Judiciary Act of 1801," 22 *William & Mary Q.* (3d Ser.) 3 (1965).

these pages."[20] The dimensions of the problem became apparent this year as regards publication of court records. As Erwin C. Surrency suggests, "Legal documents by their very nature have caused historians generally to omit them in their researches and have generally been left to the genealogist. . . ."[21] More serious than this is the fact that they are sometimes edited for the genealogist and ignore entirely the needs of the legal historian. George L. Haskins used the Essex County records to illustrate this conflict of interests:

> The Editor, Mr. G.F. Dow, states in his Introduction to the first volume that the records and files have been "printed in abstracted form, free from needless verbiage, but every essential particular is retained so that the historian, genealogist and sociologist may be assured that nothing of value has been omitted." Unhappily, examination of the original manuscript reveals that, in fact, much of value to the legal historian has been deliberately excluded. Frequently the form of action, though clearly stated in the manuscript record, is not given in the printed version; two suits, for example, appear as burglary and theft, although the clerk in fact labeled them, respectively, trespass and case. . . . Among other important omissions which may be noted is his exclusion of references to damages and costs. The costs assessed, while unimportant to a genealogist, are certainly significant to the legal historian.[22]

This complaint will not be directed against the new set of records from Prince Georges County, Maryland, since they were edited by a legal historian, Joseph H. Smith.[23] The problem encountered by Smith and his

---

[20] James Rabun, "Book Review," 70 *Am. Hist. Rev.* 569 (1965) (reviewing Paul C. Nagel, *One Nation Indivisible: The Union in American Thought* (1964)). Along the same line compare, 3 Philip Sheldon Foner, *History of the Labor Movement in the United States — The Policies and Practices of the American Federation of Labor* 338-348 (1964) with Philip Taft, *Organized Labor in American History* 215-19 (1964).

[21] Erwin C. Surrency, "Book Review," 22 *William & Mary Q.* (3rd Ser.) 366, 367 (1965).

[22] George L. Haskins, "The First American Reform of Civil Procedure" in *Perspectives of Law: Essays for Austin Wakeman Scott* 173, 185-86 (1964). This was a result which Maitland sought to avoid in the Seldon Society's publications. When the Jewish Historical Society of England suggested it might support a volume on the Jewish Exchequer rolls, Maitland warned: "I take it that our Jewish allies will want an abstract or note of all entries, as they will be in search rather of names and pedigrees than of legal matters." Letter From F.W. Maitland to B.F. Lock, 26 May 1895, in *The Letters of Frederic William Maitland* 136 (C.H.S.Fifoot ed. 1965).

[23] Although it is amusing to note that the reviewer for the local legal periodical suggested that the book "should be of interest to historians studying colonial history and to certain families in Prince George's [?] County." John B. Gray, "Book Review," 25 *Md. L. Rev.* 86 (1965).

co-editor, Philip A. Crowl, was whether to write their introduction for historians or for lawyers:

> The original intention was to have both an historical and a legal introduction to the records. However, this gave rise to a number of editorial difficulties which threatened to halt publication. The present editors finally decided to pool their efforts and to cover the historical and legal aspects in one introduction. . . . In this introduction we have attempted to integrate such material as the acts of the provincial legislature, the records of the Governor and Council and the House of Delegates, the records of other provincial courts, various other records of the colony and English law and practice.[24]

This is a matter in which legal historians have a legitimate concern. The introductions to court records constitute as important a collection of writing as exist anywhere in American legal history. The one by Smith and Crowl is a model which, if emulated, would serve as justification for demanding more publications of this type. A different, but valuable, introduction is that prepared by Neal W. Allen for the records of the home county of York on the banks of the old Piscataqua. It adopts a different approach and shows how legal records can be used for writing the social history of a rural people.[25]

The best historiographic study published in a legal periodical this year was written by John G. Wofford. While limiting his discussion to the use of history to interpret the federal constitution, he has much to say about legislative history in general as well as the techniques for employing it. His purpose is to dethrone theory as an exclusive tool of interpretation not merely for the often-cited reason that it is seldom used objectively, but for the more subtle reason that it is simply not adaptable to judicial decision making — even in the hands of totally impartial judges. His indictment of "history" is impressive, though based largely on the obvious inadequacies of the source materials most frequently used by constitutional scholars.[26] "The choice," he argues, "is not between the judgment of the individual and the judgment of history: History makes no judgment; only individuals do. History should be merely one aid in

---

[24] *Court Records of Prince Georges County, Maryland 1696 - 1699* vii-viii (Joseph H. Smith & Philip A. Crowl eds. 1964).

[25] *The Court Records of York County, Maine: Province of Massachusetts Bay April, 1711 — October, 1718* (Neal W. Allen ed. 1964) (volume 5 of Province and Court Records of Maine).

[26] An appraisal of one such source is Julius Goebel, "Melancton Smith's Minutes of Debates on the New Constitution," 64 *Colum. L. Rev.* 26 (1964).

helping that individual come to a sensible — but necessarily personal — judgment."[27]

In what was the strangest legal historiographic notion to be expressed this year, George Anastaplo agreed that history is personal, but insisted it should still be controlling — as long as it supports his side of an issue. Attacking Leonard Levy's revisionist account of civil rights in early America, Anastaplo suggests that historical scholarship which uncovers evidence disproving the traditional myths which have served as argumentative tools for modern-day liberals, is scholarship better left unpublished. If Levy's research convinced him that there was a legacy of suppression during the later eighteenth century he should have ignored the evidence and left the myths undisturbed.[28] This, of course, is a problem which plagues legal history today — the liberal insistence that legal history be treated as poetry, not as a science. In sum it is a rejection of the tenet that a legal historian's posture must be one of ethical detachment; it denies that the legal historian has responsibilities as a craftsman which transcend his responsibilities as an adherent to a moral or political philosophy currently rife. After contemplating such intellectual rubbish it is refreshing to note that polemical legal history can still be written with a graceful touch.[29]

II

CONSTITUTIONAL HISTORY

The liberal predilections which Anastaplo feels legal historians should not question are, of course, "those that we have, with gross historical inaccuracy, come to associate with the name of Mr. Justice Hugo Black."[30] Reviewing another of Dean Levy's "revisionist" books, Willmoore Kendall takes the opposite position from Anastaplo and argues that the publication of studies which expose the erroneous assumptions bequeathed to our generation by writers like Alexander Meikeljohn and

---

27 John G. Wofford, "The Blinding Light: The Uses of History in Constitutional Interpretation," 31 *U.Chi. L. Rev.* 502, 532 (1964).

28 George Anastaplo, "Book Review," 39 *N.Y.U.L. Rev.* 735 (1964) (reviewing Leonard W. Levy, *Legacy of Suppression — Freedom of Speech and Press in Early American History* (1960)).

29 See Jo Desha Lucas, "Flood Tide: Some Irrelevant History of the Admiralty," in 1964 *Supreme Court Rev.* 249 (Philip Kurland ed.)

30 Willmoore Kendell, "Book Review," 16 *Stan. L. Rev.* 753 (1964) (reviewing Leonard W. Levy, *Jefferson and Civil Liberties: The Darker Side* (1963)).

Zechariah Chafee is a "wholesome development in our public debate" since they will oblige Americans "in the future to argue these questions on their merits, that is, on the level of political philosophy."[31] Of course, it is not merely the liberal persuasion which misuses history. Charles E. Rice made history a weapon to support an argument as polemical and debatable as those who oppose his position on church and state; a position which might have been stronger had it been "put together in any careful and objective historical analysis."[32] The lawyer may use history to brief a constitutional case, but he must use it as history and not as precedent.

The collection of documents to sustain a constitutional position seems to be a growing trend. One of the very best was compiled this year by the Virginia Commission on Constitutional Government.[33] Since it is designed to sustain an argument which most scholars reject out of hand, it will not receive the attention which it deserves. Alpheus Thomas Mason, on the other hand, has taken the popular side in the states-rights debate which he is able to settle to his own satisfaction by finding that the record "overwhelmingly" supports the "Federalists" — the tenth amendment is "a constitutional tranquilizer, an empty declaration."[34] If this be "history" we would be hard pressed to define the place of an excellent volume produced by the New Jersey Historical Series. While the constitutional history of the states once attracted some attention it has been sadly neglected during this century. Julian P. Boyd has restated the case for its importance by successfully editing the fundamental laws and constitutions of his state.[35]

An illuminating collection of documents centering on the trial of Roger Williams and edited by Theodore P. Greene was published by the "Problems in American Civilization" series. It astutely balances contemporary accounts and nineteenth-century interpretations against more-recent reappraisals with the intention of shedding light on the origin and development of attitudes toward American freedoms. In overall perspective, the collection serves to warn historians against dogmatic judgments

---

[31] Id. at 757.

[32] Alfred Kelly, "Book Review," 70 *Am. Hist. Rev.* 564 (1965) (reviewing Charles F. Rice, *The Supreme Court and Public Prayer: The Need for Restraint* (1964)).

[33] Virginia Commission on Constitutional Government, *We the States: An Anthology of Historical Documents and Commentaries thereon, Expounding the State and Federal Relationship* (1964).

[34] Alpheus Thomas Mason, *The States Rights Debate: Antifederalism and the Constitution* (1964).

[35] *Fundamental Laws and Constitutions of New Jersey 1664 - 1964* (Julian P. Boyd ed. 1964).

based on the values prevalent to their own times. Yet, with a touch of irony, the editor has arranged the materials with an eye on current issues:

> After the Security Act of 1950 the many official investigations, dismissals, and even deportations of recent years, Americans cannot look upon the actions of the Massachusetts magistrates with quite the same easy condescension which characterized some historians of the nineteenth and early twentieth century. If we are honest with ourselves, we cannot fail to give the John Winthrop of 1635 a hearing. If we care about the quality and vitality of our national life, however, we cannot dismiss a Roger Williams simply as a "subversive." To understand fully what was at stake in 1635 may give us a fuller perspective on what is at stake under different circumstances, when fears for security lead us to curtail liberty today.[36]

The need to make things meaningful to present problems may explain Alan F. Westin's lament: "Most of the innovative books being written on the Supreme Court and constitutional law are by political scientists; as for the historical side, a contemporary convention of American constitutional history specialists could be held on a Greyhound bus."[37] Perhaps so, but to legal historians their number seems disproportionately large since such a high percentage of historical scholarship in law is devoted to the constitutional area. Indeed, at times it seems excessive, as for example this survey year which, aside from Willard Hurst's books, was almost totally dominated by constitutional works.[38] Carl Brent Swisher complains that too many of these have been written to satisfy curiosity "aroused by decisions in the fields of civil rights and personal liberty." This has had the unfortunate "effect of largely eliminating from treatment the hosts of important cases dealing with property rights, federalism, international relations, and other significant topics."[39] On the other side of the coin is the tendency of lawyers to see constitutional history in terms of Supreme Court decisions. Judge Edward Dumbauld's new book stresses the intention of the framers behind each clause of the constitution and goes on to annotate subsequent interpreta-

---

36 *Roger Williams and the Massachusetts Magistrates* viii (Theodore P. Greene ed. 1964).

37 Alan F. Westin, "The Business of the Court," *N.Y. Times*, Mar. 7, 1965, § 7 (Book Review), p. 3.

38 E.g., Donald Barr Chidsey, *The Birth of the Constitution: An Informal History* (1964); John A. Garraty, *Quarrels that have Shaped the Constitution* (1964); Merrill Jensen, *The Making of the American Constitution* (1964); Broadus Mitchell & Louise Pearson Mitchell, *A Biography of the Constitution of the United States: Its Formation, Origin, Adoption, Interpretation* (1964).

39 Carl Brent Swisher, "Book Review," 352 *The Annals* 190 (1964) (reviewing Rocco J. Tresolini, *Justice and the Supreme Court* (1963)).

tions. He was criticized for denying "out of hand the idea of executive prerogative, largely on the basis of the 1952 Steel Seizure Case, while virtually ignoring the great body of practice and precedent to the contrary."[40] It may be that the political scientist and the lawyer demand different results as well as different techniques from the constitutional historian.

Is it legitimate to complain that these works either re-examine issues previously researched or are fashioned not for the light they shed on "history" but for the arguments which "history" can lend to current political debates? Does it matter? One consequence may be that we are left with a partly-told tale. There is much to learn concerning our "constitutional" antecedents, but since this is an area requiring original research it is something we cannot expect from the current writers of constitutional history. This is a pity. As Herbert A. Johnson reminds us, the scope of constitutional history "is much broader than the analytical study of a written constitution or judicial precedents."

> Our associates in the field of British constitutional history are well aware of the many facets of the term "constitutional history"; lacking a document analogous to the Constitution of 1787, they do not suffer from the malady of "Constitution" fixation which burdens their fellows in American history with the handicap of being unable to distinguish between "constitutional history" and "the history of the 1787 Constitution."

In an article, Johnson surveys the materials available for pre-1787 history of American constitutional institutions. For historians this may be the one work of interest to appear this year in the area of constitutional history.[41]

But if writers insist on limiting their investigations to civil rights and personal liberty, there is still no need to rehash the same great cases or narrow discussion to the same familiar issues. There is potential even here for fresh research and original discoveries. Rudolph M. Lapp, for

---

[40] Alfred H. Kelly, "Book Review," 358 *The Annals* 206, 207 (1965) (reviewing Edward Dumbauld, *The Constitution of the United States* (1964)).

[41] Herbert A. Johnson, "Toward a Reappraisal of the 'Federal' Government: 1783-1789," 8 *Am. J. Legal Hist.* 314 (1964). See also a study of New York's first organic act to be framed by a representative convention and why it failed of approval; a failure blamed more on the constitutional principles which dominated London politics during 1684 (e.g., those of Lord Jeffreys) rather than the ill-will of the Duke of York. This study shows that American interest in the rights enjoyed by Englishmen was strong well before the eighteenth century. David S. Lovejoy, "Equality and Empire — The New York Charter of Libertyes, 1683," 21 *William & Mary Q.* (3d Ser.) 493 (1964).

example, while explaining some of the dilemmas facing Negroes in gold-rush California (e.g., was a colored man brought into the territory as a slave a "fugitive" who had to be returned to the south *after* the adoption of California's free-soil constitution?) and some of the remarkable judicial decisions (e.g., the *Lee* case in which a Negro was held within his rights to abandon his master's service, but since this was the first case of its kind the master was permitted to return him to slavery), point out that the civil-rights issue which aroused the most forceful Negro demands was one which historians often overlook and which pertained painfully to the legal system.

> While the Fugitive Slave Act and the exclusion bills drew their protests and indignation, nothing mobilized their concerted statewide actions more thoroughly than their demand for the right of testimony in cases involving white persons. The persistence of the California Negro in this campaign reflects a number of elements peculiar to California in this period. First, the turbulence of society in California at this time placed life and property in constant jeopardy. Second, the Negro population had accumulated more wealth in a shorter period of time in California than anywhere else in the nation. And, third, Negro leadership was well-organized, well-educated, articulate, and possessed a great deal of unity, especially on this question.

The Franchise League was formed, devoted to this one problem. It reported that Negroes in California had accumulated wealth totaling $2,375,000. As Lapp dryly observes, "It is clear from this that the Negro felt a need for legal defense of his growing assests as important as the legal rights to guarantee full citizenship."[42] Indeed, since this is the only issue which seems to have produced a state-wide gathering of colored citizens, it seems fair to conclude it was felt to be either more important or else more realistically obtainable. Can studies which concentrate on issues familiar to today's generation produce a true "history" of the struggle for civil rights in America?

III

LEGAL BIOGRAPHY

The interest in constitutional matters dominates even the field of legal biography, since most of the few biographies that are written today

---

[42] Rudolph M. Lapp, "The Negro in Gold Rush California," 49 *J. Negro Hist.* 81, 94-96 (1964).

deal with men who have played some part in constitution making or constitutional interpretation.[43] Happily this year attention was paid to some of the less significant judges to have sat on the federal Supreme Court.[44] We must have studies of the justices who sat beside the giants. While writers concentrate on the class of Holmes, Taney, and Marshall, the class of Woodbury, Day, and Todd has been completely neglected. For this reason alone, John P. Frank's biography of Peter V. Daniel[45] is of value. Yet we may wonder if this justifies the warm praise it received from the critics. Reviewers may have been so charmed by encountering a genuine Southern agrarian that they overlooked the unimaginative way in which the biographical material was presented.[46]

Of course the familiar "giants" were not neglected and as could have been predicted more fuel was fed this year to the furnace which fires the Holmes legend. Remarkable as it may be, 1964 saw the publication of yet another collection of his letters. These are addressed to a friend untrained in law and thus present a comprehensive appreciation of Holmes's cultural interests. "Well, dear boy," the Justice concluded one letter in which his thoughts had ranged from art to Haldane, "I must shut up and turn to applications for *certiorari* of which I suppose I must be ready to recite on about fifty by next Saturday. If you ask what a *certiorari* is I must answer with Jeremiah Mason to a client: 'That is something that your Heavenly Father never meant you to know.'"[47] Holmes's humor has even charmed punster devotees of Mr. Dooley.[48]

An article which evaluates the role of Salmon P. Chase in the trial of Andrew Johnson won the Phi Alpha Theta prize for the best undergraduate history essay submitted during the year. M. Kathleen Perdue examines the struggle between the Chief Justice who sought to make the impeachment a judicial hearing and the Radical Republicans who saw it

---

43 Samuel J. Konefsky, *John Marshall and Alexander Hamilton: Architects of the American Constitution* (1964); Fowler Vincent Harper, *Justice Rutledge and the Bright Constellation* (1965).

44 D. Stanley Eitzen, *David J. Brewer, 1837 - 1910: A Kansan on the United States Supreme Court* (1964).

45 John P. Frank, *Justice Daniel Dissenting: A Biography of Peter V. Daniel, 1784 - 1860* (1964).

46 Wisconsin's Stanley I. Kutler, who thought Frank's work "captivating," suggested that, "Daniel's judicial career might be viewed as a clue to what his good friend and Virginia compatriot, Spencer Roane, might have done in John Marshall's place." Stanley I. Kutler, "Book Review," 27 *The Historian* 96 (1964).

47 Letter From O.W. Holmes to L. Einstein, 10 October 1920, in the *Holmes - Einstein Letters: Correspondence of Mr. Justice Holmes and Lewis Einstein 1903 - 1935,* at 194 (James B. Peabody ed. 1964).

48 See Edward J. Bander, "Holmespun Humor,"10 *Vill. L. Rev.* 92 (1964) and 10 *Vill. L. Rev.* 299 (1965).

as a political proceeding; a struggle symbolized by the prosecution addressing Chase as "Mr. President," and the defense referring to him as "Mr. Chief Justice"; a distinction which Chase himself did not always honor as when he insisted on casting a tiebreaking vote, usually against the Radicals. Asserting that Chase's role in Johnson's acquittal should not be overestimated Miss Perdue concludes:

> To some extent, whether Chase remained strong or wavered during the trial was unimportant. His very presence at the impeachment trial and his adherence to the rules adopted to govern it gave the proceedings a semblance of dignity. His concern was less for Andrew Johnson the President than for the rendering of "an honest and impartial judgment, according to [the] Constitution and the laws, upon the facts proven before them [the Senators]." He felt sympathy for Andrew Johnson the man, and his own judgment and feeling favored acquittal. But even he . . . was "entirely uncertain as to the result."[49]

A persistent problem for legal biographers is how to deal with their biographee's career at the bar. In the important biography of 1963, Mark De Wolfe Howe eased around the difficulty by paying scant heed to Holmes's law practice except for those aspects which could be related to Holmes's general intellectual development.[50] Henry M. Holland is much bolder. He argues that the corpus of Cardozo's "legal thought can be found in his work as a lawyer." Undoubtedly Cardozo, who was living under the scandal of his father's corruption, displayed the "highest scruples in the practice of the lawyer's craft." But Professor Holland asks too much of his evidence when he asserts that Cardozo's later briefs

> show an inclination to move from self-interest in his client to disinterestedness and to be more conscious of the larger issues behind the litigation. In many of these briefs there is a keen awareness of the social context of the lawyer's work. . . . Indeed, Cardozo's briefs are instinct with the thought that the lawyer's work is a prime instrument for the achievement of justice.[51]

Must this always be the standard by which biographers measure law practice? Foster C. Nix apparently does not think so. He is preparing a

---

[49] M. Kathleen Perdue, "Salmon P. Chase and the Impeachment Trial of Andrew Johnson," 27 *The Historian* 75, 89 (1964) (the quotations are from Chase's private correspondence).

[50] See chapter 3, at 50-60. (discussing Mark DeWolfe Howe, *Justice Oliver Wendell Holmes — The Proving Years 1870 - 1882* (1963)).

[51] Henry M. Holland, "Mr. Justice Cardozo and the New Deal Court," 12 *J. Public L.* 383 (1963).

biography of Andrew Hamilton and does not ask whether Hamilton was able to rise above the petty interests of his clients (that is, whether he practiced law without performing the duties of a lawyer). Moreover, he presents valuable insights into the legal business of a colonial attorney and shows how much can be discovered by tracing through the local records of Virginia, Maryland, and Delaware the actions of a man who left no personal papers — no letters and no diaries.

> The Andrew Hamilton who emerges here in his early years from the official records is clearly recognizable as the man who becomes a very important figure in his later years in Pennsylvania. Recognizable too are the qualities such as loyalty, forthrightness, and strong devotion to his profession which Benjamin Franklin extolled in his obituary of Hamilton. Particularly evident in these early years is the last of these, his singular devotion to his chosen profession of law, which persisted throughout his life.[52]

The major publication of this survey year in the area of legal biography, and indeed of the year in legal history, helps to solve the logistics of this problem. While only the individual biographer can determine whether, when writing of a statesman or a judge, it is worthwhile to include material on his subject's early career at the bar, Julius Goebel, Jr., has shown him what can be done. We have noted previously how the editors of the multi-volume collections of private papers now being produced by university presses have neglected the "legal" in favor of the "historical."[53] Of course there have to be omissions. Dean Levy pointed to the need for ruthless editing when, contemplating the third volume of Madison's papers, he warned about "being smothered by tons of trivia":

> Madison was thiry-one years old in 1781. A long life, to 1836, and the great years of constructive achievement lie ahead of the editors. If these ten months are worth a volume in the life of a young congressman, who in these pages remains a shadowy and relatively unproductive figure, will we get a book for each month of the life of the mature constitutionmaker and congressman, a book for every week of the Secretary of State and a book for each day of the Presidency? Given their present rate of progress and incapacity to judge what is

[52] Foster C. Nix, "Andrew Hamilton's Early Years in the American Colonies," 21 *William & Mary Q.* (3d Ser.) 390, 407 (1964). For an excellent article on the libraries of colonial attorneys, see Edwin Wolf, "The Library of Ralph Asheton: The Book Background of a Colonial Philadelphia Lawyer," 58 *Papers of Bibliographical Soc'y of America* 345 (1964). See also Joseph H. Smith & Philip A. Crowl, supra note 24, at xxxii.

[53] Chapter 2, 41.

> worthy of inclusion and of annotation, the editors have plunged headlong into making the profession of editing look purely pedantic.[54]

Yet, while editorial judgment must be realistic, legal historians cannot accept the premise that legal papers should be the first deleted — especially when so many of the men whose papers are being published were lawyers. The decision to include many of the records from Henry Clay's law practice, for example, has provided us with an invaluable account of the nature of the legal profession in frontier Kentucky.[55] Thus the decision to produce the law papers of Alexander Hamilton in a separate series by Goebel was a welcomed compromise. As Professor Swindler says:

> Goebel's editorial approach might well be followed by others working in these fields. The very reason that has prompted, or threatens to tempt, some scholarly editors to omit legal materials from a man's collected papers — their cryptic technicality when "set down in their nakedness" — makes them richly revealing when given the necessary background by that rarest of specialists, the legal historian.[56]

In Goebel's hands the experiment proves to be a triumph, not a compromise. In his comprehensive introductions to each practice book and set of pleadings, he gives us our first detailed look at a post-Revolutionary law practice.[57] This may be understating the matter. It is our first detailed look at any American law practice. It is this which makes the year 1964 notable for legal historians.

---

[54] Leonard W. Levy, "Book Review," 51 *J. Am. Hist.* 299, 301 (1964) (reviewing 3 *The Papers of James Madison: 3 March 1781 - 31 December 1781* (William M.E. Hutchinson & William Rachal eds. 1963)).

[55] See 3 *The Papers of Henry Clay — Presidential Candidate, 1821 - 1824* (James F. Hopkins ed. 1963).

[56] William F. Swindler, "Book Review," 74 *Yale L.J.* 752, 754 (1965).

[57] 1 *The Law Practice of Alexander Hamilton* (Julius Goebel ed. 1964). The emphasis is on practice and procedure. A second volume will consider constitutional law, admiralty, land and commercial litigation.

Chapter Five

1965

John Phillip Reid

The cause of legal history made some unexpected advances during 1965. In November, just a few short years after the American Bar Association refused to become associated with the publication of John Marshall's papers because it was not interested in history as such, the American Bar Foundation announced plans for encouraging research in the history of Anglo-American law by establishing "American Bar Foundation Fellowships in Legal History." At about the same time Harvard University inaugurated an institute for the study of American history named for Charles Warren, the Pulitzer Prize-winning legal historian. One of its prime functions will be to stimulate and advance legal history. These two events make 1965 a notable year and the day may soon arrive when writers will cease repeating the tired lament that American historical scholarship has neglected its legal heritage.

I

LEGAL HISTORIOGRAPHY[1]

It may be hoped that the advisory committee of the American Bar Foundation Fellowships and the directors of Harvard's Charles Warren program will consciously strive to broaden the scope of legal history scholarship by encouraging studies in fields other than constitutional law. As Alpheus Mason noted during this survey year, "The torrent of

[1] Although this article is limited to American legal history, it seems appropriate to note a significant study by Professor Ralph V. Turner on the origins of the central common-law courts. Remarking that most textbooks still follow the theories of Stubbs and Maitland, Turner surveys newer works of rather limited circulation (chiefly introductions to editions of the rolls) and summarizes their findings, at the same time casting doubt on the dogmatic assertions of Richardson and Sayles regarding the role which the Exchequer played in the creation of Common Pleas. Ralph V. Turner, "The Medieval English Royal Courts: The Problem of Their Origins," 27 *The Historian* 471 (1965).

books about the Supreme Court seems unending."[2] Indeed, it seems to be a misuse of limited energies and resources when there are so many other jurisdictions and issues crying for treatment.

Yet constitutional matters continued to dominate legal history, and, therefore, legal historiography. The current emphasis on civil rights is a main influence on historians searching for themes. Thus we find James M. McPherson trying to infuse new meaning into the Civil Rights Act of 1875 by depicting it as "an historical bridge between the Fourteenth Amendment and the Civil Rights Act of 1964."[3] Richard E. Welch, Jr. went even further when he asked that "the Federal Elections Bill of 1890 be reinterpreted by historians in the light of current realities and a lengthened perspective."[4] Welch's "perspective" is not history but current events. It is his contention that defeat of the Federal Elections Bill of 1890 was tied to passage of the McKinley tariff. Prior historians have associated passage of the tariff with western votes won through eastern support of the Sherman Silver Purchase Act, but now that civil rights are to be reemphasized in historical studies, Welch says that "the compromise to be associated with the McKinley Act more properly concerns the Elections Bill."[5] It was the South rather than the West with whom the East had to do business. But all civil-rights history has not been left to the revisionists. An interesting lesson in scholarly objectivity as well as in the proper tools of constitutional historiography is found in a comparison of William Gillette's reluctant conclusion that legislative history shows that the fifteenth amendment was not intended to carry the weight of 1965's civil-rights legislation with Warren M. Christopher's thesis that the meaning of the amendment can be derived from enforcement legislation enacted by subsequent Congresses and need not depend on its own legislative history.[6] Undoubtedly the Supreme Court will ignore Gillette's

---

[2] Alpheus Thomas Mason, "Book Review," 71 *Am. Hist. Rev.* 303 (1965) (reviewing Marjorie Fribourg, *The Supreme Court in American History* (1965) and Leo Pfeffer, *This Honorable Court: A History of the United States Supreme Court* (1965)).

[3] James M. McPherson, "Abolitionists and the Civil Rights Act of 1875," 52 *J. Am. Hist.* 493 (1965).

[4] Richard E. Welch, "The Federal Elections Bill of 1890; Postscripts and Prelude," 52 *J. Am. Hist.* 511, 526 (1965).

[5] Id. at 515.

[6] Compare William Gillette, *The Right to Vote: Politics and the Passage of the Fifteenth Admendment* (1965) with Warren M. Christopher, "The Constitutionality of the Voting Rights Act of 1965," 18 *Stan. L. Rev.* 1 (1965). Gillette favors such legislation as the abolition of literacy tests, but insists that history shows they must be brought about by constitutional amendment. Christopher, on the other hand, insists that to meet arguments against the Voting Rights Act

findings. If it does so by holding that the intent of the drafters of the fifteenth amendment cannot be used to narrow the plain meaning of the words which they enacted, then historians may rejoice. The canons of constitutional construction are the judges' business. But if the Court continues to rewrite history to suit contemporary predilections, historians have a duty to protest as did Lewis Mayers when, evaluating the Supreme Court's interpretation of the Habeas Corpus Act of 1867,[7] he accused the Court of deliberately misrepresenting legislative history.[8] Mayers' study is perhaps the most outstanding critique of judicial abuse of the historical method since Charles Fairman commented on Justice Black's dissent in *Adamson* v. *California.*[9]

While the civil-rights approach to legal history has become more and more evident in recent years, the behaviorist interpretation has been in decline. Yet it received a slight revival in 1965 from Lawrence M. Friedman, a member of Willard Hurst's Madison Circle, in an article which demonstrated that the Hurstian school of legal history is capable of joining the constitutional revisionists. True to the Madison creed, Friedman selects an economic topic — occupational licensing statutes and their challenge in turn-of-the-century courts (both state and federal). He rejects the familiar thesis that the judges who invalidated these laws were guilty of class bias or were disciples of a laissez-faire economic theory. Friedman is too careful an historian to accept the traditions without investigating the facts. Rather he describes these judges as responding to the teachings of their profession (their training and method of argumentation led them to pursue a line of least resistance through accepted legal concepts) and of following the mentality (though not the blind interests) of their middle-class economic position.[10] Professor Fried-

---

of 1965, "we need only examine how the fifteenth amendment has been construed in the past, both as self-executing and as a reason for congressional legislation." Id. at 15.

[7] See *Fay v. Noia*, 372 U.S. 391 (1963) and *Townsend v. Sain*, 372 *U.S.* 293 (1963).

[8] "The words 'it is a bill of the largest liberty,' occurring in [Congressman] Lawrence's last sentence, are of special interest. In its desire to attribute marked significance to them, the Court saw fit to omit all mention of the military prisoner proviso and to quote part of Lawrence's original sentence as a seemingly complete and independent statement; it accomplished this surgery by substituting a period for a comma." Lewis Mayers, "The Habeas Corpus Act of 1867: The Supreme Court as Legal Historian," 33 *U. Chi. L. Rev.* 31, 38 (1965).

[9] Charles Fairman, "Does the Fourteenth Amendment Incorporate the Bill of Rights? —The Original Understanding," 2 *Stan. L. Rev. 5* (1949).

[10] Donald M. Roper makes a similar point with regard to an earlier era when he argues that: "the term conservative can be discarded when talking about economic ideas and the Marshall Court, for the line of division was over

man's historical method is convincing. His conclusions are less so. A reader who is surprised by the blending of a Hurst-type choice of economic topic with a partial explanation borrowed from Charles Beard,[11] may be startled by the broad generalizations with which Friedman gives his reasons why the courts of that era became activistic. It was, he says, because they felt an urge to define and protect areas of exclusive jurisdiction just as did other groups such as barbers and horseshoers:

> No one, it is true, threatened the economic position of the judges. But their power and prestige were threatened. The increasing volume of legislation began to undermine the earlier role of the judges as leading makers of public policy. Codification and enactment undercut the importance of the judge as a creator of living law. Judges reacted by seeking out an area of exclusive competence, just as the barbers did. The power of judicial review over legislation, sparingly used before the Civil War, gave them the doctrine. The enactment of the vague language of the Fourteenth Amendment gave them the opportunity. Current social concepts, particularly middle-class values and inherited doctrines of law, provided the limiting banks within which the course of judicial power ran.[12]

Professor Friedman is a young man. If he can discipline himself to avoid such speculations, he may have something to contribute to American legal history in the years to come.

---

policy rather than between liberal and conservative, with Johnson, Thompson, and Livingston believing that debtor relief laws were beneficial to commercial enterprise, while Marshall believed they destroyed 'all confidence between man and man'." Donald M. Roper, "Judicial Unanimity and the Marshall Court—A Road to Reappraisal," 9 *Am. J. Legal Hist.* 118, 133 (1965).

[11] It would be a mistake to bracket the Madison Circle with Charles Beard, yet it was said during 1965: "Professor Hurst apparently subscribes to the economic interpretation of history—that men are primarily motivated by economics (the pocket-book nerve). Perhaps factors of individual psychology and other values motivating the minds of men have been too long ignored." Harold J. Marquis, "Book Review," 9 *Am. J. Legal Hist.* 250, 257 (1965) (reviewing J. Willard Hurst, *Law and Economic Growth* (1964)). If "the economic interpretation of history" (which has certainly not been ignored for many years) has a generic meaning it should not be associated with the emphasis upon economic topics which characterizes Professor Hurst and his school. To this date, at least, the Madison theory seems to be that economics need not be the dominant motivation behind legislation; that economic exploitation pervaded nineteenth-century law because there was not yet an American tradition of planned regulation. Hurst is not enough of a cynic to sell himself to Beard.

[12] Lawrence M. Friedman, "Freedom of Contract and Occupational Licensing 1890-1910: A Legal and Social Study," 53 *Calif. L. Rev.* 487, 531 (1965).

Recent studies illustrated the diverse sources of American legal history as well as its methods and its schools. Professor Sidney Fine, for example, using the personal papers of Justice Murphy, showed how an in-depth paper can explore the resolution and consequences of a single judicial decision.[13] Peter J. Coleman, tracing the insolvent debtor laws of early Rhode Island, developed not only an excellent account of how changes in creditor statutes may reflect fluctuating social attitudes, but also demonstrated how court records can furnish the raw materials for an economic history of their times.[14] And B. Katherine Brown, in her study of democracy in colonial Massachusetts, employed an examination of statutes and of the absence of litigation to establish her various arguments.[15] Maurer, on the other hand, offered a remarkable specimen of the dying tradition which believes that legal history can be written from materials usually associated with brief writing. In discussing the court martial of civilians during World War I, he limited himself entirely to cases, statutes, and executive opinions. Aside from a few wild and unsubstantial statements (e.g., "armed mobs ruthlessly suppressed every tendency towards political and economic nonconformity") he presented no background, no insight into the sociological issues or human tragedies tossed up by the official policy of embracing all military employees within the definition of camp followers and by the judicial policy of according a wide construction to the term "in the field." His article is, in fact, almost a clinical example of what legal history is not supposed to be.[16]

The lawyer's tendency to write "history" from judicial records or with the method of an advocate, has been severely questioned of late.[17] One

---

[13] Sidney Fine, "Frank Murphy, The Thornhill Decision, and Picketing as Free Speech," 6 *Labor Hist.* 99 (1965).

[14] Peter J. Coleman, "The Insolvent Debtor in Rhode Island 1745-1828," 22 *William & Mary Q.* (3d Ser.) 413 (1965).

[15] B. Katherine Brown, "Puritan Democracy: A Case Study," 50 *Miss. Valley Hist. Rev.* 377 (1963).

[16] Maurer Maurer, "The Court-Martialing of Camp Followers, World War I," 9 *Am. J. Legal Hist.* 203 (1965).

[17] "Unfortunately, the general public is not so well aware of the accepted and acknowledged deficiencies of history written by lawyers. Because they are not forewarned against it, they sometimes take seriously its sweeping conclusions. . . . History therefore may become what the lawyers mistakenly said it was theretofore. The lawyers then will become not only judges of the law, and the judges of history, but the makers of history." James Russell Wiggins, "Lawyers as Judges of History," 75 *Proceedings Mass. Hist. Soc'y* 84, 104 (1963). Wiggins describes "history" as employed by lawyers as an ". . . unfortunate muse, harried by subpoena, harrassed by cross examination, subjected to *ex parte* proceedings, and lectured by the courts. . . . " Id. at 84.

historian has even suggested that constitutional history is too serious a matter to be left to the lawyers.[18] The division was noted by Alfred A. Kelly when commenting on a constitutional treatise written by a professor of law:

> If this reviewer may venture a criticism of so fine a study, it is that the "historical" portions of the book are presented in a fashion adequate enough to the legal profession but on occasion highly unsatisfactory from the point of view of the professional historian. This includes, among other things, documentation of historical points by citation to Supreme Court opinions in which the Court has animadverted upon the matter in question — "proof" enough for the lawyer's brief, but for the historian hardly proof at all.[19]

Even some of our most astute legal historians have allowed themselves to adopt the lawyer's tendency to judge past institutions in terms of their approximation to today's standards and values. Thus Wilcomb E. Washburn observes:

> George Lee Haskins . . . occasionally refers to the "improvement upon English practices" of various provisions of Massachusetts [colonial] law. I would suggest that these provisions, *for the historian*, represent changes rather than improvements.[20]

Among the historiological thoughts of the years, both wise and foolish, are Gerald Garvey's wishful suggestion that the historian can count in the world of constitutional affairs (although, writing of Edward S. Corwin, he fails to distinguish between the historian as historian and the historian as political propagandist);[21] Julius Stone's surprising suggestion that Willard Hurst may be curiously reluctant to accept as correct his basic explanation of nineteenth-century legal history ("that legal process has often been shaped by unplanned and 'mindless' social forces");[22] Mark DeWolfe Howe's suggestion that, "Historians of Ameri-

---

[18] Paul L. Murphy, "Time to Reclaim: The Current Challenge of American Constitutional History," 69 *Am. Hist. Rev.* 64, 77 (1963).

[19] Alfred H. Kelly, "Book Review," 52 J. *Am. Hist.* 352, 353 (1965) (reviewing Bernard Schwartz, *A Commentary on the Constitution of the United States. Part II, The Rights of Property* (1965)).

[20] Wilcomb E. Washburn, "Law and Authority in Colonial Virginia," in *Law and Authority in Colonial America* 116, 134 n.30 (George A. Billias ed. 1965).

[21] Gerald Garvey, "Edward S. Corwin in the Campaign of History: The Struggle for National Power in the 1930's," 34 *Geo. Wash. L. Rev.* 219 (1965).

[22] "Even when his Wisconsin legislators and judges seem (in our eyes) to have been simply unresponsive to the challenges of rational social ordering that shriek out their presence to *our* hindsight and *our* values, Hurst seems to write as if they had bent the law to rational planning for the pursuit of *their* rational

can law have always been confronted by, and have never been able to resolve, a rather large question concerning their special field of knowledge. Does it exist?";[23] and Irving Brant's justification of the extreme argument that legislative history may be based on gratuitous comments by leading politicians, connected with neither ratification nor implementation of the legislation in question.[24]

For the strangest-thought-of-the-year department we turn to a New York lawyer named Malcom S. Mason who suggests that, in the classroom, legal history should be taught backwards. His theory is that history is the handmaiden of current events and is included in the curriculum "because we hope to achieve depth of focus that will aid understanding of present legal processes and awareness of legal changes now occurring."[25] This is precisely the danger of which Maitland warned. But then Mr. Mason does not belong to the Maitland school.[26] After all, he confuses the legal institutions course (now being required by several law schools for first-year students) with legal history.

---

values. He too often attributes evidence that seems to negate vision and rationality altogether to the exigencies of Wisconsin's edge-of-the-wilderness location, and to limitations upon available procedures and techniques." Julius Stone, "Book Review," 78 *Harv. L. Rev.* 1687, 1688 (1965) (reviewing, J. Willard Hurst, *Law and Economic Growth* (1964)).

[23] "It is arguable that the history of American law is in fact the story of fifty-one identifiable legal systems, which, though they may share a common tradition, have known and been affected by so many variable influences that he who endeavors to unify the chronicles produces a structure of theory and not a record of reality," Mark De Wolfe Howe, "Book Review," 65 *Colum. L. Rev.* 1309 (1965) (reviewing *Court Records of Prince Georges County, Maryland: 1696-1699* (Joseph H. Smith & Philip A. Crowl eds. 1964)).

[24] Irving Brant, "Edmond Cahn and American Constitutional History," 40 *N.Y.U.L. Rev.* 218 (1965). For another evaluation of the late Professor Cahn's theories concerning the legal historian's trade see, J.W. Peltason, "Supreme Court Biography and the Study of Public Law," in *Essays on the American Constitution* 215, 225 (Gottfried Dietze ed. 1964).

[25] Malcom S. Mason, "On Teaching Legal History Backwards," 18 *J. Legal Ed.* 155 (1966).

[26] Nor does Julius G. Getman who, though less extreme than Mason, argues that books on constitutional law "must be judged by whether they have anything new to teach us about the workings of our institutions." Julius G. Getman, "Book Review," 52 *J. Am. Hist.* 177 (1965) (reviewing Richard C. Cortner, *The Wagner Act Cases* (1964)).

II

COLONIAL LEGAL HISTORY

It is possible that the writing of American legal history runs in cycles. Last year the bulk of material deemed worthy of comment came under the heading of "Legal Biography." This year, biographical works do not loom large, while colonial legal history, a topic we have not treated since the 1962 Survey, commands our exclusive attention. Most noteworthy of all is the fact that many of the recent studies in American colonial law have been motivated by a revisionist spirit willing to use legal materials as a tool for questioning some long-accepted and deeply-entrenched traditions. Moreover, there may be an increasing tendency to extend research beyond the familiar; something which has not characterized colonial legal historical scholarship for some time. Thus Alden T. Vaughan of Columbia published during this survey year a pioneering study of one of our most neglected topics, law and the American Indian. Examining the relationship of Puritan law to the native population, Vaughan concludes that the Indians of early New England were treated quite fairly. When we see them not only protected by statute and policy in their land rights, but even serving on Massachusetts juries, it is evidence that the spirit and administration of the law was drastically different from what it would become when the frontier moved further west. As Professor Vaughan makes clear, this was not forced on the Puritans by necessity. They always held the upper hand.[27]

A debate seems to be taking shape as to the nature of colonial law. Robert Emmet Wall, Jr., attempts to impose restraint on the enthusiasm of recent revisionists intent on proving that, since new evidence shows that the franchise was more widely distributed in Colonial America than has been previously suspected, the tradition of democratic value was greater and the reality of class rule was less than has been assumed. Wall agrees that there was a wide distribution of the right to vote, but this fact, he asserts, may have to be tempered if future investigations show that the colonies were governed by a political elite which drew its members from one social class.[28] The importance of legal history on this issue was highlighted at a meeting of general historians when it was suggested that a study of colonial laws would help clarify the speculation

---

[27] Alden T. Vaughan, *New England Frontier: Puritans and Indians 1620 - 75* (1965).

[28] Robert Emmet Wall, Jr., "A New Look at Cambridge," 52 *J. Am. Hist.* 599 (1965).

now popular concerning American nationalism being rooted in middle and lower-class values.[29]

In the most valuable colonial-law article of the year, Mark DeWolfe Howe advanced the theory that the settlers of early Massachusetts conceived of the common law (which they knew was but one of several categories of English law) as a fixed set of semi-constitutional principles which defined and limited public power.[30] In a more particular study of the impact of English law on the colonies, George William Pilcher, discussing the struggle by Presbyterians for religious liberty in Virginia, tells how, once the Toleration Act of 1689 was extended to Virginia, both the established church and the Presbyterians turned to prevailing customs in contemporary England to sustain arguments on how the law should be interpreted.[31] Also writing of church and state in colonial times, Clifford K. Shipton revises the accepted view of the Puritan establishment in Massachusetts Bay. "There never was an established church in Massachusetts," he asserts, "there was no agreed-upon body of dogma, and serious moral deviation was punished by the state, not by the church."[32] This is true enough, and admittedly the Massachusetts system created no discomfort during an era of conformity. But the fact that each parish, by the democratic process of majority rule, could select their preacher and their creed, made it no less an established religion when dissenters became more numerous.

That the church-state relationship would, in time, cause acute dissatisfaction, is demonstrated in two valuable discussions, one by Bernard Bailyn[33] and the other by William G. McLoughlin.[34] An essay closely

---

[29] Allan G. Bogue, "The Fifty-Seventh Annual Meeting of the Mississippi Valley Historical Association," 51 *J. Am. Hist.* 267, 282 (1964).

[30] Mark De Wolfe Howe, "The Sources and Nature of Law in Colonial Massachusetts," in *Law and Authority in Colonial America* 1 (George A. Billias ed. 1965) (hereinafter cited as *Law & Authority*).

[31] George William Pilcher, "Samuel Davies and Religious Toleration in Virginia," 28 *The Historian* 48 (1965).

[32] Clifford K. Shipton, "The Locus of Authority in Colonial Massachusetts, in *Law & Authority,"* supra note 30, at 137.

[33] Bernard Bailyn, "General Introduction: The Transforming Radicalism of the American Revolution," in I *Pamphlets of the American Revolution 1750 -1776,* at 151-68 (Bailyn ed. 1965).

[34] William G. McLoughlin, "The Bench, The Church, and The Republican Party in New Hampshire, 1790 to 1820," 20 *Historical New Hampshire* 3 (Summer 1965). When the Republicans moved to disestablish the church, Congregationalists argued that to do so would violate the contract clause of the federal Constitution. "[T]he towns and parishes had previously made contracts with their ministers to pay their salaries, it was [therefore] unconstitutional for the legislature to invalidate these contracts. What would have happened I wonder had some Congregational minister hired Daniel Webster to present such a case to John Marshall?" Id. at 29.

echoing Shipton's and written by Darrett B. Rutman, is especially noteworthy in that it reveals the contribution which legal history can make to the revision of colonial general history. Rutman seeks to discredit the traditional concept of a cohesive, stable, authoritarian Puritan society which scholars such as Perry Miller have made popular. Where Miller relied on the writings of Massachusetts-Bay intellectuals, Rutman turns to contemporary law and the day-to-day operation of political institutions. His picture of the average man as the consumer of law is remarkably different from that which Miller and his disciples would have us accept.[35] Reinforcing Rutman's contentions is a study by Jules Zanger which casts serious doubts on the legendary sternness usually attributed to Massachusetts-Bay magistrates. Zanger contends that an acute labor shortage produced a reluctance to punish wrongdoers when punishment would deprive the colony of the defendant's labor (as a result suspension of punishment was frequently employed), and that a shortage of money led to the remission of more than half of all fines. Moreover, he concludes that Puritan justice does not deserve its reputation of impartiality.

> The General Court frequently sentenced a wrongdoer to a whipping, and the whipping usually followed hard on the sentence. Once administered, it could not very well be remitted. Servants, men without property, were sentenced to this form of corporal punishment, by its nature unremitable, whereas gentlemen, men of property, who were by the Body of Liberties exempt from whipping, were fined, disfranchised, or even exiled all penalties easily, and frequently, remitted.[36]

Erwin C. Surrency came into his own as a legal historian by publishing (as one of the fruits of his year in the British Isles) a study of colonial statutory revision, showing how the interplay between imperial control and American reservations concerning the royal prerogative, joined with the eighteenth-century legal mind, to retard what in our times might seem a necessary and progressive undertaking.[37] Anton-Hermann Chroust made a substantial contribution to our knowledge of colonial legal conditions and especially of the colonial legal profession. While he admits that his discussion is neither original nor pioneering, his collection

---

[35] Darrett B. Rutman, "The Mirror of Puritan Authority, in *Law & Authority,*" supra note 30, at 49.

[36] Jules Zanger, "Crime and Punishment in Early Massachusetts," 22 *William & Mary Q.* (3d Ser.) 471, 476 (1965).

[37] Erwin C. Surrency, "Revision of Colonial Laws," 9 *Am. J. Legal Hist.* 189 (1965).

of source material, fully and wisely cited in clear, consistent footnotes, will be invaluable to future researchers. His two-volume book, *The Rise of the Legal Profession in America*, furnishes the raw stuff with which others can begin to build studies of individual states.

The last *Survey* reported as the big event of 1964 the publication of *The Law Practice of Alexander Hamilton.*[38] This year we received the three-volume *Legal Papers of John Adams.* They are edited by L. Kinvin Wroth and Hiller B. Zobel who did in every respect as fine a job as did Julius Goebel with the Hamilton book. There are many more Adams papers extant than there are Hamilton papers (indeed, many which could easily be labelled "legal" are, because of their wider interest, to appear in the general series edited by L. R. Butterfield — otherwise we would have more than three "legal" volumes), and as a result the editorial techniques offer some interesting contrasts. Professor Goebel used documents partly as a peg upon which to hang long explanatory introductions which amount to a history of the legal institutions and of the ways of law practice during Hamilton's time. Wroth and Zobel, on the other hand, while they have an excellent (though brief) general introduction, have faced the problem of a wealth of papers by providing separate introductions for each particular litigation. True, this restricts the comprehensiveness of their coverage, at least as compared to Goebel's treatment of legal institutions. Yet if this be a deficiency, it is more than compensated for by the fact that discussion of each case in relation to its total background permits them to blend social and political history into the context of legal developments.[39]

The art of editing historical papers has now reached such a point that Lester J. Cappon feels it is time to begin training professionals.[40] Whether or not the volume of legal publications ever expands to the extent that professional legal editors can feasibly be trained is doubtful, but there is not doubt that the Hamilton and Adams projects introduce

---

[38] Chapter 4, at 76-77.

[39] Their arrangment is to group the papers under the familiar divisions of the law, torts, contracts, property, etc. I *Legal Papers of John Adams* (L. Kinvin Wroth & Hiller B. Zobel eds. 1965).

[40] "Somehow the idea persists that, while for the historical writer primary documents are the means to a worthy end climaxed by significant conclusions, for the editor the documents themselves suffice and are an end in themselves. The editor whose comprehension of the sources fails to identify any significant meaning in or beyond them has his counterpart in the historian whose narrative never transcends the facts." Lester J. Cappon, "A Rationale for Historical Editing Past and Present," 23 *William & Mary Q.* (3d Ser.) 56, 73 (1966).

to legal history exciting new dimensions which have already borne fruit[41] and which, as primary sources, will take their place beside the infrequent, often uneven, yet indispensible colonial court records series. In the most important bibliographical review of 1965, Michael G. Kammen surveyed the publication of colonial court records, concluding that they have forced us to revise our conceptions regarding early American law,[42] and asking:

> Why has the process of maturation in this field been so slow? One reason is immediately obvious: the lack of qualified scholars. Capable lawyers in professional practice are reluctant to undertake such laborious tasks because there is so little remuneration. Judges are too busy, and members of law school facilities prefer to write scholarly articles on more contemporary problems for law journals. But there are two deeper causes basically responsible for this deficiency: courts acting as historians and the pervasive influence over several generation by the legal thought of the late Roscoe Pound.[43]

Kammen's conclusions are flattering neither to the courts[44] nor to Dean Pound.[45]

---

[41] E.g., articles by the editors based on material drawn from their Adams research. L. Kinvin Wroth, "The Massachusetts Vice-Admiralty Court, in *Law & Authority," supra* note 30, at 51-57 and Hiller B. Zobel, "Law Under Pressure: Boston 1769-1771" in id. at 187.

[42] "The editors of several volumes of colonial court records have found no evidence to support older theories of a reign of crude, untechnical law in the provinces. Careful examination of the bench and bar, even on the county level, has brought about a rejection of the traditional suggestion that the men who pleaded before the courts were terribly inferior and that a species of 'frontier jurisprudence' had thrust aside all semblance of orderly procedures derived from English practice.'" Michael G. Kammen, "Colonial Court Records and the Study of Early American History: A Bibliographical Review," 70 *Am. Hist. Rev.* 733, 739 (1965).

[43] Id. at 737.

[44] "The notion has persisted that after the Revolution judges undertook to decide what rules had been adopted in colonial times, acting on the assumption that their function to declare the law included a knowledge of its history. Since so little was known of what actually transpired in the seventeenth and eighteenth centuries, the results of the early courts came to be regarded as worthless for historical purposes." Ibid.

[45] "Meanwhile Dean Pound's enormous influence . . . also tended to persuade potential scholars that the period before independence was not worth close examination." Id. at 738.

III

THE AMERICAN REVOLUTION

Since John Adams's law practice came to an end while he was arguing a case in the New Hampshire Court Maritime during December, 1777, it can be said that his legal career belongs to the colonial period. He left the law to serve the Revolution as a Commissioner to France; and it is that event, the American Revolution, which is once again emerging as a primary topic for legal historians. Margaret A. Banks echoed the current theme when she recently wrote:

> Although the causes of the American War of Independence were many and varied, it is, in general, correct to say that the thirteen colonies rebelled not because they disliked the British system of government, but because they liked it and were being deprived of some of its fundamental characteristics.[46]

Some warnings are beginning to be sounded against this, the neo-Whig approach to the American Revolution. Gordon S. Wood, for one, feels that the neo-Whig revival may be going too far in its reaction to the behaviorist historians of the Progressive era.[47]

> By describing the Revolution as a conservative, principled defense of American freedom against the provocations of the English government, the neo-Whig historians have come full circle to the position of the Revolutionaries themselves and to the interpretation of the first generation of historians.[48]

William H. Nelson, a Canadian historian, agrees that a new historiography of the Revolution is developing. Rejecting the imperialistic school of Andrews, the economic interpretation of Beard, and the world-revolution

---

[46] Margaret A. Banks, "Attitudes in the Philadelphia Convention Towards the British System of Government," 10 *Am. J. Legal Hist.* 15 (1966).

[47] "If any catch phrase is to characterize the work being done on the American Revolution by this generation of historians it will probably be 'the American Revolution considered as an intellectual movement.'" Gordon S. Wood, "Rhetoric and Reality in the American Revolution," 23 *William & Mary Q.* (3d Ser.) 3 (1966). "Precisely because they sought to understand both the Revolutionary ideas and American society, the behaviorist historians of the Progressive generation, for all their crude conceptualizations, their obsession with class and hidden economic interests, and their treatment of ideas as propaganda, have still offered us an explanation of the Revolutionary era so powerful and so comprehensive that no purely intellectual interpretation will ever replace it." Id. at 32.

[48] Id. at 15.

theory of Becker, the new approach, which seeks to trace a conservative "consensus" through American history, is nearer to the nationalistic tradition of Bancroft.

> It is nationalist and particularist; it emphasizes the unique character, not only of the Revolution, but of American political and social life before and after it. The main issue of the Revolution has become once again, not, in Becker's phrase, "who should rule at home," but "home rule" — independence from Britain. The character of the Revolution appears again, not exactly as Bancroft saw it, but in a rather more subdued light as the sober affirmation of their rights by a mature and rational people. And the Constitution has become once again the logical fulfillment and necessary completion of the Revolution.[49]

While the neo-Whigs make Professor Nelson as uneasy as they make Mr. Wood,[50] Nelson does not go as far as does Wood; he does not label the new emphasis as purely an "intellectual interpretation." The progressive era has not, after all, been forgotten. Writers may be revising Beard's interpretations, but they are using Beard's techniques to do so. What is significant to legal historians is that they have broadened Beard's range of inquiry by placing more emphasis upon the law and upon legal institutions.[51] Moreover, the "intellectual approach" is focusing our attention once more on the constitutional debates which preceeded the Declaration of Independence. A few historians may complain, [52] but

---

[49] William H. Nelson, "The Revolutionary Character of the American Revolution," 70 *Am. Hist. Rev.* 998, 1000 (1965).

[50] "A trace of unease arises, however, simply from recalling the habit that successive generations had of viewing the Revolution in their own needs and concerns. . . . If Beard could mistake a founding father for an early twentieth-century capitalist, how can we be certain not to confuse General Washington with General Eisenhower? Living ourselves in an age of pitiless change, may we not have developed an excessive yearning for historic continuities? And, preoccupied as we are with defending our institutions, may we not mistake ancestral attackers for defenders too?" Id. at 1001.

[51] See, e.g., B. Katherine Brown, supra note 15, and Robert E. Brown & B. Katherine Brown, *Virginia, 1705 - 1786; Democracy or Aristocracy* (1964).

[52] Asking why events in Boston assumed a more general significance than did local events in other regions of America, Richard Buel argues: "Past experience suggests that this problem will not be solved, let alone perceived, while we confine ourselves to the literature that formally discussed the constitutional relationship with Great Britain; yet until we solve it, we shall continue to have difficulty in understanding why American Independence became an idea and in the end a reality." Richard Buel, "Book Review," 23 *William & Mary Q.* (3d Ser.) 160, 162 (1966) (reviewing Thomas R. Adams, *American Independence: The Growth of an Idea: A Bibliographic Study of the American Political*

Bernard Bailyn makes it indisputably clear that constitutional issues were the unifying force behind the Revolution. During 1965 he published the first of his four-volume series entitled *Pamphlets of the American Revolution 1750-1776*. "Study of the pamphlets," he writes, "confirmed my rather old-fashioned view that the American Revolution was above all else an ideological-constitutional struggle and not primarily a controversy between social groups undertaken to force changes in the organization of society."[53] Bailyn, who agrees with Professor Howe that the colonists regarded the common law as a collection of semi-constitutional, public-law principles,[54] argues that the Revolutionary literature, while it did depend on the familiar notions of social contract,[55] inalienable rights, and natural law, placed great emphasis on common-law doctrines viewed from the constitutional perspective. "The great figures of England's legal history, especially the seventeenth-century common lawyers, were referred to repeatedly—by the colonial lawyers above all, but by others as well. Sir Edward Coke is everywhere."

> The Common law was manifestly influential in shaping the awareness of the Revolutionary generation. But, again, it did not in itself determine the kinds of conclusions men would draw in the crisis of the time. . . . The law was no science of what to do next. To the colonists it was a repository of experience in human dealings embodying the principles of justice, equity, and rights; above all, it was a form of history — ancient, indeed immemorial history; constitutional and national history; and, as history, it helped explain the movement of events and the meaning of the present. Particularly revealing, therefore, though vague in their intent, are the references in the pamphlets to the seventeenth-century scholars of the law, especially of the history of the law, whose importance in the development of English historical thought we have only recently come aware; Henry Spelman, Thomas Madox, Robert Brady, and William Petyt. English law — as authority, as legitimatizing precedent, as embodied principle, as the framework of historical understanding — stood side by side with Enlightenment rationalism in the minds of the Revolutionary generation.[56]

Pamplets between 1764 and 1776 Dealing with the Dispute between Great Britain and Her Colonies (1965)).

[53] I *Pamphlets of the American Revolution 1750 - 1776* viii (Bernard Bailyn ed. 1965). See also id. at 190-93.

[54] Id. at 103, 106-07.

[55] For an excellent survey of the social-compact theory in Revolutionary America see Thad W. Tate, "The Social Contract in America, 1774-1787: Revolutionary Theory as a Conservative Instrument," 22 *William & Mary Q.* (3d Ser.) 375 (1965).

[56] I *Pamphlets of the American Revolution 1750 - 1776,* at 26-27 (Bernard Bailyn ed. 1965).

Reexamination of the revolutionary character of the Revolution in terms of law will call for reexamination of the role played by lawyers. There is an apparent inconsistency which must be resolved. To reestablish the theory that lawyers were the leaders of the American Revolution may too easily lend support to the conclusion that the Revolution was not revolutionary. "Lawyers are naturally conservative," Catherine Drinker Bowen has written. "If change must be accomplished they choose history as their guide, in preference to destruction and a total sweeping-out, believing that fact and experience carry more conviction than the fluty voice of a newly erected Goddess of Reason."[57] Richard B. Morris had this tradition in mind when he observed that "the lawyer-dominated American Revolution was to be distinguished by its concern for an emphasis upon legality."[58] Morris admits that the Revolutionary period had "a seamier side," and mentions the treatment of the Tories as an example. But even this aspect of legal history is being questioned, as seen by an article in which Richard D. Brown contends that since eighty percent (in value) of the sales of confiscated Tory property in Massachusetts were conducted on the initiative of creditors, under an "Act to Provide for the Payment of Debts," the Whig policy was not so much revenge as "conformity with the conservative view of property rights which dominated Massachusetts."[59] Thus the evidence furnished by the operation of law and by the role which lawyers played may in time prove, as Morris says, "that the entire Revolutionary movement was encompassed within the framework of legality."[60] But what of the eventual reaction which some day will seek to rejuvenate the revolutionary perspective of the Revolution? Rather than return to the world-revolution theme, it may seek answers in changes brought about in legal and political institutions. In any event, the American Revolution once more belongs to legal history.

---

[57] Catherine Drinker Bowen, "Historians Courageous" in Wilbur D. Dunkel, *William Lambarde, Elizabethan Jurist, 1536 - 1601* xx (1965).

[58] Richard B. Morris, "Foreward," in *Law & Authority,* supra note 30, at viii.

[59] Richard D. Brown, "The Confiscation and Disposition of Loyalists' Estates in Suffolk County, Massachusetts," 21 *William & Mary Q.* (3d Ser.) 534, 550 (1964). In a related article, Beatrice G. Reubens presents a study of the Revolutionary confiscation of the Tory Philipsburgh Manor in New York. While primarily an economic and social survey of results (she concludes that small farmers and former tenants received a democratically-healthy proportion of the estate), it demonstrates once again the challenge that awaits the legal historian who writes the vital monograph on security of tenure in colonial America. Beatrice G. Reubens, "Pre-Emptive Rights in the Disposition of a Confiscated Estate: Philipsburgh Manor, New York," 22 *William & Mary Q.* (3d Ser.) 435 (1965).

[60] Richard B. Morris, supra note 58, at viii.

Chapter Six

1966: LEGAL HISTORY

John Phillip Reid

This *Survey* year of 1966 saw the two disciplines which legal history serves — law and history — come into direct conflict when Helen C. Frick filed suit in the Cumberland County Court of Pennsylvania against an historian, S.K. Stevens. In the action Miss Frick asserts the right to protect her father's memory which, it is alleged, Dr. Stevens injured when he drew conventional historical judgments concerning Frick's actions during such events as the Homestead strike. The very fact that the case was placed on the docket caused such concern among professional historians that they organized the Joint Committee for the Defense of the Rights of Historians under the First Amendment, which failed in its initial legal maneuver — to have the United States District Court for the Southern District of New York enjoin the Pennsylvania proceedings. While the statements released by the Committee and its two parent groups, the Organization of American Historians and the American Historical Association, betrayed a misapprehension regarding both the judicial process and the legal issues at stake, the Committee has been encouraged by counsel to believe that the time is now ripe and that this particular suit is opportune for establishing important precedents protecting historians in the publication of their historical judgments.[1] It may be, however, that the questions raised by Frick-Stevens litigation will prove too narrow to settle much more than what may be a foregone conclusion. More basic are such matters as the use of quotations from unpublished manuscripts and private correspondence and the widening of such definitions as "fair use" and "historical value." These topics are currently being submitted to Congress in the guise of reforming the copyright laws, and here also, the prospects for a determination favorable to historical scholarship seems quite likely.[2]

---

[1] See Notes, 5 (#2) *A.H.A. Newsletter* 12-13 (1966).

[2] Henry Bartholomew Cox, "The Impact of Proposed Copyright Law upon Scholars and Custodians," 29 *Am. Archivist* 217-27 (1966). See also Ira B. Selsky, "Biography and the Copyright Law," 22 *N.Y.U. Intra. L. Rev.* 208 (1967).

I

LEGAL HISTORIOGRAPHY

"It is unfortunate," Richard Wells writes, "but a general dearth of attention to the uses of history by courts has characterized American legal history."[3] This familiar lament was out-of-date even before it was penned. If anything, legal historiography is for the first time emerging as a subject of interest to historians and perhaps even as a topic of controversy among lawyers. While Calvin Woodward may detect an "a-historical outlook" among lawyers "that acknowledges the existence of, but makes no use of, and has no need for, 'Legal History'."[4] the late Mark De Wolfe Howe took the opposite view and warned about the United States Supreme Court's increasing use of the "historical method of adjudication," which, he argued, is simplistic, unhistorical, and without method.[5] In fact, the current use and abuse of history by the Supreme Court has stimulated studies into the nature and purpose of legal, constitutional, and legislative historiography which are unprecedented when compared to the output just a decade ago.

In brief, the main theme of the new school of legal historiography has been that the use of history by Supreme Court justices (termed "magestical historiography" by Dallin H. Oaks[6] and "law-office" history by Alfred H. Kelly)[7] to support many of their recent law-making pronouncements has been as questionable as some of the pronouncements themselves. The use of history "as a precedent-breaking device"[8] ". . . supplies an apparent rationale for politically inspired activism that can be indulged in the name of constitutional continuity."[9] Even worse,

---

[3] Richard Wells, "Legal History and Politics — The Case of Lawyers' Special Status," in *Essays in Legal History in Honor of Felix Frankfurter* 567, 579 (Morris N. Forkosch ed. 1966).

[4] Calvin Woodward, "History, Legal History and Legal Education," 53 *Va. L. Rev.* 89, 96 (1967).

[5] Mark De Wolfe Howe, "Split Decisions," *New York Rev. of Books* 17 (July 1, 1965). Howe indicts the current court of "dishonoring the arts of the historian and degrading the talents of the lawyer." Mark De Wolfe Howe, *The Garden and the Wilderness — Religion and Government in American Constitutional History* (1965).

[6] Dallin H. Oaks, "Legal History in the High Court — Habeas Corpus," 64 *Mich. L. Rev.* 451 (1966).

[7] "By 'law-office' history, I mean the selection of data favorable to the position advanced without regard or concern for contradictory data or proper evaluation of the relevance of the data proffered." Alfred H. Kelly, "Clio and the Court — An Illicit Love Affair," 1965 *Sup. Ct. Rev.* 119, 122 n.13.

[8] Id. at 155.

[9] Id. at 131.

their method is adopted by so-called historians such as Irving Brant who, "eager to defend an 'activist' role for the Supreme Court,"[10] attack liberals such as Leonard W. Levy who are honest enough to insist that history is a method of scientific proof, not an excuse to be manipulated as the occasion arises. A "Marxist-type perversion of the relation between truth and utility," law-office history assumes "that history can be written to serve the interests of libertarian idealism."[11] Thus, all too often, the "nonlibertarian" dissenter is forced to fall back on historical materials for rebuttal which, on examination, proves to be a perversion of history equally objectionable.[12] Legal rules fashioned to meet "new and growing social problems," the critics argue, "should be cloaked in reason, not garbed in a regal patchwork of history that, on close examination, proves as embarrassingly illusory as the Emperor's new clothes."[13]

> The Court, in performing its self-assumed roled as a constitutional historian, has been, if not a naked king, no better than a very ragged one. From a professional point of view, most, if not all, of its recent historical essays are very poor indeed. Like the efforts of Taney in *Dred Scott* and Fuller in *Pollock,* they are essentially pieces of special pleading. Too often they reach conclusions that are plainly erroneous. More often they state as categorical absolutes propositions that the historian would find to be tentative, speculative, interesting, and worthy of further investigation and inquiry, but not at all pedigreed historical truth.[14]

Since it is generally agreed that Felix Frankfurter ". . . was undoubtedly the most history-minded Justice ever to sit on the Supreme Court, . . ."[15] it came as a shock to find Morris D. Forkosch, in a *festschrift* honoring Frankfurter's contributions to legal history, placing Hugo Black's pseudo-history on a level equal with Frankfurter's more acceptable scholarship.[16] In fact, poor Justice Frankfurter was not well served

---

[10] Sanford Levinson, "Book Review," 76 *Yale L.J.* 249, 252 (1966) (reviewing Irving Brant, *The Bill of Rights* (1965)). See also chapter 7, at 118-124. Surprisingly there are some historians who still on occasion accept a Supreme Court version of "history" as history. See, e.g., Maurice G. Baxter, *Daniel Webster and the Supreme Court* 143 (1966).

[11] Alfred H. Kelly, *supra* note 7, at 157.

[12] William Van Alstyne, "The Fourteenth Amendment, The 'Right' to Vote, and the Understanding of the Thirty-Ninth Congress," 1965 *Sup. Ct. Rev.* 33; Alfred H. Kelly, supra note 7, at 137.

[13] Dallin H. Oaks, *supra* note 6, at 472.

[14] Alfred H. Kelly, *supra* note 7, at 155.

[15] Id. at 129.

[16] Morris N. Forkosch, "What is Legal History?," in *Essays in Legal History in Honor of Felix Frankfurter* 2, at 21 n.71 (Morris N. Forkosch ed. 1966) (hereinafter cited as *Frankfurter Essays*).

even by his former law-clerks who described his method of legal history as; (1) the use of precedent which is old,[17] (2) the utilization of "historical" arguments in an advocacy context, (3) the assertion that conditions have changed and hence rules must be applied differently,[18] (4) the fact that he sought guidance on techniques from Holmes, Brandeis and Cardozo,[19] and (5) that he wrote such sentences as—

> . . . Ninety years ago this Court unanimously announced that a licensee under a patent is estopped from challenging the validity of that patent. . . . Beginning with the Interstate Commerce Act in 1887, it became a conventional feature of Congressional regulatory legislation to give administrative agencies authority to issue subpoenas for relevant information. . . . More than seventy years ago this Court upheld the regulation of grain warehousing rates by Illinois.[20]

That Justice Frankfurter insisted on the distinction between precedent and history apparently made little impression on some lawyers who profess to have learned from him.

The familiar theme concerning a dichotomy of law and history thus remains a fertile topic in legal historiography and it was Francis S. Philbrick who provided this year's focus for that division. Reviewing the book in which Philbrick sums up his theories regarding frontier history,[21] W.H. Masterson (who refers to the dichotomy as "historical diffraction") both praises and complains:

> Philbrick's life with the law decisively influences the character of the book. This professional outlook provides corrective precision to such usually carelessly treated topics as treaty making (and breaking), the ethics of preemption laws, William Johnson and George Rogers Clark, "Indian lands," and frontier democracy. However, when the author proceeds from his narrowly correct view that "as for important institutions of social organization or activity, all are created and regulated by law," to his apparent conclusions that creation and regulation constitute the real character of the institutions, then Philbrick gets into difficulties with history. It is, for example, because he bases his case on the legally definable in western society that his long, passionate denunciation of Turner's theories is unconvincing. Turner talked about institutions, but the dynamics of his theories came from a perception of social and intellectual attitudes that

---

17 Howard Kalodner, "Mr. Justice Frankfurter's Views and Use of Legal History," id. at 29-38.

18 Irving J. Helman & Albert J. Rosenthal, "Mr. Justice Frankfurter, Legal History, and Law Clerks," id. at 48-49.

19 Louis Henkin, "The Uses of History," id. at 64.

20 Id. at 58.

21 Francis S. Philbrick, *The Rise of the West, 1754 - 1830* (1965).

> cannot be defined in legal norms or proved by the usual historical evidence.[22]

W. Turrentine Jackson was more blunt:

> Because he is a lawyer, Professor Philbrick has a predilection for treaty negotiations and legislation, which leads to an emphasis on these subjects. . . . His views on legal affairs are succinct. Knowledgeable historians would welcome an opportunity to debate the author's interpretations and rigorous opinions expressed in every chapter.[23]

What makes this *Survey* year memorable, however, is that for the first time, the myth of Frederic William Maitland has been challenged on historiological terms. Though perhaps inevitable, it was nonetheless a shock to find both Roy Stone de Montpensier and Calvin Woodward casting doubts on the legacy of the master. Professor de Montpensier's appraisal defies summation. For example, consider his treatment of Maitland's oft-praised retroductive approach to pre-Conquest institutional history. When discussing the meaning and measurement of "hides," de Montpensier notes, Maitland used documents from the time of Edward the Confessor to show that Anglo-Saxon hides corresponded to the later definition of hides used in Domesday Book.

> Here Maitland attempts to verify the hypothetico-deductive premises. Having thus verified them, he does not need to challenge the assumption or hypothesis contained in *Domesday Book [and Beyond]* and which he is using to "retroduce" to Anglo-Saxon times. However, suppose the evidence of fact in earlier time refuted the conclusion retroduced from the hypothesis of the later time, then, as in hypothetico-deductive systems in science, it would be necessary to re-examine and perhaps change the hypotheses of the later time. We shall see that in writing the *Constitutional History* this important feature is neglected. We may say that Maitland has shown us how to use a retroductive logic in *Domesday Book and Beyond* but how to abuse it in his *Constitutional History*. Further, it would be a matter for the philosophy of history and an important consideration in this subject to say by what laws, rules, arguments, and for what reasons, this had to be done. Suppose, however, that Maitland did not have to proceed retroductively, that it was not an inexorable move in the writing of history, then another question arises. It is this: Was Maitland not really a Macaulay of the Medieval? Was he not a Whig

---

[22] W.H. Masterson, "Book Review," 53 *J. Am. Hist.* 118-119 (1966).

[23] W. Turrentine Jackson, "Book Review," 71 *Am. Hist. Rev.* 1429, 1430 (1966).

> interpreter of history? Did he not use twelfth-and thirteenth-century concepts and institutions to interpret the past?[24]

Professor Woodward's concern is that legal history is too tied to "development" as a theme and to "institutions" as a frame of reference.[25] This he blames on Maitland (and Maine). The consequence is that today legal history as a law-school course is a failure; it bores rather than stimulates.[26]

While Maitland was being slightly downgraded, Willard Hurst was being lionized. "With five books in fourteen years, Willard Hurst has moved himself into the ranks of the great creative jurisprudential thinkers of this country," Russell E. Brooks eulogized. "My only fear is that he will try to deny his own rightful place by claiming to be a mere historian."[27] John P. Frank disagrees. Calling Hurst's *Law and Economic Growth* "the most significant work on legal history ever produced in the United States," Frank claims for Hurst the mantle of America's greatest legal historian and uses the same evidence employed by Brooks to substantiate his argument.[28] Brooks, however, seems to have the better case, for Frank selected shaky grounds upon which to make a stand for history.

Both Brooks and Frank take as the pivotal point of their respective positions, the Hurst concept of "drift." Professor Hurst explained this concept when (writing of the nineteenth-century Wisconsin lumber business), he said that the federal and state governments "offered the industry a subsidy in fixed capital, minimized its working capital needs, held down operating costs by foregoing any attempt to impose minimum standards of efficient forest use, and relieved the industry of any obligation to create depletion reserves against the costs of a substitute economy for the cut-over region."[29] Frank approves of this historical method by pointing out:

> This, as Hurst emphasizes, does not warrant particular criticisms of Nineteenth Century lawmakers or Nineteenth Century lumber barons;

---

[24] Roy Stone De Montpensier, "Maitland and the Interpretation of History," 10 *Am. J. Legal Hist.* 259, 262-63 (1966).

[25] Thus disagreeing with Frederick G. Kempin who finds the "development" theme unsatisfactory but apparently without an acceptable alternative. Frederick G. Kempin, "Book Review," 10 *Am. J. Legal Hist.* 321, 322-23 (1966) (reviewing Frederick G. Hogue, *Origins of the Common Law* (1965)).

[26] Calvin Woodward, *supra* note 4, at 108-09.

[27] Russell E. Brooks, "The Jurisprudence of Williard Hurst," 18 *J. Legal Ed.* 257, 273 (1966).

[28] John P. Frank, "American Legal History — The Hurst Approach," 18 *J. Legal Ed.* 395 (1966).

[29] J. Willard Hurst, *Law and Economic Growth — The Legal History of the Lumber Industry in Wisconsin, 1836 - 1915,* at 502 (1964).

> conservation and the multi-purpose project are Twentieth Century ideas and there is neither justice nor profit in criticizing an earlier generation for failure to know what we have learned. Indeed, our lesson is in large part the product of their experience.[30]

All very well, yet Frank sums up the Hurstian lessons of "drift" and "inertia" by saying, "Nineteenth Century man had not yet learned how to create and manage a legal system to preserve a resource," and quotes Hurst (with approval) as concluding that this "was part of the environment of policy derived from sweeping delegation of social functions to the market."[31] This is exactly why Brooks's "jurisprudent" emerges as a stronger case than Frank's "historian." Willard Hurst's comments are astute, his argument is convincing, and his lesson for today's law is philosophically valuable. But his standard of judgment, though presented in objective terms, is still twentieth century. At least in the passages upon which Frank relies, Hurst's conclusions regarding nineteenth-century "drift" and "inertia" are premised on the realization that both he and his reader are familiar with twentieth-century regulatory experiments. Perhaps he is unfortunate in his apologist and undoubtedly a stronger defense of Hurst as an historian can be presented, but Frank's evaluation shows us a legal philosopher who employs history to develop theories regarding "drift" and "inertia" by applying today's standards to yesterday's actions.

Perhaps we are disagreeing not only on the definition of "historical method," but also on the uses and functions of legal history — another topic which received attention during 1966. "The uses of history," a professor of government suggested, "delineates styles of political behavior, both institutional and individual. History serves the purposes of the court as a whole insofar as a posture of objectivity forms a major element through legal categories. History also serves the respective purposes of the major parties in conflict."[32] A law professor was more realistic:

> The true function of Legal History, I submit, is to help lawyers and legal scholars, who are essentially concerned with current problems, to be meaningfully aware of the past as a healthy check on our often overly-optimistic and unfounded hopes; to provide gentle redress in our moments of frustration and disappointment; . . . and, above all, to provide awareness and appreciation of the value and meaning of "civilization."[33]

---

[30] John P. Frank, *supra* note 28, at 403.

[31] Id. at 398.

[32] Richard Wells, *supra* note 3, at 579.

[33] Calvin Woodward, *supra* note 4, at 105-06.

"It may be that we know too much of legal history already," a second law professor argued. "In certain corners of the law, 'ignorance is the best of law reformers'."[34] A social historian disagreed:

> For the daily work of the courts in applying legal rules real history may be unnecessary; but hardly when it comes to making and changing the law. For law is not, or ought not to be, the product of itself, but of a past society (that is, history), and it is difficult to see how things can be changed without knowing how they came to be as they are. Further, and unexpectedly, the historical approach introduces the element of irreverence which keeps the law alive, for it shows by what absurd shifts and accidents much of the law has been arrived at. . . .
>
> Perhaps the main practical value of legal history is simply to remind law that it exists for society and must constantly be reforming itself up to date with social change (that is, history).[35]

Among the varied historiological thoughts of the year, both wise and foolish, are William Jeffrey's suggestion regarding law-school curricula — "The legal history course has enough to do in presenting viewpoints and materials not even remotely approached in other courses, without being saddled with major responsibility for the historical aspects of the land";[36] S.F.C. Milsom's suggestion that too formal a law training may hamper the (English) legal historian — "The legal historian is fortunate in having an abundance of truly original materials which, though often complex and intractable, can be relied upon to give consistent answers when asked the right question; and a major difficulty is to avoid anachronism in framing the questions";[37] Russell E. Brook's suggestion that the Hurst method obviates the skepticism which attaches to the use of the extraordinary example (e.g., *Dred Scott*) in legal history — "If a theory can be documented by the history of milk regulation, it can

---

[34] Dallin H. Oaks, *supra* note 6, at 471-72.

[35] Alan Harding, *A Social History of English Law* 8 (1966). "Legal history has more workaday relevance than as a diagnostic aid for the law reformer. . . . The history of law, like its philosophy, enables the lawyer to see his subject from the outside, otherwise a very difficult thing for him to do." S.F.C. Milsom, "Theodore Frank Thomas Plucknett 1897-1965," 51 *Proc. British Acad.* 505, 517 (1965). "If law is cut off from its history, the student tends to emerge as a limited technician, who may find himself at sea as the law he has learned in school vanishes before his eyes." Eugene Rostow, *Yale Law School — Report of the Dean* 15 (1966).

[36] William Jeffrey, "Book Review," 10 *Am. J. Legal Hist.* 253, 256 (1966) (reviewing Joseph H. Smith, *Cases and Materials on the Development of Legal Institutions* (1965)).

[37] S.F.C. Milsom, *supra* note 35, at 506.

probably be documented by anything";[38] Alfred H. Kelly's suggestion that, "When a court ascertains the nature of the law to be applied to a case through an examination of a stream of judicial precedent, after the time-honored Anglo-American technique, it plays the role of historian";[39] and Alan Harding's counter-suggestion that, "While the historian goes to the past for evidence and prizes every bit he finds, the lawyer is after the single authority which will settle the case in hand."[40]

For the strangest-thought-of-the-year department, we turn to the Chief Justice of the Ohio Supreme Court who feels that "a desire for *stare decisis* is the reason for Ohio legal history."[41] His idea of legal history is almost a caricature.

> Perhaps, fortunately, there is no record of committee reports of legislative debates in Ohio which can tempt our courts to revise the interpretation ordinarily called for by the language of a statute. Hence, it is probably fair to state that Ohio legal history is found largely in the reports of opinions of our courts.[42]

Finally, we note the happy fact that this *Survey* article shows no sign of influencing opinion. At least the behaviorists continue to go their unembarrassed way.[43]

II

COLONIAL LEGAL HISTORY

The colonial era continued to dominate the attention of historians of America's laws and institutions. In a study which contrasts with Sumner Chilton Powell's masterful book, *Puritan Village,*[44] Philip J. Greven, Jr., has added to our knowledge of the use of freehold and partible inheritance in seventeenth-century Massachusetts. Where Powell employed town records to show how parental control of available land in Sudbury led to conflict between generations and to the migration of the younger

---

[38] Russell E. Brooks, *supra* note 27, at 259.

[39] Alfred H. Kelly, *supra* note 7, at 121.

[40] Alan Harding, *supra* note 35, at 8.

[41] Kingsley A. Taft, "The Use of Legal History in the Ohio Supreme Court," in *Frankfurter Essays,* supra note 16, at 113.

[42] Id. at 111.

[43] See Lawrence M. Friedman, "An American Tragedy — The Trial of Jack Ruby," 1966 *Wis. L. Rev.* 1188, 1191-94.

[44] Sumner Chilton Powell, *Puritan Village: The Formation of a New England Town* (1963).

generation to new towns, Greven employs probate records to demonstrate how other fathers, by retaining control of land in Andover long after the second generation had established nominal independence through marriage and separate households, not only kept their sons in Andover but manipulated their ownership of the land as an economic foundation upon which they maintained the family as a unit.[45] Although David J. Rothman argues that the seventeenth-century colonial household was more nuclear than extended "and there is every reason to suspect that this change increased rather than lessened the family's importance,"[46] the Andover records lead Professor Greven to conclude that, "The characteristic family structure which emerged in Andover with the maturing of the second generation during the 1670's and 1680's was a combination of both the classical extended family and the nuclear family."[47]

In colonial substantive law, the area of crime received the most attention during 1966. A fine collection of all the sources of early Massachusetts criminal law with a detailed discussion of some of the more notorious prosecutions was published by Edwin Powers.[48] The book, however, is marred by failure to offer interpretation or to place legal institutions within a social or intellectual background, such as is done in Kai T. Erikson's *Wayward Puritans*.[49] "His appreciations and his criticisms of the Puritan rulers and their laws," the late Professor Howe said of Powers, "seem scarcely distinguishable from those which came from the filiopietistic scholarship of the nineteenth century." Among other matters, Howe was troubled that Powers did not give attention to "the nature and the effectiveness of the ecclesiastical authority over the sins and offenses of the convenanted member of the churches."[50] Though perhaps this was not Power's purpose, yet it is a vitally significant aspect of colonial criminal jurisdiction and a topic to which George Lee Haskins has turned with penetrating results.

Professor Haskins employs the now well-established technique of searching for colonial antecedents among English contemporary institutions by looking for precedents of Massachusetts criminal punishments

---

[45] Philip J. Greven, "Family Structure in Seventeenth-Century Andover, Massachusetts," 23 *Wm. & Mary Q.* (3d ser.) 234 (1966).

[46] David J. Rothman, "A Note on the Study of the Colonial Family," 23 *Wm. & Mary Q.* (3d ser.) 627, 632 (1966).

[47] Philip J. Greven, *supra* note 45, at 255.

[48] Edwin Powers, *Crime and Punishment in Early Massachusetts, 1620 -1692 — A Documentary History* (1966). For a similar work, valuable for its sources, yet unimaginative and rudimentary, see Hugh F. Rankin, *Criminal Trial Proceedings in the General Court of Colonial Virginia* (1965).

[49] Kai T. Erikson, *Wayward Puritans — A Study in the Sociology of Deviance* (1966).

[50] Mark De Wolfe Howe, "Book Review," 80 *Harv. L. Rev.* 279, 280 (1966).

in English ecclesiastical practices.[51] Not only does Haskins offer new evidence of the value of comparative-law methods in reconstructing colonial legal history (as introduced by Julius Goebel in 1931), but he uses criminal law to cast a fresh light on Puritan concepts regarding church-state relationships thereby reinforcing some of the theories advanced last year by Clifford K. Shipton.[52]

Most of the 1966 studies relating to colonial legal history were in the area of constitutional or institutional history. As usual, however, constitutional issues are not always recognized, and when they are they are sometimes misunderstood. Paul R. Lucas, for example, presents an excellent account of the Royal Commission sent to Boston in 1665 by Charles II to investigate Massachusetts Bay's status within the constitutional structure of the empire. Lucas clarifies the identity of political groupings by comparing the legal arguments which each faction advanced in protest against the decision by the Commissioners to sit as an appellate court, a jurisdiction some New Englanders would have denied even to the king. The more extreme colonists, the Commonwealth men, Lucas suggests, took this antiprerogative position because to permit appeals "would be admitting that the government of Massachusetts was not sovereign on its own soil," whereas the more moderate faction stressed the fact that the charter did not provide for this appellate jurisdiction. "Through a bit of tortured logic," Lucas concludes, "the moderates had refused the Commission's request not on the basis of the General Court's sovereignty but on the grounds that to consent would somehow be a denial of the King's sovereignty."[53]

The records of Dedham and Watertown have been examined by Kenneth A. Lockridge and Alan Kreider who report that, "in the 'middle period' of colonial history, the locus of effective political power in these two towns shifted from one body — the board of selectmen — to another — the town meeting — and that the locus of power remained firmly with the meeting thereafter."[54] This shift was manifested by a remarkable increase in the number of meetings held each year after 1680 (while the meetings of the selectmen became increasingly brief and uneventful); the fact that the meeting assumed direct control over the levying of taxes and

---

[51] George Lee Haskins, "Precedents in English Ecclesiastical Practices for Criminal Punishments in Early Massachusetts," in *Frankfurter Essays,* supra note 16, at 321.

[52] Clifford K. Shipton, "The Locus of Authority in Colonial Massachusetts," in *Law and Authority in Colonial America* 137 (George Billias ed. 1965).

[53] Paul R. Lucas, "Colony or Commonwealth: Massachusetts Bay, 1661-1666," 24 *Wm. & Mary Q.* (3d ser.) 88, 105 (1967).

[54] Kenneth R. Lockridge & Alan Kreider, "The Evolution of Massachusetts Town Government, 1640 to 1740," 23 *Wm. & Mary Q.* (3d ser.) 549, 550 (1966).

the appropriation of the proceeds; and the practice of the meetings to appoint *ad hoc* committees to resolve or investigate specific matters.

> In Dedham and in Watertown, then, the town meeting as we like to think of it was not at all an automatic result of the law which gave it existence. It had to evolve slowly, over a period of a century and more. Not until 1690 could one begin to say that it positively held sway over the selectmen. Certain definite events helped it to emerge as the essential body of town government, to assert itself in various spheres of local power. Among these was the law itself, but of considerably greater significance were the passing away of the first generation of leaders, the emergence of difficult problems . . . , and the growth of the population.[55]

Little of interest was written regarding other colonies except for Pennsylvania, about which some revisionistic theories were advanced. Joseph E. Illick reappraised William Penn's relations with the crown, the Board of Trade, the Privy Council, and with Parliament, and suggests that on the whole, Penn's colonial experiment was "democratic."[56] By showing that the Board of Trade's attempt at resumption of the proprietary charters during the years from 1699 to 1702 had the support of many Whigs, I.K. Steele challenged the traditional view that resumption was a Tory program frustrated by the antiprerogativism of the Whigs. Indeed, he suggests, it was to bolster the concept of parliamentary authority that the Whigs supported legislation to abrogate agreements between the crown and proprietors. Professor Steele attributes the Board's defeat partly to divisions within the ranks of both parties, partly to the death of William III, and largely to the effective lobbying of Quakers who made the cause of proprietary charters the cause of religious dissent.[57]

The major emphasis of colonial constitutional studies during 1966 was from the imperial perspective.[58] More significant, the neglected topic

---

[55] Id. at 573.

[56] Joseph E. Illick, *William Penn, The Politician — His Relations with the English Government* 96 (1965). But see, the study where William Penn's constitutional philosophy is described as an evolution from the "liberal" to the "illiberal" and which criticizes historians who have praised the democratic tendencies of "the Frame of 1682" for reading "twentieth-century democracy back into seventeenth-century documents." Gary B. Nash, "The Framing of Government in Pennsylvania — Ideas in Contact with Reality," 23 *Wm. & Mary Q.* (3d ser.) 183, 201 (1966).

[57] I.K. Steele, "The Board of Trade, The Quakers and Resumption of Colonial Charters, 1699-1702," 23 *Wm. & Mary Q.* (3d ser.) 596 (1966).

[58] Note especially B.D. Bargar, *Lord Dartmouth and the American Revolution* (1965) (concerning one of the key officials who formulated constitutional

of the military received some attention. Stephen Saunders Webb examined the career of Francis Nicholson, the soldier-governor (Virginia, Maryland, Nova Scotia, New York, South Carolina) who, along with others of his breed, was sent to America during Stuart times on behalf of "royalization, centralization, and the imposition of authority,"[59] and who established the Anglican church while complaining about such matters as "the ill Consequence of having Custom and Common Law in these parts."[60] Webb demonstrates the process by which the royal governors came out of the ranks of officers formerly stationed at such posts as Tangier, where military rule over civilians conditioned them for authoritarian attitudes and actions.[61]

> Institutionally, governorships were similar throughout the empire, and the traditions of town government [i.e., English garrison towns] were a major source of precedent for colonial government. Governors were the instruments who united military and civil authority in the interests of the Crown. They made up the iron fist of royal absolutism and it was their work, more than memories of Cromwell, that underlay the cry against standing armies coming from every part of the empire during virtually all of Nicholson's imperial career.[62]

Yet as John Shy makes clear in the most important study of this *Survey* year, this opposition was not a major factor in the 1763 decision to maintain a standing army in America.[63] The French and Indian War "had produced a basic change in military policy, and that change raised constitutional problems that could not be solved."[64] Among the problems not solved was the constitutional status of the newly-instituted office of

---

policy during the years when the doctrine of parliamentary supremacy forced the colonies to regard revolution as inevitable); Franklin B. Wickwire, *British Subministers and Colonial America, 1763 - 1783* (1966) (concerning the effect of British patronage and American lobbyists upon politics leading to Independence).

[59] Stephen Saunders Webb, "The Strange Career of Francis Nicholson," 23 *Wm. & Mary Q.* (3d ser.) 513, 546 (1966).

[60] Id. at 537.

[61] Thus see Nicholson's constitutional antics toward law officers, in Hugh F. Rankin, *supra* note 48, at 20. Also, he was a leader of the "resumption" movement. I.K. Steele, *supra* note 57, at 598, 601.

[62] Stephen Saunders Webb, *supra* note 59, at 517-18.

[63] Shy contends that the army was maintained "to prevent illegal settlement on Indian land, to regulate the fur trade, and to assist the customs officers." It was not primarily to be a means of defense against Indian attacks, but rather to help enforce imperial laws protecting the nations against colonial provocations. In a sense, it was a police force maintaining constitutional order. John Shy, *Toward Lexington — the Role of the British Army in the Coming of the American Revolution* 82-83 (1965).

[64] Id. at 418.

commander-in-chief (held by Amherst and Gage), which led to a weakening of the governor's prestige. The extent of this weakening has not yet been measured, but, as Shy notes, "No American Commander in Chief ever lost a battle with a royal governor."[65] The vagueness of "the legal question", Shy believes, played "a great part in the deterioration of British control." For example, in 1774,

> Both Gage and the cabinet had persisted in the error that marked more than a decade of military policy: they had failed to distinguish between the legality and the capability of using force. Gage, after saying more to the King than he really believed about the capability of controlling colonists [i.e., Bostonians] with soldiers, had emphasized the legal obstacle in his discussion with the ministers. The latter thought they had met his objections by making him both Commander in Chief for North America *and* Governor of Massachusetts, and by deriving a third office for him from the second — "first Magistrate," though they failed to make clear whether explicit legal restrictions on one office could be circumvented by invoking the powers of another.[66]

Once the war had begun, different legal problems arose. Henry J. Young, in a significant article, demonstrates the type of research which must be conducted if we are to understand the legal history of the Revolutionary era. While argeeing with other recent studies which emphasize the mildness of Whig treatment of Tories (a fact he attributes to respect for precedent, legal experience, and defense attorneys such as James Wilson), Young doubts whether a true picture can be reconstructed from the records of treason trials and confiscation hearings. Political prosecutions were often disguised in conventional indictments which provided severer penalties and were more certain of punishment.[67] Moreover,

> It is paradoxical that, during the Revolution, neither prosecutions for treasonable offenses, nor acts of attainder, were initiated against Pennsylvanians by the British government, while in the same period headstrong Pennsylvania Whigs proscribed, or prosecuted as traitors, hundreds of citizens who had never deviated from the allegiance in which they were born.[68]

---

[65] Id. at 422.

[66] Id. at 409.

[67] "For example, when it was made clear that Abijah Wright, a captured loyalist, had entered a man's house by night to kidnap him for the British, the charge against him was changed from treason to burglary, and he was quickly convicted and hanged." Henry J. Young, "Treason and its Punishment in Revolutionary Pennsylvania," 90 *Penn. Mag. Hist. & Bio.* 287, 298 (1966).

[68] Id. at 288.

III

THE NINETEENTH CENTURY

The problem of treason and the doings of the Pennsylvania bar during the postrevolutionary era also received attention.[69] In a convincing paper, Robert K. Faulkner destroyed Edward S. Corwin's generally accepted thesis that John Marshall, hoping to embarrass President Jefferson, abandoned his former views and laid down an overly stringent interpretation of the constitutional provision requiring two witnesses to the act of treason, when he ruled in the *Burr* case that they must be witnesses to the overt act of the accused. Building on principles developed by Willard Hurst and Bradley Chapin, Faulkner argues that "Marshall's opinions amount to an accurate grasp of the Constitution's tenor, that there is no contradiction between Marshall's views at the Burr trial and his opinions previously expressed, and that the imputation of obscure and biased motives is unsupported by any other evidence worthy of the name."[70] Indeed, if Marshall showed any bias, "it was only a prudent bias toward the popular clamor and toward Jefferson."[71]

> Admitting Marshall's violent dislike of Jefferson, one might have expected him to choose better ground for embarrassing the President than that occupied by Burr. Popular fever ran uproariously against Burr, not for him. It was the Chief Justice, not the President, who after the decision was the object of almost universal vituperation from the press, who was hung in effigy, whose impeachment was covertly threatened in Jefferson's annual message, not to mention the more explicit first draft . . . . Moreover, neither traitors in general, nor Burr in particular, were any favorites of the Chief Justice.[72]

The late Perry Miller brought his unique genius to bear on the nineteenth-century legal profession by writing an intellectual history drawn from the speeches and essays of an elite, far beyond the thoughts of the common practitioner on the practicalities of institutional life.[73] Legal historians must be grateful for Miller's effort; even those who agree

---

[69] For a comprehensive study see Thomas R. Meehan, "Courts, Cases, and Counselors, in Revolutionary and Post-Revolutionary Pennsylvania," 91 *Penn. Mag. Hist. & Bio.* 3 (1967).

[70] Robert K. Faulkner, "John Marshall and the Burr Trial," 53 J. Am. Hist. 247, 248 (1966).

[71] Id. at 258.

[72] Id. at 255-56.

[73] Perry Miller, *The Life of the Mind in America From the Revolution to the Civil War* 99-265 (1965).

with Norman Gash's warning against the trap "of mistaking ideas for forces."

> Few things in historical writing are easier than the collection of ideas and opinions. Few things on the other hand are more difficult than the assessment of their actual influence on events; for the ideas which accompany political actions and attitudes are usually either overlaid by more material motives and interests or used as a pretext to disguise them.[74]

Somewhat in the same vein was an exhaustive study of the academic influence of civilian writings on emerging American law during the years when it was most impressionable and ready for a reception. To the familiar names of James Kent, Joseph Story, and Hugh Swinton Legare, Peter Stein adds those of David Hoffman, Edward Everett, and Caleb Cushing. While offering no details as to the impact of the civil law upon legal practice (or even an analysis of the sales of the books and translations which he cites as evidence of an interest), Stein does conclude:

> The 1820's and 1830's were the hey-day of the civil law in the United States. The publication of Edward Livingston's Civil Code for Louisiana in 1825 seemed to assert its ascendancy and to presage an extension of its influence among the common-law states. Yet by 1850, it had probably ceased to be a real force in the development of American law.[75]

Why? Stein's answer is that civil law was supported by an elite of Federalists and Whigs while the practicing bar had a vested interest in maintaining the *status quo*. In addition, he suggests that codification drained away the reforming enthusiasm of some intellectuals, while others, after the triumph of Roman law, turned their attention to an antiquarianism which "was motivated by 'elegance' rather than 'utility'."[76]

In the area of biography, Gerald T. Dunne continued his excellent series of articles dealing with the world of Joseph Story.[77] Mr. Dunne's interpretation of the *Dartmouth College Case*, limited as it is to the

---

[74] Norman Gash, "Book Review," 82 *Eng. Hist. Rev.* 186, 187 (1967) (reviewing David P. Crook, *American Democracy in English Politics 1815 -1850* (1965)).

[75] Peter Stein, "The Attraction of the Civil Law in Post- Revolutionary America," 52 *Va. L. Rev.* 403, 431-32 (1966).

[76] Id. at 433.

[77] Gerald T. Dunne, "Joseph Story — The Great Term," 79 *Harv. L. Rev.* 877 (1966); Gerald T. Dunne, "The Story-Livingston Correspondence (1812-1822)," 10 *Am. J. Legal Hist.* 224 (1966); Gerald T. Dunne, "Joseph Story — The Salem Years," 101 *Essex Institute Hist. Coll.* 307 (1965).

contract-clause aspect, is less satisfactory than that of a non-lawyer, Maurice G. Baxter, who published a pioneering study by adopting as his biographical format the role of one advocate upon constitutional history.[78] Baxter's book is excellent, and while it says little that is new, it does prove that forensic history, even in the constitutional-law area, deserves a better reputation than it has enjoyed since 1942 when Benjamin Twiss made it an iconoclastic weapon to sum up most of the historical cliches of the 1930s.[79]

One of the historical prejudices reminiscent of the New Deal generation which Twiss fostered on constitutional tradition, was his attack upon Thomas M. Cooley as an originator of economic due process. Alan Jones now revises this glib picture and, examining Chief Justice Cooley's judicial opinions, concludes that his *Treatise on Constitutional Limitations* "should be understood as a classic statement of Jacksonian constitutional theory rather than a legal apology for the judicial protection of property rights";[80] and that the Cooley image must be reshaped to recognize that Cooley "believed in the future rather than the past, in the defense of the public interest rather than the protection of private right, in the ideal of a more humane equality rather than the dogmatism of an unfettered liberty."[81]

Among other important revisionist papers presented this *Survey* year, was Stanley I. Kutler's convincing argument that the Act of 1866 reducing the Supreme Court from ten to seven members was a result neither of Radical Republican opposition to President Johnson nor of Congressional vindictiveness toward the judiciary;[82] William Wirt Blume's

---

78 Maurice G. Baxter, *Daniel Webster and the Supreme Court* (1966). For a questionable interpretation of *Dartmouth College*, premised upon the assumption that the origins of a judge's decisions may be found in his forensic arguments as a practicing attorney see, Florian Bartosic, "With John Marshall From William and Mary to Dartmouth," 7 *Wm. & Mary L. Rev.* 259 (1966).

79 Benjamin Twiss, *Lawyers and the Constitution — How Laissez-Faire Came to the Supreme Court* (1942).

80 Alan Jones, "Thomas M. Cooley and the Michigan Supreme Court — 1865-1885," 10 *Am. J. Legal Hist.* 97, 109 (1966).

81 Alan Jones, "Thomas M. Cooley and the Interstate Commerce Commission — Continuity and Change in the Doctrine of Equal Rights," 81 *Pol. Sci. Q.* 602, 627 (1966). See also Alan Jones, "Thomas M. Cooley and 'Laissez-Faire Constitutionalism': A Reconsideration," 53 *J. Am. Hist.* 751 (1967).

82 Stanley I. Kutler, "Reconstruction and the Supreme Court: The Numbers Game Reconsidered," 32 *J. So. Hist.* 42 (1966).

> A careful and thorough re-examination of the whole role and place of the Supreme Court during Reconstruction might well impair the traditional views. In any event, the existence of careless assumptions, preconceptions, and incorrect conclusions regarding the judicial legislation of 1866 and 1869 points to the need for such study.

exhaustive treatment of California's civil-procedure codes which he concludes owed less to the model furnished by David Dudley Field than to the initiative and favorable interpretations of Stephen Field;[83] and Theodore B. Wilson's revision of the revisionists (or return to the traditionalists) which places the post-Civil War black codes in a softer light than has been fashionable, arguing that the myth of their harshness was exaggerated by Radicals bent on forcing Reconstruction by any pretense.[84]

Id. at 58. See also Stanley I. Kutler, "Ex Parte McCardle: Judicial Impotency? — The Supreme Court and Reconstruction Reconsidered," 72 *Am. Hist. Rev.* 835 (1967).

[83] William Wirt Blume, "Adoption in California of the Field Code of Civil Procedure — A Chapter in American Legal History," 17 *Hastings L.J.* 701 (1966). "In its enactment of the Court and Practice Acts of 1851 and of the Code of Civil Procedure of 1872 the California Legislature did not adopt or copy New York legislation, but, in reality, originated a new code of civil procedure." Id. at 708.

[84] Theodore B. Wilson, *The Black Codes of the South* 147 (1965). For a book by a lawyer-historian which deals with many of the legal (land ownership, bequeathing property, the right to contract for labor) as well as social and political aspects of slavery in New York see, Edgar J. McManus, *A History of Negro Slavery in New York* (1966). Also, Richard B. Morris, employing court records, traces the extent of involuntary servitude (quasibondage and felon labor) during the ante-bellum era, especially among poor, uneducated whites and negroes who lived in a shadowland between freedom and slavery. Richard B. Morris, "The Courts, The Law, and Social History," in *Essays in Legal History in Honor of Felix Frankfurter, supra* note 3, at 409."

Chapter Seven

1966: CONSTITUTIONAL HISTORY

William E. Nelson

I

POLITICS IN THE CONSTITUTIONAL PROCESS

"[A]lthough the [Supreme] Court uses the jargon, patterns and rituals of a judicial tribunal, its influence upon the evolution of the American system has been basically in its role as a political rather than judicial institution."[1] So writes Leo Pfeffer, expressing a theme of much of the past year's writing in constitutional history.

Pfeffer concludes that "the makers of the Constitution did not anticipate . . . the importance the judiciary . . . would have in the political and economic evolution of the nation . . . ,"[2] but conceived of the Court as a purely judicial organ. He sees Chief Justice Marshall as the man who "took a Supreme Court which had been considered . . . as of little value and . . . hopelessly impotent, and single-handedly made of it a powerful instrument" for furthering political ends.[3] Pfeffer considers the Court as political essentially on the basis of its decisions which, in addition to their political effects, are those made in most societies by legislative or executive, rather than judicial bodies. His approach, however, is too narrow. In determining the extent to which the Supreme Court over the course of its history has been a political institution, it is necessary to take into account factors in addition to the effects of the Court's decisions. Meriting consideration are the politics behind appointments to the bench, the reactions of politicians to decisions and then of the Court to the politicians, and finally, the extent to which politicians look to the Court to solve problems which they themselves are unable to solve.

During the past year, two articles have dealt with the matter of Supreme Court appointments. While recognizing that politics always

[1] Leo Pfeffer, *This Honorable Court — A History of the United States Supreme Court* 19-20 (1965).

[2] Id. at 26.

[3] Id. at 119-20.

plays a role in high judicial appointments, they find different political considerations decisive under different Presidents. One article concerned an appointment to the Court by Theodore Roosevelt.[4] The contest for the vacant seat was between Attorney General William Moody, supported by Senator Henry Cabot Lodge, and Circuit Judge Horace Lurton, supported by Secretary of War, William Howard Taft. Lurton had the inside track, until the President learned that he "was decidedly not 'right' on the 'great' question of the national commerce power, at least by Roosevelt's standards."[5] "[T]he President's fear that Lurton's constitutional philosophy was incompatible with his own was the main, if not the sole reason, for not going through with . . . [his] appointment" and for choosing Moody instead.[6] Thus, for Roosevelt, a man's ideological preconceptions and the preview they gave of his potential political role on the bench were decisive in determining his suitability.

President Madison, on the other hand, was not especially concerned with ideology when he appointed Justice Joseph Story.[7] Although Story was nominally a Jeffersonian Republican, Jefferson and others had warned Madison that ideologically he was a Federalist and hence ought not be appointed to the High Court. Nevertheless, Madison appointed him because factors of "geographical location, religion, [and] interest group affiliation" were uppermost in the President's mind.[8] Perhaps Madison did not see the Court's decisions as sufficiently important politically to justify ignoring such factors. Or perhaps he realized that as the ideological divisions of 1800 were fast becoming irrelevant, it made no difference whom he appointed because the Court, as Donald Roper now contends, would have been in fundamental agreement on economic issues and questions of the scope of national power[9] — the chief political questions confronting it.

Political reactions to Supreme Court decisions received consideration in two other recent articles. One attempted to analyze statistically seven periods of what it termed "Court-curbing" activity on the part of Congress.[10] Its author compiled a list of "factors which have an affirma-

---

[4] Paul T. Heffron, "Theodore Roosevelt and the Appointment of Mr. Justice Moody," 18 *Vand. L. Rev.* 545 (1965).

[5] Id. at 564.

[6] Id. at 567.

[7] Morgan D. Dowd, "Justice Joseph Story and the Politics of Appointment," 9 *Am. J. Legal Hist.* 65 (1965).

[8] Id. at 285.

[9] Donald Roper, "Judicial Unanimity and the Marshall Court— A Road to Reappraisal," 9 *Am. J. Legal Hist.* 118 (1965).

[10] Stuart S. Nagel, "Court-Curbing Periods in American History," 18 *Vand. L. Rev.* 925 (1965).

tive correlation with the occurrence of Court-curbing bills" and their suc- ess,[11] concluding:

> Although an accurate measurement of the relative importance of these factors to Court-curbing cannot be made, a behavior pattern which invariably occurs in such conflicts can be described. The sequence of events involves judicial provocation, the existence of circumstances which act as catalysts or as retarders, a set of congressional and presidential responses, and judicial counteraction. This model which is based on the psychological model of stimulus, organism, response, and feedback can perhaps also be profitably applied to analyzing other legal and political phenomena.[12]

The application of methodology of this sort to the study of constitutional history portends much for the future, and may some day yield valid results. But for the present, apart from any questions about the validity of the method itself, too many difficulties stand in the way of its successful use. For example, one of the seven periods classified by the article as Court-curbing is the Andrew Johnson administration. Allegedly the principal Court-curbing bill of this period was the Judiciary Act of 1866,[13] which reduced the membership of the Supreme Court from ten to seven. It was shown in an excellent article,[14] however, that some very eminent historians have been wrong in concluding that the primary purpose of that act was to strike at the Court or at the President. The article's author, Stanley Kutler, implies that the late 1860's were not a Court-curbing period at all; thereby casting doubt upon "the standard accounts of a weak, frightened, intimidated and pliant Supreme Court during Reconstruction"[15] and upon use of that period in attempting to synthesize generalizations about Court-curbing activity.

A third problem considered during the past year involved attempts and failures by politicians to solve questions ultimately resolved only in the Supreme Court. C. Peter Magrath, in a book on the Yazoo land controversy,[16] which "for three decades . . . troubled Congress and the administrations of Washington, Adams, Jefferson, and Madison,"[17] devotes a full chapter to Congressional attempts to resolve the dispute. The

---

[11] Id. at 944.

[12] Ibid.

[13] 14 Stat. 209 (1866).

[14] Stanley I. Kutler, "Reconstruction and the Supreme Court—The Numbers Game Reconsidered," 32 *J. So. Hist.* 42 (1966).

[15] Id. at 58.

[16] C. Peter Magrath, *Yazoo - Law and Politics in the New Republic, The Case of Fletcher* v. *Peck* (1966).

[17] Id. at vii.

attempts failed, and the matter was finally settled by the Supreme Court in the collusive suit of *Fletcher v. Peck.*[18] Magrath writes:

> The Yazooists of the New England Mississippi Land Company were very likely the first organized group to see the Supreme Court — then a tribunal of still uncertain powers — as an institution that might be a source of valuable political decisions. The judicial path trod by the Yazooists in the early 1800's has since been followed by many other organized interests: railroad corporations . . . , Liberty Leaguers . . . , the American Civil Liberties Union and the National Association for the Advancement of Colored People.[19]

What effect do these articles have upon the formulation of a coherent view of the political role of the Supreme Court over the course of American history? Some of them contain material lending support to the view that the Court has been primarily a political institution, others indicate that in some instances such a view would be unsound. President Theodore Roosevelt, for example, viewed the Court as very much a political institution; President Madison, on the other hand, very possibly did not, although some of his contemporaries did. In sum, the articles on politics and the Court tell us that we know very little about the Court's political role and that a meaningful appraisal of that role is at present impossible. Nevertheless, the articles constitute a significant beginning.

Several other of this year's books which were essentially politically oriented dealt not with the Supreme Court and its work, but with the adoption and amendment of the Constitution. The most significant was William Gillette's *The Right to Vote: Politics and the Passage of the Fifteenth Amendment.* Gillette's thesis is that in 1866, at the time of the passage of the fourteenth amendment, there existed a "treacherous current of racial prejudice and opposition to Negro suffrage" throughout the entire nation.[20] However, by early 1867, the Republicans in Congress had secured the enfranchisement of the Negro throughout the South, the territories and the District of Columbia. It was only in the North that the Negro could not vote. The principal purpose of the fifteenth amendment, as Gillette sees it, was the enfranchisement of northern Negroes, who held the balance of power between the Republicans and Democrats.[21] Gillette argues that the amendment was adopted by Congress and ratified by the states because the Republicans, interested in future national office,

---

[18] 6 U.S. (Cranch) 87 (1810). On the collusive nature of the suit, see C. Peter Magrath, supra note 16, at 54-55.

[19] Id. at vii.

[20] William Gillette, *The Right to Vote* 25 (1965).

[21] Id. at 46-49.

realized that its passage would guarantee their party's dominance in the North, and thus in the nation. As Gillette concludes:

> Most constitutional historians have argued that the Fifteenth Amendment failed. It did not guarantee southern Negro voting and, in the former Confederate states, became ineffectual through successful evasion. But it is not altogether fair to condemn the Amendment because of the weakness with which it was enforced. . . . During the nineteenth century the practical effect of the Amendment was to bring the ballot to the northern Negro and power to the Republicans. The Negro was started along the road to first-class citizenship. He could vote in the North, and the Republicans benefited from a solid Negro vote in the close elections of the 1870's and 1880's. . . . Partisan but enlightened self-interest was the motive of most Republican politicans, and mutual interest was to develop as a result. The Fifteenth Amendment was thus a shotgun marriage of practical idealism to political realism.[22]

Another worthwile study of original source material is Robert Rutland's monograph on the struggle over the ratification of the Constitution.[23] Rutland argues that the Federalists won the ratification contest due to their superior organization, their willingness to compromise on the issue of a bill of rights, and the fact that the Antifederalists offered no counterproposal to the Constitution.[24] As Clinton Rossiter's discussion of the background of 1787 indicates, however, the Federalists' victory is perhaps not so easily explained.[25] Victory for the Constitution was by no means fore-ordained; indeed, it was almost miraculous. For, although Americans in the 1780's thought of themselves as citizens of one nation, there was within the context of the times no reason why a nation had to have an effective government: Many nations, among them Germany, did not.[26] In fact, Americans saw the nations of Europe which did have strong governments — Spain, France and, to an extent, Great Britain — as tyrannies, this view being confirmed by American experience with British central authority between 1763 and 1775. The framers of the Constitution, as Rossiter puts it, "made a gamble with the destiny of the American people . . . hazardous and yet . . . calculated"[27] — a gamble in which they attempted to secure the blessings of centralization and yet avoid the pitfalls of tyranny. Their success over a period of almost 175 years is a measure of the miracle of 1787.

---

22 Id. at 163-65.

23 Robert A. Rutland, *The Ordeal of the Constitution* (1965).

24 Id. at 311-13.

25 Clinton L. Rossiter, *1787: The Grand Convention* (1966).

26 Id. at 23, 37-38.

27 Id. at 20.

II

THE HISTORICAL BACKGROUND OF CONSTITUTIONAL DOCTRINE

The historian of the law, like the practitioner, must approach issues and frame problems so that he does not "in the process of writing . . . [discover] . . . [he] has given the right answers to the wrong questions."[28] Answering the wrong questions adds nothing to our store of knowledge of the past — the primary goal of history, nor does it aid in the decision of present-day legal issues — a goal of much legal history. It is unfortunate, therefore, that the bulk of recent work on the historical background of constitutional doctrines consists of often excellent scholarship addressed, however, to useless questions.

Analysis of three works, among the best of the year's publications will illustrate and, it is hoped, offer some insight into one way of framing historical problems in order to provide a means of isolating proper questions. The three are Lewis Mayers, *The Habeas Corpus Act of 1867: The Supreme Court as Legal Historian;*[29] Dallin H. Oaks, *Legal History in the High Court — Habeas Corpus;*[30] and Daniel John Meador, *Habeas Corpus and Magna Carta.*[31] The first two are well-written, thoroughly researched investigations of primary source material. The third is a notably readable survey of the history of habeas corpus from the twelfth century to the present.

Mayers' article addresses itself to only one question — whether the 1867 Act,[32] which extended federal habeas corpus to persons in state custody, was intended to permit federal habeas corpus review of state criminal convictions. His evidence establishes beyond a doubt his claim that Congress never contemplated that the act would have such an effect. He therefore concludes that "the process by which the Court has converted the proceeding authorized by the 1867 statute into a unique and anomalous procedure for review of state court convictions . . . [belies its] claim of merely fulfilling the intentions of the 1867 Congress [and] is without historical foundation."[33]

---

[28] Bernard Bailyn, "The Problems of the Working Historian—A Comment," in *Philosophy and History — A Symposium* 92, 97 (Sidney Hook ed. 1963).

[29] 33 *U. Chi. L. Rev.* 31 (1965).

[30] 64 *Mich. L. Rev.* 451 (1966).

[31] Daniel J. Meador, *Habeas Corpus and Magna Carta* (1966).

[32] Habeas Corpus Act of 1867, 14 Stat. 385 (1867).

[33] Lewis Mayers, "The Habeas Corpus Act of 1867," 33 *U. Chi. L. Rev.* 31, 58 (1965).

The essential thrust of Oaks is that the historical authorities cited by the Court in *Fay v. Noia*[34] provide no support for its statement that "'the historic office of the Great Writ [has been] to redress detentions in violation of fundamental law.'"[35] From this he implies that *Fay* is historically unsound.

Meador's approach is quite different. He begins with a discussion of the early history of habeas corpus, which shows that by the beginning of the seventeenth century the common law courts were using the writ to compel the production and release of persons held in custody by other authorities.[36] Then, during the course of the century, "the writ . . . [became] established as *the* mode for vindicating the liberty of the subject by protecting him against confinement contrary to due process of law."[37] Meador and Oaks both consider whether, "when habeas corpus practice was codified in the Habeas Corpus Act of 1679,[38] . . . [any] distinction was made between executive and judicial detentions."[39] Oaks writes:

> If a seventeenth century lawyer ever urged that the function or office of habeas corpus was the "vindication of due process," he would undoubtedly have had in mind the use of habeas corpus to review executive detentions and to release persons wrongfully imprisoned by the crown. The idea that this phrase from Magna Charta implies some supervisory review of the acts of judges of superior courts, or a broad license to "remedy any kind of governmental restraint contrary to fundamental law" originates in the United States Reports, not the annals of English history.[40]

Contrary to Meador's view that the writ was "*the* mode for vindicating the liberty of the subject," Oaks' position is unsound. It is only when men believe in the modern doctrine of separation of powers that they distinguish between executive and judicial action, and in the seventeenth century the modern doctrine had not yet developed.[41] Thus, Oaks' "seventeenth century lawyer" could not "have had in mind" the distinction between executive and judicial action which Oaks suggests; and, therefore, the Supreme Court was correct in saying that the writ gave a remedy against both types of arbitrary governmental action. This, of

---

[34] 372 U.S. 391 (1963).

[35] Dallin H. Oaks, "Legal History in the High Court — Habeas Corpus," 64 *Mich. L. Rev.* 451, 459 (1966).

[36] Daniel J. Meador, *supra* note 31, at 12.

[37] Id. at 25.

[38] 31 Car. 2, c.2.

[39] *Fay v. Noia,* 372 U.S. 391, 403 (1963).

[40] Dallin H. Oaks, *supra* note 35, at 465-66.

[41] William B. Gwyn, *The Meaning of the Separation of Powers* 67-68, 101 (1965).

course, does not mean that all judicial commitments in the seventeenth century were within the scope of habeas corpus. The Act of 1679 expressly excluded most sorts, among them cases involving persons detained pursuant to conviction of a crime by a court having jurisdiction thereof.[42] This exclusion posed an effective obstacle to habeas corpus' becoming a post-conviction remedy.

The creation of the federal system in the United States, Meador notes, raised two additional obstacles to such a remedy, at least for state prisoners. First, federal courts could grant the writ only if a man were detained in violation of federal law, and until recently there was little federal law relating to state criminal proceedings.[43] Secondly, the Judiciary Act of 1789[44] precluded the granting of the writ to any state prisoner, even one whose detention violated federal law.[45]

This last obstacle, according to Meador, was removed by the Act of 1867,[46] which gave a federal court the same power to issue a writ in the case of a state or federal prisoner. In discussing the act, Meador confirms Mayers' conclusion that no one expected it to extend federal habeas corpus to state convicts, since after its passage in 1867 the other two obstacles to its doing so still remained. But Meador in addition demonstrates that Mayers' conclusion is irrelevant: With the benefit of hindsight we can see that the elimination of the distinction between state and federal prisoners as such made the eligibility of state convicts for habeas corpus automatic once the remaining obstacles were removed. And, as Meador's tracing of history makes clear, they have been removed. One of them, the lack of federal law relating to state criminal proceedings, was removed by the fourteenth amendment and the Supreme Court's recent interpretations of it.[47] Meador concludes with an unfortunately brief sketch of the removal of the final obstacle — the prohibition of the 1679 Act against issuance of the writ to prisoners convicted of a crime.[48]

Meador's book sets much in perspective. It demonstrates the invalidity of Mayers' and Oaks' articles and in addition, it marks out the areas where the Supreme Court may be open to historical attack; (1) in

---

[42] Habeas Corpus Act of 1679, 31 Car. 2, c.2.

[43] Daniel J. Meador, *supra* note 31, at 56.

[44] 1 Stat. 73, 81 (1789).

[45] Daniel J. Meador, *supra* note 31, at 34-35.

[46] Id. at 56. The obstacle was partially revived by the subsequently enunciated rule that a state prisoner before seeking the writ must exhaust his state remedies, including remedies no longer available, and by the parallel doctrines of waiver and adequate state grounds. On the origins of the exhaustion requirement, see *Fay v. Noia,* 372 U.S. 391, 418-19 (1963).

[47] Daniel J. Meador, *supra* note 31, at 66-67.

[48] Id. at 57-66.

its modification of the exhaustion doctrine in *Fay*, (2) in its abandonment (culminating in either *Moore v. Dempsey*[49] or *Brown v. Allen*)[50] of the rule prohibiting the granting of habeas corpus to prisoners convicted of crime,[51] and (3) in its application of the Bill of Rights to the states. There is still room for properly framed historical analysis of all these questions.

The difference between Meador, on the one hand, and Mayers and Oaks on the other, is that Meador has asked the right questions whereas Mayers and Oaks have not. Thus it is necessary to examine what Meador did to obtain the right questions which Mayers and Oaks failed to do.

First let us analyze Mayers and Oaks. Essentially their method was to stand in the present time, to frame a legal issue of present-day significance and then to ask *what men of the past who were not confronted with the issue did when they were confronted with it.* The inconsistency in the italicized clause is the flaw in Mayers' and Oaks' reasoning. To take a specific example, Oaks' inconsistency lies in his asking how seventeenth century lawyers distinguished between executive and judicial detentions when they did not distinguish between the executive and the judiciary at all. Mayers' inconsistency lies in his asking whether Congress in 1867 wanted to extend federal habeas corpus to state convicts, when in fact no one in Congress ever thought about the matter.

The question which Mayers and Oaks ask — how did men of the past react to a present issue — is a natural one for lawyers and a most useful one as long as the men of the past did react. The question is meaningless, however, if the men of the past did not react. A more sophisticated question then would be how they would have reacted if they had been confronted with the issue. Yet this question too is inadequate, since it calls not for a definite and verifiable answer but for speculation — informed speculation perhaps — but speculation nonetheless. And constitutional history, like all other history, can never tell us what would have happened in the past if the past had been different; only what in fact happened in the past as it was.

Meador's method of framing his historical problem is quite different. It has been best explained, perhaps, by the historian Bernard Bailyn, who has attempted to define "true historical problems." By "true historical problems" Bailyn means "questions raised by the observation of . . . anomalies in the existing data." He gives an example as follows: In 1700,

[49] 261 U.S. 86 (1923).

[50] 344 U.S. 443 (1953).

[51] Compare *Fay v. Noia,* 372 U.S. 391, 421-22 (1963), with Justice Harlan's dissenting opinion at 457-60.

he writes, Virginia tobacco was marketed by consignment to London merchants, whereas in 1760 it was sold to local factors. About this anomaly Bailyn asks: "Why the change? The observation of the difference [between 1700 and 1760]," he continues, "creates a problem of explanation, to solve which one undertakes research and writing."[52] This is precisely what Meador did. He first looked at the writ of habeas corpus at two points in time — before 1600 and today. He saw vast differences. He then set about without attempting to solve modern legal issues, to explain how the differences occurred.

Two important new books will further illustrate the nature and superiority of Meador's approach. They are Irving Brant's *The Bill of Rights* and Leonard Levy's *Freedom of the Press from Zenger to Jefferson.*

Brant's chief concern is with the first amendment protection of free speech and free press. In dealing with this topic, he asks whether the framers of the amendment intended absolutely to prohibit goverment from making any law abridging such freedom, or whether they intended that the liberty of the individual be balanced against the needs of government. Brant sees the eighteenth century as a period of struggle between libertarian and reactionary forces. As he explains:

> Surveying the turbulent period from 1720 to 1789, . . . it is clearly evident that two great currents were in motion in the Anglo-Saxon world. One was a powerful forward motion, setting mind and body free from the political, religious and monarchic invasions of the basic rights of humankind. The other was a backward motion . . . . [T]he amendments of 1789 were gleaming libertarian cascades.[53]

Since the first amendment was such a "libertarian cascade," it must, according to Brant, be given a libertarian construction. For Brant, the absolute language of the framers — government "shall make no law" —is an indication of their libertarianism which must be taken at face value.

The difficulty with Brant's approach is that by government he means, implicitly, not only the federal government but state governments as well. Thus, he writes of a recent case in which "the English common law [the backward current of the eighteenth century] was formally rejected as a measure of the freedoms guaranteed by the First and Fourteenth Amendments," and calls that case "a return . . . to the principles that governed the framers of the First Amendment."[54] The result of his failure to distinguish between the federal and state governments is that when he

[52] Bernard Bailyn, *supra* note 28, at 96.

[53] Irving Brant, *The Bill of Rights* 219 (1965).

[54] Id. at 404.

asks, "Would the Revolutionary generation have recognized the 'balancing test' as 'the liberty for which they valiantly fought and honorably bled',"[55] he is in reality asking to what extent the framers intended to restrict both state and federal interference with freedom of expression. This question, however, is meaningless, for the framers were thinking solely in terms of a federal restriction. Brant's fault is that, like Mayers and Oaks, he asks historical figures a modern question which they did not ask themselves.

Levy, on the other hand, uses Meador's approach in his excellent introduction to his collection of documents. He begins by discussing the seventeenth century "common law's definition of criminal libels . . . that the press was free from censorship in advance of publication, but was subject to subsequent punishment for bad or wrong sentiments about the government."[56] Until 1798, this view, only slightly modified, remained predominant in America, according to Levy. "Then, in 1798, there was a sudden breakthrough in American libertarian thought on freedom of political expression."[57] "In brief, the new libertarians advocated that only 'injurious conduct,' as manifested by 'overt acts' or deeds, rather than words, should be criminally redressable."[58] Levy argues persuasively that the first amendment did not achieve an equivalent breakthrough at an earlier time. The amendment, says Levy, must be viewed in the context of federal-state relations. He writes:

> The framers meant Congress to be totally without power to enact legislation respecting the press. They intended a federal system in which the national government could exercise only such powers as were specifically enumerated, or were necessary and proper to carry out those enumerated. . . . In other words, no matter what was meant or understood by freedom of speech and press, the national government . . . could not make speech or press a legitimate subject of restrictive legislation.[59]

Levy's analysis shows us that the real difficulty in interpreting the first amendment today lies in its application not to the federal government but to the states. For historically the amendment, when adopted, was neither libertarian nor anti-libertarian. It reflected its framers' views not on freedom of expression but on the nature and power of the federal government. The amendment's purpose was to guarantee that in the area

---

[55] Id. at 51.

[56] Leonard W. Levy, "Introduction," in *Freedom of the Press from Zenger to Jefferson* xxii (Levy ed. 1966).

[57] Id. at lxx.

[58] Id. at lxxvi.

[59] Id. at lvi-lvii.

of political and ideological expression the federal government would remain a government of limited powers. Although this purpose will aid today's courts in determining the scope of the amendment as applied to the federal government, it is irrelevant in cases applying the amendment to the states, for to ask about the framers' attitudes toward state regulation of free expression is to do nothing but speculate. To the extent that history is relevant in determining the amendment's scope in such cases, the history which must be looked to is that of the last century, beginning with the adoption of the fourteenth amendment. It is useless to search for answers, as Brant did, in the eighteenth century.

Levy's introduction is, of course, neither perfect nor final. Nor does it provide easy answers as to the proper scope of the first amendment today. Nevertheless it points in the right direction by showing that the first step in seeking historical assistance to answer modern constitutional questions must be an understanding of what in fact happened, and how the law changed and developed in the past. Indeed, all that history can ever do is to make clear to us the course of development in the past. Those who ask that it do more — that it provide solutions to modern problems — will find themselves asking useless, meaningless questions.

Chapter Eight

1967

William E. Nelson

The question of when an "American Maitland" will be able to write a *History of American Law* has been considered frequently for at least 40 years.[1] It is nevertheless useful to ask the question anew in an attempt to determine whether recent efforts by legal historians have brought us close to that history.

The initial requirement for such a history is the possession of sufficient factual information, and, during the past year, some writing has added to our store of knowledge. In a study of the right to trial by jury in civil cases, Edith Henderson has published useful information on the "legislative history" of the seventh amendment and on the practices of 18th century English and American courts upon pre- and post-trial motions seeking to take allegedly undisputed fact issues away from juries.[2] Dr. Henderson uses her materials to show the widely divergent rules of law which were developed to deal with such motions. Her research has been so thorough that her article should be of value as a starting point for almost any student of eighteenth-century court procedure. Another useful article on colonial procedure discusses the various stages in the civil litigation process during the 1770's in New York, as that process would have been seen through a practitioner's eyes. It finds that "civil practice in New York in the last decade of the colonial period was fairly close to the English pattern" and that "until the enactment of the procedural codes in 1848, New York courts continued to follow the colonial pattern."[3] A third article is Erwin Surrency's comprehensive study of courts and jurisdiction in the colonies.[4]

---

[1] See, e.g., Theodore Plucknett, "Book Review," 3 *New Eng. Q.* 574, 576-77 (1930); Note, 80 *Harv. L. Rev.* 1757 n.1 (1967).

[2] Edith G. Henderson, "The Background of the Seventh Admendment," 80 *Harv. L. Rev.* 289 (1966).

[3] Herbert A. Johnson, "Civil Procedure in John Jay's New York," 11 *Am. J. Legal Hist.* 69, 79-80 (1967).

[4] Erwin C. Surrency, "The Courts in the American Colonies," 11 *Am. J. Legal Hist.* 253, 347 (1967). For further discussion of this article see the text accompanying notes 34-39 infra.

Another comprehensive study is Leonard S. Goodman's history of passport law. On the basis of an extremely thorough job researching manuscript and other documentary sources for information about early passports, Mr. Goodman has concluded that, during "the Colonial, Federal, and early Republican periods" of our history, it was "not entirely true that in times of peace law-abiding citizens have always been free to leave the country without the permission of the Government. Rather, discretion to refuse passports was exercised with varying intensity during these periods."[5]

Also useful is Harold Nelson's *Freedom of the Press from Hamilton to the Warren Court*, the second of a series of two volumes collecting documents relative to freedom of the press. Unfortunately, Professor Nelson's introduction is not as good as the introduction by Leonard Levy in the companion volume.[6] Nelson is overly concerned with statistical data[7] and, as the topical organization of his documents shows, lacks Levy's fine sense of chronology. The major weakness of Nelson's introduction is his failure to probe deeply into the causes of legal change or development. In considering, for example, the increased prosecution of obscenity in the late 19th century, he merely speculates:

> There may have been widespread anxiety over the state of the nation's morality: the scandals of the Grant administration, Reconstruction frauds, and the shocking graft of Boss Tweed's Tammany Hall were spectacular evidences of corruption. The conditions that fostered the new concern probably included a considerable increase in the output of pornography.[8]

In defense of Nelson it must be observed that historians have done much less work on freedom of the press during the nineteenth than during the eighteenth century and that, despite their weaknesses, Nelson's book and introduction have much informative value.

In biography, surely the best contribution of the year is John Reid's book on Charles Doe;[9] it is a superbly written, perceptive study of a most

---

[5] Leonard S. Goodman, "Passports in Perspective," 45 *Texas L. Rev*. 221, 276 (1966).

[6] Leonard W. Levy, "Introduction," in *Freedom of the Press from Zenger to Jefferson* (Leonard W. Levy ed. 1966).

[7] See, e.g., Harold Nelson, "Introduction," in *Freedom of the Press from Hamilton to the Warren Court* (Harold Nelson ed. 1967), at xxvii-xxix, xlvi-xlvii, 1.

[8] Id. at xxix-xxx.

[9] John Phillip Reid, *Chief Justice: The Judicial World of Charles Doe* (1967). For further discussion of this book, see the text accompanying note 40 infra.

important figure in our judicial history. Another valuable piece of biographical work discusses the role of William Sampson as a propagandist in the codification movement during the 1820's and 1830's;[10] it makes a real contribution to our knowledge by pointing out differences between two groups of codifiers — those who, following Bentham, wanted radical reform and a code which all citizens could grasp without the aid of lawyers and those who, like Sampson, sought moderate reform and codification within the legal profession and aimed not at the elimination of the bar but only at the elimination of the common law's anachronisms.[11]

Without question, the most important contribution to our factual knowledge of constitutional history was made by William McLoughlin's study of the heretofore ignored *Balckom* case, decided in 1782 by a county court in Massachusetts.[12] The issue in the case was whether a Baptist, who regularly attended and contributed to his own church, could be required to pay taxes for the maintenance of the state-supported Congregational church. In what was instituted as a test case, the court held that he could not. The legal arguments in the *Balckom* case and its outcome are unimportant because in 1784-1785 the Massachusetts Supreme Judicial Court reached an opposite result on analogous facts. However, *Balckom* was very well publicized by Isaac Backus, a leading Baptist. This publicity is most significant, for it articulates a theory of church-state relations quite different from the theory which historians and the Supreme Court have usually thought underlies the first amendment.

The Baptists' essential arguments were that "'religion must ever be a matter between God and individuals, because *every one must give account for himself to God*'"[13] and "'that RELIGION was prior to all states and kingdoms in the world, and therefore could not in its nature be subject to human laws.'"[14] They further argued that the "'most essential article in the order of Christ's kingdom, is that no man *can* . . . have any right to *power* therein, until he is born again. John i.12, 13. iii 3.'"[15]

---

[10] Maxwell Bloomfield, "William Sampson and the Codifiers: The Roots of American Legal Reform, 1820-1830," 11 *Am. J. Legal Hist.* 234 (1967).

[11] See id. at 241-46.

[12] William McLoughlin, "The Balckom Case (1782) and the Pietistic Theory of Separation of Church and State," 24 *Wm. & Mary Q.* 267 (1967). A summary statement of the case may be found in the 1773-1783 manuscript volume of the Inferior Court of Common Pleas 410 (Bristol County courthouse, Taunton, Mass.). McLoughlin, *supra*, at 281.

[13] Id. at 273.

[14] Id. at 275.

[15] Id. at 276-77.

These arguments must be compared with those in the Virginia Statute of Religious Liberty, which explained:

> WHEREAS Almighty God hath created the mind free; . . . to compel a man to furnish contributions of money for the propagation of opinions which he disbelieves, is sinful and tyrannical, and even the forcing him to support this or that teacher of his own religious persuasion, is depriving him of the comfortable liberty of giving his contributions to the particular pastor whose morals he would make his pattern . . .; that our civil rights have no dependence on our religious opinions any more than our opinions in physics or geometry; that therefore the proscribing any citizen as unworthy the public confidence by laying upon him an incapacity of being called to offices of trust and emolument, unless he profess or renounce this or that religious opinion, is depriving him injuriously of those privileges and advantages to which, in common with his fellow-citizens he has a natural right; . . . that it is time enough for the rightful purposes of civil government, for its officers to interfere, when principles break out into overt acts against peace and good order; and finally, that truth is great and will prevail, if left to herself, that she is the proper and sufficient antagonist to error, and has nothing to fear from the conflict, unless by human interposition disarmed of her natural weapons, free argument and debate.[16]

As Professor McLoughlin notes: "Clearly Backus is speaking out of a different tradition from the reasoned deism of Madison. Where Madison's argument is abstract, rational, and legalistic, Backus relies directly upon scripture, faith, and the pietistic temper of the Baptist persuasion."[17] Whereas Backus was concerned chiefly with preventing the state from interfering with the proper relationship between man and God, Madison's main concern was with preventing religion from interfering with the proper relationship between man and the state. Although the Baptists were not clear as to precisely the proper role of the state in enforcing Christian morality, they did not question that the state had some such duty.[18] Or, as McLoughlin concludes: "Backus insisted that the United States of America was and should be a Christian nation. Thomas Jefferson said it was definitely not a Christian nation."[19]

McLoughlin's article raises many interesting questions about the history of the first amendment's establishment clause; e.g., perhaps it

---

[16] An Act for Establishing Religious Freedom, Va. Laws of 1785, ch. 34 (presently, Act for Religious Freedom, 8 *Va. Code Ann. Sec.* 57-1 (1950)).

[17] William McLoughlin, *supra* note 12, at 274.

[18] Id. at 277, 280.

[19] Id. at 280.

prohibits merely the establishment of one religion in preference to another, without prohibiting government aid to religion as a whole. It would be interesting for historians to study the attitudes of the Congressmen and state convention members who voted upon the first amendment, as well as the attitudes of those who authored and worked toward the adoption of the fourteenth. If, as seems possible, the great majority of these men accepted the Baptist rather than the deist position, a good historical argument might be advanced against some recent Supreme Court opinions.

Regrettably, these eight works constitute the only materials which have added significantly during the year to our factual knowledge of our law's past, since many of the year's writings were devoted to topics about which much had previously been written. For example, an entire book was written on the already well-known history of New York's ratification of the federal constitution.[20] Nevertheless, the book does contribute to historical interpretation when it suggests:

> When the exaggerations of campaign propaganda are torn away, the essential practical difference between the Federalists and the Antifederalists was when and how to amend the Constitution. . . . [I]t is clear that both parties favored increasing the power of the central government and doing so on the basis of the Philadelphia Constitution. Both parties, however, recognized imperfections in the plan, and their differences, although clouded with emotion during the campaign, can be reduced to disagreement over whether the imperfections were so critical as to require immediate correction or whether it would be more dangerous to attempt amendment before the plan was ratified.[21]

A second study of the same topic makes a somewhat less useful contribution when it accepts the standard interpretation that the New York antifederalists who joined with the federalists to create a majority in favor of ratification of the Constitution were forced to do so to prevent isolation of the state and the probable secession of New York City, but then argues that these antifederalists were persuaded not by the speeches of Alexander Hamilton but by one of their own leaders, Melancton Smith, a delegate from Manhattan who was personally aware of the dangers of isolation and secession and who made some of his fellow antifederalist delegates similarly aware.[22]

---

[20] Linda Grant DePauw, *The Eleventh Pillar: New York State and the Federal Constitution* (1966).

[21] Id. at 176.

[22] Robin Brooks, "Alexander Hamilton, Melancton Smith, and the Ratification of the Constitution in New York," 24 *Wm. & Mary Q.* (3d ser.) 339 (1967).

The authors of these two studies could have made a greater contribution had they worked upon some of the many subjects in our constitutional history which have never been studied. This is even more true in the case of three biographical articles on two much studied nineteenth-century lawyers — Daniel Webster and Joseph Story. One of the articles deals again with Daniel Webster and the *Dartmouth College* case. However, it offers a new twist by showing how Webster, relying on a coterie of able lawyer-politicians, used the *Dartmouth* case to launch his own career in law and politics, during which he continued to draw upon other minds — sometimes without acknowledgment.[23] Of the two articles on Justice Story, one rather superficially analyzes Story's judicial opinions,[24] while the other, one of Gerald Dunne's series on the Justice, probes quite deeply into Story's life and into the society in which he did his work.[25]

Even more distressing are articles which contribute significantly neither to factual knowledge nor to historical interpretation. One such article adds further documentation, but little else, to the already well-known fact that by 1700 English common law formed the basis of the colonial legal system;[26] another reviews the historical background of the first amendment;[27] and a third surveys leading antitrust statutes and cases since the late 19th century.[28] Perhaps the worst of this type of article is one which reviews the legislative history of the fourteenth amendment and then reaches the not very profound conclusion that this history is inconclusive upon certain issues currently before the Supreme Court.[29]

Similarly distressing are articles investigating topics which are not relevant to the main factual outline of our legal history. One work in this vein presents previously unpublished background facts in *Chisholm v. Georgia* — facts, however, which were not relevant in the court's decision.[30] A second piece offers a charming and entertaining account of

---

[23] R. Kent Newmyer, "Daniel Webster as Tocqueville's Lawyer: The Dartmouth College Case Again," 11 *Am. J. Legal Hist.* 127 (1967).

[24] Morgan Dowd, "Justice Story and the Slavery Conflict," 52 *Mass. L.Q.* 239 (1967).

[25] Gerald T. Dunne, "Joseph Story: The Middle Years," 80 *Harv. L. Rev.* 1679 (1967).

[26] Note, 80 *Harv. L. Rev.* 1757 (1967),

[27] Note, 61 *Nw. U.L. Rev.* 760 (1966).

[28] John E. Schefter, "Historical Policy of the United States Toward Monopoly," 43 *N.D.L. Rev.* 17 (1966).

[29] Edward M. Goldberg, "Mr. Justice Harlan, The Uses of History, and the Congressional Globe," 15 *J. Pub. L.* 181 (1966).

[30] Doyle Mathis, "Chisholm v. Georgia: Background and Settlement," 54 *J. Am. Hist.* 19 (1967).

the escape from a British port of the *Alabama*, the famed Confederate commerce raider;[31] it is unfortunate, however, that a law professor who purports to be interested in legal history should devote his time and a law review, its space, to a study of the *Alabama's* exploits rather than to a study of the legal problems which those exploits raised. Their approach to history would appear to be the same as that of a man who, after spending 37 years in practice, recently became a law school dean. As he explained:

> Not the least of the reasons which entered into my decision to wind up my practice and embark upon a new life in the law was the thought that at a law school I would have the opportunity, seldom or never enjoyed in practice, of following up the tangent items and questions which tease the curiosity of the active practitioner when encountered in practice, but which the demands on his time will not permit him to pursue.[32]

Sentiments of this type within the legal profession go far toward explaining why only one-half of a year's published work makes any significant contribution to our knowledge of the legal past and why legal history continues to make little progress. Most lawyers persist in refusing to treat legal history seriously unless they seek to use it to answer a current legal question. Dilettantism, of course, will rarely produce worthwhile scholarship, while study of the past in order to solve present problems will often lead to distorted, anachronistic history.[33] Legal history will not make significant progress until enough serious scholars have gone to work with the aim of doing no more than adding to our knowledge of the law's past. Only then will that knowledge grow rapidly.

A second major problem confronting legal historians is that of formulating a comprehensive framework for a future "History of American Law." Such a framework is essential so that research can be pointed in potentially useful directions and so that our legal history, when it is written, will not be a mere collection of unrelated facts.

In his article on colonial courts,[34] Erwin Surrency did a thoroughly competent job in constructing a framework which comprehends a substantial segment of our legal history. Abandoning historical theories, Surrency concentrated instead upon finding a proper perspective from

---

[31] Brunson MacChesney, "The Alabama and the Queen's Advocate — A Mystery of History," 62 *Nw. U.L. Rev.* 568 (1967).

[32] Robert M. Figg, "Of Caroline Quiddities, Quillets and Cases," 18 *S.C.L. Rev.* 719-20 (1966).

[33] See ch. 7 *supra,* at 118-124.

[34] Erwin C. Surrency, "The Courts in the American Colonies," 11 *Am. J. Legal Hist.* 253, 347 (1967).

which to view the colonial judicial structure. His obvious problem was to avoid writing 13 disjointed histories of separate colonies. The perspective he selected was that "of the British official seeking an understanding of the courts in all the colonies."[35] This perspective enabled him "when comparing judicial systems of the American colonies" to search for "the similarities in the systems,"[36] for, as he notes, "the British Government tended to look upon their colonies as one unit."[37] Looking through the eyes of a London administrator, Surrency could see and describe a single unified historical pattern, a pattern which in fact existed, since "the courts in the American colonies were patterned after those in England"[38] — American justices of the peace, for example, took their guidance from books published for English justices.[39]

Surrency's technique does, however, have a weakness. It tends to ignore the changes which took place in the court system during the course of the colonial period and thus fails to indicate the exact point in time from which the system is being surveyed. Surrency, in short, stresses continuity and almost ignores development. He cannot be criticized severely for doing this, if it be appropriate to criticize him at all, since his article appears to describe primarily the first two-thirds of the eighteenth century, when change in the judicial system was minimal. However, when we attempt to write about our law's entire history, change will have to be taken into account, for today's law is vastly different from that of the seventeenth century. In order to avoid writing a disjointed description of a series of unrelated changes, we will need a technique for finding the relationships and ties between them — a technique which Surrency has failed to provide.

John Reid's *Chief Justice: The Judicial World of Charles Doe* tells us where to look. The excellence of Reid's book lies in the fact that it is not only a biography but also a comprehensive history of legal change in New Hampshire during the second half of the nineteenth century. Chapters 7 through 10 consider developments in civil procedure, torts, evidence, criminal law, and the rules for construing legal instruments. In these chapters Reid discusses, as he must, changes in individual New Hampshire rules of law, but he also identifies the force behind the individual changes — Judge Doe's notion that justice is thwarted when "rules of law decide . . . issues which might reasonably have been

---

35 Id. at 253.
36 Id. at 266.
37 Id. at 353.
38 Id. at 266.
39 Id. at 350.

determined as questions of fact."[40] Reid repeatedly stresses this jurisprudential view of Doe's; as a result, he paints a picture not of disjointed change but of coherent development from the New Hampshire law of 1860, governed by precedent and strict rules, to the law of 1900, free to achieve justice in accordance with the facts of each individual case. Reid was able to describe this central change because he realized that Judge Doe — or more specifically, Judge Doe's intellect — was the link connecting the various minute changes Reid had seen.

The writings of Professors Surrency and Reid, taken together, suggest an approach to building a framework for a "History of American Law." Surrency tells us that an initial step is to view our law at a number of static points in time from the vantage point of an outsider searching for similarities and unities among the laws of various states. To adopt the perspective of a hypothetical Englishman, as Surrency does, is particularly useful, for then the historian must search for his similarities and unities not only in our shared common law heritage but also in our law's uniquely American characteristics. Reid, meanwhile, tells us to search in the world of the intellect for unities at particular points in time as well as for causes of the changes occurring between these points in time. When we realize that throughout our history lawyers across the nation have read many of the same legal texts and received similar legal educations, often at the same schools, it is not surprising that our law should have a certain amount of intellectual coherence. Of course, not all of our legal development is the result of this coherence; as Lawrence Friedman recently suggested, we may also find explanations for legal unity and change in our nation's changing economic and social aspirations.[41]

What conclusion, then, can we draw about the prospects for a "History of American Law?" Any conclusion should not be too pessimistic. By looking for appropriate links, it should be possible to construct a framework for a history. Our greater obstacle is our lack of factual data — a lack due in large part to the failure of lawyers and historians to engage in serious work upon useful, new topics. While we particularly need study of the mundane legal developments occurring during the nineteenth century, for example, historians continue to study the law laid down by the Supreme Court. If, however, they will turn to local law, seek to discover changes occurring in it even over brief periods of time, and attempt to isolate the underlying causes of the changes, we will obtain much new knowledge and will soon be able to perceive the unities

---

[40] John Phillip Reid, *Chief Justice: The Judicial World of Charles Doe* 122 (1967).

[41] Lawrence M. Friedman, "History and the Future Law School Curriculum," 44 *Denver L.J.* 43, 46 (1967).

and central trends around which to write our history. Then legal history can begin to make a contribution to the law similar to the contribution which history in general makes to society.

Chapter Nine

1968

William E. Nelson

A dominant goal of students of legal history is to search for links between legal development, on the one hand, and the political, economic, and social context of that development, on the other. Because judges and lawyers rarely articulate the preconceptions underlying their analytical arguments, such links are obscure in contemporary society. History, however, facilitates the perception of relationships between disparate phenomena. This year's scholarship in American legal history, perhaps because it was written largely by professional historians rather than by lawyers, contained many such perceptions.

Oscar and Mary Handlin's revised edition of *Commonwealth* offers a model for scholars seeking to link legal with broader social change. The Handlins' discussion of the doctrine of limited liability for corporate shareholders will illustrate.[1] It suggests that the doctrine arose in response to certain economic and social facts: first, that in the decades after the American Revolution men expected government to promote economic growth; second, that they were unwilling to pay higher taxes to cover the cost of the services they expected government to provide; and third, that private citizens were willing to provide the services in return for a profit. The legislature accordingly made use of an old device, the corporation, which it had used in the past to organize towns and similar agencies for the performance of governmental services; it now gave corporate status to those individuals willing to assist the state in promoting economic growth.[2]

The new corporations — banks, turnpikes, certain industrial establishments, and the like — although still conceived of as performing governmental functions,[3] were, however, quite different in purpose from the older bodies politic. The older municipal corporations had been organized essentially to provide government services to their members; the new corporations, on the other hand, were organized to provide

[1] Oscar Handlin & Mary F. Handlin, *Commonwealth, A Study of the Role of Government in the American Economy: Massachusetts, 1774 - 1861,* at 87-160 (rev. ed 1969).

[2] Id. at 97-99, 111.

[3] See id. at 130-33.

profits to their members and services only to others. Legal changes flowed logically from this central change in purpose. Receipt of services had been essential to members of municipal corporations, and accordingly such corporations had been given power to assess their members for the cost of the services. Corporations formed for profit, on the other hand, would not have obtained members if membership had cost rather than returned money; as a result, it became established, after some initial confusion, that business corporations could not assess members in excess of the amount they agreed to contribute upon joining. Logically, if a corporation could not assess its shareholders, neither could the corporation's creditors.[4] With the taking of this step, the trend toward limited liability, which had begun with the need to promote economic growth, was complete.

Another book which similarly links legal to social change is Roger Lane's *Policing the City*. A study of the shift in Boston between 1822 and 1885 from non-professional, citizen enforcement of the law to enforcement by a well-organized, professional police force, Lane's book argues that professionalism stemmed from the growing complexity of municipal problems.[5] One such problem — mob violence springing on the whole from antagonism between Yankee natives and Irish immigrants — led directly to the 1838 creation of professional police.[6] Originally conceived as a riot-curbing force, the police posed no threat to civil liberties until they began to act affirmatively to ferret out vice. The difficulty of obtaining evidence of such vice soon led to infringement of privacy and other individual rights, and by the 1850's the police were conducting mass arrests and notorious line-ups, often solely for the purpose of publicity.[7] When such activity led to controversy, the marshal of the police was fired and the activity curbed, but, as a result, vice continued to flourish in the city.[8] This excited the fears of rural voters and led to a protracted struggle in the state legislature over whether the police should be controlled by the city or by the state. With the enactment in 1885 of legislation establishing state control, local citizen control of law enforcement came to an end in Boston.[9]

Stanley Kutler's study of the political background of Civil War and Reconstruction statutes dealing with the Supreme Court uses techniques similar to those of Lane and the Handlins. Kutler contends, contrary to

---

[4] Id. at 134-60.

[5] Roger Lane, *Policing the City: Boston 1822 - 1885* , at 4-13 (1967).

[6] Id. at 29-37.

[7] Id. at 39, 43-45, 48, 64-68.

[8] Id. at 79-84, 88, 110-17.

[9] Id. at 119, 122-25, 141, 195-98, 213-19.

the traditional historical view, that few Republicans in Congress during the 1860's were hostile to the Supreme Court as an institution and that most were firm supporters both of the Court and of the doctrine of judicial review.[10] Kutler rejects the view that the legislation of 1862, 1866, and 1869 altering the size of the Court stemmed from a policy of controlling the Court's membership; he finds no evidence that such a policy existed either during the 1860's as a whole or during the particular years in which legislation was enacted. He suggests instead that the legislation was motivated by a policy of realigning the federal judicial circuits so as to reduce Southern influence on the Court — a policy which the secession of the South and its later defeat in war made both necessary and possible.[11]

Kutler also contends that the legislation which deprived the Court of jurisdiction in the *McCardle* case[12] similarly did not reflect any long-term hostility to the Court, but merely the Republican party's determination to protect its Reconstruction legislation.[13] This argument is somewhat strained and largely semantic; it appears that a determination to protect legislation has been at the heart of all congressional attacks on the Court. Nonetheless, the argument adds a new and insightful dimension to our constitutional historiography.

Several of this year's articles also documented suggestive historical insights. One showed how the desire of the Mormons in Utah for effective political independence led to their giving territorial probate judges, who unlike federal district judges were elected by local voters, plenary civil and criminal jurisdiction concurrent with that of the district courts — a clear illustration of how politics can alter normal judicial institutions.[14] Another article suggested possible explanations for changing crime patterns by looking closely at Boston crime statistics over a hundred-year period and observing the precise times at which the incidence of specific crimes rose and fell.[15] It found a "persistent downward tendency in the rate of every major crime except forcible rape and manslaughter . . . in stark contrast to the popular belief that crime is growing more rampant and more serious every year."[16] The increases in

---

[10] Stanley I. Kutler, *Judicial Power and Reconstruction Politics* 10-13, 41-47 (1968).

[11] Id. at 14-20, 48-63.

[12] Ex parte McCardle, 73 U.S. (6 Wall.) 318 (1868).

[13] Stanley I. Kutler, note 10 *supra,* at 77-88.

[14] James B. Allen, "The Unusual Jurisdiction of County Probate Courts in the Territory of Utah," 36 *Utah Hist. Q.* 132 (1968).

[15] Theodore N. Ferdinand, "The Criminal Patterns of Boston since 1849," 73 *Am. J. Sociology* 84 (1968).

[16] Id. at 98.

rape and manslaughter were attributed to the automobile.[17] The decrease in theft, on the other hand, was thought to have followed from the "gradually rising standard of living during nearly the entire period of . . . [the] study"[18] — a correlation confirmed by the tendency of burglaries to increase in times of economic depression.[19] A third article, studying the background of the eleventh amendment, demonstrated that the amendment was a response not, as previously thought, to Supreme Court decisions compelling the payment of state Revolutionary war debts, but only to cases challenging the sovereign power of states named as parties defendant to control the disposition of loyalist lands seized during the Revolution.[20]

In addition to the writing illustrating the effects of social change upon the law, there was some writing during the year which showed the effects of legal change upon society. An article on *Buchanan v. Warley,*[21] a 1917 case holding unconstitutional municipal ordinances requiring residential segregation, pointed out, for example, that the case was a landmark in the history of the N.A.A.C.P. The decision raised the association's prestige and membership and assisted in the development of techniques still in use, such as the acceptance of aid from sympathetic whites and the employment of Negro churches as focal points for local organization.[22] Another article showed how poorly drafted customs legislation helped intensify Anglo-American controversy during the 1760's,[23] while a third article studying the effects of primogeniture and entail in colonial Virginia demonstrated that rules of law will often go unheeded if they are inconsistent with economic and social needs.[24]

Sometimes, of course, legal development is a purely internal phenomenon, and legal change occurs with neither social cause nor social effect. Leonard Levy's study of the origins of the fifth amendment is illustrative.[25] Levy's book, although not as well constructed as his earlier

---

[17] Id. at 97.

[18] Id. at 98.

[19] Id. at 92-93.

[20] Clyde E. Jacobs, "Prelude to Amendment: The States Before the Court," 12 *Am. J. Legal Hist.* 19 (1968).

[21] 245 U.S. 60 (1917).

[22] Roger L. Rice, "Residential Segregation by Law, 1910-17," 34 *J. So. Hist.* 179 (1968).

[23] Herbert A. Johnson & David Syrett, "Some Nice Sharp Quillets of the Customs Law: The *New York* Affair, 1763-1767," 25 *Wm. & Mary Q.* (3d ser.) 432 (1968).

[24] C. Ray Keim, "Primogeniture and Entail in Colonial Virginia", 25 *Wm. & Mary Q.*(3d ser.) 545 (1968).

[25] Leonard W. Levy, *Origins of the Fifth Amendment: The Right Against Self - Incrimination* (1968).

study of the first amendment,[26] contains an encyclopedic amount of data on the development of the self-incrimination privilege prior to the Bill of Rights. And, in his study of the colonial American development of the privilege, Levy makes the interesting suggestion that it was applied sporadically in the colonies during the seventeenth century and became truly effective in the eighteenth only as the colonies gradually adopted and emulated common-law procedure in criminal cases. No underlying political, economic, or social explanation for the adoption of the privilege is apparent.[27] Neither did political, economic, or social causes underlie the statutes which have been adopted in all 50 states requiring foreign corporations doing business within a state to file their charters and designate local agents for service of process; an article[28] studying these statutes showed that most of them were enacted during the years following the Supreme Court's decisions in *Paul v. Virginia*[29] and *Pennoyer v. Neff.*[30] The thesis of the article was that the statutes were a response to these two cases, which gave states the power to exclude foreign corporations and at the same time prohibited a state from exercising jurisdiction over corporations which did not enter it.

Judicial biography is a particularly valuable device for studying the links between law and its social context. Two excellent biographies were published this year. One of them, on Justice Murphy, was based upon previously unpublished sources such as memoranda to and from law clerks and other justices and Murphy's notes of judicial conferences; it illustrated in specific detail the interaction in opinion writing of legal doctrine, the personal convictions of the justices, their institutional loyalty to the Court, and political events both within and without the Court.[31] The second biography, John Reid's life of Marmaduke Dent of West Virginia, is especially useful because it is about a judge whose "influence was not so great, nor . . . his thoughts so weighty that his place can be measured in anything but representational terms."[32] Like the great mass of middling American judges about whom we have precious few biographies, Dent "did not treat the decision of cases as an opportunity to apply doctrines arrived at by the development of a rational

---

[26] Leonard W. Levy, *Legacy of Suppression: Freedom of Speech and Press in Early American History* (1960).

[27] Leonard W. Levy, *supra* note 25, at 333-404.

[28] William L. Walker, "Foreign Corporation Laws: The Loss of Reason", 47 *N.C.L. Rev.* 1 (1968).

[29] 75 U.S. (8 Wall.) 168 (1869).

[30] 95 U.S. 714 (1878).

[31] J. Woodford Howard, *Mr. Justice Murphy: A Political Biography* (1968).

[32] John Phillip Reid, *An American Judge: Marmaduke Dent of West Virginia* 205 (1968).

pattern of thought," but "instead . . . reacted to problems by relying upon his cultivated sense of what was right and what was wrong."[33] Reid's study of Dent's biblicist fundamentalism — a trait out of place today but quite understandable in a late nineteenth century man from the West Virginia mountains — is an excellent example of the manner in which biography can be used to tie legal and social development together. As Reid observed, Dent's fundamentalism largely explains his criminal law classicism, his most notable contribution to the law.[34] A third biography — an article on Professor John Norton Pomeroy — was also useful in showing how surviving concepts of state sovereignty placed real limitations upon the nationalism and centralizing tendencies of post-Civil War Republicans.[35]

A number of other books and articles, although they do not document their arguments, offer suggestive historical insights and accordingly deserve mention. Arthur Sutherland's history of the Harvard Law School, which incidentally contains a great deal of useful information about early American legal education elsewhere as well, suggests that developments in legal education are at least in part a product of intellectual developments in society at large.[36] A book on the origins of American patent and copyright law, which also contains a great deal of valuable data, is of special interest for its suggestion that, historically, authors and inventors were given rights of exclusive exploitation in response to developing notions that they were entitled to such rights as a matter of fairness and that the promise of such rights would promote society's well-being.[37]

Two additional articles are worthy of note. One suggests that in order to facilitate the transportation of war material to Europe, the scope of immunity granted to foreign sovereigns by American courts was expanded during World War I to cover cases in which a sovereign was acting in a private, as distinguished from a public, capacity.[38] Another contends that complex procedural rules in colonial Louisiana were a product of a fee system in a subsistence economy, in which fees from judicial office were the only road to wealth.[39]

---

[33] Id. at 199.

[34] Id. at 167-96.

[35] Phillip S. Paludan, "John Norton Pomeroy, State Rights Nationalist," 12 *Am. J. Legal Hist.* 275 (1968).

[36] Arthur E. Sutherland, *The Law at Harvard* (1967).

[37] Bruce W. Bugbee, *The Genesis of American Patent and Copyright Law* 27-43, 49-83 (1967).

[38] Note, "The American Doctrine of Sovereign Immunity," 13 *Vill. L. Rev.* 583 (1968).

[39] James D. Hardy, "Probate Racketeering in Colonial Louisiana," 9 *La. Hist.* 109 (1968).

The principal difficulty with these suggestive pieces is that their authors do no more than establish the plausibility of their suggestions. They do not offer detailed evidence in support of them, nor do they consider and rule out alternative explanations for the legal developments they have studied. Such suggestive writing is, however, of value, unlike writing which seeks merely to state historical facts,[40] to analyze old cases,[41] or to show that contemporaries misread the cases.[42] We study the past for the insight it gives us into the present, and mere details extracted from the past alone give no insight. Suggestive writing, however, does offer insight, and, once we have an insight, we can always amass the detail to determine whether it is sound. Because detail will often make rough insights more precise, the value of detail cannot be ignored. Insight refined by detail must remain our standard of historical excellence. This year much of the writing in American legal history attained that standard.

---

[40] Stephen B. Wood, *Constitutional Politics in the Progressive Era: Child Labor and the Law* (1968); J.R. Saylor, "'Court Packing' Prior to FDR," 20 *Baylor L. Rev.* 147 (1968).

[41] Alfred Avins, "The Right to Bring Suit under the Fourteenth Amendment: The Original Understanding," 20 *Okla. L. Rev.* 284 (1967); Doyle Mathis, "Georgia Before the Supreme Court: The First Decade," 12 *Am. J. Legal Hist.* 112 (1968).

[42] Joseph C. Burke, "What Did the Prigg Decision Really Decide?", 93 *Pa. Mag. Hist. & Bio.* 73 (1969).

Chapter Ten

1969/70

John Phillip Reid and William E. Nelson

A *Survey* of American law is unable to give attention to developments in English legal history, despite our common heritage. This year, however, there appeared two books of such significance that they cannot be allowed to pass unnoticed. The first is Samuel E. Thorne's *Bracton.*[1] Perhaps the most important publication in English legal-historical scholarship since Maitland's *History,* this work is the first competent translation of *Bracton* and contains a masterful introduction in which Professor Thorne put to rest much of the polemics that have characterized "Bractonian studies." Thorne has done even more: he has transformed a task of editing into a work of history. Working from his own vast knowledge of thirteenth century law and upon the theory that Bracton's original manuscript was a coherent and intelligent whole, Thorne has accomplished a feat of historical imagination in piecing together that manuscript from a series of deviant copies.

The second book was S.F.C. Milsom's *Historical Foundations of the Common Law.*[2] Milsom's new book, which is the first comprehensive treatment of English legal history since T.F.T. Plucknett's *Concise History,* supersedes the earlier work. Although Milsom's style is often elliptical and as a result his book is somewhat difficult for the beginning student, *Historical Foundations* is superior to the *Concise History* first, because of Milsom's thorough knowledge of recent historical scholarship, including work not yet completed,[3] and, even more important, because Milsom makes the attempt, which Plucknett rarely made, to trace broad patterns of legal change and to suggest how those patterns may have been related to social change.[4]

---

[1] 1 & 2 *Bracton on the Laws and Customs of England* (Samuel E. Thorne transl. 1968). Only two of a projected five volumes were published in 1968, but volume one contains the scholarly introduction. Volume two prints about one-third of the text. Volume five promises to give us our first complete index.

[2] (1969).

[3] See, e.g., id. at 377 (citing Helen Maud Cam's 1969 volumes for the Selden Society), 382 (citing William J. Jones' 1967 study of the Elizabethan Chancery), 391 (citing Catherine McCauliff's still to be completed study of the maritagium and fee tail), and 428 (citing J.M. Kaye's 1967 study of malice.)

[4] See, e.g., id. at 82-83 (suggesting that the seventeenth century conflict between law and equity resulted in part from the Reformation's secularization of

I

LEGAL HISTORIOGRAPHY

No other historiographical topic received as much attention this year as the subject of publication and use of court records. While for some of us the appearance of court records may seem few and far between (as scholarly attention apparently shifts to the preparation of private law papers such as those of Marshall, Adams, Hamilton and Webster), David H. Flaherty nevertheless raised a timely issue regarding priorities when he wrote:

> Given the current underdeveloped state of American legal history, one may argue that there has been too much emphasis on the editing of court records for publication. Whether the editing of such records should remain a major outlet for the energies of legal historians is an important question. . . . Instead of editing one volume of county court records that span a decade, the legal historian might be better advised to employ all the manuscript records of the county in an extensive monograph. Surely the editing of court records should not cease completely, but at least for the moment it is to be hoped that mature scholars will shun this outlet for their energies in favor of some of the more pressing needs of early American legal history.[5]

In another context, Nigel Walker reinforced Professor Flaherty's concern by warning:

> . . . [T]he published documents have their own dangers. In comparison with most of the sources of social history they have the virtue of considerable accuracy; but this very accuracy distracts attention from their chief deficiency. By their nature they are almost always reports of atypical cases. It is of course atypical cases which are supposed to make legal history, but . . . when we reach the age of statistics, the most celebrated cases seem to have remarkably little effect on the numerical trends.[6]

Walker, to be sure, raises a different issue than does Flaherty, yet by criticizing selective editing he suggests that all cases should be printed,

---

the Chancellor's conscience), 203-04 (explaining the Rule Against Perpetuities as the quasi-legislative culmination of a centuries-long struggle between settlors seeking to tie up land and descendants seeking to break the ties).

[5] David H. Flaherty, "An Introduction to Early American Legal History," in *Essays in the History of Early American Law* 3, 31 (David H. Flaherty ed. 1969).

[6] 1 Nigel Walker, *Crime and Insanity in England: The Historical Perspective* 11 (1968).

thus calling for an even larger expenditure of energy than Flaherty thinks we can now afford.

Flaherty's question itself raises a second question: If legal historians cease to publish court records, where will they and the general historians find materials for writing the more wide-ranging works that he contemplates? One solution might be to go to the original sources, and the National Archives has instituted a pioneer project in this field. Since March, 1969, accession inventories for 16 United States Court districts have already been prepared, covering from 1716 (colonial admiralty records inherited by the federal judiciary under its juridictional grant) through 1943.[7] Fresh efforts are being made to interest social historians in these records. Telling general historians what they can expect to find in the regional Federal Records Centers, Gerald T. White leaves little doubt that the chief yield is in legal material.[8] It is Professor White's premise "that historians generally have been remarkably slow in discovering how rich court records can frequently be for research purposes."[9] Walter Rundell, Jr., agrees:

> Court records, like other types of local sources, excite considerable emotion and enthusiasm among those historians who have used them. Graduate students are not more conversant with court records, Philip D. Jordan contends, because most professors have not been inside courthouses except to complain about their taxes and because most historians have a blind spot concerning legal records. . . . Aubrey C. Lands says, "Court records probably constitute the most valuable local source we have." He thinks students shun them because of their dryness, technical language, and repetitiveness. But he agrees . . . that court records can be extremely rich in social and economic information. Land explains that in two weeks students can learn to identify types of legal action, to distinguish between parts of a set of proceedings, and to find and extract historical data.[10]

Basic to Professor Rundell's theme is the proposition that "legal history in a broader sense has been undernourished." In an unkind, though

---

[7] Note, 1 (#2) *Prologue: The Journal of the National Archives* 51 (1969).

[8] Gerald White, "Government Archives Afield: The Federal Records Centers and the Historian," 55 *J. Am. Hist.* 833 (1969).

[9] Id. at 838 n.7. "The hundreds of thousands of bankruptcy cases in the records of the inferior federal courts provide a parallel opportunity for meaningful studies utilizing quantitative techniques. A careful scruntiny of the impact of financial disaster on different groups, individual or corporate, and by regions, could deepen our understanding of the effect of major depressions on American society in both the nineteenth and twentieth centuries. Such studies would be an important contribution to social, economic, and business history." Id. at 842.

[10] Walter Rundell, Jr., "Southern History from Local Sources: A Survey of Graduate History Training," 34 *J. So. Hist.* 214, 222 (1968).

truthful, cut at his legal brethren, he expresses the hope that "[t]he exploitation of these records by nonlegal historians may even broaden the traditionally narrow scope of legal historians."[11]

The troublesome topic of the relationship between history and the judicial process received its usual attention during 1969. In the least meritorious article to appear this year, Robert M. Spector (who confuses "legal history" with the ability to cite "old precedents") drew a line between the legal historian on and off the bench when he observed: "The important thing about a judge on the bench is not so much what he does with history as that he have knowledge of it."[12] Why? — Spector does not say.[13] Considering the controversies of the last decade, a case could be made for the judge who ignores history completely. A compromise between the two extremes was suggested by Hans W. Baade, when he argued: "[W]hile courts cannot help deciding micro-historical questions, they should try to stay away from macro-historical issues."[14]

Concerning the problem of judge-made history, Robert M. Ireland raised some of the correct issues when he criticized Alfred Avins' latest contribution to the "reconstruction amendments" debate. Ireland found fault on three points:

> In the first place it is questionable whether the Constitution is an embodiment of immutable principles to be discovered by simply uncovering legislative intention.
>
> Secondly, it is not clear that the prevailing spirit of the debates as compiled by Avins lends itself irrevocably to the propositions he has so prodigiously advanced. . . . [M]any of the orators spoke so vaguely about the statutory language they had molded that no precise meaning is extractable from their comments.

---

[11] Id. at 222.

[12] Robert M. Spector, "Legal Historian on the United States Supreme Court: Justice Horace Gray, Jr., and the Historical Method," 12 *Am. J. Legal Hist.* 181, 208 (1968).

[13] Perhaps what he meant was said by another who wrote: "Indeed, the gradual and general demise of the study of legal history in law school throughout this country is unfortunate. The production of lawyers who have only scant knowledge of their 'professional cultures' threatens a proliferation of mere legal technicians." Victor H. Li, "Book Review," 67 *Mich. L. Rev.* 179, 195 (1968).

[14] Hans Wolfgang Baade, "Hoggan's History," 16 *Am. J. Comp. L.* 391, 401 (1968). ". . . [I]t seems clear that respect for higher authority, the imprecise line between holdings, *dicta,* and determination of fact, and pure inertia will usually combine to give adjudications of historical fact, at least by courts of last resort, an unmistakable aura of finality — a patently absurd situation in the opinion of historians (and, let it be added, of thoughtful lawyers)." Id. at 397.

Finally, . . . is it possible to determine "legislative intent" in the broader sense of the term by simply amassing Congressional debates? Ofttimes congressmen are not particularly candid in their congressional oratory. . . . In some instances they express their true feelings in extra-legislative sources. In short, there is no iron law of judicial interpretation which requires a judge to examine only the printed records of a legislature to find legislative intent, especially when the Constitution is concerned.[15]

The problems, however, are much more difficult than Professor Ireland realizes.

In *The Supreme Court and the Uses of History*[16] Charles A. Miller raises those problems. Although Miller, who is not a lawyer, shows occassional signs of legal naivete[17] and ultimately fails to resolve the questions he raises, these failings should not obscure the real merits of his book. Precisely because he is not a lawyer Miller eschews the jargon — words such as "motive," "purpose," "intent," and "original understanding" — which lawyers use in discussing constitutional and legislative construction. Defining his concepts carefully, he articulates two valuable insights. First is the insight implicit in much of Professor Bickel's work;[18] that one must distinguish between the meaning of a document and the intentions of its authors or, as Miller explains succinctly, "between documents and people,"[19] since documents such as constitutions acquire a meaning of their own over the course of time. Miller's second insight, which is the central point of his book, is that the Supreme Court uses history in two strikingly different ways:

The history that searches for the "original understanding" of a constitutional clause is a history that recognizes and places high value on the "intent theory" of documentary interpretation. The intent theory holds that a document, such as the Constitution, should be construed in agreement with the intentions of the person or persons who wrote it. To discover these intentions for the Constitution one must turn to the history of the late eighteenth century. Since it is the Constitution that commands the Supreme Court to decide one way

---

[15] Robert M. Ireland, "Book Reviews," 25 *Wash. & Lee L. Rev.* 354, 356-57 (1968).

[16] (1969).

[17] See, e.g., id. at 8, where he completely misses the point of Justice Holmes' statement that, as a justice, he worked "'with no thought but that of solving a problem according to the rules by which one is bound.'"

[18] See, e.g., Alexander M. Bickel, "The Original Understanding and the Segregation Decision," 69 *Harv. L. Rev.* 1, 59-65 (1955).

[19] Charles Allen Miller, *The Supreme Court and the Uses of History* 153 (1969).

> or another, since the Constitution should mean what it was intended to mean, and since intent is ascertainable only by resort to historical material, history as intent is essentially history as command. The other history, ongoing history, is not to be viewed as determining the command of the Constitution but as demonstrating the currents and lessons of experience. Ongoing history does not say "this is what was expected," but "this is what the nation has become."[20]

Usually, "history as intent" has been "a restraining force in constitutional law and . . . ongoing history . . . the champion of progress."[21] But Miller notes:

> [B]ecause the Court writes opinions in order to explain its decisions and not with respect to developing a consistent philosophy of the uses of history, this natural implication has sometimes proved misleading and the roles of the two histories have been reversed. Intent history has been invoked in the name of change and ongoing history in the name of the existing order.[22]

Miller's analysis can be particularly useful in helping historians and lawyers to understand better each other's work, for it suggests that each profession chooses one or the other form of history for reasons which are internal to the profession and not to history itself.

A college professor complained this year that too much of the imaginative writing in constitutional history is locked away in law reviews unobtainable on most American campuses.[23] If a present trend continues, legal historians may soon be complaining that a good deal of judicial history appears in periodicals not found in all law libraries. Among newer trends in legal historiography, none is currently more dynamic than that represented by various studies stressing judicial behavior. A fine example is John D. Sprague's study of Supreme Court voting patterns.[24] One reviewer sums up the Sprague technique as follows:

> The author's orientation is statistical, his emphases are upon questions of methodology and technique, and his data are grouped in chronologically sequenced subsets for what he calls longitudinal analysis. He is unconcerned with those facets of judicial behavior that heretofore have been of interest to constitutional historians. In direct opposition to their method, John Sprague has analyzed quantitatively, almost

---

[20] Id. at 25-26.

[21] Id. at 28.

[22] Ibid.

[23] William F. Zornow, "Book Reviews," 31 *The Historian* 642 (1969).

[24] John D. Sprague, *Voting Patterns of the United States Supreme Court: Cases in Federalism, 1889 - 1959* (1968).

> 3,000 Supreme Court cases; and he cites not a single one. Indeed, he is unconcerned with the previous work of historians, lawyers, or philosophers; his citations are, instead, to political scientists, political sociologists, and psycho-metrically inclined psychologists.[25]

It is evident that studies of this character will encounter skepticism from both historians and lawyers. In a well-reasoned article, for example, J. Woodford Howard has questioned the very assumption (so basic to the behaviorist theory) that a judge's values are accurately mirrored in his votes on the court.[26] And consider Hiller B. Zobel's appraisal of Richard B. Morris's commendable study, *John Jay , The Nation , & The Court.*[27]

> . . . A lawyer feels a bit uncomfortable at his insistence on treating the seriatim judicial opinions in *Chisholm* in terms of the prior political attitudes of the judges. Admittedly, *Chisholm,* like many Supreme Court cases since, raised a purely political issue, in this instance, should a state be subject without its consent to private suit? It is also true that all of the judges who concluded that the question should be answered affirmatively were in fact of a nationalist outlook. Nonetheless, taken in context, the problem can be regarded as entirely one of construction: Should language authorizing the federal courts to entertain suits "between a state and citizens of another state" be construed to cover cases in which the state was the defendant rather than the plaintiff? Even an antifederalist judge might fairly conclude that "between" looked in two directions.[28]

It is too early to say what the behaviorists will contribute to legal history. All too often they seem to be talking in their own jargon to a closed, select circle interested primarily in academic structuring. One point, however, seems fairly clear: Judicial behaviorism is becoming a norm for testing political theory, just as constitutional history was once the debating ground of the economic determinists. Carl J. Friedrich warns us not to expect much:

> . . . [A] curious paradox is involved here as far as the relation of law to history is concerned. For while all cases are history and history is supposed to provide precedents, they are not treated historically. The reason is that if, in accordance with sophisticated notions of what we like to think of as scientific history, the historical aspect is taken seriously, then no precedent exists, because the events of the past and their setting are unique. . . .

---

[25] Glendon Schubert, "Book Review," 55 *J. Am. Hist.* 879 (1969).

[26] J. Woodford Howard, "On the Fluidity of Judicial Choice," 62 *Am. Pol. Sci. Rev.* 43 (1968).

[27] (1967).

[28] Hiller B. Zobel, "Book Review," 42 *New Eng. Q.* 303-04 (1969).

> . . . But if not to history, where are we to turn? To the behavorial [sic] sciences, so called? The present inclination is to stress the importance of the behavorial sciences. . . . The trouble, however, is that in contrast with the historical learning . . . the teachings of these behavorial sciences are extremely controversial. Take, for example, psychology. Above a certain very elementary kind of psychology that could almost be called prejudicial folkviews of the role of man, all is all disagreement. We have, as one text has it, seven schools of psychology. You can also say seventy schools of psychology. And each of them says something different on any given problem of law or government. . . . What, in other words, among their actual findings is actually applicable to the law?[29]

I

COLONIAL LEGAL HISTORY

In the area of colonial history, the past year was dominated by Professor Flaherty of the University of Virginia, who edited two books of merit: one was the text of the laws of Virginia from 1609 to 1612[30] and the other was a collection of the leading articles on colonial legal history.[31] Flaherty did a spendid job. All the important periodical literature is included — Haskins, Goebel, Morris, and many more. Gathered for the first time within one cover, they give an opposite impression from what one might expect. Instead of showing how much has been accomplished, this collection points up how little has been written and how much remains to be done.

A quick glance at Flaherty's selections brings immediately to our attention two overriding facts, one surprising, the other not. The surprising fact is the almost total lack of recent scholarship: "For his choice of essays include only two written in the 1960's, in 1961 and 1962 — by the prolific Joseph Smith and the even more productive George Haskins respectively. The other selections, and there are twenty-seven more, are all drawn from earlier published works, some going back three decades

[29] Carl J. Friedrich, "Discussion," in *The Law School of Tomorrow: The Projection of an Ideal* 56 (David Haber & Julius Cohen eds. 1968).

[30] *For the Colony in Virginia Britiannia: Lawes Divine, Morall and Martiall* (David H. Flaherty ed. 1969).

[31] *Essays in the History of Early American Law* (David H. Flaherty ed. 1969).

or more."[32] Not so surprising is the fact that more than half the book deals with the Puritan colonies, and primarily with Massachusetts Bay.[33] Such, after all, is the state of colonial legal history scholarship, a condition further reflected in the fact that most of the new work continues to be of New England, building upon what is already known, while non-specialists are able to say more about New England colonial law than they are of the law of other provinces.[34]

Taking a fresh look at the first great constitutional decision of the colonial era, William G. Robbins concludes that the transfer of the government of Massachusetts Bay from the undertakers in London to the planters in New England was made for pragmatic reasons. The move did not constitute a sudden break in policy during 1629, for affairs continued to be conducted with a "remarkable degree of continuity and consistency," and harmony was maintained between the two groups. The legal issue was debated but opposition was overcome by practical considerations. The planters were largely men of means reluctant to trust their governance to others, while the undertakers were at least as interested in the religious aspect of colonization as in its commercial possibilities, and both sides were aware of the difficulties in communication experienced by the Plymouth planters whose General Court remained in London.[35]

Another book seeking to take a new look at old cases is one by Sanford J. Fox[36] which reconsiders the witchcraft trials that occurred at Salem and elsewhere in the American colonies. Fox's concern, however, was not with presenting new historical insight into the witchcraft cases, but with analyzing those cases as an example of the enduring relationship between law and science. He finds that "law enforcement against witches [in no way] actually conflicted with science,"[37] for

---

[32] Milton Cantor, "Book Review," 27 *Wm. & Mary Q.* (3d ser.) 146 (1970).

[33] Of the New England Puritans, Gene Wise suggests themes still remain to be developed: "Using 1630 as one base line and 1776 as the other, the cultural historian may view the period in between as an abundant source for interpreting the evolution from a doctrinally and structurally closed society directed upward toward God to a doctrinally and structurally open society looking outward toward man." Gene Wise, "Implicit Irony in Perry Miller's *New England Mind*," 29 *J. Hist. of Ideas* 579, 586 (1968).

[34] Thus the best discussion, in a work of general history, of colonial laws and colonial courts had to do with Connecticut. M.J.A. Jones, *Congregational Commonwealth Connecticut, 1636 - 1662* (1968).

[35] William Robbins, "The Massachusetts Bay Company: An Analysis of Motives," 32 *The Historian* 83 (1969).

[36] Sanford J. Fox, *Science and Justice: The Massachusetts Witchcraft Trials* (1968).

[37] Id. at 110.

> . . . it is not our scientific sophistication that prevents us from taking witchcraft seriously now. We could term Elizabeth Kelley's terminal illness bronchial pneumonia or diphtheria, but the question of its spiritual causation would remain open. Science still remains the provider of only penultimate answers if we concede the potency of supernatural forces, as one may assume most persons who are orthodox in their religious beliefs would. It can be suggested that the principles of religion that were at the heart of the neglect of science in the death cases, far from being a demonstration of seventeenth-century fanaticism, were hardly more than an acknowledgment of the omnipotence of God that continues to be recognized today. The view that the universe of things is not merely a matter of insensible physical particles is commonly found among men of science, past and present. In one form or another, the scientist's rejections of thoroughgoing materialism lent much support to the view that witches could cause the elements of nature to combine in fatal proportions.[38]

The law's attitude toward science, Fox seems to suggest, is determined more by people's theological biases than by their scientific ones, yet his ultimate conclusion is that American law schools should give increased training in the sciences to overcome the current ineptness of our courts in coping with scientific data.[39]

Concentrating upon the eighteenth-century, Pauline Maier investigated the currently popular topic of violence, mobs, and riots. Her conclusions lend support to Willard Hurst's theme that violence in the form of extra-judicial self-help constitutes a legitimate strain in the history of American law:[40]

> Eighteenth-century uprisings were in some important ways different than those of today — different in themselves, but even more in the political context within which they occurred. As a result they carried different connotations for the American Revolutionaries than they do today. Not all eighteenth-century mobs simply defied the law: some used extralegal means to implement official demands or to enforce laws not otherwise enforceable, others in effect extended the law in urgent situations beyond its technical limits. Since leading eighteenth-century Americans had known many occasions on which mobs took on the defense of the public welfare, which was, after all, the stated purpose of government, they were less likely to deny popular upheavals all legitimacy than are modern leaders. While not advocating popular uprisings, they could still grant such incidents an established and necessary role in free societies, one that made them

38 Ibid.

39 Id. at 115-16.

40 J. Willard Hurst, "The Uses of Law in Four 'Colonial' States of the American Union", 1945 *Wis. L. Rev.* 577, 583-87.

an integral and even respected element of the political order. These attitudes, and the tradition of colonial insurrections on which they drew, not only shaped political events of the Revolutionary era, but also lay behind many laws and civil procedures that were framed during the 1780's and 1790's, some of which still have a place in the American legal system.[41]

In the area of legal argument perhaps the most interesting specimen from the colonial era to turn up this year was found in the journal of a physician who, writing aboard a slave ship off the Gold Coast in 1750, cited native African law as a justification for the slave trade in which he was engaged:

> A king very often takes it into his head to kill anybody, when he dies numberless poor unhappy creatures are sacrificed to him, out of whose skulls they drink Rum as soon as clean'd. Since I have been here Jno King of the Coranties whom in his Illness I attend has sacrificed several on his recovery from it, and will soon will [sic] more go, that I say they are better in being servants to the English then in this continuall dread of Death.[42]

III

THE REVOLUTIONARY ERA

More work was done on the American Revolution than on the colonial era — perhaps a result of the renewed emphasis upon the legal and constitutional causes of the rebellion. Yet Jackson Turner Main reminds us that we have no grounds for satisfaction. In a long article he discusses the many results of the Revolution, touching most bases and showing numerous changes, without considering or mentioning legal reforms or legal continuity. There is perhaps, no better demonstration of how little work has been done by legal historians in this, the most critical era of formative law.[43]

Much of the current scholarship continues in the "consensus" or "legal" trend that began to develop a few years ago. Indeed, Arthur M.

---

[41] Pauline Maier, "Popular Uprisings and Civil Authority in Eighteenth-Century America", 27 *Wm. & Mary Q.* (3d ser.) 3, 4 (1970).

[42] Darold D. Wax, "A Philadelphia Surgeon on a Slaving Voyage to Africa, 1749-1751," 92 *Penn. Mag. Hist. & Bio.* 465, 491 (1968).

[43] Jackson Turner Main, "The Results of the American Revolution Reconsidered," 31 *The Historian* 539 (1969).

Schlesinger, Sr., seems to have come round full circle from his earlier interpretation of the American Revolution, for now he says it was a constitutional struggle to protect, not create, a free equalitarian society.[44] He is supported by Ira D. Gruber who added significant evidence to the argument that the American Revolution was essentially a legal-constitutional struggle with his finding that "ministeries and members of parliament had . . . little interest . . . in the nature of colonial resistance," and were upset by it simply because the "colonists were challenging the supremacy of Parliament."[45]

There are, however, signs that a reaction to the consensus school has begun to find favor. No less an authority than John R. Alden insists that the old view was correct after all: colonial society was essentially unequal.[46] He is supported by John M. Head, who stresses the economic rather than the legal causes of the Revolution,[47] and David Curtis Skaggs who offers evidence from Maryland to support the thesis of a "social" revolution. Maryland, he argues, was not a middle-class democracy:

> A study of the revolutionary movement in Maryland indicates that the most influential segment of society desired the preservation of the existing social, economic, and political order and that it was willing to exert extensive energies and talent to preserve that society from threats directed against it either by the British government or by domestic malcontents. Evidence also shows that in the years just prior to the Declaration of Independence, other social elements began to demand a more drastic revision of society than the gentry believed necessary to end parliamentary tyranny.[48]

Charles F. Mullett dismissed the new left's historical assumptions by observing that "[t]he Boston Tea party was only a Columbia sit-in two centuries ahead of itself."[49] Historians outside the new left took the topic of taxation much more seriously. It has always been accepted that Great Britain was staggering under an oppressive debt and that most people in the mother country felt taxation of the colonies was not only the best but

---

[44] Arthur M. Schlesinger, Sr., *The Birth of the Nation: A Portrait of the American People on the Eve of Independence* 250 (1968).

[45] Ira D. Gruber, "The American Revolution as a Conspiracy: The British View," 26 *Wm. & Mary Q.* (3d ser.) 360, 372 (1969).

[46] John Richard Alden, *A History of the American Revolution* (1969).

[47] John M. Head, *A Time to Rend: An Essay on the Decision for American Independence* (1968).

[48] David Curtis Skaggs, "Maryland's Impulse Toward Social Revolution: 1750-1776", 54 *J. Am. Hist.* 771, 785-86 (1968).

[49] Charles F. Mullett, "Book Review", 35 *J. So. Hist.* 77 (1969) (reviewing *Toward A New Past: Dissenting Essays in American History* (B.J. Bernstein ed. (1968)).

also the fairest solution to money problems. A related theme was the belief that, compared to Great Britain, America was lightly taxed. Marvin L. Michael Kay now casts doubt on that idea, arguing that taxes in pre-Revolutionary North Carolina "were far from negligible. . . ."[50] Mark Thompson, on the other hand, finds that stamp taxes levied by colonial legislatures in the 1750's were neither particularly unpopular nor burdensome and "may very well have encouraged George Grenville . . . to extend the English Stamp Act to all the colonies. . . ."[51]

Grenville and his colleagues soon learned their mistake. A milestone in the formulation of basically antagonistic positions by the colonists and the British on the role of Parliament was, of course, the Townshend Acts of 1767. Robert J. Chaffin, taking a fresh look at the political infighting that led to these acts,[52] argues that there was general agreement on the principle of parliamentary supremacy and, therefore, on the constitutional power to tax the colonies. The disagreement was over the method and wisdom of taxation, and not over the right.[53] Repeal of the stamp act was the turning point which persuaded the Whigs as well as the Tories that a stand on behalf of parliamentary supremacy would have to be made sooner or later. It was also the "greatest triumph" of the agents who represented the colonial assemblies in London.[54] Although these agents have received much attention from historians, Michael G. Kammen now writes that as a constitutional institution linking the colonies with Great Britain, they proved no stronger than "a rope of sand,"[55] leading William B. Willcox to remark that "[c]olonial agencies in London were a developing institution that, like feudalism, began to decay before it developed."[56]

---

[50] Marvin Kay, "The Payment of Provincial and Local Taxes in North Carolina, 1748-1771," 26 *Wm. & Mary Q.* (3d ser.) 218, 240 (1969).

[51] Mark Thompson, "Massachusetts and New York Stamp Acts," 26 *Wm. & Mary Q.* 253, 257 (1969).

[52] Another revisionist study of this period examines the unpublished views of Thomas Hutchinson and throws doubt on the long-accepted belief that John Adams's defense of the accused soldiers in the Boston Massacre trial is the apogee of the American legal profession. Hiller Zobel, "Newer Light on the Boston Massacre," 78 *Proc. Am. Antiquarian Soc.* 119 (1968). [Zobel's thesis was rejected in John Phillip Reid, "A Lawyer Acquitted: John Adams and the Boston Massacre Trials," 18 *Am. J. Legal Hist.* 189 (1974).]

[53] Robert J. Chaffin, "The Townshend Acts of 1767," 27 *Wm. & Mary Q.* (3d ser.) 90, 119-20 (1970). See also, Derek Watson, "The Rockingham Whigs and the Townshend Duties," 84 *Engl. Hist. Rev.* 561 (1969).

[54] Benjamin W. Labaree, "Book Review," 27 *Wm. & Mary Q.* (3d ser.) 150, 152 (1970).

[55] Michael G. Kammen, *A Rope of Sand: The Colonial Agents, British Politics and The American Revolution* (1968).

[56] William B. Willcox, "Book Review," 74 *Am. Hist. Rev.* 1356 (1969).

One of the best articles supporting the "constitutional" or "legal" school of revolutionary history was by Donald C. Lord and Robert M. Calhoon.[57] While showing that legal arguments lay at the core of the Whig-Tory dispute, they nevertheless strangely appraise the controversy between the Massachusetts General Court and Governor Hutchinson. The legislators, when contending with the governor over exercise of the prerogative, are said to have used ambivalence as they "preferred to construct an unsystematic set of tangible precedents."[58] In other words, the tenacious clinging in official messages to phrases like "according to usage" and "ancient and legal seat" emphasized the "preservative, traditional sources of the [General] Court's favorite ideas."[59] Perhaps so, but how else could the argument be conducted? In the language of confrontation? A legal premise is defended best in legal language, and in debates over the meaning of an unwritten constitution, custom and usage are the strongest points on which to stand. As Robert E. Brown remarked, "One should not be surprised that Americans defended their position in terms of 'British liberties,' as they would have gotten nowhere by insisting on 'American liberties.'"[60] Yet Lawrence H. Leder felt that reliance on the rights of Englishmen was ill-judged, because it meant that Americans failed to identify with any precision the theoretical foundations of their institutions.[61] Even if we concede the argument, it is impossible to think of any other premise upon which the colonists could have debated. They were, after all, traditional whigs, and in the eighteenth century the whig tradition offered them strong grounds for winning British allies, a point Gordon S. Wood may have had in mind when he wrote:

> . . . Leder misinterprets the meaning of several conceptions of political theory . . . and misses the incredible subtlety and complexity of the English constitutional tradition, which allowed both the colonists and crown officials to appeal to disparate strains of the same heritage even at the moment of revolution. Only an appreciation of this complicated heritage can explain how most Americans in 1776, even with their invocation of natural rights, could justifiably believe they were revolting not against the English constitution but on behalf of it.[62]

---

[57] Donald C. Lord & Robert M. Calhoon, "The Removal of the Massachusetts General Court from Boston, 1769-1772," 55 *J. Am. Hist.* 735 (1969).

[58] Id. at 753.

[59] Ibid.

[60] Robert E. Brown, "Book Review," 74 *Am. Hist. Rev.* 1357, 1359 (1969).

[61] Lawrence H. Leder, *Liberty and Authority: Early American Political Ideology, 1689-1753,* at 116-46 (1968).

[62] Gordon Wood, "Book Review," 74 *Am. Hist. Rev.* 1078, 1079 (1969).

IV

CONSTITUTIONAL HISTORY

Not only did the new school of "legal-constitutional" historiography continue during 1969 to dominate writing on the Revolution, it also made its first real impact on the history of the Constitution itself with the publication of Gordon Wood's *The Creation of the American Republic,*[63] the sequel to Bernard Bailyn's *Ideological Origins of the American Revolution.*[64] Wood can be criticized for adhering too rigidly to Bailyn's work and, as a result, simply repeating much of it in his opening chapters, and further, for failing fully to achieve his original objective of demonstrating the ties between Revolutionary "rhetoric and reality."[65] Nonetheless, *The Creation of the American Republic* is an outstanding work — the best book in American constitutional history of this year and, perhaps, the best general study ever written of the Founding Fathers' legal and political theory. Setting forth in immense detail the transformation under pressure of events of pre-Revolutionary ideology into the essentially democratic ideology of the framers, Wood's book is a "must" for lawyers interested in constitutional history.

The Creation of the American Republic was not the only scholarly work on our constitutional origins written during the past year. Questioning the importance of ideology upon those origins, Jackson Turner Main wrote:

> In tracing the origin and consequences of ideas, the historian naturally sees ideology as antecedent to a particular historical situation and as profoundly affecting the course of events, while he tends to ignore or to underestimate the degree to which ideas develop out of the environment and the extent to which events are shaped by non-ideological factors.[66]

One historian willing to challenge familiar theories and to reappraise the origin of ideas and the impact of events was Robert A. Feer. Suggesting that no one has ever looked to see just what it was that Shays's Rebellion "caused," he breaks radically with past scholarship and convincingly argues that it contributed nothing to the calling or to the work of the Constitutional Convention:

---

[63] (1969).

[64] (1967).

[65] See Gordon S. Wood, "Rhetoric and Reality in the American Revolution," 23 *Wm. & Mary Q.* (3d ser.) 3 (1966).

[66] Jackson Turner Main, "Book Review," 26 *Wm. & Mary Q.* (3d ser.) 604, 606 (1969).

> There is no evidence that state legislatures moved one whit faster to choose delegates to the Philadelphia Convention because of Shays's Rebellion. . . . Five states, including Massachusetts, did not act until after Shays's Rebellion had been all but suppressed. These five states delayed in choosing delegates partially because the proposed Convention smacked too much of the sort of extra-legal conventions which the Shaysites were using. The Articles of Confederation specified that amendments were to be proposed by Congress and to become operative when approved by the states. There was no provision for by-passing Congress and holding a constitutional convention. States such as New York, Connecticut, and Massachusetts refused to appoint delegates until Congress had sanctioned the Convention, thereby giving it the color of legality and removing from the shoulders of state officials the burden of explaining why they opposed extra-legal conventions when the Shaysites called them but supported extra-legal conventions when their own friends summoned them.[67]

Adding that there is no evidence that Shays's Rebellion contributed to the growth of the movement toward nationalism, or even to Washington's decision to go to Philadelphia, and that in fact Shays's Rebellion became as much an argument to support the anti-Federalists as the Federalists,[68] Feer concludes:

> Historians can say little, if anything, with complete certainty, least of all in the realm of causation. But, in all likelihood, the Constitutional Convention would have met when it did, the same document would have been drawn up, and it would have been ratified even if Shays's Rebellion had not taken place. If by a "cause" we mean something necessary to the occurrence of a particular event, Shays's Rebellion was not a cause of the Constitution of the United States.[69]

In another vein, Raoul Berger has published a massive study of *Marbury v. Madison* in *Congress v. The Supreme Court.*[70] Berger establishes beyond any doubt that "[t]hroughout the [Constitutional] Convention the availability of judicial review was repeatedly asserted by the leadership, while the voices of dissenters were few and feeble"[71] and

---

[67] Robert A. Feer, "Shays's Rebellion and the Constitution: A Study in Causation," 42 *New Eng. Q.* 388, 393-94 (1969).

[68] The Federalists argued: "Shays's Rebellion, because it had thrown one of the 'large' states into confusion, seemed to show that a strong government covering the entire United States could not survive and remain democratic." Id. at 408. The Anti-Federalists argued: ". . . [H]aving come through Shays's Rebellion unscathed, American society must be so stable and healthy that a stronger government was not necessary. . . ." Id. at 404.

[69] Id. at 410.

[70] (1969).

[71] Id. at 335.

"many silent members favored it. . . ."[72] He also shows that in the ratifying conventions ". . . the promise of judicial review as a check on unbridled Congressional power emerged more clearly and without dissent."[73] Berger's conclusions are more than amply justified; with Crosskey-like thoroughness he has examined, evaluated and explained every scrap of evidence pertinent to his conclusion and has done so with a sound instinctive understanding of the mentality of the late 1780's. His work should leave no doubt as to what was in the minds of most leaders of that time. Yet Berger fails to meet the stringent standard of showing ". . . just exactly where the collective judgment [of the framers] — which alone is decisive — came to rest."[74] He does not recognize history's ultimate inability to control the current course of events or that constitutional history merely ". . . represents a choice that men have made and [that] . . . we must justify . . . in our own time."[75]

The Reconstruction Era also received its usual attention. Tracing the growth of the law granting the federal courts exclusive jurisdiction in all cases arising under the Civil Rights Act of 1875, J. David Hoeveler, Jr., considers it "very likely" that "the Senate passed the Civil Rights Act as a memorial to Charles Sumner."[76]

> The Congressional debates on the court provisions of the Civil Rights Bill are revealing. They indicate both that Congressmen were often confused on the issue, uncertain of the virgin territory they were exploring, but at the same time aware that the resort to the federal courts was producing a major change in the federal system.[77]

A second article, seeking to show that *Brown v. Board of Education*[78] was "contrary to the intent of the framers" of the fourteenth amendment, analyzes federal aid to education during the twenty years after the

---

[72] Id. at 222.

[73] Ibid.

[74] Alexander M. Bickel, *The Least Dangerous Branch: The Supreme Court at the Bar of Politics* 16 (1962).

[75] Ibid.

[76] David J. Hoeveler, Jr. "Reconstruction and the Federal Courts: The Civil Rights Act of 1875," 31 *The Historian* 604, 612 (1969).

[77] Id. at 613. "One consequence of the act was a flood of new business for the federal courts. Justice under the Reconstruction legislation, for this and other reasons, was therefore painfully slow. While Congress wisely turned to the federal courts as reliable agencies, its failure to expand the courts and the number of court officials actually weakened the enforcement provisions." Id. at 616.

[78] 349 U.S. 294 (1954).

amendment.[79] Its author, Alfred Avins, concludes that the amendment's framers ". . . manifested an unwavering determination that colored people should receive their fair proportion of school funds and quality education at all levels. But they never believed that Negroes had a right to be educated together with white persons."[80] Like Berger, Avins fails to appreciate the limitations of history; he also has another fault which he shares with many other constitutional historians in that he writes upon topics which are momentarily the fashion of the day with an eye to proving some preordained legal conclusion,[81] rather than to adding to our store of historical knowledge. It is the rare historian who selects a neglected topic in constitutional history and gives it the scholarly consideration it merits.

V

THE NINETEENTH CENTURY

The nineteenth century was the subject of the most thorough and complete work of scholarship of this year: Paul W. Gates's monumental *History of Public Land Law Development.*[82] Gates discusses seemingly every statute dealing with public lands passed by Congress prior to the twentieth century, as well as the debates leading up to each statute, the administrative implementation of the statute, and the consequences of the statute for land settlement and exploitation. He concludes:

> American land policy from Independence to the end of the 19th century had four objectives inherited from the colonial period: (1) to

---

[79] Alfred Avins, "Federal Aid to Education Policies, 1865-1888: Some Reflected Light on School Segregation and the Fourteenth Amendment," 21 *Ala. L. Rev.* 61, 118 (1968).

[80] Ibid.

[81] See, e.g., Leon Friedman, "Conscription and the Constitution: The Original Understanding," 67 *Mich. L. Rev.* 1493 (1969); Carl Brent Swisher, "The Supreme Court and Conscription," 54 *Current Hist.* 351 (1968). The most interesting of these studies, from an historiological point of view, was undertaken for the New York Civil Liberties Union to prove that the draft is unconstitutional. It is a marvellous example of the "special-pleading" or "assumed conclusion" approach to legal history that remains so popular with legal scholars. The absurdity of such "scholarship" is demonstrated by the fact that the brief for the N.Y.C.L.U. was met by a brief for the government whose "history" was equally inaccurate.

[82] (1968).

> produce revenue for the government; (2) to facilitate the settlement and growth of new communities; (3) to reward veterans of wars and (4) to promote education, the establishment of eleemosynary institutions, and the construction of internal improvements by grants of land.[83]

Gates traces in full detail the shifts in emphasis from one to the other of these objectives. Without doubt his book and, in particular, his complete bibliography, will be the starting point for future historians of public land law.

The recent interest among intellectual historians in the legal profession, symbolized by the last published work of Perry Miller, continued unabated this year. In an essay on "Anxiety and Despair in American History," dealing with what he describes as the "deep streaks of morbidity" shared by many "of the figures about whom we knew most in American history," Page Smith observes: "At the time of the American Revolution another anxiety-producing factor had been added to the American sense: competition. A young man in the period between 1760 and 1800 who wished to be something other than a farmer or a minister had, generally speaking, one option — to be a lawyer."[84]

> The consequence was that law was egregiously overcrowded and the competition was fierce. It took John Quincy Adams, one of the most brillant Americans in our history, years of painful austerity before he finally made the most modest living. The correspondence between John Quincy Adams and his father is filled with the son's despair of ever establishing himself and with the father's efforts to keep up the young man's spirits in the face of discouragingly little progress. Thomas Boylston Adams, another of John Adams's sons, was never able to establish himself as a lawyer and lived off parental handouts and minor offices. Charles tried and gave up and drank himself to death. These were the sons of a president of the United States, connected by marriage to many of the most prosperous and influential families in New England. . . .
>
> In other societies in the nineteenth century, competition was muted or virtually non-existent. A man was born to a certain class or caste, to a certain trade and station in life, and that was where, by and large, all but the most able stayed.[85]

While these intellectual appraisals of the earlier legal profession are valuable and welcome, it is distressing to note signs that Perry Miller's

---

[83] Id. at 765.

[84] Page Smith, "Anxiety and Despair in American History," 26 *Wm. & Mary Q.* (3d ser.) 416 (1969).

[85] Id. at 420-21.

overly broad generalizations may be seeping into historical writing —and unfortunately adopted by lawyers.[86] A law note, for example, challenges some of the myths surrounding *Swift v. Tyson* and finds that Justice Story did not think in terms of a general, federal common law existing as a separate entity. What he wanted was "that federal courts could draw on cases arising in all jurisdictions, English, state, and federal, and need not consider themselves limited to cases arising in the state where the action was brought."[87] The theme is sound and the documentation, convincing. What is jarring is the semi-behaviorist theory which the writer lifted from Miller without determining whether it conformed to the legal materials he was analyzing. *Swift v. Tyson,* we are told, was "a judicial response to social and intellectual forces embodied in the movement to codify the common law, which appeared to Story to threaten the integrity of the entire legal system." The decision "gave federal courts the power to develop the common law in isolation from the confusion and ideological partisanship of the state judicial systems."[88]

> . . . Story might well have feared for American law in the hands of state court judges. Even though what he regarded as the disaster of codification might be avoided, state judges were less accomplished as technicians of the law than federal judges, and they were increasingly likely to be elected, and therefore subject to the pressures of popular emotion and political interest to an extent unknown in the federal system. Insofar as Story's attempted accommodation of the Heart and the Mind [Miller's counterpoints for framing the intellectual struggles between schools of legal theory] failed, it did so because he overestimated the capacity of national institutions to perform the task he set them.[89]

---

[86] Actually, in this case, by a law student, who does wisely observe: "While lawyers may write better legal history than intellectual historians, a law degree does not insure historical writing of high quality. . . ." [Mark Tushnet], Note, "Swift v. Tyson Exhumed," 79 *Yale L.J.* 284, 305 n.92 (1969).

[87] Id. at 295.

[88] Id. at 297.

[89] Id at 310. "*Swift v. Tyson* responded to deep needs in the legal profession for a defense against the social and intellectual forces which transformed the codification movement from a lawyers' to a popular movement. A desire to protect the profession against popular demands, and not only a desire to exalt national over state power, lay behind Justice Story's attempt to provide a legal framework in which judges could respond to the claims of the Mind to which the profession adhered and to the appeals of the Heart which the populace put forth.

". . . *Swift* was superseded as an intellectual endeavor not by the economic growth of the nation, which made forum-shopping a practical problem, but by a change in the lawyers' approach to the task of reconcilling the Heart and the Mind." Ibid.

The most interesting study of the year, at least from a jurisprudential viewpoint, related to acculturation in Hawaii. William Davenport, taking a new look at the "Hawaiian Cultural Revolution" of 1819, concludes that the arrival of the Europeans had placed the Islands under great economic and political stress, creating a cultural crisis with legal implications. The monarchy and aristocracy had been supported by the traditional laws, particularly the kapu or religious laws. By 1819 it was recognized that new times called for new laws, that the old ways were not suitable for the new trade economy, and that constitutional change had to be brought about. The problem was that as the kapu was based on sacred taboos there was no machinery for legal reform. Thus, the radicals among the upper class, led by the queen mother and supported by the paramount chief, deliberately violated the kapu by publicly eating proscribed foods. Even the high priest took part, thus destroying his own function in life. By violating the law, they used the only means available to repeal it. As even those in command could not change the law without rebelling, their action constituted a legal as much as a cultural revolution undertaken from the top.[90]

Among the historical premises that may be questioned are (1) whether anyone in 1842 thought state judges inferior to federal judges, and (2) whether codification ever became a "popular" movement.

[90] William Davenport, "The 'Hawaiian Cultural Revolution': Some Political and Economic Considerations," 71 *Am. Anthropologist* 1 (1969).

Chapter Eleven

1971/72

William E. Nelson

THE two years that have elapsed since the most recent legal history survey[1] have produced at least one major landmark of scholarship in the field — the fifth volume of *Perspectives in American History*,[2] devoted entirely to law and consisting of ten monographic articles and an introduction dealing with various topics in its history. That students of the law's past could assemble such an impressive collection of articles in a single volume is a tribute to the evolving discipline of legal history. More importantly, the volume makes a significant contribution to our knowledge of and insight into the development of American law.

In his Introduction to the *Perspectives* essays,[3] Justice Byron R. White puts forward a tentative hypothesis "that although legal institutions have educative functions and may reinforce certain interests and weaken others they have only marginal influence in effecting significant and enduring legal and social change. . . ."[4] "[B]asic change," he further suggests, "at least in a country like ours, occurs only with changes in the social order."[5] Both the essays in the *Perspectives* volume and other recent scholarship underscore the fruitfulness of this hypothesis as a medium for ordering data in legal history.

The endless variety of political, social and economic factors that contribute to the passage of legislation is illustrated in Charles O. Jackson's fine new book, *Food and Drug Legislation in the New Deal.*[6] Jackson traces the five-year struggle that culminated in the passage of the Food and Drug Act of 1938. He details the numerous impediments that confronted the act and prevented its passage during the first four years after it had been proposed: the opposition of powerful drug industry lobbies; the jurisdictional dispute between the Federal Trade Commission and the Food and Drug Administration, each of which wanted control over food and drug advertising; the President's lack of interest in the

[1] See ch. 10 above, at 143-163.

[2] 5 *Perspectives in American History* (Donald Fleming & Bernard Bailyn eds. 1971) [hereinafter cited as *Perspectives*].

[3] Id. at v.

[4] Id. at x-xi.

[5] Id. at xi.

[6] (1970).

legislation and unwillingness to press for it in Congress; the public's similar lack of interest; and finally, a number of personality struggles and conflicts within the Congress. Jackson proceeds to show how over a five-year period each of these obstacles was overcome. An initial step was to convince the industry lobbies that some form of legislation ultimately would be enacted. Once this was accomplished, portions of the industry gradually changed lobbying tactics, seeking less to prevent the passage of any legislation than to influence the content of what would untimately be passed. Even more important was a 1937 disaster in which 107 people died from taking a drug that had been placed on the market without adequate testing; as a result, the public immediately became interested in drug reform and brought sufficient political pressure to bear upon Congress to impel it to act. In essence, formal legal institutions were able to revise the law only after a fundamental change in public opinion, whereas, faced with strong economically motivated opposition, they had been unable or unwilling to act before that change occurred.

Three recent articles on the subject of federal-state relations indicate that Congresses of the nineteenth century exhibited a similar response to public needs. Charles A. Lindquist's "The Origin and Development of the United States Commissioner System,"[7] maintains that the absence of any perceived need for federal justices of the peace in the nation's early history, when states were willing to enforce federal law, resulted in Congress granting only minimal powers to the first United States Commissioners. It was only during the fugitive slave crisis beginning in the 1840's that Congress granted to commissioners the powers of justices, including the power to authorize arrest and imprisonment and to set bail.[8] This grant was necessary, and, in fact, occurred only because the underlying harmony between the state and federal governments had been destroyed. When that harmony was subsequently restored after the Civil War and Reconstruction, however, legislative inertia thwarted return to the pre-1840 commissioner system — absent further change in political conditions, the legislature could not be induced to act.

Similarly, as William M. Wiecek demonstrates,[9] special political conditions had to exist before Congress would broaden the removal and habeas corpus jurisdiction of the federal courts. As initially established, federal courts lacked power to issue habeas corpus to prisoners in state custody or to prevent the hearing in state court of suits against federal officials. But in 1833, when South Carolina threatened nullification of

---

[7] 14 *Am. J. Legal Hist.* 1 (1970).

[8] Act of Aug. 23, 1842, ch. 188, §1, 5 Stat. 517.

[9] William M. Wiecek, "The Great Writ and Reconstruction: The Habeas Corpus Act of 1867," 36 *J. So. Hist.* 530 (1970).

the federal revenue laws, Congress authorized federal officers acting pursuant to federal law to remove to federal court suits or criminal prosecutions brought against them in state court.[10] Then in the early 1840's when New York refused to release British agents who had violated state law, thereby creating a moderate international crisis, Congress authorized federal courts to grant habeas corpus to foreigners acting under the authority of a foreign nation.[11] Finally, when it appeared during Reconstruction that states, despite the thirteenth amendment, would imprison blacks in order to perpetuate slavery, Congress authorized federal courts to issue habeas corpus on behalf of prisoners in state custody.[12]

The third article, a recent study by Catherine Tarrant of the nineteenth-century law of seditious conspiracy,[13] outlines the political infeasability of enacting federal sedition legislation before the Civil War when the nation was politically divided and each potential minority felt threatened by such laws. As Tarrant observes, however, once the South left the Union, it became possible for Congress to legislate concerning sedition,[14] for the North then arrived at a sufficient consensus to enable proponents of the legislation to identify as potential traitors only those who lacked power to block it and who did not have to participate in its adoption.

As Herbert Schreiber's study of late nineteenth-century labor legislation suggests,[15] state legislatures, like Congress, act only in response to forceful and genuine political pressures. A scholar of the development of the doctrine unique to American labor law that representatives of the majority of workers in any bargaining unit should be the exclusive bargaining agents for all workers in that unit, Schreiber argues that the doctrine initially developed in state arbitration statutes of the 1880's and 1890's in part in response to majoritarian concepts in American political theory and in part under persistent pressure and lobbying by organized labor groups seeking to strengthen their bargaining power.

Like legislatures, both executive and administrative agencies are responsive to social pressures originating outside formal legal institutions. A series of books and articles written during the past two years regarding the development of modern police forces lends support to this notion. Pauline Maier, in her study, "Popular Uprisings and Civil Authority in

---

[10] Act of March 2, 1833, ch. 57 §3, 4 Stat. 633.

[11] Act of Aug. 29, 1842, ch. 257, §1, 5 Stat. 539.

[12] Act of July 31, 1861, ch. 33, §1, 12 Stat. 284.

[13] Catherine Tarrant, "To 'Insure Domestic Tranquility': Congress and the Law of Seditious Conspiracy, 1839-1861," 15 *Am. J. Legal Hist.* 107 (1971).

[14] See Act of July 31, 1861, ch. 33, §1, 12 Stat. 284.

[15] Herbert Schreiber, "The Majority Preference Provisions in Early State Labor Arbitration Statutes, 1880-1900," 15 *Am. J. Legal Hist.* 186 (1971).

Eighteenth-Century America,"[16] explains that professional police forces did not exist in colonial America because they were viewed as a threat to a free society; crime and disorder were quelled only by the individual and corporate efforts of private subjects acting temporarily in an official capacity. Although riots and incidents of mob rule occasionally resulted from the absence of official means of coercion, such ferment was explained as a product of misgovernment and seen as insurance that government would remain beneficient and free. But after the Revolution, according to Maier, Americans became more satisfied with government and less willing to explain riots as a result of misgovernment. Furthermore, there also developed a new concern for minority rights, which mobs had always imperilled. It thus became possible to develop professional police.

James F. Richardson in his book, *The New York Police: Colonial Times to 1901,*[17] notes that professional forces also became necessary in major eastern cities when after 1820 they grew in size and changed in ethnic composition, and traditional methods of community crime control failed. New York, for example, created a professional police force in 1845. Regrettably, as Richardson notes, the new force quickly became highly political in nature, for the basis of both appointment to and, initially, retention on the force was subserviency to the politicans running city government. The political nature of the force, as colorfully documented by Gerald Astor in *The New York Cops: An Informal History,*[18] led to massive graft and corruption and to systematic looting of the city and its residents. Most surprising is that efforts at reform during the nineteenth and early twentieth centuries occurred only briefly and intermittently. Astor demonstrates that movements to eliminate police corruption have become commonplace only in the mid-twentieth century, although he does not explain why this new concern for police honesty is only a recent development.

Another series of books and articles on the enforcement of criminal law develops a similar theme — the tendency for the law to reflect a society's underlying cultural values. Chadwick Hansen, in *Witchcraft at Salem,*[19] puts forward a quite arresting thesis that, because people in the seventeenth-century Western world believed in witches, it was possible for individuals to become true witches and to commit the crime of witchcraft. Hansen contends that victims of witchcraft so feared witches that when someone who acted like a witch threatened to bewitch them

---

[16] 27 *Wm. & Mary Q.* (3d ser.) 1 (1970).
[17] (1970).
[18] (1971).
[19] (1969).

they developed genuine, though psychosomatic, symptoms of illness. Given such fear of the supernatural, it was entirely rational and predictable that society would punish witchcraft as a crime. It was only when people ceased to believe in a supernatural, nonmaterial world that the law relating to witchcraft became irrational, and at that point, as Hansen notes, the law of witchcraft simply expired.

Two of the essays in the *Perspectives* volume further attest that, whatever the written rules of law, society will often use either formal or informal mechanisms to punish those whom it deems guilty of immorality and to exculpate those whose moral standards it approves. In "Legal and Behavioral Perspectives on American Vigilantism,"[20] Richard Brown contends that Americans' belief in the iniquity of interracial sex and of other activities perceived as immoral led many otherwise law-abiding citizens in the late nineteenth century, despite the restraints of the formal legal system, into vigilante and white-capping movements of the most reprehensible sort. David Flaherty, on the other hand, argues in "Law and Enforcement of Morals in Early America"[21] that the willingness of eighteenth-century Americans to tolerate similar acts of "immorality" made it extremely difficult for formal legal institutions to punish those acts despite unflinching efforts at doing so.

In one of the clearly outstanding works of recent legal history scholarship, a two-volume series entitled *Court and Constitution in the Twentieth Century,*[22] William F. Swindler develops the premise that courts, like the legislature and the executive, are susceptible to noninstitutional pressures from society at large. Swindler does an admirable job integrating the development of constitutional doctrine by the Supreme Court with political, social and economic development in the nation at large and the development of constitutional theory among intellectuals. Swindler begins by observing that the Supreme Court of the late nineteenth and early twentieth centuries based its judgments upon absolute and immutable principles reflecting standards of right and morality widely shared among the Eastern establishment — standards whose preservation the establishment thought vital in suppressing the socialist menace thought to be posed by the lower classes. As Swindler recognizes, however, the jurisprudential standards of the turn of the century could not last. For a few like Holmes, Brandeis and Cardozo, these standards were discarded early under pressure of their skepticism, their wide-ranging law practices and their observation of the nature of the judicial

---

[20] *Perspectives, supra* note 2, at 95.

[21] Id. at 203.

[22] William F. Swindler, *Court and Constitution in the Twentieth Century: The Old Legality, 1889 - 1932* (1969); William F. Swindler, *Court and Constitution in the Twentieth Century: The New Legality, 1932 - 1968* (1970).

process. But most Americans continued to accept the principles developed by nineteenth-century jurisprudence well into the 1920's, when, as Swindler explains in a fascinating chapter, the experiment of prohibition created doubts among previously secure people. When the eighteenth amendment was adopted, Americans, according to Swindler, viewed it like the rest of their Constitution as an articulation of moral principle which would be assured permanence by its very inclusion in the Constitution. The difficulty of enforcing prohibition, however, and the pressure which that enforcement placed upon other fundamental principles, notably the Bill of Rights, led to doubt in the permanence and even the reality of all legal principle. The Great Depression was the next and ultimate event contributing to the destruction of the old jurispudence of lasting principles, for it revealed that both the laws of economics and the laws regulating the relationship of government to the economy had simply ceased to function and that new laws would be needed in their stead. However, the prospect of developing new law was troubling, for as Swindler shows in his brillant chapter entitled, "Experimental Constitutional Law," this new law would be nebulous and forever fluctuating —for example, far more cases have been overruled in the thirty years since 1937 than in the preceding 140 years. In short judges, under the pressure of a changing world have had to abandon the fiction that "the meaning of the constitution is fixed when it is adopted, and is no different at any subsequent time when a court has occasion to pass upon it."[23]

An excellent student note, "American Slavery and the Conflict of Laws,"[24] indicates that nineteenth-century judges similarly accommodated legal doctrine, in this instance, choice of law rules, to social and political considerations. The note suggests that the pre-Civil War era can be subdivided into two periods: a pre-1830 period in which judges were often willing to accommodate the conflict rules of th ir own states to the policies of other states and apply out-of-state law, ar a post-1830 period in which judges increasingly disposed of slavery cases only on the basis of their own local law. The note theorizes that this change occurred partly in response to the publication of Joseph Story's conflicts treatise,[25] which

[23] William F. Swindler, *Court and Constitution in the Twentieth Century: The New Legality, 1932 - 1968,* at 32 (1970).

[24] 71 *Colum. L. Rev.* 74 (1971). On the same topic, see also Harold Horowitz, "Choice-of-Law Decisions Involving Slavery: 'Interest Analysis' in the Early Nineteenth Century," 17 *U.C.L.A.L. Rev.* 587 (1970), which fails, however, to explain why "interest analysis" was used by the courts in the early nineteenth and mid-twentieth centuries, but not in other periods of time.

[25] Joseph Story, *Commentaries on the Conflict of Laws* (3d ed. 1846).

favored a territorial approach, but largely in response to the increasing virulence of the slavery controversy.

A still clearer example of the receptiveness of courts to political and intellectual change is portrayed in Morton Horwitz' "The Emergence of an Instrumental Conception of American Law, 1780-1820,"[26] an unusually noteworthy article which traces the shift in judges' understanding of the nature of the common law in post-Revolutionary America. In the 1780's, Horwitz explains, judges viewed the common law as a body of permanent and immutable principle and precedent, but by the 1820's they were coming to see it as a flexible instrument of social policy and as a mechanism for judicial ordering of society. Horwitz argues that the change occurred largely between 1790 and 1810 as a result of changes in political ideology during the post-Revolutionary period — changes which established consent as the basis of American law and weakened natural law theories, thereby undermining belief in the permanence of law.[27]

If the work of judges is in fact responsive to changes in society, it follows that their work is also a mirror of social reality at any given point in time. Richard Ellis in *The Jeffersonian Crisis: Courts and Politics in the Young Republic*[28] utilizes law as such a mirror. His book attempts to study Jeffersonian attitudes toward courts and judicial reform during the first decade of the nineteenth century primarily in order to understand the divisions within the Jeffersonian party. Ellis divides the party into two groups: the moderates, who desired reforms that would make the legal system more useful to commercial interests chiefly by promoting speedier disposition of cases, and the radicals, who sought to abolish the common law, destroy the legal profession and create an elected judiciary. Ellis views law reform as a key issue upon which moderate and radical Jeffersonians divided and hence as a useful tool in identifying the personages on each side and the reasons underlying the division.

An analogous approach is taken by A.E. Keir Nash in two articles[29] on the disposition of racial cases by Southern judges before the Civil War. In both articles Nash argues that, even after 1830, many Southern

---

[26] *Perspectives, supra* note 2, at 287.

[27] Horwitz' study raises a question why judges who early in the nineteenth century had abandoned a jurisprudence which viewed law as a permanent and immutable body of precedent should again adopt that jurisprudence by the end of the nineteenth century. The present writer is currently engaged in studying that question.

[28] (1971).

[29] A.E. Keir Nash, "A More Equitable Past? Southern Supreme Courts and the Protection of the Antebellum Negro," 48 *N.C.L. Rev.* 197 (1970); A.E. Keir Nash, "Fairness and Formalism in the Trials of Blacks in the State Supreme Courts of the Old South," 56 *Va. L. Rev.* 64 (1970).

judges maintained attitudes of relative decency and dealt fairly with blacks. Finding that judges were not blind and monolithic in defense of slavery, Nash accordingly questions the conclusion of previous historians that Southern white society shared uniform convictions. Indeed, Nash discovered that judges who had been raised in humble circumstances in the Upper South were often quite sympathetic toward the rights of black litigants — a finding consistent with the fact that the impoverished inhabitants of West Virginia and eastern Tennessee often opposed secession. That the South was not a monolith finds further support in an article[30] suggesting that Justice Campbell, who sat on the Supreme Court from 1853 until 1861, rejected the conventional Southern view that slavery was a positive good and recognized instead that the South must ultimately abolish slavery.

The responsiveness of judges to extralegal pressures generated in society at large is not, of course, a new discovery. As Gerald Gunther points out in a brief introduction[31] to newly republished documents relating to the case of *McCulloch v. Maryland,*[32] John Marshall was well aware of that responsiveness and, in order to insure favorable public opinion, wrote under a pseudonym a series of essays in defense of his *McCulloch* decision. Thus John Marshall recognized that the totality of law was not to be found in formal judicial institutions.

Only recently, however, Willard Hurst has found it necessary again to remind us of this same truth and to urge us to look beyond formal legal institutions — the legislature, executive and administrative agencies, and the courts — in the writing of legal history. We must, as he urges "relat[e] the formal operations of law — passing statutes, deciding cases, making administrative orders or rules — to the life that flowed outside the legal forms." We must study the "relations of formal operations of legal processes to the total behavior of those who worked or used those processes."[33] When we do, we will see that the informal elements of the legal system, like the formal ones, are responsive to social and intellectual change.

The legal profession provides an example of the type of phenomena which Hurst asserts we must examine. George Martin, in his book, *Causes and Conflicts: The Centennial History of the Association of the*

---

[30] Justine S. Mann, "The Political Thought of John Archibald Campbell: The Formative Years, 1847-1851," 22 *Ala. L. Rev.* 275 (1970).

[31] Gerald Gunther, "Introduction," in *John Marshall's Defense of McCulloch v. Maryland* (G. Gunther ed. 1969).

[32] 17 U.S. (4 Wheat.) 316 (1819).

[33] J. Willard Hurst, "Legal Elements in the United States History," *Perspectives, supra* note 2, at 3, 14-15 (1971).

Bar to the City of New York, 1870-1970,[34] adds to the evidence that many lawyers in the late nineteenth century ceased to be litgators and became instead business advisors. This was chiefly in response to the development of large national business entities, but also resulted in part as a consequence of the arrival of new office procedures produced by typewriters and telephones. Similarly, Maxwell Bloomfield in "Lawyers and Public Criticism: Challenge and Response in Nineteenth-Century America,"[35] questions the view of the mid-nineteenth century bar as one plagued by increasingly diluted standards; on the contrary, he contends that standards escalated as economic development created an ever increasing need for skilled and sophisticated professionals. Gerald Gawalt's study, "Sources of Anti-Lawyer Sentiment in Massachusetts, 1740-1840,"[36] confirms that the profession in the nineteenth century was organizing itself, controlling entry to the bar and thereby raising standards — a trend which combined with lawyers' increasing wealth and their increasing power in the government to produce considerable popular resentment and hostility toward the profession. Still further confirmation of Bloomfield's thesis occurs in Elizabeth G. Brown's survey of the prestatehood Wayne County, Michigan, bar which maintains that early Detroit lawyers "knew and practiced their craft as competently and advisedly, with a careful regard for forms and precedents, as their contemporaries practicing law along the eastern seaboard."[37] In short, the early nineteenth-century Michigan bar, like a majority of the American bar, was a well trained, highly skilled body of professionals.

The development of the law teaching profession, like that of the practicing bar, has responded to casual factors originating outside the profession. So argues Jerold Auerbach in his recent *Perspectives* article entitled "Enmity and Amity: Law Teachers and Practitioners, 1900-1922."[38] Auerbach observes that law teachers in the early twentieth century ceased to be mere practitioners and, as a result of the confluence of the social sciences and the Progressive Movement, became instead experts in the new science of effecting social change. Similarly, Robert Stevens finds that developments in law schools have paralleled developments in the "outside" world.[39] He observes that law schools in the late

---

[34] (1970).

[35] 15 *Am. J. Legal Hist.* 269 (1971).

[36] 14 *Am. J. Legal Hist.* 283 (1970).

[37] Elizabeth Gaspar Brown, "The Bar on a Frontier: Wayne County 1796-1836", 14 *Am. J. Legal Hist.* 136, 155 (1970).

[38] *Perspectives, supra* note 2, at 551.

[39] Robert Stevens, "Two Cheers for 1870: The American Law School," *Perspectives, supra* note 2, at 405.

nineteenth century abandoned the policy of teaching their students an entire and coherent body of American law as the nation had developed to the point that a comprehensive body of law had ceased to exist. Rather, law schools began to teach a body of analytical skills needed by business litigators and business counselors. Currently, as the legal profession is entering into many nonbusiness, social fields, law schools have begun to teach what are known as "clinical" skills.

Moreover, Gerhard Mueller's *Crime, Law and the Scholars*[40] suggests the existence of parallels between legal scholarship and scholarship at large. Mueller has traced the history of American criminal law scholarship, observing the criminal law scholars of the mid-nineteenth century sought to study substantive criminal law systematically and analytically, but that thereafter substantive analysis declined to the extent that the only work of significance in criminal law prior to the 1930's, apart from detailed scholarship dealing with narrow and prosaic topics, was done by criminologists. Mueller is rather critical of what he sees as a downward trend in criminal law scholarship since the mid-nineteenth century, although he regrettably makes no attempt to analyze the causes of the decline. In all probability, however, this trend in the study of criminal law parallels trends in other areas of academic scholarship. The mid-nineteenth century, it seems, was in most fields of scholarly endeavor an age of systematization; the twentieth century, on the other hand, has been an age of empirical study. Developments in criminal law scholarship may thus have been little different from developments in other scholarly fields.

Herman Belz' study[41] of the origins of realism in American constitutional scholarship confirms the likelihood of similarity between legal and academic thinking. Belz describes the study of the Constituton in the first two-thirds of the nineteenth century as being primarily legalistic; constitutional scholars of that era saw as their task the articulation of how the Constitution meshed with traditional concepts of political theory and the development of a systematic body of American theory. But, beginning in the end of the nineteenth century, professional scholars began to view the Constitution as a working political institution and to describe how government in fact operated. In essence, constitutional scholarship became an empirical discipline. Belz attributes this change to the rise of professional historical scholarship, but, while his explanation seems

---

[40] (1969).

[41] Herman Belz, "The Constitution in a Gilded Age: The Beginnings of Constitutional Realism in American Scholarship," 13 *Am. J. Legal Hist.* 110 (1969); Herman Belz, "The Realist Critique of Constitutionalism in the Era of Reform," 15 *Am. J. Legal Hist.* 288 (1971).

viable when developments in constitutional scholarship are viewed alone, it is not convincing when one also tries to explain parallel developments in other fields of legal scholarship.

We have so far seen how formal legal institutions and the legal profession often respond to political, economic and social pressures; we have now to survey how legal institutions and legal concepts in their entirety can change in response to such pressures. David Rothman's outstanding book, *The Discovery of the Asylum,*[42] portrays precisely such a change. Rothman's book, which traces the rise of penitentiaries, mental hospitals, alms houses and orphanages in Jacksonian America, first observes that in the colonial period crime, insanity, poverty and orphanage were considered natural phenomena which inevitably existed in society and whose effects could only be minimized, not cured. Nineteenth century Americans, on the the other hand, with utopian vision, thought that all social ills could be eliminated. Their response was to create asylums as a means of effecting a cure for society's ills. Any of Rothman's several types of asylums can be taken as illustrative; mental hospitals, for example, emphasized giving patients a well-ordered regular life of work and exercise so they could avoid the stresses of their former lives and hence be cured. Of course, the hopes and ideals of Jacksonians could not be translated into reality. One problem was that asylums were normally given custody only of the incurable. Penitentiaries, for example, did not receive first offenders, but multiple offenders, while mental hospitals were similarly asked to treat only the hopelessly insane. Other problems were lack of staff and lack of adequate financial support from the legislatures. In short, by the end of the nineteenth century what had begun as institutions of hope and promise had turned into mere institutional custodians keeping the sores of society hidden from its people.

In an equally extraordinary study of the effect of cultural conditions on law, John Phillip Reid explains how the legal system of the Cherokee Indians was totally dependent upon Cherokee cultural values. Reid's book, *A Law of Blood,*[43] the first volume of a projected multi-volume study of the Cherokee legal system, analyzes the various branches of primitive Cherokee law in detail, contrasting it with modern American law and with the law of the eighteenth-century colonies. Then, in the concluding chapters, Reid demonstrates the dependence of the law upon cultural values, especially upon the value of obtaining obedience from Cherokee warriors through informal social pressures, notably ostracism,

---

[42] (1971). The same change is portrayed in Robert S. Pickett, *House of Refuge: Origins of Juvenile Reform in New York State, 1815 - 1857* (1969). Pickett indicates that there was some reason to believe that the New York House of Refuge was successful in its early years.

[43] (1970).

rather than through coercion. In the coming volumes, Reid will show how increased contact with white Americans led to the breakdown of these cultural values and consequently to the breakdown of the Cherokees' primitive law and the adoption in its place of a modified version of the common law.

Other historians have voiced perceptions similar to those of Rothman and Reid concerning the cultural background of law. Edwin Gaustad, for one, perceives that the principle of separation of church and state resulted from a complex interaction of forces arising outside the law.[44] In the same vein Willard Hurst argues in his most recent book:

> . . . The organization and procedures of legal agencies, the structure of federalism, the inherited dignity of precedent, the inertia of familiar legal concepts and practices, as well as our attitudes toward the market and the proper autonomy of private will — all had effect upon the development of law affecting the business corporation.[45]

Likewise, James Patterson writes that, as a result of the Great Depression, a new concept of cooperative federalism arose when new programs financed and administered jointly by the federal government and the states were established,[46] while Jonathan Alpert further confirms that the law of slavery arose in seventeenth-century Maryland from a variety of economic and intellectual pressures.[47] Finally, George Haskins reiterates the theme that representative government in Massachusetts resulted from the twin influences of the corporate and parliamentary traditions of government in England.[48]

If it appears that the law will respond to social change, then it also appears that, absent any particular trend or direction of social change, the legal system likewise will not be amenable to palpable change in any one direction. Two recent studies of the Freedmen's Bureau during Reconstruction illustrate this latter thesis: William S. McFeeley's *The Yankee Stepfather,*[49] which is both a biography of General O.O. Howard,

---

[44] Edwin Gaustad, "A Disestablished Society: Origins of the First Amendment," 11 *J. Church & State* 409 (1969).

[45] J. Willard Hurst, *The Legitimacy of the Business Corporation in the law of the United States, 1780 - 1970,* at 153 (1970).

[46] James Patterson, *The New Deal and the States: Federalism in Transition* (1969).

[47] Jonathan Alpert, "The Origin of Slavery in the United States — The Maryland Precedent," 14 *Am. J. Legal Hist.* 189 (1970).

[48] George L. Haskins, "Parliamentary Aspects of Representative Government in Early Massachusetts," in *Liber Memorials Georges de Lagarde* 203 (1970).

[49] (1968).

the head of the Freedmen's Bureau, and a truly distinguished study of the Bureau itself, and Howard A. White's *The Freedmen's Bureau in Louisiana,*[50] a detailed study of the racial, economic and social history of Louisiana during the immediate post-Civil War years. These two books illustrate that the South from 1865 to 1870 was in the throes of a revolution. Antebellum social bonds had been torn assunder, and the task of postwar political leaders in state government, in the Freedmen's Bureau, and in the military was to create a new social order. In the field of labor relations, for example, old procedures for caring for slaves in times of economic distress and unemployment had ceased to function. When the year 1866 saw bad harvests, planters no longer felt obliged to feed their workers as they had before the war when workers had been slaves; thus the government had to organize large-scale relief. Similarly, the old rules of race relations had broken down. It was clear that blacks would no longer be slaves, but whether their status would materially improve remained unclear — they might become an inferior caste, a segregated but equal group, or a superior, if not dominant, group. What is painfully apparent from both books is that the regression to a status approximating slavery occurred largely because the blacks and their white allies could never agree upon and mobilize society behind a particular course of change. The only faction with a coherent plan was the white racists who had ruled the South before the Civil War. Consequently, this group made use of its opponents' lack of direction to insure that the law of race relations made little progress and that blacks remained in a legal position substantially analogous to their pre-Civil War position of slavery. A somewhat related article notes the failure of an attempt to achieve Negro suffrage in New York before the Civil War because of similar division and lack of mobilization in society.[51]

Two excellent studies by Harry N. Scheiber on law and economic development further confirm the thesis that the law will remain static when extralegal, specifically economic forces cut against change. One of his studies, *Ohio Canal Era: A Case Study of Government and the Economy 1820-1861*[52] traces in great detail the consequences of legal decisions to build canals and railroads in Ohio between 1820 and 1860, to build them in particular places and to set tolls at particular levels. According to Scheiber, those legal decisions usually exerted the economic impact which the decision-makers intended. When economic conditions in a region were unfavorable to development, however, then the decisions did not have their intended pro-developmental effect. For example, the

---

50 (1970).

51 John L. Stanley, "Majority Tyranny in Tocqueville's America: The Failure of Negro Suffrage in 1846," 84 *Pol. Sci. Q.* 412 (1969).

52 (1969).

Ohio canals failed to bring about economic development in the Scioto region because land distribution patterns there were unfavorable to development. In his second study[53] Scheiber asserts that nineteenth-century eminent domain law reveals a persistent conflict between two policy goals: the insistence that the rights of individuals in private property be secure versus the belief that property should be freely available for economic development. During the nineteenth century the courts alternated in preferring first one and then the other goal, seeking reconciliation whenever possible.

In developing the law relating to tax titles, the legislature and courts in Iowa struggled throughout the nineteenth century with a similar conflict between the policy goal of creating a viable tax system and the competing goal of protecting private property rights. As Robert Swierenga maintains,[54] the legislature generally leaned toward protection of the tax system, whereas the courts usually favored private property interests; it was not until after the Civil War that the legislature finally emerged victorious, as the courts realized the pernicious effects of their past decisions upon the public fisc. Even then, however, Swierenga indicates that the legislative triumph was incomplete.

Two articles appearing in the recent *Perspectives* volume also examine the tendency on the part of legal institutions to accommodate conflicting interests whenever possible rather than to advance one in preference to the other. One article is Stanley Katz' study of colonial equity courts.[55] Katz demonstrates that Americans living in the colonies and royal authorities in England agreed substantially upon the need for equity courts in the colonies, but that constitutional disputes over whether the crown or the colonial legislatures had jurisdiction to create chancery courts often prevented both from acting. When the Massachusetts legislature created courts of equity in the 1690's, for example, the privy council disallowed its legislation, and, as a result, Massachusetts throughout the eighteenth century had a legal system without equity jurisdiction. The experience in other colonies, such as New York and Pennsylvania, was not substantially different. In New York a chancery court functioned only intermittently during the last third of the seventeenth and first third of the eighteenth centuries and was subject to frequent politically-

[53] Harry N. Scheiber, "The Road to Munn: Eminent Domain and the Concept of Public Purpose in the State Courts," *Perspectives, supra* note 2, at 329.

[54] Robert Swierenga, "The 'Odious Tax Title': A Study in Nineteenth Century Legal History," 15 *Am. J. Legal Hist.* 124 (1971).

[55] Stanley Katz, "The Politics of Law in Colonial America: Controversies over Chancery Courts and Equity Law in the Eighteenth Century," *Perspectives, supra* note 2, at 257.

motivated challenges, while in Pennsylvania no equity court sat after the 1730's and equitable remedies, to the extent they were available, were available only in common law proceedings. In sum, a major legal innovation, the formal establishment of a colonial equity jurisdiction, could not occur in the face of political division, although partial, albeit informal, use of equitable procedures did occur.

The second article, John Elliff's study[56] of federal civil rights enforcement subsequent to the establishment of the Civil Rights Section of the Justice Department in 1939, traces the conflict between the Civil Rights Section and the Federal Bureau of Investigation. Since its establishment, what is now the Civil Rights Division has sought consistently to protect citizens, especially ethnic and political minorities, in the enjoyment of their federal constitutional rights against police and other official state infringement. The F.B.I., on the other hand, while not hostile to the Division's policy, possesses a competing policy of its own — the preservation of harmonious and cooperative ties with local law enforcement officers. As a result, there has existed constant tension within the Justice Department between these two competing agencies — a tension which has never been fully resolved and which has only been placated by occasional movement at the top levels of the Department in prefering first one policy and then the other, a movement seemingly occurring in response to immediate yet temporary political pressures.

Our historical experience thus suggests that formal legal institutions are frequently unable to resolve social policy conflicts fully and irrevocably until society itself first resolves those conflicts and resulting changes occur in societal structure or ideology. This does not mean, however, that role of formal institutional decision-makers is unimportant. As Charles Miller exhibits in "Constitutional Law and the Rhetoric of Race,"[57] one vital function which decision-makers can serve is to educate the public about the ideals and aspirations of reformers. Surely one of the outstanding contributions of the first Justice Harlan was to keep before the nation by his dissents in cases such as *Plessy v. Ferguson*[58] and *Berea College v. Kentucky*[59] the ideal of racial equality. Similarly one of the important results of *Brown v. Board of Education*[60] was to kindle the national awareness of the reality of racial discrimination.

A statute or favorable judicial decision in a particular case can also serve an important function by materially aiding the advancement of a

---

[56] John T. Elliff, "Aspects of Federal Civil Rights Enforcement: The Justice Department and the FBI, 1939-1964, *Perspectives, supra* note 2, at 605.

[57] *Perspectives, supra* note 2, at 147.

[58] 163 U.S. 537, 552 (1896).

[59] 211 U.S. 45, 58 (1908).

[60] 347 U.S. 483 (1954).

particular policy goal. As John Elliff demonstrates, the decision of the Supreme Court in *Screws v. United States*[61] aided the Civil Rights Division in its struggle with the F.B.I. to obtain vigorous enforcement of civil rights laws.[62] Furthermore, a consistent line of statutes, executive orders and judicial decisions, even when they do not fully resolve conflicts between competing policy goals, can further one goal in preference to another; as set forth by Harry Scheiber in both his book and his article, nineteenth-century legal institutions, even while continuing to recognize the importance of private property rights, did much to further economic development.[63] Finally, decisions taken by formal legal institutions can delay and impede the implementation of social changes accepted by the vast majority of society; as William Swindler's study of the Supreme Court suggests, the Court played precisely such a role in the 1930's.[64] As Hiller Zobel argues in his superbly written study of the Boston Massacre, formal legal institutions, while delaying the implementation of social change, can also save favored individuals from the adverse consequences of the forthcoming changes.[65]

While formal institutions thus are important, the historical writing of the past two years does nonetheless suggest that these institutions lack power to bring about fundamental legal change in periods of sharp political division or upon issues productive of such divisions. If this is in fact true, then an interesting line of argument arises for interpreting statutory and constitutional provisions enacted in such periods or upon such issues. William L. Richter makes such an argument in his article[66] discussing the perennial issue whether the fourteenth amendment was intended by its authors to incorporate the Bill of Rights. In essence, he maintains that the amendment could not have been intended to bring about any major change in the structure of the federal system since the North was narrowly divided on the issue whether such change was appropriate; specifically, he argues that Congressman Bingham, the author of section one, could not have meant to propose any radical change since he himself represented a very closely divided constituency.

---

[61] 325 U.S. 91 (1945).

[62] John T. Elliff, *supra* note 56, at 619.

[63] Harry N. Scheiber, *supra* note 52; Harry N. Scheiber, *supra* note 53.

[64] William F. Swindler, *supra* note 22.

[65] Hiller B. Zobel, *The Boston Massacre* (1970).

[66] William L. Richter, "One Hundred Years of Controversy: The Fourteenth Amendment and the Bill of Rights," 15 *Loyola L. Rev.* 281 (1969). On the same perennial issue, see also Ronald Mykkeltvedt, "Justice Black and the Intentions of the Framers of the Fourteenth Amendment's First Section: The Bill of Rights and the States," 20 *Mercer L. Rev.* 432 (1969), which adds nothing to the already extant literature on the subject.

Before concluding, note must also be taken of several other books and articles which, although not addressing themselves directly to the question of the relationship of law to social change, nonetheless constitute valuable additions to our knowledge of American legal history. Much of this work is in the field of constitutional history. Thus, there is a new book[67] on *Marbury v. Madison*[68] which, although offering no new knowledge, is a highly readable summary of existing scholarship; two books have appeared republishing earlier works — John T. Horton's *James Kent, A Study in Conservatism 1763-1847,*[69] first published in 1939, and Howard Jay Graham's *Everyman's Constituion: Historical Essays on the Fourteenth Amendment: The "Conspiracy Theory" and American Constitutionalism*[70] containing many of Graham's previously published essays; and finally, Gerald Dunne's long-awaited biography of Justice Joseph Story[71] was published, most of which has already appeared in a series of law review articles over the past seven years. Some of the recent constitutional scholarship, moreover, contains either new information or new interpretation. Herman Belz, for example, in *Reconstructing the Union: Theory & Policy During the Civil War,*[72] has written a thorough and detailed factual account of various theories of Reconstruction put forward in Congress during the course of the Civil War, while Albie Burke has written an article[73] compiling previously unknown and unavailable data about an 1871 Congressional act[74] giving federal officials power to prevent fraud in federal elections in Northern cities. Unlike much contemporaneous voting legislation, this act was not concerned with ensuring civil rights and minority voting rights, but with preventing improper voting — notably voting by unnatualized immigrants and double voting by qualified citizens.

Three other articles increase our knowledge concerning early American judicial review: the first by Leonard B. Rosenberg argues that Justice William Paterson was a committed advocate of judicial review as early as

---

[67] Donald E. Dewey, *Marshall Versus Jefferson: The Political Background of Marbury v. Madison* (1970).

[68] 5 U.S. (1 Cranch) 137 (1803).

[69] (1969).

[70] (1968).

[71] Gerald T. Dunne, *Justice Joseph Story and the Rise of the Supreme Court* (1971).

[72] (1969).

[73] Albie Burke, "Federal Regulation of Congressional Elections in Northern Cities, 1871-94, 14 *Am. J. Legal Hist.* 17 (1970).

[74] Act of Feb. 28, 1871, ch. 99, 16 Stat. 433.

the 1780's;[75] the second by Craig C. Murray[76] analyzes the opposition of Pennsylvania's Chief Justice Gibson to judicial review in the 1825 case of *Eakin v. Raub;*[77] while the third article by Gordon M. Bakken describes the counterattacks of territorial legislatures upon the jurisdiction of federally appointed judges of territorial supreme courts who had reviewed and declared territorial legislation unconstitutional.[78] Another article presents new information about James Madison's views concerning the most authoritative historical sources for a valid understanding and interpretation of the Constitution.[79] Finally, there are three worthwhile articles reinterpreting familiar materials: the first, arguing that no real popular support existed in colonial New Jersey for the colonial political leaders who were seeking to secure good behavior tenure for judges;[80] the second, maintaining that nationalists at the Constitutional Convention used southern support for the three-fifths clause as a means of weakening state financial control of the proposed federal government;[81] and the third, noting that opponents of the Alien and Sedition Acts, at the grass roots level in Kentucky, were uninterested in the theoretical constitutional questions raised by Jefferson and Madison and sought joint action by the states only for the purpose of securing Congressional repeal of the Acts.[82]

Finally, note must be taken of three books and one article presenting information of essentially local interest only: James Johnston's *Race Relations in Virginia and Miscegenation, 1776-1860;*[83] Philip Jordan's

---

[75] Leonard Rosenberg, "Constitutional Supremacy: An Early Advocate of Judicial Review," 7 *Duquesne L. Rev.* 515 (1969). His data seems unsound for the 1780's, at which time Paterson's thinking had not progressed much, if any, beyond that of James Otis during the 1760's. See 1 Bernard Bailyn, *Pamphlets of the American Revolution* 409-17 (1965). See generally Samuel E. Thorne, "Dr. Bonham's Case", 54 *L.Q.R.* 543 (1938); Gordon S. Wood, *The Creation of the American Republic, 1776 - 1787,* at 456-62 (1970). But his material on Paterson during the 1790's is convincing.

[76] Craig C. Murray, "Chief Justice Gibson of the Pennsylvania Supreme Court and Judicial Review," 32 *U. Pitt. L. Rev.* 127 (1970).

[77] 12 S. & R. 330 (Pa. 1825).

[78] Gordon Bakken, "Judical Review in the Rocky Mountain Territorial Courts," 15 *Am. J. Legal Hist.* 56 (1971).

[79] Donald E. Dewey, "James Madison Helps Clio Interpret the Constitution," 15 *Am. J. Legal Hist.* 38 (1971).

[80] Jerome J. Nadelhaft, "Politics and the Judicial Tenure Fight in Colonial New Jersey," 28 *Wm. & Mary Q.* (3d ser.) 46 (1971).

[81] Howard A. Ohline, "Republicanism and Slavery: Origin of the Three-Fifths Clause in the United States Constitution," 28 *Wm. & Mary Q.* (3d ser.) 563 (1971).

[82] James Morton Smith, "The Grass Roots Origins of the Kentucky Resolutions," 27 *Wm. & Mary Q.* (3d ser.) 221 (1970).

[83] (1970).

Frontier Law and Order: Ten Essays;[84] Paul Vanderwood's *Night Riders of Reelfoot Lake;*[85] and Henry Cohn's "Connecticut Divorce Mechanism: 1636-1969."[86] All four of these studies fail to give anything but a purely chronological or topical organization to the data offered and hence are of little interest to the general historian, but Vanderwood's book in particular is a lively, well-written account of a vigilante movement in early twentieth-century rural Tennessee.

---

[84] (1970).
[85] (1969).
[86] 14 *Am. J. Legal Hist.* 35 (1970).

Chapter Twelve

1973/74

William E. Nelson

In a provocative article entitled "The Conservative Tradition in the Writing of American Legal History,"[1] Morton Horwitz raises an issue that has permeated much of the literature of the field during the two years since the last *Survey* article was written. That issue, fundamentally, is whether rules of law at any point in time merely reflect current policy preferences of politically dominant social groups or whether law, at least in part, embodies an autonomous value structure that remains constant over all but prolonged periods of time.

The main thrust of Horwitz' article is a criticism of what he calls "lawyer's legal history."[2] Horwitz suggests that the "most characteristic mark" of this dominant form of legal history "has been an emphasis on continuity and a corresponding deemphasis of change."[3] Lawyer's legal history has assumed "that the basics of legal thought" are "governed by historically unchanging criteria."[4] Although he agrees that law is "to some extent autonomous of political and economic change,"[5] Horwitz would have legal historians deemphasize this autonomy, abandon the conservative "insistence on a radical separation between law and politics,"[6] and instead view "legal and jurisprudential change as a product of changing social forces,"[7] recognizing that all law has an "obvious political content."[8].

I

Many scholars in the past two years have not self-consciously addressed the question of law's autonomy, remaining content to pursue

[1] 17 *Am. J. Legal Hist.* 275 (1973).
[2] Id. at 276.
[3] Id. at 275-76.
[4] Id. at 278.
[5] Id. at 277.
[6] Id. at 281.
[7] Ibid.
[8] Id. at 275.

the central historical task of finding and reporting facts that subsequently can be synthesized into a comprehensive picture of the American legal past.[9] Others, however, have done synthetic and interpretative work. A review of this work leads one to doubt Horwitz' conclusion that the conservative tradition is dominant in the writing of American legal history.

---

[9] On the colonial and revolutionary periods, see Dwight Henderson, *Courts for a New Nation* (1971); Alan V. Briceland, "Ephraim Kirby: Pioneer of American Law Reporting, 1789," 16 *Am. J. Legal Hist.* 297 (1972); Charles T. Cullen, "New Light on John Marshall's Legal Education and Admission to the Bar," 16 *Am. J. Legal Hist.* 345 (1972); James W. Deen, Jr., "Patterns of Testation: Four Tidewater Counties in Colonial Virginia," 16 *Am. J. Legal Hist.* 154 (1972); David H. Flaherty, "Virginia and the Marginal Sea: An Example of History in the Law," 58 *Va. L. Rev.* 694 (1972); M. Leigh Harrison, "A Study of the Earliest Reported Decisions of the South Carolina Courts of Law," 16 *Am. J. Legal Hist.* 51 (1972); Herbert A. Johnson, "The Prerogative Court of New York, 1686-1776," 17 *Am. J. Legal Hist.* 95 (1973); Charles McKirdy, "A Bar Divided: The Lawyers of Massachusetts and the American Revolution," 16 *Am. J. Legal Hist.* 205 (1972); Hermine H. Meyer, "Constitutionality of Pretrial Detention" (pts. 1-2), 60 *Geo. L.J.* 1139, 1381 (1972); Stefan A. Riesenfeld, "Enforcement of Money Judgments in Early American History," 71 *Mich. L. Rev.* 691 (1973); Joseph H. Smith & Leo Hershkowitz, "Courts of Equity in the Province of New York: The Cosby Controversy, 1732-1736," 16 *Am. J. Legal Hist.* 1 (1972); Erwin C. Surrency, "The Court's Place in History," 43 *Penn. B.A.Q.* 440 (1972); "Comment, More Light on an Old Court: The Kent County Court, 1647-1655," 68 *Nw. U.L. Rev.* 110 (1973). On the nineteenth century, see Elizabeth Gaspar Brown, "Frontier Justice: Wayne County, 1796-1836," 16 *Am. J. Legal Hist.* 126 (1972); George M. Dennison, "Thomas Wilson Dorr: Counsel of Record in Luther v. Borden," 15 *St. Louis U.L.J.* 398 (1971); Jurij Fedynskyj, "State Session Laws in Non-English Languages: A Chapter of American Legal History," 46 *Ind. L.J.* 463 (1971); Michael H. Harris, "The Frontier Lawyer's Library: Southern Indiana, 1800-1850, as a Test Case," 16 *Am. J. Legal Hist.* 239 (1972); Raymond B. Marcin, "Nineteenth Century De Jure School Segregation in Connecticut," 45 *Conn. B.J.* 394 (1971); George L. Priest, "Law and Economic Distress: Sangamon County, Illinois, 1837-1844," 2 *J. Legal Studies* 469 (1973); John S. Schuchman, "The Political Background of the Political-Question Doctrine: The Judges and the Dorr War," 16 *Am. J. Legal Hist.* 111 (1972); Donald Senese, "Building the Pyramid: The Growth and Development of the State Court System in Antebellum South Carolina, 1800-1860," 24 *S.C.L. Rev.* 357 (1972); D. Grier Stephenson, "Chief Justice as Leader: the Case of Morrison Remick Waite," 14 *Wm. & Mary L. Rev.* 899 (1973); Erwin C. Surrency, *supra;* "Comment, The Influence of Bentham's Philosophy of Law on the Early Nineteenth Century Codification Movement in the United States," 22 *Buffalo L. Rev.* 253 (1972). In addition to these articles on the development of nineteenth century American law, a useful symposium on James Kent and Joseph Story was published in 17 *Am. L. Legal Hist.* 221 (1973). For articles on the twentieth century, see James M. Graham, "Law's Labor Lost: Judicial Politics in the Progressive Era," 1972 *Wis. L. Rev.* 447; John T. Hubbell, "The

Surely Lawrence Friedman's *A History of American Law,*[10] the most important book of the biennium, cannot be faulted from Horwitz' perspective. Friedman writes that his book is "a *social* history of American law," which "takes nothing as historical accident, nothing as autonomous, everything as relative and molded by economy and society,"[11] and his path-breaking survey of procedure, property, contract, administrative and social welfare law conforms to this pronouncement. Others, writing on narrower topics, also heed Horwitz' advice. J. Willard Hurst, for example, has continued his study of the social history of law in the United States in his most recent book,[12] whose consistent theme is the impact of "public policy"[13] upon various legal rules regulating the supply and control of money. Likewise, Nathan Levy shows how colonial courts' awareness "of the necessity of molding their laws to suit their own circumstances" led to simplification of the American law of mesne process;[14] Jonathan Lurie, how private commodity exchanges "escaped progressive regulation because they reflected much of the progressive ethos";[15] and Kermit Hall, how efforts to reform the federal judiciary during the 1850's broke down because the South feared that various reform proposals would weaken the judiciary as "the most viable mechanism for furthering . . . [its] interests."[16] Finally, Horwitz himself shows how an urge to develop the American economy in the early nineteenth century led to the rejection of many inherited rules of property law that were thought to impede such development, such as the rules of eminent domain.[17]

Desegregation of the University of Oklahoma, 1946-1950," 57 *J. Negro Hist.* 370 (1972). See also Stanley Feldstein, *The Poisoned Tongue: A Documentary History of American Racism and Prejudice* (1972); Stanley I. Kutler, *John Marshall* (1972); Cynthia Owen Philip, *Imprisoned in America: Prison Communications: 1776 to Attica* (1973), three valuable collections of articles and documentary source material.

[10] Lawrence M. Friedman, *A History of American Law* (1973).

[11] Id. at 10 (emphasis in original).

[12] J. Willard Hurst, *A Legal History of Money in the United States, 1774-1970* (1973).

[13] See id. at ix-xvii.

[14] Nathan Levy, "Mesne Process in the Early American Colonies," 44 *Miss. L.J.* 671, 686 (1973).

[15] Jonathan Lurie, "Private Associations, Internal Regulation and Progressivism: The Chicago Board of Trade, 1880-1923, as a Case Study," 16 *Am. J. Legal Hist.* 215, 237 (1972).

[16] Kermit L. Hall, "Federal Judicial Reform and Proslavery Constitutional Theory: A Retrospect on the Butler Bill," 17 *Am. J. Legal Hist.* 166, 183 (1973).

[17] Morton J. Horwitz, "The Transformation in the Conception of Property in American Law, 1780-1860," 40 *U. Chi. L. Rev.* 248 (1973). A student note suggests that the logically analogous concept of state police power was unaffected

Three local studies also detail the relationship between legal and social change. In an article on South Carolina legislation, James W. Ely reaches "some general conclusions about law and society in post-Revolutionary Carolina." He argues that the period was one of "striking continuity" rather than of "legal upheaval," and that the legal change that did occur was a product of a "sustained concern for economic enterprise."[18] Similarly, John D. W. Guice,[19] although interested primarily in proving that judges in the Rocky Mountain States made a significant contribution to the region's development, also assumes "that law is founded upon necessities of those whom it is to serve,"[20] and then shows how the necessities of the Rocky Mountain Region led to substantial modification of the inherited common law rules of mining and water law. In a like vein Kathianne Knaup demonstrates the way in which a huge influx of common-law-oriented American settlers in Missouri forced a transition from Spanish law to common law.[21]

Writers on the legal profession have also recognized the impact of social change upon the bar. Thus Alan Day attributes the increasing professionalization of the bar in late seventeenth century Maryland largely to the economic development of colonial society,[22] while Gerald Gawalt attributes the change from office study to university preparation for the law in nineteenth century Massachusetts primarily to the increasing complexity of commercial law and to the emergence of a view of law as a science.[23] Authors concerned with the influence of ideas have shown how the post-revolutionary urge for independence from English common law precedent led lawyers to work for publication of American judicial opinions,[24] and how the idealism of the early New Deal led a new

---

because of the historical accident that few police power cases arose during the period when the urge for development was strongest. Note, "Land Use Regulation and the Concept of Takings in Nineteenth Century America," 40 *U. Chi. L. Rev.* 854 (1973).

[18] James W. Ely, "American Independence and the Law: A Study of Post-Revolutionary South Carolina Legislation," 26 *Vand. L. Rev.* 939, 969-70 (1973).

[19] John D.W. Guice, *The Rocky Mountain Bench, The Territorial Supreme Courts of Colorado, Montana & Wyoming, 1861-1890* (1972).

[20] Id. at 125.

[21] Kathianne Knaup, "The Transition from Spanish Civil Law to English Common Law in Missouri," 16 *St. Louis U.L.J.* 218 (1971).

[22] Alan Day, "Lawyers in Colonial Maryland, 1660-1715," 17 *Am. J. Legal Hist.* 145, 163 (1973).

[23] Gerald Gawalt, "Massachusetts Legal Education in Transition, 1766-1840," 17 *Am. J. Legal Hist.* 27, 42 (1973).

[24] Alan V. Briceland, "Ephraim Kirby: Pioneer of American Law Reporting, 1789," 16 *Am. J. Legal Hist.* 297, 303 (1972).

generation of lawyers to abandon corporate practice for government and other public service work.[25]

As Horwitz himself recognizes, the writing of constitutional as distinguished from legal history has long "been involved in controversy over fundamental political questions concerning the nature of American society and the meaning of the American past."[26] Much of the work of the past two years continues the tradition of debating the political underpinnings of constitutional doctrine. This has been true of all time periods to which constitutional historians have turned their attention.

Some of the best work of the biennium was done by students of the revolutionary and post-revolutionary periods. William McLoughlin, for example, wrote a detailed and thorough two-volume analysis of the breakdown of the Congregational religious establishments of New England in which the theological, political and religious causes of disestablishment are all carefully integrated.[27] An article by Jon Teaford on the changing relationship between states and municipalities during the same period shows how beliefs in republicanism and majority rule led states to repeal colonial municipal charters despite arguments that they lacked power to do so,[28] while an article by Norman Rosenberg demonstrates that acceptance of notions of political conflict and legitimate political opposition turned libel and slander law into an insignificant restraint on political debate in Jacksonian America.[29] Even the late Julius Goebel on occasion viewed law as a product of social forces in *Antecedents and Beginnings to 1801*, the first volume of the Holmes devise, *History of the Supreme Court of the United States.*[30]

---

[25] Jerold S. Auerbach & Eugene Bardach, "'Born to an Era of Insecurity': Career Patterns of Law Review Editors, 1918-1941," 17 *Am. J. Legal Hist.* 3 (1973).

[26] Morton J. Horwitz, *supra* note 1, at 275.

[27] William G. McLoughlin, *New England Dissent, 1630-1833: The Baptists and the Separation of Church and State* (1971).

[28] Jon Teaford, "City versus State: The Struggle for Legal Ascendancy," 17 *Am. J. Legal Hist.* 51 (1973).

[29] Norman Rosenberg, "The Law of Political Libel and Freedom of Press in Nineteenth Century America: An Interpretation," 17 *Am. J. Legal Hist.* 336 (1973). Even some less satisfactory books viewed the constitutional law of the early nineteenth century as a product of changing social and political realities. See Francis N. Stites, *Private Interest and Public Gain: The Dartmouth College Case, 1819* (1972), in which Stites writes the first complete analysis of that case, but fails to add any new research or insights. Stites argues that the Dartmouth College decision ultimately rested upon "a conviction that the legal order should protect and promote . . . productive energy and that it should help create an environment that would increase opportunity." Id. at 100.

[30] Julius Goebel, Jr., *History of the Supreme Court of the United States: Antecedents and Beginnings to 1801* (1971).

Unfortunately, Charles Fairman did not do the same in his companion volume, *Reconstruction and Reunion, 1864-88,*[31] one of several studies covering post-Civil War constitutional development. On the other hand, relationships between politics and constitutional doctrine were considered in three articles which discussed a shift by several Supreme Court justices between the 1870's and 1880's from a broad to a narrow view of the scope of the fourteenth amendment's protection of blacks from private as well as state-imposed discrimination. John Anthony Scott argues that the shift was a result of the compromise of 1877, which led Justice Bradley and Chief Justice Waite to recognize that in return for the South's acceding to Republican political control of the nation, the North had to permit southern control of its own race relations law. Scott sees the *Civil Rights Cases* as the judicial confirmation of this compromise.[32] Michael Horan and Philip Paludan both disagree, maintaining that the genesis of the more limited view of the fourteenth amendment lay in the Jacksonian backgrounds of the laissez-faire Republicans who were the dominant force on the Court and in the nation in the 1880's. Men raised in the 1830's and 1840's, when liberty meant the absence of legal regulation and equality meant only equal non-intervention by government in the affairs of all, could not have made federal law dominant in day-to-day relations among individuals without violating their most strongly held political beliefs.[33] Another article covering the post-war period, by Carl Pierce, relates how political considerations totally unrelated to the functioning of the Supreme Court led to rejection of two of President Cleveland's nominees and finally compelled him to nominate a member of the Senate, Edward D. White, to the Court.[34] Finally, the best book on the period, Loren P. Beth's *The Development of the American Constitution, 1877-1917,*[35] details the growth of a national economy in the last third of the nineteenth century and the resultant need for responsive governmental policies — a need which led to concentration of power in the federal government, and ultimately, in

---

[31] Charles Fairman, *History of the Supreme Court of the United States: Reconstruction and Reunion, 1864-88* (pt. 1) (1971).

[32] John Anthony Scott, "Justice Bradley's Evolving Concept of the Fourteenth Amendment from the Slaughterhouse Cases to the Civil Rights Cases," 25 *Rutgers L. Rev.* 552, 565-69 (1971).

[33] Michael Horan, "Political Economy and Sociological Theory as Influences upon Judicial Policy-Making: The Civil Rights Cases of 1883," 16 *Am. J. Legal Hist.* 71 (1972); Phillip S. Paludan, "Law and the Failure of Reconstruction: The Case of Thomas Cooley," 33 *J. Hist. Ideas* 597 (1972).

[34] Carl Pierce, "A Vacancy on the Supreme Court: The Politics of Judicial Appointment, 1893-94," 39 *Tenn. L. Rev.* 555 (1972).

[35] Loren Beth, *The Development of the American Constitution, 1877-1917* (1971).

the office of president. This new entrant in the New American Nation Series "assume[s] that social and economic development, and social, economic, and political theories, are forcing beds for constitutional change,"[36] and continually details the ties between political reality and constitutional change. It can do this largely because it views "the American constitution not merely as the document written in 1787, but as the whole set of written and unwritten rules and practices which govern the way our political system operates."[37]

In comparison, another entrant in the series — Paul L. Murphy's *The Constitution in Crisis Times, 1918-1969*[38] — is disappointing. Like Beth, Murphy is concerned with "the historical and social context in which vital developments took place" and "seeks explanations as much within the value structure of the American people as in the formal record of legal adjudication and congressional action."[39] Although it usefully surveys the jurisprudence and constitutional law of the last half century, Murphy's book is little more than a rehash of the familiar events and equally familiar interpretations of the Supreme Court's aboutface during the late 1930's.[40] Nor is a second book by Murphy, *The Meaning of Freedom of Speech,*[41] vastly different from his first. Although it is a useful survey of constitutional jurisprudence on the subject of free speech during the first third of the twentieth century, and it traces carefully the links that existed between legal and political communities, it lacks any new, overarching conceptual apparatus. Far superior to these two books on twentieth century federal constitutional history are two state histories, Albert B. Saye's *A Constitutional History of Georgia, 1732-1968,*[42] and Janet Cornelius' *Constitution Making in Illinois, 1818-1970.*[43]

The most interesting application of Horwitz' prescription that historians should study law as a product of social forces is a series of four articles tracing changes in American jurisprudential thought during the nineteenth and twentieth century. The first article in the series was Horwitz' own "The Emergence of an Instrumental Conception of Ameri-

---

36 Id., at xv.

37 Ibid.

38 Paul L. Murphy, *The Constitution in Crisis Time, 1918-1969* (1972).

39 Id. at xvii.

40 Charles A. Leonard, *A Search for a Judicial Philosophy: Mr. Justice Roberts and the Constitutional Revolution of 1937* (1971), is vulnerable to the same criticism.

41 Paul L. Murphy, *The Meaning of Freedom of Speech: First Amendment Freedoms from Wilson to FDR* (1972).

42 Albert B. Saye, *A Constitutional History of Georgia, 1732-1968* (rev. ed. 1970).

43 Janet Cornelius, *Constitution Making in Illinois, 1818-1970* (1972).

can Law, 1780-1820,"[44] in which he argued that political ideas about consent as the basis of all law — ideas associated with the American Revolution — produced by the 1820's a conception that law should serve as an instrument for the advancement of felt social needs. As I have argued elsewhere, however, instrumentalism did not remain the dominant American style of judicial reasoning throughout the nineteenth century. By the end of the century a perceived need to have judicial opinions appear less overtly political had produced a new formalistic conception of law which viewed the task of the judge as the deduction of results in individual cases from autonomous ethical principles or autonomous judicial precedents.[45] Finally, Bruce A. Ackerman and G. Edward White have traced the decline of formalism during the twentieth century.[46] They detail the early years of the century in which a series of critics such as Oliver Wendell Holmes, Roscoe Pound, and Felix Frankfurter saw that "legal doctrine was basically the historical product of social conflict and political compromise" and "emphasized the need for social experiment"[47] in formulating rules of law. Ackerman and White then trace the emergence of the realist school in the 1930's in the context of what Ackerman calls a national "failure to develop a coherent social philosophy,"[48] which was related in turn to the failure of the nation as a whole to develop common political and cultural traditions. In light of these failures the realists sought "to look within themselves and. . . to understand the nonrational well-springs of their own conduct."[49] But, White continues, realisms's "relativistic approach to morals and ethics"[50] was not suited to the 1940's, after the court-packing plan of 1937 and the presence of totalitarianism in Europe had demonstrated the need for a legal order based on moral and ethical principles. What Ackerman calls the legal process school, and White, the school of reasoned elaboration, then sought to revive principle as the basis of adjudication.

---

[44] 5 *Perspectives in American History* 287 (Donald Fleming & Bernard Bailyn eds. 1971).

[45] William E. Nelson, "The Impact of the Antislavery Movement upon Styles of Judicial Reasoning in Nineteenth Century America," 87 *Harv. L. Rev.* 513 (1974).

[46] Bruce A. Ackerman, "Law and the Modern Mind," 103 *Daedalus* 119 (1973); G. Edward White, "From Sociological Jurisprudence to Realism: Jurisprudence and Social Change in Early Twentieth-Century America," 58 *Va. L. Rev.* 999 (1972); G. Edward White, "The Evolution of Reasoned Elaboration: Jurisprudential Criticism and Social Change," 59 *Va. L. Rev.* 279 (1973).

[47] Bruce A. Ackerman, *supra* note 46, at 121.

[48] Id. at 125.

[49] Id. at 122.

[50] G. Edward White, "The Evolution of Reasoned Elaboration: Jurisprudential Criticism and Social Change," 59 *Va. L. Rev.* 279, 280 (1973).

II

These four studies of jurisprudential trends during the past two centuries of American history suggest the need for further analysis of the issue raised by Horwitz' critique — whether the rules of law at any point in time merely reflect the current policy preferences of politically dominant social groups or whether law is, at least in part, the embodiment of an autonomous system of values that remains constant over all but prolonged periods of time. On the one hand, the four articles suggest that American lawyers have at times viewed law as the embodiment of an autonomous structure of values. On the other hand, as G. Edward White maintains, the articles show that jurisprudential ideas, including the idea that law is an autonomous system of values, "reflect the social needs and ideological concerns of various points in time."[51] While Horwitz thus seems correct in his view that ultimately law reflects the policy preferences of politically dominant social groups, legal historians will err if they fail to recognize that dominant groups at times in the past have understood law to be autonomous of social change and that Americans of today may have reason to adopt a similar understanding.

James McClellan argues for an autonomous view of law in *Joseph Story and the American Constitution,*[52] a book of which Horwitz is sharply critical.[53] McClellan's central hypothesis is that the American legal system traditionally has looked to natural law, a system of jurisprudence clearly autonomous of transient social and economic policy preferences, as a basis of its decisions. McClellan, however, advances this thesis in a more limited form: he does not argue that all American judges have incorporated natural law into their jurisprudence, but only that Joseph Story, clearly one of the great judges of our past, "sought to establish an ethical and moral basis for authority through the incorporation of traditional natural law principles into America's institutional framework."[54]

Although McClellan presents substantial evidence of Story's natural law beliefs, a convincing case can be made that Story was also a believer in positivism. There is evidence of Story's positivism that is quite as substantial as the evidence of his natural law beliefs. Kent Newmyer describes Story as "neither moral and idealistic, scientific and rational,

---

[51] Id. at 279.

[52] James P. McClellan, *Joseph Story and the American Constitution* (1971).

[53] See Morton J. Horwitz, *supra* note 1, at 284-93.

[54] James P. McClellan, *supra* note 52, at xii.

nor pragmatic and instrumental — [he] . . . was all of these together."[55] Horwitz thus seems correct in arguing the McClellan misconstrues Story's thought, which, like the thought of the American legal profession as a whole, is too complex to be described by a single label.

Although McClellan the historian misunderstands the subtleties of Story's thought, McClellan the jurisprude wisely argues that, in order to avoid "the intellectual and moral anarchy underlying the realist's conception of the law," it is necessary "to establish an ethical and moral basis for authority through the incorporation"[56] into American jurisprudence of at least some autonomous values. Much of the literature of the past biennium underscores the need for incorporation of such values. The need emerges most clearly in the law of race relations, where the notion that law takes its content solely from the political and economic goals of society has led to outrageous conduct by people possessing power. Some of the outrages and excesses are portrayed in Wilcomb E. Washburn's fine summary of the history of white-Indian relations[57] in which he shows that white men, fearing no restraints from moral principle, simply molded law to wipe out Indian tribes. The same picture emerges in a collection of emotionally charged photographs by Maisie and Richard Conrat[58] showing how white Americans in possession of political and military power placed 110,000 Japanese Americans in concentration camps during World War II, without justification and in total violation of American constitutional principles.[59]

But while the history of American racial and ethnic relations illustrates the need for incorporating into our jurisprudence autonomous moral values that can serve as restraints upon legal decision-making, that history fails to identify a source of such values. In view of the secular nature of twentieth-century American society, natural law is not a promising source. The value of another possible source — the language of the federal and state constitutions — is likewise diminished by its ambiguity.

---

[55] Kent Newmyer, "Justice Joseph Story, The Charles River Bridge Case, and the Crisis of Republicanism," 17 *Am. J. Legal Hist.* 232, 242 (1973).

[56] James P. McClellan, *supra* note 52, at xii.

[57] Wilcomb E. Washburn, *Red Man's Land — White Man's Law — A Study of the Past and Present Status of the American Indian* (1971). See also Manuel P. Servin, *An Awakened Minority: The Mexican Americans* (2d ed. 1974).

[58] Maisie Conrat & Richard Conrat, *Executive Order 9066: The Internment of 110,000 Japanese Americans* (1972).

[59] The same story of injustice emerges in another recent collection of photographs, this one unfortunately not as well done. Alice Dickinson, *The Sacco-Vanzetti Case, 1920-27: Commonwealth of Massachusetts vs. Nicola Sacco and Bartolomeo Vanzetti* (1972).

However, there is one form of historical scholarship, frequently practiced by both judges and professional historians and epitomizing what Horwitz has called lawyer's legal history, which seeks the meaning of ambiguous constitutional language in the intentions of its authors. During this biennium, as in the past, a number of scholars have taken this approach. Thus, Alan Scheflin determined whether juries have a right as well as a power to acquit defendants who are guilty under the law by analyzing the rights and powers of juries in the eighteenth and nineteenth centuries, the period in which constitutional provisions concerning the right to trial by jury were written.[60] But the most important works of this genre since the last *Survey* article are two recent books on impeachment by Raoul Berger and Irving Brant.[61] Analyzing essentially the same bodies of source material, they come to opposite conclusions. Brant takes the view that impeachment is limited only to offenses which are indictable in a court of law. Berger, on the other hand, is of the view that a judge or other official can be impeached for certain sorts of maladministration in office. Both base their argument essentially upon the textual language of the Constitution, upon the debates of the constitutional and ratifying conventions, and upon the English background.

Given Berger's reputation for precise and thorough scholarship one is inclined to trust him over Brant. However, a closer look at their positions suggests that resolution of the controversy cannot occur on the basis of evidence alone. The key piece of evidence was an amendment to the impeachment clause made on the floor of the Constitutional Convention. Brant describes the events leading to the amendment as follows:[62]

> . . . The clause as it came from the committee read as follows:
>
> 'He [the President] shall be removed from his office on impeachment by the House of Representatives, and conviction by the Senate, for treason, or bribery.'
>
> George Mason of Virginia promptly asked:

---

[60] Alan Scheflin, "Jury Nullification: The Right to Say No," 45 *S. Cal. L. Rev.* 168 (1972). Similarly, a student note on whether Section 1981 provides a remedy against private as well as state-abetted discrimination sought to answer the question by showing that the framers of the section meant it to embrace private discrimination. Note: "Section 1981 and Private Discrimination: An Historical Justification for a Judicial Trend," 40 *Geo. Wash. L. Rev.* 1024 (1972).

[61] Irving Brant, *Impeachment: Trials and Errors* (1972); Raoul Berger, *Impeachment: The Constitutional Problems* (1973).

[62] Irving Brant, *supra* note 61, at 18.

> 'Why is this provision restrained to treason and bribery only? Treason as defined in the Constitution will not reach many great and dangerous offenses. Hastings [governor of India, lately impeached and then awaiting trial] is not guilty of Treason. Attempts to subvert the Constitution may not be treason as above defined. As bills of attainder which have saved the British Constitution are forbidden, it is necessary to extend the power of impeachments.'
>
> Mason moved to add, after 'bribery,' the words 'or maladministration.' Elbridge Gerry seconded him.
>
> Madison objected. 'So vague a term,' he said, 'will be equivalent to a tenure during the pleasure of the Senate.' Mason gave up his attempt. He withdrew 'maladministration,' Madison recorded, and substituted 'other high crimes and misdemeanors against the State.'

He finds this ". . . conclusive proof that the term 'high crimes and misdemeanors' was not meant to be synonymous with 'maladministration.' Impeachment was to be grounded on high criminality."[63] Berger likewise concludes from this evidence "that the Framers . . . intended to confer a *limited* power."[64] But he does not find this evidence alone controlling. Berger also looks to old English precedents and finds that at common law the term "high crimes and misdemeanors" encompassed, in addition to criminal conduct, "misapplication of funds, abuse of official power, neglect of duty, encroachment on or contempts of Parliament's prerogatives."[65] For Berger it follows that, since "'high crimes and misdemeanors' had an ascertainable content at the time the Constitution was adopted, that content furnishes the boundaries of the power."[66]

Two questionable assumptions underlie Berger's analysis, however. The first is that the framers had the common law in mind when they wrote and ratified the impeachment clause. With indefatigable energy, Berger has amassed the available circumstantial evidence bearing upon this point, but the point never can be truly proved since we never can know the state of mind of all those who participated in the writing and ratification of the Constitution. Berger's second assumption is that we are bound to adhere to the framers' meaning. Although there may be special reason to adhere to any meaning that was imparted to the impeachment clause, I have suggested elsewhere that the Constitution as a whole cannot and was not expected to be binding for all time;[67] the

---

[63] Id. at 18-19.

[64] Raoul Berger, *supra* note 61, at 86.

[65] Id. at 70.

[66] Id. at 87.

[67] William E. Nelson, "Continuity and Change in Constitutional Adjudication," 78 *Yale L.J.* 500 (1969).

framers expected the Constitution to be capable of ready amendment as the needs of the nation changed. The fact that changes in the nature of politics in the early nineteenth century resulted in the breakdown of the amendment process should not lead us to conclude that the framers meant to bind us or that we are necessarily bound by decisions they made some two centuries ago.

It thus seems doubtful that resort to the intentions of the framers of constitutional or statutory language can consistently give meaning to that language sufficient to transform it into an effective restraint upon the discretion of decisionmakers. Although the need for restraints remains, the question arises whether historians can be of any help in searching for them. Historians may, in fact, be able to help by identifying those legal traditions which are an essential part of our legal culture. For if those traditions can be identified, judges and other decisionmakers, for reasons suggested below, will feel constrained to follow them in order to avoid initiating revolutionary changes in that culture.

Of course, identifying and describing our legal traditions is a difficult matter. One pitfall in searching for traditions emerges from a careful and thorough compilation of existing secondary literature in the field of church-state law by Elwyn A. Smith.[68] To one who had not read Smith's book, it would seem easy to identify religious liberty as a tradition to which Americans, except in seventeenth century Massachusetts, have always adhered. Smith, however, demonstrates that it is necessary to distinguish, for example, between mere toleration of religious dissent and a legal system in which all religious sects, and indeed, non-religious persons, are on an equal footing. In short, even in a field where the American historical record is rather clear, the search for traditions can lead to overgeneralizations and oversimplifications.

Other difficulties in searching for traditions emerge in David Flaherty's excellent study of *Privacy in Colonial New England.*[69] Flaherty sought to identify a tradition of privacy in the seventeenth and eighteenth century — a "time period . . . when so many of our contemporary values were taking shape."[70] He concluded that a concern for privacy existed throughout the colonial period, but that it grew stronger in the eighteenth century as improved material conditions and the decline of Puritanism made the practice of privacy more feasible. His evidence, however,

---

[68] Elwyn A. Smith, *Religious Liberty in the United States: The Development of Church-State Thought Since the Revolutionary Era* (1972).

[69] David H. Flaherty, *Privacy in Colonial New England* (1972). Flaherty's study grew out of a larger study of the Association of the Bar of the City of New York, which was seeking to bring "historical perspective, the logic of experience," to bear upon the problems of how best to protect privacy today, id. at vii.

[70] Id. at viii.

presented a problem. While he found such evidence as Massachusetts' statutory acceptance in 1641 of the privilege against self-incrimination to support the view that individuals were entitled to keep some facts private from the state and the community, he also found contrary indications, such as the early Puritan ideal of mutual neighborly watchfulness. Flaherty resolved this conflict only by arguing that, while a concept of privacy existed in the seventeenth century, it was often overcome by competing Puritan concepts. A potentially more fruitful approach for Flaherty might have been a comparative one. Had he taken a comparative approach, he would not have asked whether American law has been hospitable to a tradition of privacy, but rather, whether it has been more hospitable than some comparable culture, like that of Western Europe. Such comparative questions can be asked on several levels. The first is to ask how the Western legal tradition differs from legal traditions elsewhere in the world — to identify the values and principles emphasized in Western legal culture. The second is to ask how the common law tradition differs from that of other Western legal systems. Finally, one can ask how the American legal tradition differs from that of other common law jurisdictions.

Mirjan Damaska's excellent comparative study[71] that is part historical suggests that common law systems traditionally have been more concerned than those of Continental Europe with procedural protections for criminal defendants and less concerned with finding truth. Unlike attempts to identify a society's tradition in a noncomparative context, Damaska's study is careful and precise and does not ignore relevant evidence or result in overgeneralization. Unfortunately, Flaherty ignored the opportunities which a comparative approach would have offered, although in one of his most persuasive passages he took note that Indians, who simply opened closed doors and walked into houses without knocking, had to be taught New Englanders' concern for protecting privacy by knocking first.[72] He did not, however, use a comparative approach to demonstrate that New Englanders had a greater concern for privacy in the seventeenth century than did Englishmen or inhabitants of the Western world generally — an approach that would have given much more content to his ultimate conclusion that an early concern for privacy did exist.

A more explicitly comparative approach to similar data was adopted by Rennard Strickland in his analysis of the attitudes of Indians and

---

[71] Mirjan Damaska, "Evidentiary Barriers to Conviction and Two Models of Criminal Procedure: A Comparative Study," 121 *U. Pa. L. Rev.* 506 (1973).

[72] David H. Flaherty, *supra* note 69, at 88-89.

Puritans toward the wilderness.[73] Indians, according to Strickland, "viewed the world in terms of the Spirit Beings." For them, "law was simply the earthly representation of the divine spirit order."[74] For the white man, in comparison, law was an "ongoing social process [that] could . . . be manipulated to achieve policy goals," a process by which man was "able to create laws."[75] We thus learn from Strickland that however much our Puritan ancestors may have believed in God as the ultimate source of all human law, they had much greater confidence than the Indians, whom they supplanted as masters of the American continent, in their ability to master God's nature. In short, the American legal and cultural heritage, at least in comparison with that of some other peoples, has been one of mastery of the wilderness and control over nature.

Where does such comparative study lead us? As Strickland's essay on Puritans and Indians paradoxically suggests, we must recognize first that our cultural heritage assumes that man can control nature and can use law to reshape the world. Unless we can assume that we have a capacity to abandon our heritage, we must recognize that we will continue to remake our law to meet our changing needs, and hence that our law, as Horwitz urges, will continue to have political content. Comparative study, in short, does not lead to any easy implication of restraints upon lawmakers.

But comparative study can lead to a more complete understanding of relationships between seemingly discrete areas of law. The three studies to which I have referred, for example, together may tell us something basic about Anglo-American assumptions concerning the relationship of man to the world and about the common law's view of the relation of law to the individual. While Strickland, that is, tells us of the vast power which Anglo-American thought gave the individual over nature, Damaska tells us of the power which the common law gives the individual in relation to government, and Flaherty stresses the power of the individual against the community. Taken together, the three studies may thus suggest that a central assumption of Anglo-American law and thought is the exaltation of the individual. They may also suggest that to denigrate the power of the individual in one area could result in the denigration of the individual elsewhere.

Of course, this is a fundamentally conservative hypothesis. It tends to stress the interrelationships between various facets of the law and the fact

---

[73] Rennard Strickland, "Puritan, Indian, and Agrarian: A Critical Essay on the History of Law, Environmental Values, and Rhetorical Strategy," 3 *St. Mary's L. Rev.* 231 (1971).

[74] Id. at 244.

[75] Ibid.

that rejection of some legal principles felt by those in power to be socially undesirable may impair the validity of others thought to be more desirable. The hypothesis suggests, for example, that before we undergo the ecological revolution, which Strickland among others urges, and abandon our ideas about man's power over nature and his right to change nature, we must consider whether we will not be impairing the hegemony of the individual over government and the community. The hypothesis also suggests that, while the hegemony of the individual, like other basic values underlying much of the law, is a product of social choice made in the distant past, that hegemony has developed into an almost autonomous value that cannot be abandoned without revolutionary changes in American law and society.

Although it thus seems true that all legal rules are a product of policy choices which ultimately reflect the long-range preferences of politically dominant social groups, it is also true that some legal rules and traditions survive beyond the time when they serve the immediate interests of those in power. They may survive because they are related to other rules and traditions which dominant groups wish to preserve. Alternatively, the dominant groups, along with others, may adhere to longstanding traditions because they wish to preclude, or cannot even conceive of, radical alternatives to the existing legal culture of which those traditions are an important part. Other reasons could also be found. The key point, however, is that legal rules and traditions do survive beyond the period of their immediate usefulness to dominant groups and, in doing so, take on a status that is autonomous of the immediate political interests of those groups. This semi-autonomous body of law, which can and does serve as a restraint on decisionmakers, surely is a legitimate object of historical study.

Chapter Thirteen

1976

William E. Nelson

A decade ago I contributed to the *Annual Survey of American Law* my first review of the literature in the field of American legal history.[1] This year I would like to look back over the past ten with the hope of identifying at least some of the continuities and changes in the literature during that period.

Continuities in the Literature. — Many legal historians continue to concentrate on discussions of factual data in their writings about the American legal past. Some legal historians, such as Robert Mennel in *Thorns and Thistles: Juvenile Delinquents in the United States, 1825-1940,*[2] have enlarged our factual knowledge on a variety of narrow topics.[3] Others are still writing books and articles which do little other than cover familiar factual ground.[4] Such works include Alan Reitman's

---

[1] Ch. 7 *supra,* p. 113-124.

[2] Robert Mennel, *Thorns and Thistles: Juvenile Delinquents in the United States,* 1825-1940 (1973).

[3] See Ira G. Clark, "The Elephant Butte Controversy: A Chapter in the Emergence of Federal Water Law," 61 *J. Am. Hist.* 1006 (1975); David R. Colburn, "Governor Alfred E. Smith and the Red Scare, 1919-20," 88 *Pol. Sci. Q.* 423 (1973); William K. Holdsworth, "Adultery or Witchcraft? A New Note on an Old Case in Connecticut," 48 *N. Eng. Q.* 394 (1975); Ludwell H. Johnson, "The Business of War: Trading with the Enemy in English and Early American Law," 118 *Proc. Am. Phil. Soc'y* 459 (1974); David J. Langum, "Pioneer Justice on the Overland Trails," 5 *Western Hist. Q.* 421 (1974); Philip Mackey, "An All-Star Debate on Capital Punishment, Boston, 1854," 110 *Essex Inst. Hist. Coll.* 181 (1974); Gary Planck, "Lincoln's Assassination: More Forgotten Litigation—Ex parte Mudd (1868)," 75 *Lincoln Herald* 86 (1974); Jonathan Prude, "Portrait of a Civil Libertarian: The Faith and Fear of Zechariah Chafee, Jr.," 60 *J. Am. Hist.* 633 (1973); Nile Stanton, "The Presidency and the Purse: Impoundment, 1803-1973," 45 *Colo. L. Rev.* 25 (1973); H. Brauglin Taylor, "The Foreign Attachment Law and the Coming of the Revolution in North Carolina," 52 *N.C. Hist. Rev.* 20 (1975).

[4] See Henry J. Abraham, *Justices and Presidents: A Political History of Appointments to the Supreme Court* (1974); George Dargo, *Roots of the Republic: A New Perspective on Early American Constitutionalism* (1974); Michael Les Benedict, "Perserving the Constitution: The Conservative Basis of Radical Reconstruction," 61 *J. Am. Hist.* 65 (1974); G. Sidney Buchanan, "The Quest for Freedom: A Legal History of the Thirteenth Amendment," 12

book, *The Pulse of Freedom: American Liberties, 1920-1970's,*[5] which deals with the struggle for civil liberties in the United States during the past fifty years; Walter Trattner's, *From Poor Law to Welfare State: A History of Social Welfare in America,*[6] which discusses the history of the nation's social welfare system over the past three centuries; and, Milton Read's article on land tenure in colonial Georgia[7] which retells how the efforts of Georgia's trustees "to eliminate economic privilege within their model community in America"[8] resulted in their restricting the size of farms and the tenure by which they were held.

Other essentially factual writing makes a more substantial contribution. In this regard, a valuable contribution is the third volume of *North Carolina Higher-Court Records, 1702-1708,*[9] part of a series of the records of the General Court of basic common law jurisdiction, the Chancery Court, and the Admiralty Court of North Carolina. The single most important factual contribution has probably been made by Harold Hyman in *A More Perfect Union: The Impact of the Civil War and*

Houston L. Rev. 1, 331, 592, 843, 1069 (1974-75); Thomas P. Campbell, "Chancellor Kent, Chief Justice Marshall and the Steamboat Cases," 25 *Syracuse L. Rev.* 497 (1974); Paul Crawford, "A Footnote on Courts for Trial of Negroes in Colonial Pennsylvania," 5 *J. Black Stud.* 167 (1974); James C. Duram, "The Labor Union Journals and the Constitutional Issues of the New Deal: The Case for Court Restriction," 15 *Labor Hist.* 216 (1974); Walter Ehrlich, "The Origins of the Dred Scott Case," 59 *J. Negro Hist.* 132 (1974); Daniel J. Flanigan, "Criminal Procedure in Slave Trials in the Antebellum South," 40 *J. So. Hist.* 537 (1974); John J. Gibbons, "The Interdependence of Legitimacy: An Introduction to the Meaning of Separation of Powers," 5 *Seton Hall L. Rev.* 435 (1974); Jonathan Grossman, "Wage and Price Controls During the American Revolution," 96 *Monthly Labor Rev.* Sept. 1973, at 3; William Leuchtenburg, "A Klansman Joins the Court: The Appointment of Hugo L. Black," 41 *U. Chi. L. Rev.* 1 (1973); Charles R. Morgan, Hope Eastman, Mary Ellen Gale & Judith Areen, "Impeachment: An Historical Overview," 5 *Seton Hall L. Rev.* 689 (1974); Steven J. Novak, "The College in the Dartmouth College Case: A Reinterpretation," 47 *N. Eng. Q.* 550 (1974); Paul Oberst, "The Strange Career of Plessy v. Ferguson," 15 *Ariz. L. Rev.* 389 (1973); Norman K. Risjord, "Virginians and the Constitution: A Multivariant Analysis," 31 *Wm. & Mary Q.* (3d ser.) 613 (1974); David B. Roe & Russell K. Osgood, "United States Supreme Court, February Term 1824," 84 *Yale L.J.* 770 (1975); Frank R. Strong, "The Economic Philosophy of Lochner: Emergence, Embrasure and Emasculation," 15 *Ariz. L. Rev.* 419 (1973); William Van Alstyne, "A Critical Guide to Ex parte McCardle," 15 *Ariz. L. Rev.* 229 (1973).

[5] (1975).

[6] (1974).

[7] Milton Read, "Land Tenure in Trusteeship Georgia," 48 *Agric. Hist.* 353 (1974).

[8] Ibid.

[9] *North Carolina Higher Court Records, 1702-1708* (W. Price ed. 1974).

Reconstruction on the Constitution.[10] Hyman's erudition is immense; moreover, he conceives of constitutional history as including not only lawyers' law but political theory and administrative development as well. Adrian Cook's detailed study, *The Armies of the Streets: The New York City Draft Riots of 1863,*[11] is of special note for its two chapters describing the dreadful conditions of life among the poor of mid-nineteenth century New York.

Five other factually oriented books are also particularly important: Peter Fish's *The Politics of Federal Judicial Administration,*[12] which studies the Judicial Conference of the United States, the Administrative Office of the Courts, the Federal Judicial Center, and various administrative agencies at the circuit level; William H. Harbaugh's *Lawyer's Lawyer: The Life of John W. Davis,*[13] which is a thoroughly detailed study of the life, personality, and career of Davis; Robert M. Ireland's *The County Courts in Antebellum Kentucky,*[14] which contains a wealth of new information about the structure and functioning of the Kentucky county courts; R. Alton Lee's *A History of Regulatory Taxation,*[15] which is a detailed discussion of various federal taxes enacted during the last century for purposes of regulation; and William Twining's *Karl Llewellyn and the Realist Movement,*[16] which includes an introductory section of some seventy pages on the background of the realist movement.

David M. Billikopf, with his *The Exercise Of Judicial Power, 1789-1864,*[17] makes a substantial contribution to early nineteenth century constitutional history by placing largely unknown antebellum circuit and district court decisions in juxtaposition with some more widely known Supreme Court cases. George Fiedler in his general study, *The Illinois Law Courts in Three Centuries, 1673-1973: A Documentary History,*[18] presents new information on the French judicial system that existed during the first century of Illinois's history. He also discusses the jurisdictional confusion that existed between 1764, when the British assumed control of Illinois from the French, and 1790, when the mechanisms of American territorial government finally reached Illinois.

Three articles are also of interest in expanding our available factual information. One, by Robert Seddig, locates the origins of the Supreme

[10] (1973).
[11] (1974).
[12] (1973).
[13] (1973).
[14] (1972).
[15] (1973).
[16] (1973).
[17] (1973).
[18] (1973).

Court's unique role in American government in the practice developed by Chief Justice Ellsworth of disposing of cases by unanimous rather than seriatim opinions, in the special political skills of Chief Justice Marshall, and in the need of the Federalist Court to present a united front to the Jefferson administration during the years 1801-1804.[19] An article by Albert Cowdrey[20] describes how Section 13 of the Rivers and Harbors Act of 1899, which has recently become a mainstay in the federal statutory scheme of environmental protection, originated as legislation that gave the government power to prevent the obstruction of navigation without having to prove that any particular discharge had, in fact, obstructed a waterway. Steven Schlossman discusses the New York House of Refuge,[21] an institution established in 1825 as both a prison and a school, a place to "punish as well as to teach."[22]

The single most interesting factual claim was made by Harold Chesnin and Geoffrey Hazard concerning the practice of English Chancery courts in the eighteenth century.[23] Chesnin and Hazard reported that issues of fact were ordinarily referred to juries sitting at law whenever there was a substantial conflict in the evidence; they claim that it was only during the nineteenth century that "referral to a jury . . . [became] wholly discretionary and the jury verdict merely advisory."[24]

This claim has been challenged, however, by John Langbein.[25] Langbein concedes that in most cases the Chancellor did refer disputed questions of fact to juries, but contends that the Chancellor had a residual power to decide such questions by himself. It is somewhat difficult to resolve the issue drawn between Langbein, on one hand, and Chesnin and Hazard, on the other, on the basis of the evidence they present. In the few cases that Langbein cites in which the Chancellor did seem to find facts, such findings have a greater resemblance to the granting of summary judgment on a clear written record than to the weighing of credibility and probability of oral testimony in a closely

---

[19] Robert Seddig, "John Marshall and the Origins of Supreme Court Leadership," 36 *U. Pitt. L. Rev.* 785 (1975).

[20] Albert Cowdrey, "Pioneering Environmental Law: The Army Corps of Engineers and the Refuse Act," 44 *Pac. Hist. Rev.* 331 (1975).

[21] See Steven Schlossman, "Juvenile Justice in the Age of Jackson," 76 *Teach. Col. Rec.* 119 (1974).

[22] Id. at 133.

[23] See Harold Chesnin & Geoffrey Hazard, "Chancery Procedure and the Seventh Amendment: Jury Trial of Issues in Equity Cases Before 1791," 83 *Yale L.J.* 999 (1974).

[24] Id. at 1011.

[25] See John Langbein, "Fact Finding in the English Court of Chancery: A Rebuttal," 83 *Yale L.J.* 1620 (1974).

balanced case. More research is needed — research in which American legal historians should be eager to participate. If the Chesnin-Hazard position should turn out to be correct, their position could explain why the crown's program of conferring fact-finding powers on colonial equity judges, powers the Chancellor himself did not possess, seemed to be an unusually "aggressive measure"[26] to the colonials and would explain the vigorous opposition in the colonies to the equity courts.

The area in which the largest number of important factual contributions was made is that of black legal history. In her new book, *Black Resistance/White Law,*[27] Mary Berry details innumerable instances of the use of federal power, often in a quite bloody manner, to repress blacks. Three valuable articles spell out the important role that blacks played in late nineteenth century efforts to secure racial equality. First, John Hope Franklin writes of the efforts of blacks to secure enforcement of the Civil Rights Act of 1875 — efforts which failed because of doubts about the Act's constitutionality and the lukewarm attitude of federal enforcement officials.[28] The successful efforts of a black state legislator in Ohio, in conjunction with white proponents of equality, to obtain passage of an anti-lynching law in the mid 1890's were examined by David Gerber in a 1974 article.[29] Finally, Dale Somers explores the development of new equalitarian racial attitudes in New Orleans as a result of effective black leadership supported by black voters and the use of federal power during the two decades after the Civil War.[30] He notes that, although racial discrimination did persist during the period of 1865-1900, flexible racial practices arose based on day-to-day needs and demands of ordinary citizens. For at least two decades after the war, "residents from the rank and file of both races played and worked together on amicable, harmonious, even equalitarian terms."[31] Toward the end of the century, these individual practices were reversed by legislation as whites demanded and imposed racial segregation.

Another article, discussing the controversy in Kentucky between state and federal authorities concerning whether testimony of blacks should be admissible in trials, shows that even in border states federal officials

[26] See Harold Chesnin & Geoffrey Hazard, *supra* note 23, at 1019.

[27] (1971).

[28] See John Hope Franklin, "The Enforcement of the Civil Rights Act of 1875," 6 *Prologue* 225 (1974).

[29] See David Gerber, "Lynching and Law and Order: Origin and Passage of the Ohio Anti-Lynching Law of 1896," 83 *Ohio Hist.* 33 (1974).

[30] See Dale Somers, "Black and White in New Orleans: A Study in Urban Race Relations, 1865-1900," 40 *J. So. Hist.* 19, 35-38 (1974).

[31] Id. at 30.

worked hard for black equality.[32] According to its author, Victor Howard, "by January, 1869, the docket of the federal court had become largely a calender of cases tried under state law by the federal court due to the denial of equality of testimony in state courts. Besides the large number of cases that were taken directly before the federal court, many were transferred before trial and others on appeal from state courts."[33]

Despite these efforts, however, the post-Civil War drive for racial equality failed and blacks were subjected to a new system of involuntary servitude.[34] According to William Cohen,

> Far less rigid than slavery, the system of involuntary servitude that emerged after the Civil War was a fluid, flexible affair which alternated between free and forced labor in time to the rhythm of the southern labor market. Employers had the legal and social tools to compel labor from blacks, but the use of such measures was not obligatory. When labor was plentiful, Draconian powers were unneeded. When it was scarce, they were readily at hand. Thus, whites had no reason to impede black mobility except when faced with a real or anticipated shortage of hands, and the system had something of a "now you see it, now you don't" quality about it. Still, compulsion was frequent enough. Even when unused, force posed an omnipresent threat which had a pervasive effect upon the tone of the southern labor system.[35]

While several of these factually oriented articles are important, none of them is different in kind from the sort of literature that was being published a decade ago. The book which perhaps best illustrates the similarity of recent factually oriented writing to earlier writing is Carl B. Swisher's *The Taney Period, 1836-64.*[36] This volume, like the two earlier volumes in the Oliver Wendell Holmes Devise *History of the Supreme Court of the United States,*[37] is encyclopedic in its research and in its coverage of topics, but, unfortunately, does little to illuminate the significance of the past. Swisher's *The Taney Period, 1836-64*, in short, is a book that is vital as a reference source for anyone who needs information about the mid-nineteenth century Supreme Court; like most of the

---

[32] See Victor Howard, "The Black Testimony Controversy in Kentucky, 1866-1872," 58 *J. Negro Hist.* 140 (1973).

[33] Id. at 157.

[34] See William Cohen, "Negro Involuntary Servitude in the South, 1865-1940: A Preliminary Analysis," 42 *J. So. Hist.* 31 (1976).

[35] Id. at 33.

[36] (1974).

[37] See Charles Fairman, *Reconstruction and Reunion, 1864-88, Part One* (1971); Julius Goebel, Jr., *Antecedents and Beginnings to 1801* (1971).

writing of a decade ago, it is not a book that one would examine for its ideas.

Also similar to the literature of ten years ago are most of the articles surveying such matters as the methodology of legal history,[38] available source materials,[39] or the existing literature.[40] One such article, which summarizes the legal source materials that have been microfilmed by the Mormon Genealogical Society, is quite important since it indicates how historians may obtain access to the film and even gives the hours during which various Mormon libraries are open and the means by which film may be purchased.[41] While articles of this sort offer promise for the future development of the field of legal history, they are not in themselves indications that important developments have already begun to occur.

Professionalization of Legal History, — In fact, significant changes have begun to occur in the field of American legal history as a result of increasing professionalization. Professionalization is most visible, perhaps, in the pages of the *American Journal of Legal History*, in which many articles ten years ago were addressed not to academic legal historians but to practicing attorneys. In the last two years, however, the *Journal* has become a publication in which academic historians speak to each other. Since virtually every one of the many articles in the *Journal* has become essential reading for those wishing to keep current in the field, I have not included them in this review. The professionlization of the *Journal* has not been a unique development, but has been paralleled by the creation of a legal history series by the Harvard University Press — a series which has published two monographs in the past two years.[42]

---

[38] See, e.g. Graham Parker, "The Masochism of the Legal Historian," 24 *U. Toronto L.J.* 279 (1974); Hiller B. Zobel, "The Joys and Uses of Legal History," 84 *Mass. Hist. Soc'y Proc.* 53 (1972).

[39] See, e.g., Gloria I. Main, "Probate Records As a Source for Early American History," 32 *Wm. & Mary Q.* (3d ser.) 89 (1975); Daniel Smith, "Underregistration and Bias in Probate Records: An Analysis of Data from Eighteenth-Century Hingham, Massachusetts," 32 *Wm. & Mary Q.* (3d ser.) 100 (1975).

[40] See Wythe Holt, "Now and Then: The Uncertain State of Nineteenth-Century American Legal History," 7 *Ind. L. Rev.* 615 (1974); Marvin Laurence Winitsky, "Roger B. Taney: A Historiographical Inquiry," 69 *Md. Hist. Mag.* 1 (1974).

[41] Larry R. Gerlach & Michael L. Nicholls, "The Mormon Genealogical Society and Research Opportunities in Early American History," 32 *Wm. & Mary Q.* (3d ser.) 625 (1975).

[42] See George M. Dargo, *Jefferson's Louisiana: Politics and the Clash of Legal Traditions* (1975); William E. Nelson, *Americanization of the Common Law: The Impact of Legal Change on Massachusetts Society, 1760-1830* (1975).

The appearance of a professionally oriented body of literature is a central element in the emergence of any genuine profession.[43]

Signs of professionalization can also be seen in the methodological literature of the past two years. Several methodological articles make a point, not generally accepted when I made it in these pages ten years ago,[44] that we cannot resolve current legal questions by asking how the past intended us to resolve them when the past never asked the question which concerns us and therefore left no answer.[45] William Wiecek recognizes the power of this truism in his book *The Guarantee Clause of the U.S. Constitution.*[46] Wiecek devotes relatively few pages to an analysis of the intentions of the Constitution's framers, but instead concentrates on how the Guarantee Clause has evolved over time.

Those articles which do seek to examine "the original intent"[47] — and they are far fewer in number than they were a decade ago — do so with considerable sensitivity and with an explicit recognition of the limits of their analysis. Charles Wolfram, for example, in an excellent article on "The Constitutional History of the Seventh Amendment,"[48] recognizes that we cannot answer with certainty whether the framers intended juries always to be unanimous bodies of twelve men, but argues that we can be quite certain that "[j]uries were sought to be thrust into cases to effect a result different from that likely to be obtained by an honest judge sitting without a jury."[49] Similarly Charles Lofgren, while recognizing that "the original understanding"[50] cannot always bind the present, maintains that the founding fathers expected that compulsory military service would be required only in the militia and purposely provided the federal government with sufficient means of raising revenue so that it could recruit the regular army voluntarily and thereby avoid conscription. Finally, Arthur Bestor quite rightly concludes that the Constitution's framers did not

---

[43] See Thomas Kuhn, *The Structure of Scientific Revolutions* 19-21 (2d ed. 1970).

[44] See ch. 7, *supra*, at 118-124.

[45] See Robert J. Kaczorowski, "Searching for the Intent of the Framers of the Fourteenth Amendment," 5 *Conn. L. Rev.* 368 (1972-73); Arthur Selwyn Miller, "An Inquiry into the Relevance of the Intentions of the Founding Fathers, with Special Emphasis Upon the Doctrine of Separation of Powers," 27 *Ark. L. Rev.* 583 (1973).

[46] (1972).

[47] Arthur Bestor, "Separation of Powers in the Domain of Foreign Affairs: The Original Intent of the Constitution Historically Examined," 5 *Seton Hall L. Rev.* 527 (1974).

[48] 57 *Minn. L. Rev.* 639 (1973).

[49] Id. at 653.

[50] Charles Lofgren, "Compulsory Military Service under the Constitution: The Original Understanding," 33 *Wm. & Mary Q.* (3d ser.) 61 (1976).

believe in a rigid application of the doctrine of separation of powers, but instead intended to have the branches of government checking and balancing each other by participating in various governmental functions.[51] What is implicit even in the articles that do search for original intent is an assumption that the past was not the same as the present, that people in the past did not see issues in the same light as we do in the present, and hence that the past can never yield precise, binding answers to the problems of the present.

This assumption about the essential difference between the past and the present is, of course, axiomatic for practicing historians, who generally seek not to instruct us about the answers to present problems but to explain the processes of historical evolution and the reasons for particular historical changes. Legal historians have begun to do the same. In *Jefferson's Louisiana: Politics and the Clash of Legal Traditions,*[52] George Dargo traces the evolution of American law and government in Louisiana during the first decade of the nineteenth century. Dargo explains that the American takeover of Louisiana in 1803 led to a conscious attempt to impose American culture and law on the area in order to replace the indigenous Franco-Spanish system. When many American newcomers in Louisiana sympathized with the Burr Conspiracy in 1805-07, however, the territorial administration forged an alliance with the old French settlers; Louisiana's adherence to the civil law is a product of that alliance.

In another book, *Free Men All: The Personal Liberty Laws of the North, 1780-1861,*[53] Thomas Morris brilliantly traces the gradual polarization of ideological positions in the mid-nineteenth century on the issue of fugitive slaves, with the result that room for compromise between North and South became increasingly limited. In his study of sexual morality and social control, David Pivar argues that a basic transformation in American attitudes toward power occurred between the late eighteenth and late nineteenth century.[54] He notes that the framers of American constitutions in the late eighteenth century harbored a healthy fear of all governmental power and sought to restrain its use. By the end of the nineteenth century, however, Americans were willing to use power as long as it was directed to the attainment of legitimate social goals. His argument suggests that restraints were imposed on governmental economic intervention in the late 19th century not because of any fear of

---

[51] See Arthur Bestor, *supra* note 47.

[52] See George M. Dargo, *supra* note 42.

[53] (1974).

[54] David Pivar, *Purity Crusade: Sexual Morality and Social Control, 1868 -1900* (1973).

governmental power in general, but because of a fear that power would be used for illegitimate ends, such as taking property from one individual and giving it to another. When government could intervene in the economy without redistributing wealth, however, its intervention was tolerated.

There are also some noteworthy articles which seek to explain important historical changes. One, which traces Indian-white legal relations in seventeenth century Plymouth, notes that in the 1620's Indians were treated fairly and punished equally to whites even though ethnocentric English attitudes required that English courts resolve disputes between English settlers and Indians.[55] After King Philip's War, however, many Indians were enslaved and "considerations of protection for Indian rights were ignored."[56] In another article, one of the best of the last two years, Lance Banning asks the important question why the federal constitution, to which so much opposition existed in 1787-1789, gained such quick acceptance that by the early 1790's opposition had largely disappeared.[57] Banning's answer rests upon his claim that a main element of eighteenth century thought was the fear of constitutional degeneration — a fear which resulted in an instinctive unwillingness to alter constitutional provisions once they had been written. Among the signs of corruption and degeneration to which the eighteenth century was attuned were an ambitious executive, a standing army, rising taxes, public debts, and chartered corporations. Republicans saw in Hamilton's program, which contained all these measures together with the broad construction and the social elitism of Hamiltonian Federalists, the beginnings of constitutional subversion:

> But opposition to the progress of social and political corruption traditionally required an ancient constitution against which it could measure the degeneration of the present day. A critique of constitutional corruption needed an accepted constitution that could be seen to undergo a process of decay. . . . Paradoxically, then, it was the appearance of a deeply felt opposition to the policies of our first administration which assured the quick acceptance of the Constitution. . . .[58]

Another sign of increasing professionalization among legal historians is the recognition by recent writers of one of the special powers of

---

[55] James P. Ronda, "Red and White at the Bench: Indians and the Law in Plymouth Colony, 1620-1691," 110 *Essex Inst. Hist. Coll.* 200 (1974).

[56] Id. at 213.

[57] Lance M. Banning, "Republican Ideology and the Triumph of the Constitution, 1789 to 1793," 31 *Wm. & Mary Q.* (3d ser.) 167 (1974).

[58] Id. at 187.

historical analysis — the capacity of a good historian to place two seemingly discrete events in juxtaposition and thereby understand both events more fully. Few legal historians engaged in this process of juxtaposition a decade ago, but many have in the past two years. Robert Stevens, for example, has urged that legal developments in the United States can often be better understood if they are viewed in juxtaposition with developments in England.[59] In particular, he notes that anti-lawyer sentiment in early Massachusetts was little different from anti-lawyer sentiment in Civil War England and that changes in post-Civil War England and changes in post-Revolutionary American law were part of a broader late eighteenth and early nineteenth century process of modernization of the common law. George Haskins,[60] agreeing with Stevens, has argued that Massachusetts did not become a Bible Commonwealth because

> [the settlers] remained, in their respective circumstances and backgrounds, Englishmen of their time. They brought with them outlooks and social attitudes which not only reflected contemporary England but much of the legacy and humanism of the Renaissance. Thus, except insofar as their daily life and intellectual tastes were affected by Puritan principles, and their institutions necessarily molded by the same driving concerns for which the colonial enterprise had been undertaken, they remained basically English in their outlooks, habits and understanding.[61]

Employing similar comparative modes of analysis, Scott Powe has urged that the activist role pursued by the Supreme Court from the 1890's to the 1930's under the rubric of due process can be properly understood only against the background of the Court's earlier activist role in some two hundred municipal bond cases decided between 1865 and 1890;[62] Russell Wheeler has concluded that the rejection by early federal judges of the English and colonial model permitting judges to perform a wide variety of extrajudicial functions can be understood only in conjunction with the simultaneous development of the ideal of the rule of law;[63] Jonathan Lurie has maintained that nineteenth century private

---

59 See Robert B. Stevens, "Unexplored Avenues in Comparative Anglo-American Legal History," 48 *Tulane L. Rev.* 1086 (1974).

60 See George L. Haskins, "Representative Government and the 'Bible Commonwealth' in Early Massachusetts," 9 *Akron L. Rev.* 207 (1975).

61 Id. at 216.

62 L. Scott Powe, "Rehearsal for Substantive Due Process: The Municipal Bond Cases," 53 *Texas L. Rev.* 738 (1975).

63 Russell Wheeler, "Extrajudicial Activities of the Early Supreme Court," [1973] *Sup. Ct. Rev.* 123.

commodities exchanges can be usefully analyzed as legal analogs of twentieth century administrative agencies;[64] and Milton Klein has suggested that the role of lawyers in the coming of the American Revolution was parallel to the role which Arthur Schlesinger, Sr. thought was played by merchants.[65]

The two items that use the process of juxtaposition to reach the most interesting conclusions are a book on witchcraft in Salem and an article on the jurisprudence of Justice Holmes. In *Salem Possessed: The Social Origins of Witchcraft,*[66] Paul Boyer and Stephen Nissenbaum seek to explain how the terror of witchcraft in Salem occurred. They relate it to the breakdown of a theocratically oriented society which was trying to maintain itself against the onslaught of liberal capitalism. Their position is that the farmers of Salem Village were seeking to maintain a sort of utopian community safe from the pollutions of the material world — pollutions which, like all other sin, were both evil and attractive. The farmers reacted to liberal capitalism by viewing it the same way they viewed other sin, and they punished those committing the sin with the extreme punishment of death. Only when the sin failed to go away did the villagers cease their attempt to construct a heaven on earth, turn to the next world for their solace, and thereby permit a liberal legal order to emerge in this world.

Likewise, the author of a student note, "Holmes, Peirce and Legal Pragmatism,"[67] in searching for the source of Holmes's "theory of external legal standards"[68] and his "attack, implicit throughout *The Common Law*, on the notion that private, internal standards can serve as a basis of legal liability,"[69] turns to the philosophy of Charles Peirce, a close associate of Holmes in the late 1860's. The note maintains that "Holmes's recognition that only public standards can function as legal rules is paralleled in Charles Peirce's attack on the epistemology of Rene Descartes."[70] The author continues that "Peirce sought to replace Descartes's reliance on the 'natural light' of immediate intuition of clear and distinct ideas with the process of a community of inquirers reaching agreement through application of public and accepted methods of re-

---

64 Jonathan Lurie, "Commodities Exchanges as Self-Regulating Organizations in the Late 19th Century: Some Perimeters in the History of American Administrative Law," 28 *Rutgers. L. Rev.* 1107 (1975).

65 See Milton M. Klein, "New York Lawyers and the Coming of the American Revolution," 55 *N.Y. Hist.* 383 (1974).

66 (1974).

67 Note, "Holmes, Peirce and Legal Pragmatism," 84 *Yale L.J.* 1123 (1975).

68 Id. at 1129.

69 Ibid.

70 Id. at 1130.

search."[71] This juxtaposition of Holmes and Peirce is especially important for what it suggests about a more general inquiry into post-Civil War historiography — an inquiry into the reasons for the rejection throughout American society of private moral intuitions as standards of conduct.[72]

Legal History as Philosophy. — As the literature reviewed in the past several paragraphs suggests, the growing professionalization in the field of American legal history is extremely valuable for the new insights it can yield into the nature of our legal past. Yet professionalization can also have its costs, one of which can be the withdrawal of history and its practitioners from the needs and concerns of the society in which we live today. Fortunately, however, at least some legal historians are not withdrawing into purely academic areas, but are instead directing their research and writing toward important current questions. These legal historians are attempting to write history as a form of political philosophy.

Two broad groups of philosophically oriented historians can be identified within the writing of the past two years. The first group consists of several radical critics of the existing legal order who attempt to show that the existing structure of legal thought and legal doctrine has or necessarily must oppress the weak and the poor. Jerold Auerbach, for example, has written a highly political essay in Alan Reitman's book, *The Pulse of Freedom.*[73] Auerbach's essay, entitled "The Depression Decade,"[74] argues that "the prototypical Depression victim of civil liberties infractions was an industrial worker, a union organizer, or a radical critic of capitalism."[75] This approach, however, is an unduly narrow one. While labor made an important contribution to civil liberties in the 1930's, one cannot ignore the contribution of other groups such as artists and blacks simply because such groups do not readily fit into a Marxist view of history. Auerbach's political view of history is, in short, distorted.

Similarly, Mary Berry[76] tries to argue that since federal power has often been used to repress blacks, the Constitution was formulated for the purpose of repression. She labels American constitutional law as "a

---

[71] Id. at 1131.

[72] See William E. Nelson, "Officeholding and Powerwielding: An Analysis of the Relationship Between Structure and Style in American Administrative History," 10 *L. & Soc'y Rev.* 187, 220-31 (1976); William E. Nelson, "The Impact of the Antislavery Movement Upon Styles of Judicial Reasoning in Nineteenth Century America," 87 *Harv. L. Rev.* 513, 547-66 (1974).

[73] Alan Reitman, *supra* note 5.

[74] Jerold Auerbach, "The Depression Decade," in Alan Reitman, *supra* note 5, at 65.

[75] Ibid.

[76] See Mary Berry, *supra* note 27.

handy philosophical tool for maintaining white superiority,"[77] since it is based on "essentially racist, not legal, concerns."[78] Unfortunately, Professor Berry has exaggerated her argument, failing to separate out historical cause from historical consequence.

Far more sophisticated are the writings of Morton Horwitz and Joel Brenner. In his outstanding essay, "The Historical Foundations of Modern Contract Law,"[79] Horwitz's main theme is that the modern "will theory of contract,"[80] which arose in the late eighteenth and early nineteenth century, necessarily favors capitalist entrepreneurs at the expense of the weak, the unsophisticated and the poor. To the extent that Horwitz limits his analysis to a discussion of the effects of the will theory, the position is a plausible one, for our modern experience suggests that the doctrine of freedom of contract does benefit the strong at the expense of the weak. Unfortunately, he occasionally weakens his thesis by arguing that contract law was purposely formulated to produce repressive results. This claim is much less plausible in view of the social fragmentation or mobility that existed in early nineteenth century America. That fragmentation and mobility, coupled with contemporary awareness of those phenomena, would have made it difficult for members of the small elite that Horwitz believes to have benefited from a will theory of contract to have identified each other and conspired to put that theory into practice. Nonetheless, Horwitz's article, which is part of a forthcoming book, is a powerful and important attempt to understand nineteenth century legal development from a viewpoint that is relevant to current legal concerns.

A not dissimilar article by Joel Brenner on "Nuisance Law and the Industrial Revolution"[81] asks why the common law of nuisance did not stand in the path of industrial development in nineteenth century England. Unfortunately, however, Brenner makes inconsistent claims in his attempt to decide whether judges who were seeking to promote the interests of the entrepreneurial class consciously changed nuisance law to attain that end or whether the structure of nuisance law itself, which had always "had a zoning function . . . of allocating activities to appropriate areas,"[82] merely permitted the development of industrial zones once the economy placed a demand on society for them.

---

[77] Id. at 1.

[78] Id. at ix.

[79] Morton J. Horwitz, "The Historical Foundations of Modern Contract Law," 87 *Harv. L. Rev.* 917 (1974).

[80] Id. at 936.

[81] Joel Brenner, "Nuisance Law and the Industrial Revolution," 3 *J. Legal Studies* 403 (1974).

[82] Id. at 406.

Robert Cover, like Horwitz and Brenner, also makes use of history to address current questions about the apparently repressive nature of law. The central object of his book, *Justice Accused: Antislavery and the Judicial Process,*[83] is to explain how judges were able to reject moral claims for freedom that were advanced on the part of slaves between the Revolution and the Civil War. Much of the book consists of an analysis of the formal assumptions of the judiciary — primarily the assumption that judges ought not to engage in lawmaking as an act of will — and of the moral underpinnings of those assumptions. Cover thereby shows that the choices which judges confronted in slavery cases, like most judicial choices, involved a complex conflict of competing moralities. In effect, Cover, like Auerbach, Berry, Horwitz and Brenner, is studying how instruments of oppression grow out of law which is designed as a rational tool for the attainment of desired social ends. Unlike the others, however, he recognizes that law often oppresses some in the interest of the good of others.

Two older historians — Grant Gilmore and Willard Hurst — write from a different, but equally powerful perspective. Essentially, Gilmore and Hurst reject the idea that law can be rationally designed to accomplish any end. In a recent lecture, "Thoreau, Conscience and Law,"[84] Hurst made the argument that law should never be understood as a rational process of moral choice but must be viewed instead as a process of compromising conflicting social interests. He does not appear to have found American law repressive in the past, at least when it has been made in a democratic legislative process. Since Hurst sees hope only in democratic lawmaking, he urges that the duty of the courts must be the improvement of the legislative processes through mechanisms such as reapportionment and the encouragement of free expression and association and not the articulation of fixed, morally derived doctrine.

Similarly, Grant Gilmore in a recent lecture, "The Age of Anxiety,"[85] argues "that it is not possible to make a scientific statement about . . . law,"[86] because "law is always an instinctive response to disorder, never a reasoned approach to the quite different problem of achieving order."[87] Gilmore's attitude also leads to the conclusion that we will get our best results by leaving lawmaking to the political process rather than in the hands of professionals striving to develop a scientific statement of the law.

---

[83] (1975).

[84] 19 *S.D.L. Rev.* 1 (1974).

[85] 84 *Yale L.J.* 1022 (1975).

[86] Id. at 1041.

[87] Id. at 1044.

An article on late nineteenth century railroad regulation[88] leads me, at least, to be wary of law that is hammered out in the political process. Its author, Albo Martin, summarizes recent work on railroad regulation and concludes that the Interstate Commerce Act of 1887 advanced no rational program of regulation and served little real purpose. He writes:

> What the nation required in 1887 was a body which could proceed to cartelize the railroads; but the acts of 1887 and 1890 were a bundle of contradictory compromises which prohibited every kind of concerted action the railroads had tried up to that time. In determining the outcome of the bumbling efforts to establish meaningful federal regulation, the practical desire for a stable rate structure was less important than the deep-seated mistrust, hatred, and fear of large, insulated aggregations of power. This attitude has always rested at the heart of American egalitarianism. . . . A new kind of power, in many ways more pervasive than political power, had emerged by the 1870s. If they could prevent it, Americans were not going to allow great concentrations of economic power to continue. . . . [T]he people certainly were not going to lend the support of the state to the creation and perpetuation of such power. . . . Most Americans who had to deal with the railroad problem knew the price, in dollars and cents, of a continuation of destructive competition, but they were willing, in fact insisted on being allowed, to pay the price. Railroad men themselves sensed this opposition and some, like the testy A.B. Stickney, opposed pooling. . . .
>
> Even so, railroads were "cartelized." Consolidation, which railroad men had warned against throughout the last third of the nineteenth century, was the inevitable alternative to pooling. It became a reality by the first decade of the twentieth century. By 1906 the major railroads were neatly packaged into some six or seven systems. This process had begun in earnest with the passage of the Act of 1887. . . .[89]

Martin's study of railroad regulation makes it plain, in short, that Americans must engage in rational legal ordering to avoid legal chaos and social waste. In returning to rationality, we must, of course, keep in mind the writings of critics such as Robert Cover and Morton Horwitz, who properly remind us of the repressive effects that rational legal schemes can have. But their emphasis upon the occasional repressive effects of the law must not cause us to ignore the law's accomplishments over the long course of American history. Although the few legal historians who have abandoned purely professional concerns and evalu-

---

[88] Albro Martin, "The Troubled Subject of Railroad Regulation in the Gilded Age: A Reappraisal," 61 *J. Am. Hist.* 339 (1974).

[89] Id. at 370-71.

ated our legal traditions during the past two years have been rather critical of them, their critical approach is not an inevitable one. History can also fulfill the function of identifying the legal traditions that we still value and linking them with the social conditions that underlie them. In the coming years, perhaps, legal history will begin to do so.

Chapter Fourteen

1978

William E. Nelson

Since the publication of the last "Legal and Constitutional History" survey two years ago,[1] the field has seen an extraordinary outpouring of significant literature. In part, the literature was a product of the bicentennial celebration. The *University of Pennsylvania Law Review,*[2] the *Virginia Law Review,*[3] the *De Paul Law Review,*[4] and even the *Public Contract Law Journal*[5] published bicentennial issues, each of which

---

[1] Ch. 13 *supra,* p. 201-217.

[2] Barbara A. Black, "The Constitution of Empire: The Case for the Colonists," 124 *U. Pa. L. Rev.* 1157 (1976); Herbert A. Johnson, "John Jay: Lawyer in a Time of Transition, 1764-1775," 124 *U. Pa. L. Rev.* 1260 (1976); Joseph H. Smith, "An Independent Judiciary: The Colonial Background," 124 *U. Pa. L. Rev.* 1104 (1976); William F. Swindler, "'Rights of Englishmen' Since 1776: Some Anglo-American Notes," 124 *U. Pa. L. Rev.* 1083 (1976); G. Edward White, "The Path of American Jurisprudence," 124 *U. Pa. L. Rev.* 1212 (1976).

[3] Julian P. Boyd, "On the Need for 'Frequent Recurrence to Fundamental Principles,'" 62 *Va. L. Rev.* 859 (1976); Peter Gay, "America the Paradoxical," 62 *Va. L. Rev.* 843 (1976); James E. Herget, "The Missing Power of Local Governments: A Divergence Between Text and Practice in Our Early State Constitutions," 62 *Va. L. Rev.* 999 (1976); James H. Kettner, "Subjects or Citizens? A Note on the British Views Respecting the Legal Effects of American Independence," 62 *Va. L. Rev.* 945 (1976); Dennis R. Nolan, "The Effect of the Revolution on the Bar: The Maryland Experience," 62 *Va. L. Rev.* 969 (1976); G. Edward White, "Foreward: Placing the American Revolution," 62 *Va. L. Rev.* 839 (1976).

[4] L. Edward Allemand, "Two European Influences on the American Revolution: Puritanism and John Locke," 25 *De Paul L. Rev.* 805 (1976); George B. Curtis, "The Checkered Career of *Parens Patriae:* The State as Parent or Tyrant," 25 *De Paul L. Rev.* 895 (1976); Terrence F. Kiely, "The Hollow Words: An Experiment in Legal Historical Method as Applied to the Institution of Slavery," 25 *De Paul L. Rev.* 842 (1976); R. Kent Newmyer, "Justice Joseph Story's Doctrine of 'Public and Private Corporations' and the Rise of the American Business Corporation," 25 *De Paul L. Rev.* 825 (1976).

[5] B. Alan Dickson, "Some Comments on Procurement Law in the Confederacy," 8 *Pub. Cont. L.J.* 191 (1976); James V. Joy, Jr., "Connecticut's Merchant Governor: Washington's Major Provisioner," 8 *Pub. Cont. L.J.* 129 (1976); James V. Joy, Jr., "Eli Whitney's Contracts for Muskets," 8 *Pub. Cont. L.J.* 140 (1976); Robert S. Moss & Paul H. Gantt, "A Steam Engine and Contract Termination Settlement Procedures," 8 *Pub. Cont. L.J.* 188 (1976);

contained several historical studies. In addition, the *Law and Society Review* published a two-issue *Festschrift* in honor of the retirement of the preeminent legal historian of the last three decades, James Willard Hurst.[6] These special issues, together with the volumes of the *American Journal of Legal History* that have been published during the past two years,[7] contain extensive and important periodical literature to which many major figures in the field have contributed. Individual comment upon the articles is impossible; all that can be said is that most of them deserve examination by any scholar seeking to remain current in the field.

The bicentennial also spawned two books on legal history. One is entitled *Milestones! 200 Years of American Law: Milestones in Our Legal History,* by Jethro K. Lieberman.[8] Although "written for the general reader,"[9] the book is surprisingly well researched. The author is well versed both in details of his subject matter and in the recent scholary literature in the field. The other book, *The Sheriff's Jury and the Bicentennial*, is a collection of essays edited by Joseph T.P. Sullivan;[10] they are of somewhat more mixed quality.

Perhaps the most significant event of the past two years was the award of a Bancroft Prize to Morton J. Horwitz for *The Transformation*

Austin G. Roe, "Lincoln: The First Board of Contract Appeals," 8 *Pub. Cont. L.J.* 179 (1976); Rudolf Sobernheim, "Contracts for the Highway Transportation of the Mails," 8 *Pub. Cont. L.J.* 157 (1976); Richard C. Solibakke, "The First Successful Government Contract for 'One (1) Heavier-Than-Air Flying Machine,'" 8 *Pub. Cont. L.J.* 195 (1976); F. Trowbrige Vom Baur, "The Origin of the Changes Clause in Naval Procurement," 8 *Pub. Cont. L.J.* 175 (1976); John H. Whelan & Steven B. Mains, "'Cost Plus' or 'I May Be a Robber But I'm Not a Thief,'" 8 *Pub. Cont. L.J.* 210 (1976).

[6] Lawrence M. Friedman & Robert V. Percival, "A Tale of Two Courts: Litigation in Alameda and San Benito Counties," 10 *Law & Soc'y Rev.* 267 (1976); Robert W. Gordon, "Introduction: J. Willard Hurst and the Common Law Tradition in American Legal Historiography," 10 *Law & Soc'y Rev.* 9 (1975); Mark S. Haller, "Historical Roots of Police Behavior: Chicago, 1890-1925," 10 *Law & Soc'y Rev.* 303 (1976); Charles McCurdy, "Stephen J. Field and Public Land Law Development in California, 1850-1866: A Case Study of Judicial Resource Allocation in Nineteenth-Century America," 10 *Law & Soc'y Rev.* 235 (1976); William E. Nelson, "Officeholding and Powerwielding: An Analysis of the Relationship Between Structure and Style in American Administrative History," 10 *Law & Soc'y Rev.* 187 (1976); Harry N. Scheiber, "Federalism and the American Economic Order, 1789-1910," 10 *Law & Soc'y Rev.* 57 (1975); Mark Tushnet, "The American Law of Slavery, 1810-1860: A Study in the Persistence of Legal Autonomy," 10 *Law & Soc'y Rev.* 119 (1975).

[7] 20 *Am. J. Legal Hist.* (1976); 21 *Am. J. Legal Hist.* (1977).

[8] (1976).

[9] Id. at xvii.

[10] (1977).

of American Law, 1780-1860.[11] Horwitz's *The Transformation of American Law* is a significant book.[12] It is a pioneering effort in its detailed analysis of doctrinal change in important areas of private substantive law in the early nineteenth century. More importantly, it demonstrates beyond doubt that there was a cohesive body of American law in the early nineteenth century;[13] that is, on most important issues, the law of the different states developed in parallel rather than divergent directions. Finally, the book constitutes a systematic attempt to relate legal change to social change — an attempt to which legal historians will be reacting for years to come. At this early date, it can be said that *The Transformation of American Law* is without doubt the most sophisticated and subtle Marxist analysis of Anglo-American legal history that has yet appeared.[14]

Horwitz's was not the only book during the two-year period that was written from an essentially Marxist perspective. Another important book — clearly the most controversial of the past two years — was Jerold S. Auerbach's *Unequal Justice: Lawyers and Social Change in Modern America.*[15] Auerbach, who states that he is not writing "a comprehensive history of the entire legal profession," but only a history of "the response of the professional elite" that dominated major law firms and controlled bar associations,[16] is clearly correct in taking note of the economic and ethnic prejudices among elite lawyers that persisted into the 1960's. The controversy about his book develops when he moves beyond his narrowly defined class of the professional elite to argue that bias in the legal profession as a whole "has had particularly serious consequences in a society that depends so heavily upon the legal profession to implement the principle of equal justice under law."[17] I do not believe that any reader will deny the existence of inequality and bias throughout much of American society, or that there were and are lawyers who share such

[11] (1977).

[12] See, e.g. Eugene Genovese, "Book Review," 91 *Harv. L. Rev.* 726 (1978); J. Willard Hurst, "Book Review," 21 *Am. J. Legal Hist.* 175 (1977); Stephen B. Presser, "Book Review: Revising the Conservative Tradition: Towards a New American Legal History," 52 *N.Y.U.L. Rev.* 700 (1977).

[13] Cf. Theodore F.T. Plucknett, "Book Review," 3 *New Engl. Q.* 156 (1930) (reviewing a republication of a 1648 edition of Massachusetts laws), in which the author assumed that the laws of different states were developed independently in the 17th century.

[14] Some readers have not been persuaded, however, by Horwitz's essentially Marxist approach. See, e.g., John Phillip Reid, "Book Review: A Plot Too Doctrinaire," 55 *Tex. L. Rev.* 1307 (1977); John E. Crowley, "Book Review," 35 *Wm. & Mary Q.* (3d ser.) 562-564 (1978).

[15] (1976).

[16] Id. at 9.

[17] Id. at 10.

social bias. Auerbach, however, seems to deny the existence of another segment of the profession, which has not shared the same bias — a corps of elite reformers, such as Louis Brandeis, Felix Frankfurter, Thurgood Marshall, and Earl Warren, who have had a profound impact upon American society. It is this apparent denial, I suspect, that has been at the root of the controversy about *Unequal Justice*.

A third piece written from a Marxist perspective is Sidney L. Harring's study of "Class Conflict and the Suppression of Tramps in Buffalo, 1892-1894."[18] In an interesting and professional way, Harring supports obvious Marxist points such as: "the police are not neutral in the class struggle, but rather are an instrument of ruling class domination."[19] But Harring, like Auerbach, fails to document some significant claims. I had always assumed that the police were controlled by a governmental apparatus that in the late nineteenth century was, in turn, under "bourgeois" control.[20] What Harring fails to do — indeed, what Marxist analysis is incapable of doing — is to ask questions such as why the working class frightened the bourgeoisie more in the 1890's than at other times in American history, and why the working class failed to turn to violence to redress its grievances.

The great bulk of legal history literature of the past two years, however, was not written from a Marxist perspective. Many writers took questions of intergroup conflict seriously, but their approach was often far removed from a Marxist one. For example, in a recent lecture, Lawrence M. Friedman agreed with Sidney L. Harring that there is "a clear connection between the goals of society's leaders and the goals of their system of criminal justice."[21] But he then continued: "American society has been unusually broad-based for centuries, and it has gotten steadily more democratic, whatever its failings and faults."[22] Friedman contended that increasing democratic participation in law-making and enforcement has produced a "puritanical" criminal code under which "*compared to the past,* the middle class is exposed to ordinary police operations in a way that would have been unthinkable in the nineteenth century."[23] He concluded that "relationships of class, crime, and order are complex."[24].

---

[18] 11 *Law & Soc'y Rev.* 873 (1977).

[19] Id. at 874.

[20] Ibid.

[21] Lawrence M. Friedman, "John A. Sibley Lecture: The Devil is Not Dead: Exploring the History of Criminal Justice," 11 *Ga. L. Rev.* 257, 270 (1977).

[22] Id. at 272.

[23] Id. at 273.

[24] Ibid.

An outstanding book by Elliot W. Brownlee, Jr.,[25] on the Wisconsin income tax law of 1911 illustrates the complexity of the general relationship between class and the legal order. Brownlee reports that, after the Republican party had been defeated in the early 1890's by Democrats who had "capitalized on the rising impact of ethnic and religious associations on political alignments,"[26] Robert M. LaFollette and "a cadre of Republican leaders" decided to restore their party's position by reestablishing "the role of economic interests in electoral politics."[27] More specifically, they proposed to charge the costs of government to the manufacturing rather than the agricultural sector of the state's economy by means of a corporate income tax in lieu of real property taxes — a method of taxation that had the effect of driving industry out of Wisconsin. Thus, a normally powerful interest group — capitalist industrialists — in the end became the victim of government power. Another unusual tale of class conflict is reported by James P. Whittenburg in "Planters, Merchants, and Lawyers: Social Change and the Origins of the North Carolina Regulation."[28] The author argues that the North Carolina Regulation was not a rebellion of the poor against the rich, but rather a struggle on the part of planters, who saw political power slipping from their hands, against merchants and lawyers who were stepping into their places.

Other writers tell of interclass cooperation and amalgamation instead of conflict. In an article on workmen's compensation in the state of Washington,[29] Joseph F. Tripp explains that, in 1909-1910, half of the state judiciary's time was spent adjudicating workers' claims even though only one in every eleven injured workers ever brought suit.[30] He also notes that sixty percent of all insurance premiums paid by industry went for insurance company administrative expenses, thirty percent went for lawyers' fees, and only ten percent went for compensation payments.[31] The result was that industry, labor, and government officials (particularly judges) wanted reform, and therefore joined together to obtain "a law

---

25 Eliot W. Brownlee, Jr., *Progressivism and Economic Growth: The Wisconsin Income Tax, 1911-1929* (1974).

26 Id. at 44.

27 Ibid.

28 James P. Whittenburg, "Planters, Merchants, and Lawyers: Social Change and the Origins of the North Carolina Regulation," 34 *Wm. & Mary Q.* (3d ser.) 215 (1977).

29 Joseph F. Tripp, "An Instance of Labor and Business Cooperation: Workmen's Compensation in Washington State (1911)," 17 *Lab. Hist.* 530 (1976).

30 Id. at 537.

31 Ibid.

suitable to their interests, which meant a compulsory law with liberal benefits."[32] In a similar vein, Susan W. Prager argues that California adopted a community property system in its 1850 constitution because the Anglo-American majority wanted to secure the support of the Spanish minority for the new state government.[33] Finally, in a study of the social backgrounds of lower-court federal judges from 1829 to 1861,[34] Kermit L. Hall notes that men of modest origins were able to assure their assimilation into the elite by being appointed to the federal bench, and that political ties rather than social origins were the keys to obtaining a judicial appointment.

By far the largest body of scholarship on the general question of intergroup relationships has been written by historians in the area of racial, ethnic, and sex discrimination. The most important study in the field is "Attorneys Black and White: A Case Study of Race Relations Within the NAACP."[35] This article, which is based upon NAACP files recently made available to historians, describes how the black community pressured the NAACP during the 1930's to use black rather than white attorneys; the article maintains the blacks assumed top positions only when well-trained black attorneys such as William H. Hastie, Charles H. Houston, and Thurgood Marshall became available in sufficient numbers to fill the positions. A related article[36] reinforces the point, showing how the absence of national leadership from black lawyers resulted in local black attorneys' loss of the first effort, in *Garvey v. Townsend,*[37] to end all-white primaries.

Two books also make important contributions to the study of race relations in American history. The more interesting one is *The Angelo Herndon Case and Southern Justice*, by Charles H. Martin.[38] Martin's book is, in essence, a story about Southern radicalism in the 1930's, especially the communist-dominated International Labor Defense (ILD) and its efforts on behalf of black equality. Martin maintains that the ILD alienated white liberals and some blacks as a result of its doctrinaire

---

32 Id. at 549.

33 Susan W. Prager, "The Persistence of Separate Property Concepts in California's Community Property System, 1849-1975," 24 *U.C.L.A.L. Rev.* 1, 16-18 (1976).

34 Kermit L. Hall, "240 Men: The Antebellum Lower Federal Judiciary, 1829-1861," 29 *Vand. L. Rev.* 1089 (1976).

35 August Meier & Elliott Rudwick, "Attorneys Black and White: A Case Study of Race Relations Within the NAACP," 62 *J. Am. Hist.* 913 (1976).

36 Darlene Clark Hine, "Blacks and the Destruction of the Democratic White Primary, 1935-1944," 62 *J. Negro Hist.* 43 (1977).

37 295 U.S. 45 (1935).

38 (1976).

position, but other blacks, although they never accepted its ideology, respected the ILD for its efforts on their behalf. The second book, *The Anti-Lynching Movement: 1883-1932*, by Donald L. Grant,[39] argues that blacks throughout the late nineteenth centuries perceived lynching as the ultimate recourse of white racists for keeping blacks in their assigned place, and, accordingly, fought for its elimination as their first priority. In addition to these two books, several articles make valuable contributions to the legal history of black-white relations.[40]

Three articles report on the history of women's rights. In "Barred from the Bar: Women and Legal Education in the United States, 1870-1890,"[41] D. Kelly Weisberg recites many familiar facts as well as some new ones, such as the fact that many early women law students were either wives or daughters of lawyers.[42] In "Radical Reconstruction and the Property Rights of Southern Women,"[43] Suzanne D. Lebsock makes the important new argument that married women's property acts were "a significant new form of debtor relief," which "shielded the husband while it shielded the wife,"[44] and hence the acts were not really examples of a lessening discrimination on the basis of sex. Finally, in "Who Sues for Divorce? From Fault Through Fiction to Freedom,"[45] Lawrence M. Friedman and Robert V. Percival make the point that increases in divorce rates are, in effect, an important benchmark of the progress of women toward equality.

It is also necessary to take note of writing about other sorts of discrimination. In a book[46] that is at times guilty of overstatement,

---

[39] (1975).

[40] See David W. Bishop, "Plessy v. Ferguson: A Reinterpretation," 62 *J. Negro Hist.* 125 (1977); Michael S. Hindus, "Black Justice Under White Law: Criminal Prosecutions of Blacks in Antebellum South Carolina," 63 *J. Am. Hist.* 575 (1976); Neil R. McMillen, "Black Enfranchisement in Mississippi: Federal Enforcement and Black Protest in the 1960s," 43 *J. So. Hist.* 351 (1977); S.G.F. Spackman, "American Federalism and the Civil Rights Act of 1875," 10 *J. Am. Stud.* 313 (1976); Mason W. Stephenson & D. Grier Stephenson, Jr., "'To Protect and Defend': Joseph Henry Lumpkin, The Supreme Court of Georgia, and Slavery," 25 *Emory L.J.* 579 (1976); William M. Wiecek, "The Statutory Law of Slavery and Race in the Thirteen Mainland Colonies of British America," 34 *Wm. & Mary Q.* (3d ser.) 258 (1977).

[41] 28 *J. Legal Educ.* 485 (1977).

[42] Id. at 494-95.

[43] 43 *J. So. Hist. 195* (1977).

[44] Id. at 202-03.

[45] Lawrence M. Friedman & Robert V. Percival, "Who Sues for Divorce? From Fault Through Fiction to Freedom," 5 *J. Legal Stud.* 61 (1976).

[46] Richard Gambino, *Vendetta: A True Story of the Worst Lynching in America, the Mass Murder of Italian-Americans in New Orleans in 1891, the Vicious Motivations Behind It, and the Tragic Repercussions That Linger to This Day* (1977).

Richard Gambino traces the actions of an anti-Italian mob that lynched several Italian immigrants who had been charged with murdering the police chief of New Orleans. Gambino's main argument is that the mob's prejudice was motivated by a desire to keep Italians from achieving the economic success they were beginning to attain. Gambino's book is a powerful one, but it regrettably fails to emphasize the fact that the Louisiana legal system's generally fair treatment of Italians resulted in many acquittals. Thus, for bigots to carry out their discriminatory aims, it became necessary to circumvent the law by assembling lynch mobs. A more balanced article by Yasuhide Kawashima[47] concludes that the legal system of Puritan Massachusetts did not discriminate against Indians who were brought before it accused of crime, but treated them the same as it treated whites. Kawashima notes that discrimination existed, however, in that the criminal justice system did little to punish crimes by whites against Indians living outside white settlements.[48] Perhaps the most interesting article on discrimination by Americans against outsiders[49] discusses the jury *de medietate linguae* — a body of six Americans and six aliens that was available in American courts to try criminal cases against aliens until well into the nineteenth century. The author, Lewis H. LaRue, argues that the jury *de medietate linguae* died out in the late nineteenth century because most aliens at that time were of a lower social and economic class, and judges, believing in the importance of having disciplined minds on juries, were unwilling to permit lower-class jurors to sit.

Issues of class conflict and of racial, ethnic, and sex discrimination have not, of course, been the only ones upon which legal historians have focused during the past two years. Indeed, they have focused upon many different kinds of issues. One group of historians has focused upon the impact of ideas on legal and social development. John P. Reid has been an extraordinarily prolific historian of the impact of ideas on the law, having published the equivalent of three books during the past two years. In one book, *A Better Kind of Hatchet: Law, Trade, and Diplomacy in the Cherokee Nation during the Early Years of European Contact,*[50] Reid continues his work on the Cherokee Indians,[51] in this instance

[47] Yasuhide Kawashima, "Forced Conformity: Puritan Criminal Justice and Indians," 25 *Kan. L. Rev.* 361 (1977).

[48] Id. at 367-68.

[49] Lewis H. LaRue, "A Jury of One's Peers," 33 *Wash. & Lee L. Rev.* 841 (1976).

[50] (1976).

[51] See John Phillip Reid, *A Law of Blood: The Primitive Law of the Cherokee Nation* (1970).

tracing how the clash between Anglo-American and Cherokee conceptions of law led to fundamental misunderstandings between the two groups. In a series of five articles[52] that constitute the core of another book, Reid studies how common law ideas, such as the principle that an advocate should "assert those arguments most calculated to win" and avoid "irritat[ing] the 'court' . . . by arguing the ultimate question,"[53] had a significant impact upon the arguments advanced by Americans during the pre-Revolutionary debate with Great Britain over the scope of parliamentary power. In a related article,[54] he suggests that British legal ideas about the limited power of the military affected both the use to which the Crown put troops in pre-Revolutionary Boston and the way in which American crowds reacted to the military's presence. But Reid's most important contribution comes in a series of six other articles,[55] which are the equivalent of a third book, in which he describes how Americans from the East transplanted legal ideas to the West — how they strove "consciously . . . to carry beyond the line of forward settle-

---

[52] John Phillip Reid, "In Accordance with Usage: The Authority of Custom, the Stamp Act Debate, and the Coming of the American Revolution," 45 *Fordham L. Rev.* 335 (1976); John Phillip Reid, "In an Inherited Way: English Constitutional Rights, the Stamp Act Debates, and the Coming of the American Revolution," 49 *S. Calif. L. Rev.* 1109 (1976); John Phillip Reid, "In Legitimate Stirps: The Concept of 'Arbitrary,' the Supremacy of Parliament, and the Coming of the American Revolution," 5 *Hofstra L. Rev.* 459 (1977); John Phillip Reid, "'In Our Contracted Sphere': The Constitutional Contract, The Stamp Act Crisis, and the Coming of the American Revolution," 76 *Colum. L. Rev.* 21 (1976); John Phillip Reid, "In the First Line of Defense: The Colonial Charters, the Stamp Act Debate, and the Coming of the American Revolution," 51 *N.Y.U.L. Rev.* 177 (1976).

[53] John Phillip Reid, "In an Inherited Way: English Constitutional Rights, the Stamp Act Debates, and the Coming of the American Revolution," 49 *S. Calif. L. Rev.* 1109, 1110 (1976).

[54] John Phillip Reid, "In a Constitutional Void: The Enforcement of Imperial Law, the Role of the British Army, and the Coming of the American Revolution," 22 *Wayne L. Rev.* 1 (1975).

[55] John Phillip Reid, "Dividing the Elephant: The Separation of Mess and Joint Stock Property on the Overland Trail," 28 *Hastings L.J.* 73 (1976); John Phillip Reid, "Knowing the Elephant: Distinguishing Property Rights on the Overland Trail," 10 *Creighton L. Rev.* 640 (1977); John Phillip Reid, "Paying for the Elephant: Property Rights and Civil Order on the Overland Trail," 41 *Huntington Lib. Q.* 37 (1977); John Phillip Reid, "Prosecuting the Elephant: Trials and Judicial Behavior on the Overland Trail," 1977 *B.Y.U.L. Rev.* 327; John Phillip Reid, "Sharing the Elephant: Partnership and Concurrent Property on the Overland Trail," 45 *U.M.K.C.L. Rev.* 207 (1976); John Phillip Reid, "Tied to the Elephant: Organization and Obligation on the Overland Trail," 1 *U. Puget Sound L. Rev.* 139 (1977).

ment a mode of social behavior learned during a remembered youth in towns and cities they had left in body but not in spirit."[56]

John Reid, it should be noted, is not alone in the emphasis he gives to the impact of Eastern ideas upon frontier law.[57] Nor is he alone in his emphasis upon ideas in general.[58] Another legal historian who treats ideas seriously is G. Edward White. This serious treatment is apparent from the title to one of his articles, "The Intellectual Origins of Torts in America,"[59] in which he makes an original contribution to legal history with a discussion of how the conceptualist impulse in Victorian America, along with factors listed by other legal historians, resulted in the emergence of torts as a discrete legal subject.[60] In his book, *The American Judicial Tradition*,[61] White emphasizes the importance of ideas generated by individual appellate judges. He maintains that there has been a distinctive American judicial tradition since the time of John Marshall — a tradition transmitted from the collective mind of one generation to the next.

The most detailed of the books studying the impact of thought on law is *A Covenant with Death: The Constitution, Law, and Equality in the Civil War Era*, by Phillip S. Paludan.[62] Paludan asks why the Civil War amendments and Reconstruction failed to give genuine equality to blacks. His answer focuses upon the desire of both conservatives and radicals within the Republican party for social stability. He suggests that conservatives fought the Civil War to save the structure of existing institutions rather than to revolutionize race relations. He then points to the radicals' conception of liberty as "the negation" rather than "the exercise of governmental power"[63] and analyzes how denial of power to the national government inevitably precluded the attainment of racial equality.[64]

---

[56] John Phillip Reid, "Prosecuting the Elephant: Trials and Judicial Behavior on the Overland Trail," 1977 *B.Y.U.L. Rev.* 327, 350.

[57] See Gordon M. Bakken, "The Development of Landlord and Tenant Law in Frontier California, 1850-1865," 21 *Pac. Hist.* 374 (1977); Joel Samaha, "A Case of Murder: Criminal Justice in Early Minnesota," 60 *Minn. L. Rev.* 1219 (1976).

[58] See Paul K. Conkin, *Self - Evident Truths* (1974); M. Marcus Cunliffe, *The Right to Property: A Theme in American History, Sir George Watson Lecture, delivered at the University of Leicester* (May 4, 1973) (1974).

[59] 86 *Yale L.J.* 671 (1977).

[60] Id. at 673-78.

[61] (1976).

[62] (1975).

[63] Id. at 261.

[64] Id. at 274-75.

A particularly excellent article traces the impact of Blackstone's ideas on American law;[65] its author, Dennis R. Nolan, concludes that "Blackstone did not bring about the Revolution or even contribute significantly to the Declaration of Independence," while his "contribution to the Constitution . . . was limited to defining a few concepts."[66] Furthermore, Nolan claims that Blackstone had only a slight effect on the outcome of the nation's early legal cases.[67] Nolan concludes, rather, that Blackstone's influence was upon legal education; he writes that "from universities to private schools to simple offices, from courts in Philadelphia to roving justices in the West, and from law students and lawyers to laymen, the *Commentaries* shaped the form and content of the law of the nation."[68] Two other noteworthy articles focusing on the relationship between ideas and the contributions of great legal thinkers are Stanley Katz's essay on "Thomas Jefferson and the Right to Property in Revolutionary America"[69] and Don Fehrenbacher's piece on "Roger B. Taney and the Sectional Crisis."[70]

Other historiographical approaches have also produced valuable work. The two best books, apart from Horwitz's *The Transformation of American Law, 1780-1860,*[71] were written by young historians who engaged in precise analyses of the workings of institutions as a means of understanding the underlying social structures. In the first of the books, *Crime and Law Enforcement in the Colony of New York, 1691-1776,*[72] Douglas Greenberg attempts to use court records to analyze the social history of law and to "illuminate the history of society itself."[73] His is a history not only of the criminal courts and their doctrine, but also of "the many citizens of the colony who stood before them in criminal pro-

---

[65] Dennis R. Nolan, "Sir William Blackstone and the New American Republic: A Study of Intellectual Impact," 51 *N.Y.U.L. Rev.* 731 (1976).

[66] Id. at 767.

[67] Id. at 768.

[68] Id. at 767.

[69] Stanley N. Katz, "Thomas Jefferson and the Right to Property in Revolutionary America," 19 *J.L. & Econ.* 467 (1976).

[70] Don Fehrenbacher, "Roger B. Taney and the Sectional Crisis," 43 *J. So. Hist.* 555 (1977). The article will also appear as a chapter in the author's forthcoming book on the *Dred Scott case*. See also Gerald Fetner, "The Law Teacher as Legal Reformer: 1900-1945," 28 *J. Legal Educ.* 508 (1977); N. Houston Parks, "Judicial Selection — The Tennessee Experience," 7 *Mem. St. U.L. Rev.* 615 (1977); Gary J. Simson, "Jury Nullification in the American System: A Skeptical View," 54 *Tex. L. Rev.* 488 (1976).

[71] See notes 11-14 supra and accompanying text.

[72] (1976).

[73] Id. at 12.

ceedings."[74] In the second book, *The Municipal Revolution in America: Origins of Modern Urban Government, 1650-1825,*[75] Jon C. Teaford presents a powerful analysis of the transformation of municipal corporations from institutions run by merchants for the promotion and regulation of trade to institutions responsible to the general populace for the provision of governmental services. A useful article that also focuses on institutional change is Barry D. Karl's essay on "Executive Reorganization and Presidential Power."[76]

Legal biographers have also made important contributions to the literature of the past two years. In *American Lawyers in a Changing Society, 1776-1876,*[77] Maxwell Bloomfield uses biography to illustrate important themes in American history. For example, his essay on Peter Van Schaack[78] illustrates the impossibility of remaining neutral during the American Revolution, and the difficulties of Loyalist emigres in reintegrating themselves into American life, their ultimate success, and their subsequent centrality in the early American conservative movement. His essay on William Sampson[79] illustrates the place of immigrants in American life, including their treatment as second-class citizens, their love for their adopted nation despite that treatment, and their ultimate accomplishments within the American system. A third essay on William Pitt Ballinger[80] shows how well-placed Confederates, even those active in the Confederate cause, were able to manipulate the postwar situation to improve their material well-being.

Two other biographies are of important twentieth-century legal figures. One is Peggy Lamson's portrait of *Roger Baldwin: Founder of the American Civil Liberties Union.*[81] The other is David Wigdor's study of *Roscoe Pound: Philosopher of Law.*[82] Both are highly readable and informative studies that focus upon the personal lives as well as the public contributions of their subjects. Another valuable biographical essay is Ellyn Ballou's article on Prentiss Mellen, the first chief justice of Maine.[83]

---

[74] Id. at 13.
[75] (1975).
[76] 1977 *Sup. Ct. Rev.* 1
[77] (1976).
[78] Id. at 1.
[79] Id. at 59.
[80] Id. at 271.
[81] (1976).
[82] (1974).
[83] Ellyn Ballou, "Prentiss Mellen, Maine's First Chief Justice: A Legal Biography," 28 *Me. L. Rev.* 317 (1977).

Also represented in the scholarship of the past two years is work that brings to legal history the techniques of other disciplines. The best of this work is a book by Eric H. Monkkonen, *The Dangerous Class: Crime and Poverty in Columbus, Ohio, 1860-1885.*[84] Monkkonen is a highly sophisticated statistician, whose very skill illustrates the limits of statistical analysis. The difficulty with his book is that a great deal of careful work led only to very narrow generalizations, such as that crime patterns in Columbus differed from those in Eastern cities[85] and that urbanization and industrialization produced an increase in thefts by trick.[86] In every other respect, however, Monkkonen's study is excellent. Two other studies are of more problematic value. One article[87] brings to legal history the tools of economic analysis, arguing that doctrines providing greater protection to private property in land, livestock, and water emerged on the Great Plains in the nineteenth century because the benefits of asserting property rights rose and the costs of asserting them declined. The other article[88] brings the tools of probability theory to history, arguing that Franklin D. Roosevelt erred in trying to pack the Supreme Court in 1937 because "the odds were already *eleven to one in his favor* that he would be able to name one or more justices by traditional means that very year."[89] Each of these studies is excessively unidimensional, ignoring factors that contributed significantly to the historical events under study.

Less common than in past years were studies that focus upon how the authors and early expounders of particular constitutional provisions intended them to apply to issues troubling legal and political decision-makers today. Two books, *Government by Judiciary: The Transformation of the Fourteenth Amendment,*[90] by Raoul Berger, and *The Rise of Guardian Democracy: The Supreme Court's Role in Voting Rights Disputes, 1845-1969,*[91] by Ward E.Y. Elliott, argue that the Supreme Court has exceeded its mandate in applying the fourteenth amendment to problems other than the narrow ones with which its authors intended it to deal. Both books have a brief-like quality, emphasizing historical

---

[84] (1975).

[85] Id. at 29-33.

[86] Id. at 92-100.

[87] Terry L. Anderson & Peter J. Hill, "The Evolution of Property Rights: A Study of the American West," 18 *J.L. & Econ.* 163 (1975).

[88] Rodney J. Morrison, "Franklin D. Roosevelt and the Supreme Court: An Example of the Use of Probability Theory in Political History," 16 *Hist. & Theory* 137 (1977).

[89] Id. at 144.

[90] (1977).

[91] (1974).

data that support their legal position and ignoring evidence about social, intellectual, and political development in the backgound that cuts in the opposite direction. Such a brief-like quality may be inevitable in any attempt to search the past for answers to current problems, because the ambiguity of the past generally can be overcome only by ignoring its richness. The real issue for historians of constitutional intention is that of identifying and evaluating permissible evidence of such intention. In the case of Berger, it appears from his previous writing[92] that he examines intention by looking to statements in debate and to the common law background of those statements; if a scholar so limits his vision, it is possible to reach narrow conclusions like those of Berger with reference to the meaning and intent of the fourteenth amendment.

More expansive approaches than Berger's and Elliott's exist for evaluating historical evidence. One approach is exemplified by Abraham D. Sofaer's book, *War, Foreign Affairs and Constitutional Power: The Origins*[93] — an analysis of the powers claimed and exercised by the legislative and executive branches in regard to war and foreign affairs from the time of the constitutional convention to 1829. Unlike Berger and Elliot, Sofaer does not come to any definitive conclusion as to the location of constitutional power; on the contrary, he argues that the framers deliberately left the powers of the two branches vague[94] and that, while each branch has been "jealous of its authority, and at times sought to increase its power," "neither branch [has] prevailed consistently enough to subordinate the other."[95] An equally judicious approach is taken by Charles A. Lofgren in "Compulsory Military Service under the Constitution: The Original Understanding";[96] Lofgren concludes that the framers intended to compel military service from all adult males, but only in the militia. In sum, both Lofgren and Sofaer seek to learn what men decided in the past in reference to issues they faced. They thereby recognize both the ambiguity and the richness of the past in a way in which Berger and Elliott do not. The cost of such an approach is, of course, a recognition that the past cannot yield simple answers to issues of the present.

Lofgren and Sofaer were not, of course, the only legal historians during the past two years who wrote history without attempting to address current legal and political issues. Indeed, as has always been true, most scholars addressed rather narrow factual questions without regard

---

[92] See Raoul Berger, *Congress v. The Supreme Court* (1969); Raoul Berger, *Executive Privilege: A Constitutional Myth* (1974); Raoul Berger, *Impeachment: The Constitutional Problems* (1973).

[93] (1976).

[94] Id. at 60.

[95] Id. at xv.

[96] 33 *Wm. & Mary Q.* (3d ser.) 61 (1976).

to their present relevance. Some of this factually oriented work is especially noteworthy.

Three articles are noteworthy because they are based upon important primary source materials — the Felix Frankfurter and Jerome Frank papers — that have made available for scholarly research only in recent years. The most newsworthy of the articles is Michael E. Parrish's "Cold War Justice; The Supreme Court and the Rosenbergs,"[97] which recounts the intrigue and political maneuvering occurring among the Justices of the Supreme Court as they faced possible review of the Rosenberg case. Important legal process insights can be obtained from the two other articles: "How Questions Begot Answers in Felix Frankfurter's First Flag Salute Opinion," by Richard Danzig,[98] and "Portrait of the Judge as an Activist: Jerome Frank and the Supreme Court," by Robert J. Glennon, Jr.[99]

Important factual contributions were also made by three books. Henry J. Bourguignon has written an extraordinarily thorough study of *The First Federal Court: The Federal Appellate Prize Court of the American Revolution, 1775-1787;*[100] subsequent historians should not find it necessary to retrace the steps he has plotted.[101] The same can be said for Peter J. Coleman's *Debtors and Creditors in America: Insolvency, Imprisonment for Debt, and Bankruptcy, 1607-1900.*[102] A third valuable book is *The Twenty-Fifth Amendment: Its Complete History and Earliest Applications*, by John D. Feerick.[103] In addition, the past two years saw many useful articles reporting research in primary sources,[104] as well as some valuable books and articles summarizing

---

[97] 82 *Am. Hist. Rev.* 805 (1977).

[98] 1977 *Sup. Ct. Rev.* 257.

[99] 61 *Cornell L. Rev.* 950 (1976).

[100] (1977).

[101] See also Henry J. Bourguignon, "Incorporation of the Law of Nations during the American Revolution — the Case of the San Antonio," 71 *Am. J. Int'l L.* 270 (1977).

[102] (1974).

[103] (1976).

[104] See James B. Boskey, "A History of Commercial Arbitration in New Jersey," 8 *Rut. - Cam. L.J.* 1 (1976); R.D. Cox, "History of the Adverse Possession Statutes of Tennessee," 6 *Mem. St. U.L. Rev.* 673 (1976); James W. Ely, Jr., "Charleston's Court of Wardens, 1783-1800: A Post-Revolutionary Experiment in Municipal Justice," 27 *S.C.L. Rev.* 645 (1976); James W. Ely, Jr., "'That no office whatever be held during life or good behavior': Judicial Impeachments and the Struggle for Democracy in South Carolina," 30 *Vand. L. Rev.* 167 (1977); Lewis L. Laska, "A Legal and Constitutional History of Tennessee, 1772-1972," 6 *Mem. St. U.L. Rev.* 563 (1976); Carol Lee, "Discretionary Justice in Early Massachusetts," 112 *Essex Inst. Hist. Coll.* 120 (1976); Thomas A. Lund, "Early American Wildlife Law," 51 *N.Y.U.L. Rev.* 703 (1976); Charles R.

existing factual knowledge.[105]

Finally, it is necessary to mention two projects that have begun the publication of important records in our nation's legal and constitutional experience. The first is a project edited by Merrill Jensen, entitled *The Documentary History of the Ratification of the Constitution*, the first two volumes of which are now in print;[106] it will include for every state both the standard materials and newspaper and private commentary on the ratification process. The second project is the publication under the editorship of Herbert A. Johnson of *The Papers of John Marshall*, the first volume of which has appeared.[107] Both of these masterful compilations are of first-rate significance.[108]

McKirdy, "Before the Storm: The Working Lawyer in Pre-Revolutionary Massachusetts," 11 *Suffolk U.L. Rev.* 46 (1976); Charles R. McKirdy, "The Lawyer as Apprentice: Legal Education in Eighteenth Century Massachusetts," 28 *J. Legal Educ.* 124 (1976); Anthony A. Morano, "Historical Development of the Interrelationship of Unanimous Verdicts and Reasonable Doubt," 10 *Val. L. Rev.* 223 (1976); Dallin H. Oaks & Joseph I. Bentley, "Joseph Smith and the Legal Process: In the Wake of the Steamboat *Nauvoo*," 1976 *B.Y.U.L. Rev.* 735; Leonard Packel, "The History of Pennsylvania's Juvenile Institutions: A Sesquicentennial Review," 22 *Vill. L. Rev.* 83 (1976-77); Graham Parker, "The Juvenile Court Movement: The Illinois Experience," 26 *Toronto L.J.* 253 (1976); Sherry Smith, "An Historical Sketch of Oregon's Supreme Court," 55 *Ore. L. Rev.* 85 (1976); Robert Vogel, "Looking Back on a Century of Complete Codifications of the Law," 53 *N.D.L. Rev.* 225 (1976).

105 See William E. Burrows, *Vigilante!* (1976); Vern Countryman, "A History of American Bankruptcy Law," 81 *Com. L.J.* 226 (1976); Barry F. Helfand, "Labor and the Courts: The Common-Law Doctrine of Criminal Conspiracy and Its Application in the Buck's Stove Case," 18 *Lab. Hist.* 91 (1977); Francis H. Heller, "Military Law in the Continental Army," 25 *Kan. L. Rev.* 353 (1977); Ginger Roberts, "Edward Livingston and American Penology," 37 *La. L. Rev.* 1037 (1977).

106 1 *The Documentary History of the Ratification of the Constitution: Constitutional Documents and Records, 1776 - 1787* (Merrill Jensen ed. 1976); 2 *The Documentary History of the Ratification of the Constitution: Ratification of the Constitution by the States, Pennsylvania* (Merrill Jensen ed. 1976).

107 1 *The Papers of John Marshall* (Herbert A. Johnson ed. 1974).

108 Another valuable compilation is *Basic Documents of American Public Administration, 1776 - 1950* (Frederick C. Mosher ed. 1976).

Chapter Fifteen

1980

William E. Nelson

A scholarly work should be judged by how well it accomplishes the author's objectives. In the field of legal and constitutional history, the past two years have witnessed scholarship having at least three different types of academic or scholarly purposes. First is the genre of lawyers' legal history,[1] in which the past is examined in an effort to find direct answers to current issues of law or policy.[2] Second is a genre of a more purist sort, in which legal materials are examined in an effort to answer questions regarding the historical development of the law, but unrelated to any current legal or policy issues. Third is a genre of a factual sort, in which an author seeks to address neither legal nor historical questions, but merely attempts to add to the interdisciplinary profession's store of factual knowledge. This survey will examine recent developments in each of these three categories of scholarship.

I

LAWYERS' LEGAL HISTORY

One common variety of lawyers' legal history involves a search for precedent by which to adjudicate current legal questions. Jay M. Feinman and Roy S. Cohen engaged in such a search for precedent in an article

---

[1] The term was coined in Morton J. Horwitz, "The Conservative Tradition in the Writing of American Legal History," 17 *Am. J. Legal Hist.* 275, 276 (1973). I use the term slightly differently than did Horwitz to apply only to work addressing current legal questions and not to work examining the origins of modern rules.

[2] It has been suggested that research which relates to current policy issues is often misread and unfairly criticized by persons with differing political positions. A.E. Keir Nash, "Reason of Slavery: Understanding the Judicial Role in the Peculiar Institution," 32 *Vand L. Rev.* 7 (1979). Such politically motivated criticism, in which the critic is rarely explicit about the nature of his or her motivation, subjects writers to political standards which neither they nor their readers accept.

entitled "Suing Judges: History and Theory,"[3] in which they carefully trace the historical roots of the doctrine of judicial immunity from suit. They conclude that at English common law only judges of courts of record were fully immune from suit and that, since most courts were not of record, few judges possessed complete immunity.[4] Hence, they argue[5] that the common law does not provide precedent, as some have suggested, for the broad rule of judicial immunity proclaimed by the Supreme Court in *Bradley v. Fisher*[6] and extended in *Stump v. Sparkman.*[7] An article with a similar approach is Peter D. Garlock's "'Wayward' Children and the Law, 1820-1900."[8] Garlock's "main purpose" is "to demonstrate that well before the invention of the juvenile court, statutes authoriz[ed] the state to intervene coercively in the lives of wayward children,"[9] and thus that the juvenile court, which has been under challenge during the last decade, is not an unprecedented way of dealing with delinquent children.[10]

Plea bargaining is a subject whose supporters and critics alike have claimed the support of historical precedent. In an article entitled "Plea Bargaining and Its History,"[11] Albert W. Alschuler argues that the history of plea bargaining demonstrates that the practice has not become sufficiently embedded in the American legal tradition to warrant the status of "a venerable institution."[12] Alschuler reports that judges discouraged defendants from pleading guilty throughout the nineteenth century and that as late as 1958 it appeared that the Supreme Court might hold plea bargaining unconstitutional.[13] Nevertheless, by the 1920's, it had become commonplace in large urban jurisdictions for defendants to bargain with corrupt prosecutors for lesser sentences,[14] and more recently the practice of plea bargaining has expanded throughout the country under the pressure of increasing criminal caseloads and the

---

3 31 *S.C.L. Rev.* 201 (1980).

4 Id. at 211.

5 Id. at 254-56.

6 80 U.S. (13 Wall.) 335 (1871).

7 435 U.S. 349 (1978).

8 Peter D. Garlock, "'Wayward' Children and the Law, 1820-1900: The Genesis of the Status Offense Jurisdiction of the Juvenile Court," 13 *Ga. L. Rev.* 341 (1979).

9 Id. at 434.

10 See id. 436-41.

11 79 *Colum. L. Rev.* 1 (1979) [hereinafter cited as "Plea Bargaining"]. An abbreviated version of the same article appears as Albert W. Alschuler, "Plea Bargaining and Its History," 13 *Law & Soc'y Rev.* 211 (1979).

12 "Plea Bargaining," *supra* note 11, at 5.

13 Id. at 7-12, 35-37.

14 Id. at 24-25.

increased difficulty, resulting from the due process revolution, of trying criminal cases.[15] In Alschuler's view, whatever precedents exist for plea bargaining are misguided,[16] and the practice undermines defendants' exercise of their right to trial by jury.[17]

Alschuler's position has not, however, gained general acceptance, as is evidenced by Lawrence M. Friedman's essay, "Plea Bargaining in Historical Perspective."[18] In this essay, Friedman presents data not dealt with by Alschuler, showing that "[p]lea bargaining does not stand by itself . . . [but] is part of a process," having "connections with other well-known historical developments — the guilty plea, the routinization of criminal justice, [and] the rise of professional control over crime and punishment."[19] Two other authors writing in the same symposium as Alschuler and Friedman also take Friedman's position. In John Langbein's view, trial by jury was abandoned as a mode of adjudicating criminal proceedings when it lost the speed and efficiency it had once possessed.[20] Mark Haller adds that plea bargaining is part of a larger evolutionary development in which courts have lost much of their ancient control over the criminal process to police, professional prosecutors and penal institutions.[21]

Other writers also engage in a search to determine whether or not particular legal conditions today have precedent in the American past. Although not explicit about her purposes, Ellen E. Guillot makes an argument similar to Peter D. Garlock's in her article entitled "What's Old, What's New in the Jail Registers of San Joaquin County, California: 1890 and 1970."[22] Guillot's article is a statistical study of the criminal charges upon which people were committed to the San Joaquin jail in the years 1890 and 1970. She concludes that the rate for crime, as measured by pretrial commitments, has declined from 6.1 to 5.3 cases per 100 residents and that most major offenses, like larceny, burglary, and assault, accounted for the same proportion of all crime in both 1890 and 1970.[23] The conclusion, which Guillot never explicitly draws, is that

---

[15] Id. at 33-34, 38-40.

[16] Id. at 42.

[17] Id. at 42-43.

[18] 13 *Law & Soc'y Rev.* 247 (1979). This article utilizes data from a study of criminal cases in the Superior Court of Alameda County, California from 1880 through 1974.

[19] Id. at 258.

[20] John Langbein, "Understanding the Short History of Plea Bargaining," 13 *Law & Soc'y Rev.* 261, 262 (1979).

[21] Mark Haller, "Plea Bargaining: The Nineteenth Century Context," 13 *Law & Soc'y Rev.* 273, 274-75 (1979).

[22] 23 *Pac. Historian* 53 (1979).

[23] Id. at 55, 58-60.

Americans today are not witnessing an unusually high crime rate and that extreme steps to repress crime accordingly are not necessary.

Richard Maxwell Brown and Robert M. Ireland agree with Guillot on the prevalence of violent crime in the late ninteenth century. In their articles, "Southern Violence — Regional Problem or National Nemesis?: Legal Attitudes Toward Southern Homicide in Historical Perspective,"[24] and "Law and Disorder in Nineteenth Century Kentucky,"[25] they observe that the nineteenth century South in general, and nineteenth century Kentucky in particular, had an unusually high rate of crime, especially of violent crime. Brown attributes this phenomenon partly to "[t]he South's historical subculture of violence and community tolerance of killing in personal disputes."[26] It is clear from the two studies, however, that the legal system also contributed to extensive criminal violence, with legal doctrines that encouraged the practice of self-defense[27] and with practices, such as the gubernatorial pardoning power, that allowed well-placed defendants to escape the consequences of their crimes.[28] Paradoxically, it is unclear whether crime could have been reduced had prosecutors, judges, and others worked harder to reduce it. Professor Brown takes note of one effort against homicide by the Alabama Supreme Court, which did not significantly reduce Alabama's homicide rate.[29]

Another author who finds guidance for the present in the past is Gary J. Jacobsohn, who, in his fine book, *Pragmatism, Statesmanship, and the Supreme Court*[30] aspires to use history to develop a theory about the proper role for the Supreme Court in the American constitutional system. Jacobsohn examines the judicial methodology of historic figures such as Stephen J. Field, Benjamin N. Cardozo, Oliver Wendell Holmes, Charles Evans Hughes, and Felix Frankfurter. After rejecting the natural rights approach of Justices like Field, the pragmatic approach of the Warren Court, and the avoidance techniques of Justice Frankfurter, Jacobsohn concludes that the Justice whose jurisprudence is most worthy of emulation was Charles Evans Hughes, who always remained faithful

---

[24] 32 *Vand. L. Rev.* 225 (1979). Brown's article is severely criticized in Dennis R. Nolan, "Comment: Southern Violence—Regional Problem or National Nemesis?: Legal Attitudes Toward Southern Homicide in Historical Perspective," 32 *Vand. L. Rev.* 251 (1979).

[25] 32 *Vand. L. Rev.* 281 (1979).

[26] Richard M. Brown, *supra* note 24, at 231.

[27] Id. at 232-34.

[28] Robert M. Ireland, *supra* note 25, at 294-98.

[29] Richard M. Brown, *supra* note 24, at 243-44.

[30] (1977).

to fixed constitutional principles while at the same time applying them flexibly to changing facts.[31]

In "The Role of a Circuit Judge in Shaping Constitutional Law: Jerome Frank's Influence on the Supreme Court,"[32] Robert J. Glennon looks with equal favor on the judicial career of Jerome Frank. Glennon, who has written previously on Frank's career, demonstrates in this article how Frank, sitting as a circuit judge, influenced the Supreme Court to consider what he thought were important issues and to resolve them in accordance with his views on the merits.[33] In particular, Glennon notes how Frank induced the Court to adopt his positions in the areas of civil liberties and criminal law and procedure.[34] A third article examining legal controversies in an historical setting, "The Antievolution Law: Church and State in Arkansas,"[35] by Cal Ledbetter, Jr., analyzes a 1928 initiative which resulted in passage of special state legislation prohibiting the teaching of the Darwinian theory of evolution in Arkansas' public schools.[36] The article also examines a litigation campaign which resulted in the Supreme Court holding the legislation unconstitutional in 1968.[37] Ledbetter illustrates how social reformers can use the litigation process to effectuate policies that have failed to sway the electorate.[38]

Others turn to history to provide guidance about how present decision makers should not act. For example, Robert J. Goldstein argues that a government that fails to disclose its repressive activities against political dissidents "seeks to maintain the structure of government at the expense of the foundation of trust which supports it . . . [and] fore-ordains not only its own collapse but [also] the collapse of [the social order] it is intended to sustain."[39] This thesis stems from Goldstein's larger study entitled *Political Repression in Modern America, From 1870 to the Present,*[40] in which Goldstein traces both the chronological de-

---

[31] Id. at 190-91.

[32] 1978 *Ariz. St. L.J.* 523.

[33] Id. at 525.

[34] Id. at 540, 547.

[35] 38 *Ark. Hist. Q.* 299 (1979).

[36] Id. at 309-14. An initiated act is passed by popular referendum and requires a two-thirds majority of the legislature to be repealed. See id. at 300.

[37] Id. at 299; see Epperson v. Arkansas, 393 U.S. 97 (1968).

[38] Cal Ledbetter, Jr., *supra* note 35, at 315-16.

[39] Robert J. Goldstein, "An American Gulag? Summary Arrest and Emergency Detention of Political Dissidents in the United States," 10 *Colum. Human Rights L. Rev.* 541, 573 (1978).

[40] (1978). The stated purpose of the book is to show the failure of American labor to achieve major power until 1930, the destruction of the radical labor movement, and the self-censorship which Americans imposed upon their own exercise of basic political freedoms. Id. at ix.

velopment of American political repression and its concomitant effect on the free market of ideas.[41] Similarly, Athan Theoharis, in "The Truman Administration and the Decline of Civil Liberties: The FBI's Success in Securing Authorization for a Preventive Detention Program,"[42] considers the impact of Cold War security practices on American constitutional values and institutions.[43] Theoharis describes the "clear indifference of justice department and FBI officials to legal and constitutional considerations" in formulating internal security policy.[44] By implication, Theoharis suggests the need for greater public surveillance of government's internal security operations.[45]

Finally, two works use history to focus upon current legal issues. Frank T. Read's and Lucy S. McGough's book, *Let Them Be Judged: The Judicial Integration of the Deep South,*[46] and Grant Gilmore's article, "Formalism and the Law of Negotiable Instruments,"[47] address two important issues: whether judges should use their power to bring about public school integration and whether judges should reason in a "formal" rather than a "grand" style.[48] Comparison of the two works suggests that Read and McGough use history rather successfully, whereas Gilmore does not.

Gilmore suspects that the American legal system may be entering upon a new period of formalism — a prospect that he views with "acute distaste."[49] His article examines formalist — and at the opposite pole "activist" — approaches to the law of negotiable instruments during the

---

[41] Ibid. In his conclusion, Goldstein asserts that the United States is headed for totalitarianism unless we heed the warnings of its onset and take measures to avert it. Id. at 574.

[42] 64 *J. Am. Hist.* 1010 (1978).

[43] Id. at 1010.

[44] Id. at 1030.

[45] See id. at 1011. Theorharis calls for further research by Cold War historians into the files of national security organizations to consider questions he believes are of transcendent importance: how the Cold War affected American values and institutions; how and why internal security bureaus came to disregard legal and constitutional sanctions in order to obstruct public knowledge of illegal activities; and how society acquiesced to government's need for secrecy and to "inherent" presidential powers which eventually precluded government accountability and insured the public's insubordination.

[46] (1978).

[47] Grant Gilmore, "Formalism and the Law of Negotiable Instruments," 13 *Creighton L. Rev.* 441 (1979).

[48] The term "grand style" was first used in Karl N. Llewellyn, *The Common Law Tradition,* 65, 75 (1960).

[49] Grant Gilmore, *supra* note 47, at 441.

nineteenth century, and seeks to demonstrate the unsoundness of legal formalism.[50] With his usual eloquence, Gilmore concludes:

> The moral of the story is that, when a cat is to be skinned, there is always a formalist, as well as an activist, way of doing the job. The only difference is that the formalist techniques of cat-skinning are more complicated. But, as I said earlier, the distinction between activism and formalism is one of style, not substance.[51]

I, for one, am not persuaded by Gilmore's claim that formalism is inherently inferior to activism or instrumentalism. The late nineteenth century generation of formalists was certainly sophisticated enough to understand the disadvantages of formalism. As I have suggested elsewhere,[52] they were attracted to formalism, despite its possibly greater complexity, because their political and intellectual experience created jurisprudential problems that a formalist reasoning style could solve better than could an activist or instrumental style. Perhaps my earlier discussion of the attractions of formalism is wrong. Even if it is correct, similar reasons arguably ought not on balance lead late twentieth century judges to turn to a formalist style. But a scholar should not, as Gilmore does, simply ignore one side of a complex issue and hope to persuade thoughtful readers of the wisdom of his view.

On the other hand, the excellence of *Let Them Be Judged* lies in its presentation of both sides of the integration issue. Read and McGough trace in moving detail the conflict between the southern resistance to desegregation and the enforcement responses of the Court of Appeals for the Fifth Circuit.[53] The authors portray the conflict in moral terms and express admiration for leading judicial figures such as Elbert Parr Tuttle, Richard T. Rives, John R. Brown, and John Minor Wisdom. However, the authors also present the opponents' side of the integration story. For example, one section shows the real hardships that massive integration imposed on both whites and blacks.[54] They explain how integration has

---

[50] Id. at 446-61.

[51] Id. at 455.

[52] See William E. Nelson, "The Impact of the Antislavery Movement Upon Styles of Judicial Reasoning in Nineteenth Century America," 87 *Harv. L. Rev.* 513 (1974). Formalistic jurisprudence sought to resolve social controversies by making deductions from basic principles on which all men have agreed. The revived attraction to formalism in the late 19th century arose primarily from society's hope that such formality and logic would eventually be able to quell the increased social disruption stemming from the Civil War. See Grant Gilmore, *supra* note 47, at 445.

[53] Frank Read & Lucy S. McGough, *supra* note 46, at 542-62.

[54] Ibid.

been only a partial success, especially in urban areas, as whites have fled the inner cities, leaving huge black ghettos in their wake.[55] Finally, they discuss how the Fifth Circuit was transformed by the pressure of its vast desegregation caseload from a traditional appellate court into something of an administrative enforcement agency disposing of cases on an expedited basis without full judicial hearings.[56] Ultimately, Read and McGough, unlike Gilmore, allow their readers to pass judgment on the wisdom of school integration.

II

HISTORIANS' LEGAL HISTORY

A far greater proportion of recent historical scholarship focuses on genuine historical questions than on current issues of law or policy. Some of this purely historical scholarship focuses on processes of historical change, some examines significant continuities, and other works address particular topics that have been of recurrent interest to legal and other historians.

Three outstanding books inquiring into the origins of current phenomena were published since this journal's last legal history survey. James H. Kettner, in *The Development of American Citizenship, 1608-1870,*[57] traces the transformation of the sixteenth century English concept of allegiance into the nineteenth century American concept of citizenship. The central idea of sixteenth century English law was that allegiance

---

[55] See id. at 166. Read and McGough attribute inner-city deterioration to massive white flight accompanied by increased development of low-rent federal housing projects. The rapidity of the process is reflected by the neighborhood of Orleans Parish. In November 1969, 35,860 whites and 77,079 blacks resided there. However, only three years later, there were approximately ten thousand fewer whites, 26,399 exactly, while the number of blacks remained fairly constant at 77,600. Ibid.

[56] See id. at 464-70. This phenomenon is discussed in a section entitled "Court Congestion and the Conservation of Judicial Energy: Summary Disposition and Standing Panels." Id. at 464-71. The key to the court's expediency was described as Chief Judge John R. Brown's "desire to get the job done." Id. at 465. During his administration, Brown initiated the following procedures to expedite his dockets: (1) divided his 15 member bench into three-judge standing panels, each responsible for the final dispositions of cases; (2) conducted initial screening procedures; (3) avoided hearing oral argument; (4) favored short opinions; (5) eliminated written opinions altogether for certain lower court judgments but not for school cases. Id. at 465-68.

[57] (1978).

involved a personal, indissoluble relationship between the king and those persons born in the territory of which he was sovereign. Allegiance was viewed as permanent because it was based upon the laws of nature. Kettner explains how this English view was transformed by practical needs into the modern concept of citizenship, according to which individual volition is paramount. America's need for settlers, coupled with Enlightenment notions of consent as the basis of government, led to the view that individuals could voluntarily choose to adopt or renounce their citizenship. This notion conflicted, however, with deep-seated prejudices against Blacks and Indians, and not until the passage of post-Civil War equality legislation were these new citizenship ideals fully articulated.

The second study is Jon C. Teaford's *City and Suburb: The Political Fragmentation of Metropolitan America, 1850-1970.*[58] Teaford notes that American dedication to local decisionmaking resulted in the proliferation of suburban polities in every major metropolitan area during the past century. Until the 1910's, the superiority of the central city's services provided a counterweight to suburban proliferation as many suburbs sought consolidation with the central cities. But the improvement of suburban services by the 1920's terminated the movement toward consolidation and led to the political, social, and cultural fragmentation of urban America.[59]

The third work is Burton I. Kaufman's *The Oil Cartel Case: A Documentary Study of Antitrust Activity in the Cold War Era.*[60] Kaufman argues, with support from extensive documentation, that the government's need for assistance from oil firms in its relations with Mideast countries has given the firms a practical immunity from the antitrust laws. Yet he rejects the "guilt by association" thesis of some writers that our foreign oil policy was a response to the private oil interests. Instead, through a detailed analysis of an antitrust proceeding against five major oil companies doing business in the Mideast during the Truman administration, Kaufman argues that Cold War concerns of a Soviet threat to Third World nations dictated domestic oil policy. American national security interests conflicted with antitrust regulation of the oil companies and caused the government to settle the litigation it had brought.

The past two years also saw the publication of several important articles concerning the origins of today's American legal system. Perhaps the most valuable is Hendrik Hartog's essay on the changing nature of

---

58 (1979).
59 Id. at 184-86.
60 (1978).

the corporation from 1730 to 1860.[61] Hartog disagrees with the established view that the modern business corporation was an offshoot of the public, municipal corporation.[62] Relying on an analysis of New York City's transformation from a traditional British corporation into a public corporation responsible for a wide system of management, Hartog favors discarding the notion that eighteenth century corporations were exclusively either public or private in nature. Corporations, he argues, began to take on either public or private characteristics beginning in the nineteenth century, and only then did the single generic corporate form break down into a public, municipal form and a private, business form.

In two jointly written articles,[63] Peter C. Hoffer and N.E.H. Hull examine a series of seventeenth and eighteenth century American impeachment cases as an aid to understanding the impeachment provisions of the United States Constitution.[64] The colonial cases show that impeachment in the colonies was used as a political device and a legislative check on the coordinate branches and that it largely lost its criminal overtones, derived from the English system. The authors, note, however, that, in creating modern American impeachment law, the framers of the Constitution's impeachment clause and the Jeffersonian Republicans, who were the first to use the clause extensively, turned to English rather than American precedent in drafting and implementing the impeachment provisions.[65] The authors propose that English precedent appeared to have more authority with the framers and the Jeffersonians, who did not wish to elevate colonial precedents to the status of constitutional law.

A recent article[66] by William K. Jones traces the origins of the

---

[61] Hendrik Hartog, "Because All the World Was Not New York City: Governance, Property Rights, and the State in the Changing Definition of a Corporation, 1730-1860," 28 *Buffalo L. Rev.* 91 (1979).

[62] Supporters of this position argue that all corporations were public institutions as derivative agencies of the state, and that gradually entrepreneurs attached themselves to the notions of limited liability and the fiction of corporate existence. See Oscar Handlin & Mary F. Handlin, "The Origins of Business Corporations," 5 *J. Econ. Hist.* 1 (1945).

[63] Peter C. Hoffer & N.E.H. Hull, "Power and Precedent in the Creation of an American Impeachment Tradition: The Eighteenth-Century Colonial Record," 36 *Wm. & Mary Q.* (3d ser.) 51 (1979) [hereafter cited as Power and Precedent]; Peter C. Hoffer & N.E.H. Hull, "The First American Impreachments," 35 *Wm. & Mary Q.* (3d ser.) 653 (1978).

[64] U.S. Const. art. II, § 4.

[65] "Power and Precedent," *supra* note 63, at 75-77.

[66] William K. Jones, "Origins of the Certificate of Public Convenience and Necessity: Developments in the States, 1870-1920," 79 *Colum. L. Rev.* 426 (1979).

certificate of public convenience and necessity[67] from 1870 to 1920. Jones argues that the certificate system emerged as part of the shift from general to specialized governmental regulation. From early movements toward specialized regulation in Massachusetts and New York,[68] there emerged a consensus by the 1920's on the desirability of imposing state controls on public service industries. Thus, the certification system emerged to meet genuine problems and not as the result of industry pressures for protection against competition.[69]

Jamil A. Zainaldin, in his article, "The Emergence of a Modern American Family Law: Child Custody, Adoption, and the Courts, 1796-1851,"[70] concludes that the law of child custody changed in response to "a developing conception of childhood and parenthood."[71] Zainaldin rejects both the traditional view, which regarded the growth of state intervention as a phase in the expansion of civil equality,[72] and the revisionist view, which argued that the reforms of the Progressive era were tinged with class interests.[73] The author argues that the new understanding of the parental role in the nurturing of children encouraged the development of discretionary determinations of custody. Proprietary parental rights based exclusively on kinship at English common law therefore gave way to parental rights as matters of conduct and reciprocity.[74]

Four other articles also have a developmental cast. In one article, Joseph J. Kalo[75] examines the development of quasi in rem and in personam principles in American jurisprudence, dividing the development of jurisdictional concepts into several phases. In another, John W. Johnson examines "The Grudging Reception of Legislative History by American Appellate Courts in the Early Twentieth Century."[76] Johnson argues that the shift in the use of legislative history paralleled the shift from common law to statutory adjudication in the early twentieth century.[77] As more statutory litigation came before the courts, and the

---

67 These certificates are utilized to regulate the entry of new companies and the expansion of existing ones in public service industries by requiring a showing of public "need" for the proposed change. Id. at 427.

68 Id. at 451.

69 Id. at 514.

70 73 *Nw. U.L. Rev.* 1038 (1978-1979).

71 Id. at 1085.

72 Id. at 1084.

73 Id. at 1057-58.

74 See Christopher Lasch, *The State of the Child* (1976).

75 Joseph J. Kalo, "Jurisdiction as an Evolutionary Process, The Development of Quasi in Rem and in Personam Principles," 1978 *Duke L.J.* 1147.

76 1978 *Det. C.L. Rev.* 413.

77 Id. at 422.

law schools shifted emphasis toward more use of statutory materials,[78] the courts were forced to resort to legislative history to better interpret the statutes put before them.

In a third article, Marcia J. Speziale traces the emergence of the modern doctrine of impossibility in contract law at the turn of the twentieth century.[79] The author argues that at the turn of the century, parallel to the Populist-Progressive reform movement, the courts began to end the laissez-faire concreteness of the concept of freedom of contract.[80] Concepts of contract interpretation and the "intent of the parties" began to take hold as courts found various exceptions to the traditional doctrine of impossiblity.[81] Finally, Maxwell Bloomfield traces the demise of the Texas open bar, to which any comer was admitted on the basis of a perfunctory examination.[82] Bloomfield observes that the bar first took on a structured, stable character in Galveston, the commercial capital of the state during the nineteenth century, and only later became organized throughout the state.

An excellent book, which has a somewhat different developmental cast than the literature thus far discussed, is G. Edward White's *Tort Law in America: An Intellectual History*.[83] White, unlike the authors whose works are discussed above, is not especially interested in locating the origins of modern doctrine. The most original and impressive parts of his book do, however, focus on doctrinal development, as White traces the impact first of the nineteenth century legal science movement and then of the twentieth century legal realist movement upon such basic tort doctrines as assumption of risk, last clear chance, and causation.

Even more impressive than the work of White and other writers who focused upon processes of historical change is the writing of several recent scholars who suggest that important legal patterns and ideas may have persisted far longer at certain times in the past than previous historians had thought. One important book, *The Constitution and the Common Law: The Decline of the Doctrine of Separation of Powers and Federalism*,[84] by Randall Bridwell and Ralph U. Whitten, concludes,

---

[78] Id. at 424.

[79] Marcia J. Speziale, "The Turn of the Twentieth Century as the Dawn of Contract 'Interpretation': Reflections in Theories of Impossibility," 17 *Duq. L. Rev*. 555 (1978-1979).

[80] Id. at 567.

[81] The doctrine traditionally stated that contingencies which rendered performance impossible, if not provided for in the contract, were not grounds for excusing performance of the contract. See id. at 557.

[82] See Maxwell Bloomfield, "The Texas Bar in the Nineteenth Century," 32 *Vand. L. Rev*. 261 (1979).

[83] (1980).

[84] (1979).

contrary to a body of previous scholarship,[85] that "judicial pragmatism of the 'instrumental' variety did not really begin to materialize in the federal courts until the late ninteenth century,"[86] when Austinian positivism first legitimated a process of judge-made law.[87] Before that time, according to Bridwell and Whitten, the prime judicial task was to decide cases arising out of private transactions in accordance with the expectations of the parties to the transaction.[88] On the basis of this conclusion, the authors proceed to reexamine *Swift v. Tyson.*[89] Historians who view early nineteenth century judges as instrumentalists tend to find *Swift* a troublesome case because the Court never addressed what an instrumentalist judge would see as the main issue: whether the power to make law in diversity cases should lie with federal or state judges.[90] Bridwell and Whitten, on the other hand, do not find the case problematic at all. They note that the main purpose of diversity jurisdiction was to protect out-of-state citizens from local bias in state-court law-finding and fact-finding, and that *Swift* merely prevented state decisions from operating to defeat the parties' settled expectations derived from their understanding of general commercial law.[91] The *Swift* court did not have to resolve the issue of which sovereign, federal or state, had power to make law because it did not conceive of law in such terms.[92]

Charles A. Heckman disagrees.[93] In his view, Justice Story, the

---

[85] See, e.g. Morton J. Horwitz, *The Transformation of American Law, 1780 - 1860,* ch. 1 (1977); Karl N. Llewellyn, *The Common Law Tradition* (1960); William E. Nelson, "The Impact of the Antislavery Movement Upon Styles of Judicial Reasoning in Nineteenth Century America," 87 *Harv. L. Rev.* 513 (1974).

[86] Randall Bridwell & Ralph U. Whitten, *supra* note 84, at 137.

[87] Id. at 123.

[88] Id. at 129.

[89] 41 U.S. (16 Pet.) 1 (1842).

[90] Bridwell and Whitten believe that commentators mistakenly evaluate *Swift* from a positivistic viewpoint. Once it was understood that judges "make" law, all nonlegislative explanations were discarded, precluding accurate understanding of the system of law actually applied by the *Swift* Court. See e.g., Frederic J. Stimson & Munroe Smith, "State Statute and Common Law," 2 *Pol. Sci. Q.* 105 (1887). Later commentators, and Justice Brandeis in *Erie R.R. Co. v. Tompkins,* 304 U.S. 64 (1938), made the error of adopting the belief that judges always "made" law, and hence, restricted their analysis of earlier cases to searching for a sovereign authority behind the rules. Since they misinterpreted the system of law actually applied in the past, they were unable to understand what *Swift* actually represented. See Randall Bridwell & Ralph U. Whitten, *supra* note 84, at 136-37.

[91] See Randall Bridwell & Ralph U. Whitten, *supra* note 84, at 129-31.

[92] Id. at 136-41.

[93] Charles A. Heckman, "Uniform Commerical Law in the Nineteenth

author of *Swift* "desire[d] to promote a uniform body of commercial law to be administered throughout the United States by federal courts."[94] Heckman finds this objective "justifiable," and argues that "[t]he problems created by *Swift* occurred when its doctrine was expanded" into other areas.[95] Since I remain convinced that early nineteenth century judges paid heed at times to policy values other than the expectations of parties and hence that an instrumental conception of law did emerge in early nineteenth century America,[96] I find Heckman's position more persuasive. Nonetheless, credit must be given to Bridwell and Whitten for their perception that older ideas may well have persisted along with the emergence of the new instrumentalism — ideas which may have made *Swift* as well as some other decisions more plausible to contemporaries.

Another historian who believes that eighteenth century attitudes persisted into the mid-nineteenth century is John P. Reid, who has authored an article about constitutional theory on the overland trail.[97] Having examined the constitutions written by the ordinary Americans who migrated west on the trail, Reid concludes that "[t]he legal and social objective shaping constitutional theory on the overland trail was mediation, not legislation, and to obtain harmony within diversity."[98] As I have argued elsewhere,[99] these were also the objectives of eighteenth-century American communities.[100]

A third historian writing about the persistence of old attitudes is Michael Les Benedict. His article, "Preserving Federalism: Reconstruction and the Waite Court,"[101] takes the position that, while the failure of the Waite Court to extend federal power to protect the rights of blacks appears regressive to the modern eye, the Court's approach was quite

---

Century Federal Courts: The Decline and Abuse of the *Swift* Doctrine," 27 *Emory L.J.* 45 (1978).

[94] Id. at 45.

[95] Id. at 55.

[96] See William E. Nelson, *Americanization of the Common Law: The Impact of Legal Change on Massacusetts Society, 1760-1830,* 144, 154-58, 171-73 (1974). For example, courts did more than rely on the expectations of the parties in early nineteenth century contracts cases. The judiciary's concern for economic growth led courts to analyze the economic needs of the business community in formulating the rules of the marketplace. Id. at 154.

[97] John Phillip Reid, "Governance of the Elephant: Constitutional Theory on the Overland Trail," 5 *Hastings Const. L.Q.* 421 (1978).

[98] Id. at 442.

[99] See William E. Nelson, "The Eighteenth-Century Background of John Marshall's Constitutional Jurisprudence," 76 *Mich. L. Rev.* 893, 917-24 (1978).

[100] "The mid-eighteenth century style of governance resolved disputes and other problems, not according to policy, but according to a widely shared consensus of values." Id. at 901.

[101] 1978 *Sup. Ct. Rev.* 39 (1979).

progressive when examined in light of early nineteenth-century ideas about federalism on which the justices of the Waite Court had been raised.[102]

In addition to this general writing focusing on the extent of both change and continuity in the American legal past, legal historians have written extensively in the past two years on four broad topics. The most extensive literature is on the topic of colonial legal history. There is also extensive literature focusing on late eighteenth- and early nineteenth-century constitutional history. Two other topics that have received attention are the history of police and the history of repressed groups.

The only book covering the colonial period, *Law and Society in Puritan Massachusetts: Essex County, 1629-1692,*[103] by David Thomas Konig, is a contribution to the history of early Massachusetts law that is equal in importance to George L. Haskins' book, *Law and Authority in Early Massachusetts: A Study in Tradition and Design.*[104] Although Konig's study lacks the geographic breadth and doctrinal detail of Haskins' treatment, it goes beyond Haskins' work in tracing not only the carrying of English law to early Massachusetts, but also the transformation of the law under the pressure of life in America during the second half of the seventeenth century. Konig is the first historian to focus attention upon the general pattern of American legal change during the period between the Civil War and the Glorious Revolution in England, and his book would be of importance for that reason alone. Equally significant, however, is Konig's use of local court records as the main source material for his study.

Three articles focus on how law functioned in seventeenth- and eighteenth-century colonial communities. In an excellent study of the town court of Newtown, New York,[105] Jessica K. Ehrlich concludes that,

---

[102] Most commentators have taken the position that the Waite Court, disregarding congressional intent, "perver[ted] what the abolitionists tried to write into the constitution." Eugene Gressman, "The Unhappy History of Civil Rights Legislation," 50 *Mich. L. Rev.* 1323, 1339 (1952). Benedict, while he does not justify the acts of the Court, believes the Court's decisions were the result of the justices' views concerning the necessity of preserving the balance of the old federal system and were not a consequence of their views on racial issues. The Court was merely protecting states' rights, which had been long understood to be an implicit element of nationalism. Michael Les Benedict, *supra* note 101, at 41. The principle of dual federalism explains the Court's support of the primary jurisdiction of the states over criminal offenses while still sustaining Congress' power to protect fundamental rights. Id. at 77.

[103] (1979).

[104] (1960).

[105] Jessica K. Ehrlich, "'To Hear and Try All Causes Betwixt Man and Man'": The Town Court of Newtown, 1659-1690," 59 *N.Y. Hist.* 277 (1978).

"[w]hile peace and harmony were the ideal, men were imperfect, and therefore, a legitimate adjudicator was needed to smooth out differences and protect the vulnerable."[106] She finds that the court served the adjudicative function, meeting "frequently," resolving "cases quickly," and making "what seemed an honest effort to be fair."[107] Overall, for its time, the court was "a capable, responsive instrument of justice."[108] M.P. Baumgartner has a somewhat different view of the earliest court of New Haven, Connecticut, as well as a different research method.[109] Baumgartner's article is a sociological study and analysis of court records that concludes that high-status persons used the court to promote their interests far more effectively than did persons of low status.[110] A.G. Roeber attempts a synthesis of these positions in his article, "Authority, Law, and Custom: The Rituals of Court Day in Tidewater Virginia, 1720 to 1750."[111] He concludes that the "courthouse was a sort of 'everyman's plantation,'" in which "authority, law, and custom mingled in ritual exchanges" to give Virginians their due, according to their rank.[112]

A similar concern, that all segments of society should receive fair treatment while simultaneously doing their duty both to the king and to their fellow subjects, emerges in Lemuel Molovinsky's study of taxation

---

[106] Id. at 302-03.

[107] Id. at 303.

[108] Id. at 305.

[109] M.P. Baumgartner, "Law and Social Status in Colonial New Haven, 1639-1665," 1 *Research L.& Soc.* 153 (1979).

[110] Id. at 172.

[111] 37 *Wm. & Mary Q.* (3d ser.) 29 (1980).

[112] Id. at 51. He concluded that,

> [T]he courthouse was a sort of "everyman's plantation." To a degree, everyone in the county "belonged" there and rightly expected to receive what was due him as he defined himself, his rank, his relationship to others. Authority, in the persons of the justices, managed to give various ranks of Virginians what was theirs, as the law was supposed to do, by a judicious mixture of "cunning, wit, and power." At its best, court day was the arena in which authority, law, and custom mingled in ritual exchanges. Deference to authority was expected all down the line. Mutual obligations had to be acted out as well, as both business and self-images were advanced in the settlement of debt. Communal sanction served to ratify authority's presence by mediating that presence by means of the grand jury, and in exchange for deference, obligations were set upon superiors as well. Over all, the public law, the public authority of the king's court loomed large in everyone's mind.

Ibid.

in colonial Pennsylvania.[113] Molovinsky observes that the "poll tax insured that all were taxed," but a selective excise tax and the exemption of the very poor from property taxes insured that burdens "would not be great on those least able to pay."[114] Molovinsky concludes cryptically that "despite theoretical concerns for equity and needs of the poor, expediency seemed to [have been] the rule."[115]

Colonial debtor-creditor law showed a like concern for the underprivileged. Tommy R. Thompson has shown that in colonial Maryland, for instance, many individuals received relief from imprisonment for debt.[116] Likewise, according to Robert A. Becker, concern for the underprivileged masses led to debtor relief legislation in the 1780's in South Carolina.[117]

The importance of ordinary people in colonial history is also affirmed by Warren M. Billings in an article entitled "English Legal Literature as a Source of Law and Legal Practice for Seventeenth-Century Virginia,"[118] a topic also examined in a book by Herbert A. Johnson.[119] Although Billings discusses Virginia's legal literature, his real theme is the reception of English law in the colony. His central claim is that the agents of reception were neither the great men sent out by the London Company to settle the colony nor the governors later sent out by the crown to administer it, but rather the waves of ordinary settlers who began to inhabit Virginia in the mid-1630's.[120] These ordinary settlers placed considerable demands on the law; by the eighteenth century, according to Frank L. Dewey, Virginia's highest court was beset by considerable delay and docket congestion.[121]

This discussion of colonial history cannot be closed without reference to a set of important articles by Hans W. Baade on the law of French-

---

[113] Lemuel Molovinsky, "Continuity of the English Tax Experience in Early Pennsylvania History," 46 *Pa. Hist.* 233 (1979). The main subjects of Molovinsky's article were the excise, poll, and property taxes. See id. at 243-44.

[114] Id. at 244.

[115] Ibid.

[116] Tommy R. Thompson, "Debtors, Creditors, and the General Assembly in Colonial Maryland," 72 *Md. Hist. Magazine* 59 (1977). These individuals often lost all their property, however, and were forced into servitude for five to seven years upon release from prison. Id. at 77.

[117] Robert A. Becker, "Salus Populi Suprema Lex: Public Peace and South Carolina Debtor Relief Laws, 1783-1788," 80 *S.C. Hist. Magazine* 65 (1979).

[118] 87 *Va. Magazine Hist. & Biography* 403 (1979).

[119] Herbert A. Johnson, *Imported Eighteenth - Century Law Treatises in American Libraries, 1700-1799* (1978).

[120] See Warren M. Billings, *supra* note 118, at 403-06.

[121] See Frank L. Dewey, "New Light on the General Court of Colonial Virginia," 21 *Wm. & Mary L. Rev.* 1, 2-3 (1979).

and later Spanish-Louisiana and of the Spanish colonies that became the southwestern United States. One of his articles focuses on marriage law in Louisiana,[122] where the Spanish sought to substitute their law for French law upon assuming jurisdiction in 1769. French customary law persisted outside New Orleans, however, in part because it was deeply entrenched among the populace, and in part because there were few trained officials with the capacity to ascertain whether any particular marriage contract exceeded the rather flexible and open-ended bounds of Spanish law.[123] On the other hand, in an article about formalities in real estate transactions,[124] Baade reports that Spanish law became effective throughout the Louisiana territory — indeed, even more effective than in Texas, New Mexico and California.

The second topic that many scholars have addressed is that of the nation's early constitutional history. A very useful book by William M. Wiecek, *The Sources of Antislavery Constitutionalism in America, 1760-1848,*[125] covers familiar ground in dealing with the history of the antislavery movement prior to 1830, but makes a unique contribution to the literature by noting that during the 1830's the antislavery movement became fragmented. Three distinct branches of the movement emerged in the 1840's according to Wiecek: moderate constitutional antislavery, which was exemplified by Salmon P. Chase;[126] radical constitutional antislavery, exemplified by Alvan Stewart, William Goodell, and Lysander Spooner;[127] and the Garrisonian critique, developed by William Lloyd Garrison.[128]

Recent scholarly work seems to abound with reinterpretations of widely-held conceptions of early constitutional development and political thought. For example, *The Massachusetts Constitution of 1780: A Social Compact,*[129] by Ronald M. Peters, Jr., examines the political theory of the Revolutionary generation in general and the framers of the Massachusetts Constitution of 1780 in particular. It concludes that the generation of 1780 subordinated individual rights to the power of the majority to govern itself. Another piece focusing on the same period argues, contrary to established ideas, that ratification of the federal Constitution

---

[122] Hans W. Baade, "Marriage Contracts in French and Spanish Louisiana: A Study in 'Notarial' Jurisprudence," 53 *Tul L. Rev.* 1 (1978).

[123] Id. at 77.

[124] Hans W. Baade, "The Formalities of Private Real Estate Transactions in Spanish North America: A Report on Some Recent Discoveries," 38 *La. L. Rev.* 655 (1978).

[125] (1977).

[126] Id. at 190-93.

[127] Id. at 254-57.

[128] Id. at 228-36.

[129] (1978).

in Pennsylvania did not become a partisan issue until its proponents tried to hurry the ratification process.[130] In addition, a study of Thomas Jefferson's reference to the "wall of separation between church and state"[131] concludes that Jefferson did not believe in a rigid partitioning of secular and religious affairs, but rather that the first amendment merely precluded the federal government from establishing any relationhip with religion, while the power to establish a nonpreferential relationship with religion was implicitly reserved to the state governments.[132] The object of the first amendment, in this view, is to further religious liberty and tolerance by establishing nonpreferential support, rather than by the complete separation of church and state.

A more important contribution to the constitutional history of the Revolutionary era came in John P. Reid's two books, *In a Defiant Stance: The Conditions of Law in Massachusetts Bay, the Irish Comparison, and the Coming of the American Revolution*[133] and *In a Rebellious Spirit: The Argument of Facts, the Liberty Riot, and the Coming of the American Revolution.*[134] In the first book, Reid suggests how the structure of institutions in America, unlike their rather different structure in eighteenth-century Ireland, limited the capacity of royal officials to enforce law as they conceived of it. Reid also shows how American colonials developed a conception of law more consistent with the structure of things than the imperial conception. Reid's later book shows how the colonial conception led Americans to view facts differently than royal officials did and how historians' failure to appreciate that conception has led to a misperception of those facts.

Four articles deal with the work of courts during the early national period, seeking to uncover the hidden motives and influences behind some otherwise obscure results. The best is Stephen B. Presser's "A Tale of Two Judges: Richard Peters, Samuel Chase, and the Broken Promise of Federalist Jurisprudence,"[135] which concludes that the jurisprudence of the High Federalists failed because, while it was framed to reflect concepts of popular sovereignty, it was administered by judges like Chase in what seemed to be a partisan, arbitrary, and tyrannical manner.[136] An

---

[130] See Owen Ireland, "Partisanship and the Constitution," 45 *Pa. Hist.* 315, 332 (1978).

[131] "Note, Jefferson and the Church-State Wall: A Historical Examination of the Man and the Metaphor," 1978 *B.Y.U.L Rev.* 645.

[132] Id. at 672-73.

[133] (1977).

[134] (1979).

[135] 73 *Nw. U.L. Rev.* 26 (1978).

[136] Id. at 109. It is claimed that this uneven administration of the law may have been caused by an inability of judges, especially Chase, to serve the

outstanding student note reinterprets Justice Story's dissent in the *Charles River Bridge* case as being concerned primarily with the issue of the Supreme Court's power to review the constitutionality of state legislation and only nominally with the substantive contract clause issue raised by the case.[137] Another fine student note, "Eminent Domain in Indiana: 1816-1865,"[138] concludes that although the judiciary acted on the basis of utilitarian policy arguments in justification of eminent domain, it "never lost its sense of dedication to legal principles which antedated modern philosophy,"[139] and it continued to pay close attention to legal formulations which traditionally had provided protection to the property owner. The fourth article traces the evolution of aboriginal rights in the American legal system during the period of the Marshall Court.[140]

Important works were also written during the past two years on police and related subjects. The leading book in this area is Robert M. Fogelson's *Big-City Police.*[141] After reviewing much familiar material, Fogelson makes two significant original contributions. First, he observes a transformation in the twentieth-century reform movement to depoliticize the police and deprive urban machines of control over local forces. Fogelson finds that what began as a movement for reform under upper middle-class leadership turned into a movement by professional police officers for bureaucratic independence. Second, Fogelson notes that the success of reformers and police officers made twentieth-century police forces less responsive than nineteenth-century forces had been to racial and ethnic groups that enjoyed political power in large cities.

Another excellent book is Wilbur R. Miller's *Cops and Bobbies: Police Authority in New York and London, 1830-1870.*[142] Miller, whose main concern is with the historical roots of the differing character of the New York and London forces, observes that the London police were

---

competing Federalist goals of "commercial progress in the law" and Federalist political hegemony. Id. at 29.

[137] "Note, Justice Story's Doctrine of Judicial Supremacy and the Uncertain Search for a Neutral Principle in The Charles River Bridge Case," 53 *Ind. L.J.* 327, 357 (1977-1978).

[138] "Note, Eminent Domain in Indiana: 1816-1865," 54 *Ind. L.J.* 427 (1979).

[139] Id. at 442. Attention to these principles was vital to the preservation of the integrity of the legal process and the credibility of judicial decisonmaking. These principles included the traditional notions of due process and vested property rights. In remaining faithful to them while accommodating change, the courts acted as "arbiter[s] of competing interests, and balancer[s] of new legal substance and ancient legal formalism." Ibid.

[140] Howard R. Berman, "The Concept of Aboriginal Rights in the Early Legal History of the United States," 27 *Buffalo L. Rev.* 637, 666 (1978).

[141] (1977).

[142] (1977).

created by Parliament in 1829 in the midst of a political crisis to help repress classes unrepresented in the political system, whereas New York's force was created to control brawling, often between different ethnic groups, in a society where democracy already held full sway. To accomplish their task, the London police tried to take themselves out of politics and to appear as neutral enforcers of an impartial law; one element of their program was to be as unprovocative as possible by using a minimal amount of force. New York's police, on the other hand, were subject to full democratic control, enjoyed unquestioned legitimacy as a result, and were free to use the force that was needed in the violent society they confronted.

Recent studies have reexamined the Western law enforcement institutions so often romanticized in popular literature. In a book entitled *The United States Marshals of New Mexico and Arizona Territories, 1846-1912,*[143] Larry D. Ball dispels the popular image of the marshals as gun-toting, horse-riding cowboys perpetually chasing outlaws in ramshackle towns. Instead, he finds that the federal marshals were not unlike their Eastern police counterparts; they were political appointees who were closely tied to local political machines and deeply involved in the real estate and other speculative activities of those machines.[144] In basic agreement with Ball, Charles A. Tracy III observes in a series of articles that the police force of Portland, Oregon, developed and changed during the third quarter of the nineteenth century pursuant to patterns quite similar to those in the East.[145] William P. Wood, on the other hand, confirms popular impressions of the San Francisco vigilantes of 1851, who "demonstrate[d] moderation, not mob passion," and whose punishments "were based upon law, not expedience."[146]

Michael Hindus deals with related topics in *Prison and Plantation: Crime, Justice, and Authority in Massachusetts and South Carolina 1767-1878,*[147] a wide-ranging study of crime and the criminal process in two states over a century-long period. Hindus' most interesting data concerns the differing patterns of crime in the two states. He finds that crimes of violence were the most common type of offense in South Carolina, whereas offenses against property and propriety accounted for

---

143 (1978).

144 Id. at 238-44. Congress had, of course, assigned to the Marshals as their primary task the service of process of the federal courts. Id. at 240.

145 Charles A. Tracy, III, "Police Function in Portland, 1851-1874," 80 *Or. Hist. Q.* 5, 134, 287 (1979).

146 William P. Wood, "The Committee of Vigilance: Justice and the Legal Order," 53 *Cal. St. B.J.* 154, 159 (1978).

147 (1980).

the bulk of Massachusetts' crime.[148] Hindus also has valuable new material on the treatment of slave crime in South Carolina.

Finally, mention must be made of several excellent studies of various repressed groups in American history. The best of these is Michael R. Belknap's *Cold War Political Justice: The Smith Act, the Communist Party, and American Civil Liberties.*[149] Belknap asks why the Communist Party of America collapsed under the legal assault mounted against it by the federal government during the 1950's. He concludes that the federal attack undermined the party in two ways. First, the use of informers made the party suspicious of all but its most trusted and dedicated members, with the result that many less committed members left the party and few new members were recruited. Second, the government sent many party leaders to jail, with the result that old ties and activities which had produced unquestioned loyalty and discipline dissolved and many party members began to think for themselves. The weakened party could not stand the strain of Khruschev's revelations of Stalin's excesses and of Russia's suppression of the 1956 Hungarian revolt, so that by the late 1950's it was rapidly falling into oblivion.[150]

Another fine book is Judith A. Baer's *The Chains of Protection: The Judicial Response to Women's Labor Legislation.*[151] Baer asks why the Supreme Court, in *Muller v. Oregon,*[152] treated legislation regulating working conditions of women as a special category. Baer argues that the goal of Justice Brewer, the author of *Muller*, was to limit the impact of the case on the line of cases spawned by *Lochner v. New York.*[153] The Court reached this result by focusing upon the special characteristics of women laborers. Baer notes that later cases based on *Muller* developed a general theory that for purposes of labor legislation women are different from men — a theory that survived the practical overruling in the 1930's of *Lochner*, which had initially given rise to the distinction. Ironically, Baer concludes that, subsequent to *Lochner's* demise, the doctrine of protection of women announced in *Muller* retarded the progress of women in overcoming the limitations imposed by protective legislation.[154]

---

[148] Id. at 59-84.

[149] (1977). See also *Dennis v. United States,* 341 U.S. 494 (1951) (upholding Smith Act against a first amendment attack).

[150] Michael R. Belknap, *supra* note 149, at 193-206.

[151] (1978).

[152] 208 U.S. 412 (1908). In *Muller,* the Court sustained, against a due process attack, an Oregon statute prescribing a maximum ten-hour workday for women employed in laundries. Id. at 423.

[153] 198 U.S. 45 (1905). *Lochner* invalidated a New York statute prescribing ten-hour workdays and sixty-hour weeks for all bakery employees. Id. at 64.

[154] Judith A. Baer, *supra* note 151, at 66-67.

Four articles also merit comment. One is Nunzio Pernicone's precise analysis of the radical Carlo Tresca's statement that Nicola Sacco was guilty but Bartolomeo Vanzetti innocent of the charges against them in the Sacco-Vanzetti case.[155] Pernicone concludes that Tresca believed his statement to be true, whatever its actual truth may have been. Another excellent article is A.E. Keir Nash's "Reason of Slavery: Understanding the Judicial Role in the Peculiar Institution,"[156] the main conclusion of which is that the law of slavery differed greatly from state to state.[157] A third article, "Race, Property Rights, and the Economic Consequences of Reconstruction: A Case Study," by Robert J. Haws and Michael V. Namorato,[158] argues that local courts in Mississippi effectively circumscribed the freedom and opportunity of former slaves and rigorously enforced laws on behalf of creditors at the expense of debtors — actions that "helped stifle" and otherwise "slowed the pace of economic recovery."[159] Finally, Marilyn Hall Mitchell's "From Slavery to Shelley — Michigan's Ambivalent Response to Civil Rights,"[160] provides a survey of how blacks fared legally in one northern state during the nineteenth and early twentieth centuries.

III

FACTUAL LEGAL HISTORY

The first task of historians is to accumulate factual data from the past, and many writers during the past two years have done precisely that without striving to articulate "overarching themes of a profoundly novel nature."[161]

One of the better books to emphasize facts without dictating how its quantitative tabulations are to be used is *The First One Hundred*

---

[155] Nunzio Pernicone, "Carlo Tresca and the Sacco-Vanzetti Case," 66 *J. Am. Hist.* 535, 547 (1979).

[156] A.E. Keir Nash, "Reason of Slavery: Understanding the Judicial Role in the Peculiar Institution," 32 *Vand. L. Rev.* 7 (1979).

[157] Id. at 205.

[158] Robert J. Haws & Michael V. Namorato, "Race, Property Rights, and the Economic Consequences of Reconstruction: A Case Study," 32 *Vand. L. Rev.* 305 (1979).

[159] Id. at 325-26.

[160] 26 *Wayne L. Rev.* 1 (1979).

[161] Milton M. Klein, "From Community to Status: The Development of the Legal Profession in Colonial New York," 60 *N.Y. Hist.* 133, 135 (1979).

Justices: Statistical Studies on the Supreme Court of the United States[162] by Albert Blaustein and Roy Mersky. The authors, as their title suggests, gathered considerable quantitative data. Among the information compiled are demographic statistics concerning the first one hundred justices,[163] a rating of the justices from worst to best,[164] and a relationship of various demographic characteristics of judges to their rated performance on the bench.[165] Blaustein and Mersky also explore the quantitative aspects of Supreme Court opinions: how many were written — concurrences, per curiam opinions, dissents — and by whom they were written.[166]

Federal Courts in the Early Republic, Kentucky 1789-1816,[167] is a substantial book for which the author, Mary Bonsteel Tachau, conducted research aimed at reconstructing the manuscript records of the federal district court for Kentucky. Tachau's work provides insights into the role the lower federal courts played in the early Republic, beginning with the Judiciary Act of 1789, by which the district and circuit courts were established by Congress. The author presents an in-depth view of the caseload of the district court for Kentucky during this period[168] and integrates this quantitative information and an exploration of the personnel of the early court with the political struggles of early America.

Similarly, Donald G. Nieman's *To Set the Law in Motion: The Freedmen's Bureau and the Legal Rights of Blacks, 1865-1868,*[169] is based on extensive research in the Freedmen's Bureau records. Two other essentially factual studies are Mary F. Berry, *Stability, Security and Continuity: Mr. Justice Burton and Decision-Making in the Supreme Court, 1945-1958,*[170] and Harold Hutton, *Vigilante Days: Frontier Justice along the Niobrara.*[171] Of course, there were also a number of articles during the past two years that examined facts without articulating overarching themes.[172]

---

162 Albert P. Blaustein & Roy Mersky, *The First One Hundred Justices* (1978).

163 Id. at 9-31.

164 Id. at 32-51.

165 Id. at 52-71.

166 Id. at 87-102.

167 (1978).

168 Litigation involving land ownership, suits brought by the United States that primarily concerned the internal revenue code, and private civil suits based on diversity jurisdiction each accounted for about one-third of the court's caseload. Id. at 149.

169 (1980).

170 (1978).

171 (1978).

172 W. Hamilton Bryson, "The History of Legal Education in Virginia," 14 *U. Rich. L. Rev.* 155 (1979); Robert Scott Davis, Jr., "The Loyalist Trials at

Some literature of the past two years focused on facts previously reported to the profession, reassembling the known data in useful and convenient ways. An excellent book of this nature is William B. Scott's *In Pursuit of Happiness: American Conceptions of Property from the Seventeenth to the Twentieth Century,*[173] which in addition to reviewing known terrain adds some new details to the previously accepted historical picture. *American Prisons: A History of Good Intentions,*[174] by Blake McKelvey, is a revision of McKelvey's work of several decades ago.[175] It integrates the vast body of recent literature on the history of prisons into McKelvey's earlier work to form a detailed and complex tapestry. The book spans the entire history of American prisons, from William Penn's prescription of imprisonment as a corrective treatment for major offenders and the early experiments with jails as an alternative to capital or corporal punishment, to the late 1960's and early 1970's when violent outbreaks, such as George Jackson's killing at San Quentin and the Attica revolt, rocked a prison system in need of major reform. Also of value is *Courts and Law in Early New York,*[176] a collection of previously published essays about the legal history of New York from 1690 to 1830.

Finally, two articles deserve mention: "Communists and Blacks: The ILO and the Angelo Herndon Case,"[177] by Charles H. Martin, and "Law Schools and Legal Education, 1879-1979: Lectures in Honor of 100

Ninety Six in 1779," 80 *S.C. Hist. Mag.* 172 (1979); James N. Giglio, "Attorney General Harry H. Daugherty and the United Gas Improvement Company Case, 1914-1924," 46 *Pa. Hist.* 347 (1979); Edmund W. Kitch & Clara Ann Bowler, "The Facts of Munn v. Illinois," 1978 *Sup. Ct. Rev.* 313; Steven L. Piott, "Missouri and Monopoly: The 1890's as an Experiment in Law Enforcement," 74 *Mo. Hist. Rev.* 21 (1979); John Phillip Reid, "Replenishing the Elephant: Property and Survival on the Overland Trial," 79 *Or. Hist. Q.* 65 (1978-1979); Joseph F. Steelman, "Origins of the Campaign for Constitutional Reform in North Carolina, 1912-1913," 56 *N.C. Hist. Rev.* 396 (1979); Carol Weisbrod & Pamela Sheingorn, *"Reynolds v. United States:* Nineteenth Century Forms of Marriage and the Status of Women, 10 *Conn. L. Rev.* 828 (1978); John Wunder, "Constitutional Oversight: *Clarke v. Bazadone* and the Territorial Supreme Court as the Court of Last Resort," 4 *Old Northwest* 259 (1978).

[173] (1977).

[174] (1977).

[175] (1936).

[176] Leo Hershkowitz & Milton M. Klein, *Courts and Law in Early New York* (1978).

[177] 64 *J. Negro Hist.* 131 (1979).

Years of the Valparaiso Law School,"[178] by Robert B. Stevens, both of which summarize earlier, lengthy studies by the same authors.[179]

[178] 14 *Val. U.L. Rev.* 179 (1980).

[179] Charles H. Martin, *The Angelo Herndon Case and Southern Justice* (1976); Robert B. Stevens, "Two Cheers for 1870: The American Law School," 5 *Perspectives in Am. Hist.* 405 (1971). Other articles that reconsider material that is already in print are Lawrence Berger, "The Public Use Requirement in Eminent Domain," 57 *Or. L. Rev.* 203 (1978); Rosezella Canty-Letsome, "John Winthrop's Concept of Law in 17th Century New England, One Notion of Puritan Thinking," 16 *Duq. L. Rev.* 331 (1977-1978); Hall Hammond, "Commemoration of the Two Hundredth Anniversary of the Maryland Court of Appeals: A Short History," 38 *Md. L. Rev.* 229 (1978); J. Willard Hurst, "Alexander Hamilton, Law Maker," 78 *Colum. L. Rev.* 483 (1978); Whittington B. Johnson, "The Vinson Court and Racial Segregation, 1946-1953," 63 *J. Negro Hist.* 220 (1978); Kathleen E. Lazarou, "'Fettered Portias,': Obstacles Facing Nineteenth-Century Women Lawyers," 64 *Women L.J.* 21 (1978); Daniel L. Littlefield, Jr. & Lonnie E. Underhill, "The Judiciary of the Western Cherokee Nation, 1839-1876," 22 *Pac. Hist.* 38 (1978); Harry N. Scheiber, "American Federalism and the Diffusion of Power: Historical and Contemporary Perspectives," 9 *Tol L. Rev.* 619 (1978); William M. Wiecek, "Slavery and Abolition before the United States Supreme Court, 1820-1860," 65 *J. Am. Hist.* 34 (1978); Note, Jury Nullification in Historical Perspective: Massachusetts as a Case Study, 12 *Suffolk U.L. Rev.* 968 (1978); "Note, Justice on the Tennessee Frontier: The Williamson County Circuit Court 1810-1820," 32 *Vand. L. Rev.* 413 (1979); "Note, The Tennessee County Courts under the North Carolina and Territorial Governments: The Davidson County Court of Pleas and Quarter Sessions 1783-1796, as a Case Study," 32 *Vand. L. Rev.* 349 (1979).

Chapter Sixteen

1981-1984

William E. Nelson

In 1977 a group of law professors and practicing lawyers held a conference on what they called critical legal studies. The conference led to the birth of the critical legal studies movement, which has had a substantial impact on legal scholarship.[1] Now, after some seven years of development, the work of critical legal studies scholars has become sufficiently important to justify its consideration as a distinct body of legal history literature. Such consideration will occupy Parts I and II of this essay.

At the same time that critical legal studies scholarship has grown to maturity, traditional legal history writing has burgeoned. Parts III and IV of this article will turn to a discussion of this legal and constitutional history scholarship. Throughout the emphasis will be on comparative analysis of the merits of the critical and traditional approaches.

I. *The Critical Legal Studies Movement*

Robert W. Gordon, who has been an eloquent spokeman for the critical legal studies movement in two recent essays,[2] has observed that "[c]ritical legal writers pay a lot of attention to history. In fact, they probably have devoted more pages to historical description . . . than to anything else."[3] But their scholarship is somewhat different from most recent legal history writing. Two qualities differentiate it.[4]

First, historians of the critical school typically believe that "law is indeterminate at its core" because "legal rules derive from structures of

---

[1] For a history of the critical legal studies movement, see John Henry Schlegel, "Notes Toward an Intimate, Opinionated, and Affectionate History of the Conference on Critical Legal Studies," 36 *Stan. L. Rev.* 391 (1984).

[2] See Robert W. Gordon, "Historicism in Legal Scholarship," 90 *Yale L.J.* 1017 (1981); Robert W. Gordon, "Critical Legal Histories," 36 *Stan. L. Rev.* 57 (1984).

[3] Robert W. Gordon, "Critical Legal Histories," 36 *Stan. L. Rev.* 57 (1984).

[4] I will identify these two qualities in the text below. It is Gordon's view, however, that two other qualities also characterize critical legal studies history. First, according to Gordon, the critical legal writers believe that law to an important extent defines relationships among individuals and groups. See *id.* at 103-05. Second, they understand the power of the law to lie "less in the force

thought, the collective constructs of many minds, that are fundamentally contradictory."[5] Since law is indeterminate and thus incapable of autonomous development, critical legal studies historians striving to understand the law focus on its political roots. In particular, they study

> how the latest of these great cultural constructs, "liberal legalism," arose and developed its own characteristic set of mediating devices . . . ; how the construct was purified of its preliberal elements and elaborated to its highest pitch in the late nineteenth century; and how, at the moment of its perfection, it started to decay under attacks from without and the pressure of its own internal contradictions — ultimately leaving us where we are now, living in its ruins, no longer believing in its mediating powers, and clinging to it still because we have found nothing to replace it, and being faithless moderns, doubting that we ever can.[6]

The second defining characteristic of critical legal history is what John Henry Schlegel labels a "note of stridency in some CLS scholarship."[7] The stridency stems from the movement's rejection of notions of objectivity and neutrality; every critical legal studies scholar proclaims

---

that it can bring to bear . . . than in its capacity to persuade people that the world described in its images and categories is the only attainable world in which a sane person would want to live." *Id.* at 109. I do not regard these two precepts as identifying characteristics of critical legal studies historians since I am convinced that they would be accepted by most historians, including many who identify themselves as outside the critical legal studies orbit.

[5] *Id.* at 114.

[6] *Id.* at 114-115. Accord, Alfred S. Konefsky, "Men of Great and Little Faith: Generations of Constitutional Scholars," 30 *Buffalo L. Rev.* 365, 382 (1981); Stephen B. Presser, "'Legal History' or the History of Law: A Primer on Bringing the Law's Past into the Present," 35 *Vand. L. Rev.* 849, 863, 867-868 (1982). Gordon notes, among others, the following recent pieces as examples of critical legal history: Elizabeth Mensch, "The Colonial Origins of Liberal Property Rights," 31 *Buffalo L. Rev.* 635 (1982); Rolf N. Olsen "The Family and the Market: A Study of Ideology and Legal Reform," 96 *Harv. L. Rev.* 1497 (1983); Lea Vandevelde, "The New Property of the Nineteenth Century: The Development of the Modern Concept of Property," 29 *Buffalo L. Rev.* 325 (1980); "Note: Tortious Interference with Contractual Relations in the Nineteenth Century: The Transformation of Property, Contract, and Tort," 93 *Harv. L. Rev.* 1510 (1980). A piece which Gordon regrettably does not cite is "Note: The White Slave Traffic Act: The Historical Impact of a Criminal Law Policy on Women," 72 *Georgetown L. J.* 1111, 1133 (1984).

[7] John Henry Schlegel, *supra* note 1, at 395. For some illustrations of this stridency, see Morton J. Horwitz, "The History of the Public/Private Distinction," 130 *U. Pa. L. Rev.* 1423, 1427-1428 (1982); Alfred S. Konefsky and John Henry Schlegel, "Mirror, Mirror on the Wall: Histories of American Law Schools," 95 *Harv. L. Rev.* 833, 844 (1982).

that "LAW IS POLITICS, pure and simple"[8] and hence finds it appropriate to discuss law in the contentious dialect of political debate rather than the gentlemanly style of scholarly journals. Moreover, the thrust of critical legal studies politics is radical, with much of the writing pointing to "capitalism" as the "heart" of our society's current problems and contradictions.[9]

These two tendencies — to focus scholarly inquiry on the rise and fall of "liberal legalism" and to report findings in strident, politically radical language — recur in many of the seminal critical legal studies writings of recent years. One such book is Jerold Auerbach's *Justice Without Law.*[10] Auerbach contends that informal, nonlegal dispute resolution occurred in American history only among inhabitants of "communities of common purpose" who were bound together "by the values of harmony and consensus." But, as "religious dissenters, political partisans, and acquisitive merchants pursued their particular advantages, new alliances of special interest" appeared, "lines of division multiplied," and "the judiciary emerged as the dominant dispute-settlement institution."[11] "In an atomistic social environment," such as we inhabit today, only courts possess "sufficient coercive power to secure the compliance of disputing parties."[12] For Auerbach, there is thus a link "between religious commitment and non-adversarial forms of disputation," on the one hand, and the protection of individual rights, "private property and litigation," on the other.[13] Since Auerbach makes clear his own dissatisfaction with the legal system,[14] it seems clear that Auerbach's work should be perceived as part of the critical legal studies effort to undermine the individualistic tenor of the American legal order.

Another book typical of those recently written by members of the movement is William C. Chase's *The American Law School and the Rise of Administrative Government.*[15] Chase suggests that American administrative law turned in the wrong direction when it developed the rule that courts would not review administrative decisions for error in the decision-making process. As a result, administrative law did not develop and hold administrators to any substantive standards, and administrative decision-making became a matter of yielding to competing interest groups rather

---

8 John Henry Schlegel, *supra* note 1, at 411 (emphasis in original).

9 Alfred S. Konefsky, *supra* note 6, at 383.

10 Jerold S. Auerbach, *Justice Without Law* ? (1983).

11 *Id.* at 47.

12 *Id.* at 134.

13 *Id.* at 65.

14 See *id.* at vii-viii.

15 William C. Chase, *The American Law School and the Rise of Administrative Government* (1982).

than adhering to substantive standards.[16] Chase's critical legal studies perspective emerges when he posits that administrative law took its wrong turn in response to the scholarly advice of law professors, who urged lawyers not to apply legal analysis to the substance of the administrative process. The professors, according to Chase, did not want to engage in substantive analysis because they had a vested interest in Socratic case discussion in the classroom — a form of discussion that left no room for policy considerations that would constitute an essential element of any substantive approach to administrative law.[17]

Another book within the rubric of critical legal studies, at least if one understands radical ideology as an essential part of the movement, is *Equality under the Constitution: Reclaiming the Fourteenth Amendment.*[18] Its author, Judith Baer, describes her work as "passionate, committed scholarship" designed "to reveal how limited our commitment to equality is, and how extensive it can and should be."[19] Like much critical legal studies scholarship, the book makes predictable arguments from familiar primary and secondary sources. Its historical thrust is "that the Reconstruction amendments were intended to write into the Constitution the [broad] principles of equality and natural rights contained in the Declaration" of Independence[20] — principles that can be used by courts today to generate progressive constitutional doctrine on issues of reverse discrimination, gender discrimination, age, disability, and sexual orientation.[21]

The critical legal studies movement has had a substantial impact on legal history scholarship during the last five years. But the impact has been different from that sought by most writers of the critical school. They aspire to generate debate and challenge received wisdom, to emphasize that there are no right answers to legal questions and that law is simply the product of political choice. It is ironic, then, that textwriters and reference librarians are embracing critical legal studies counterculture and disseminating it to others as truth.

Ideas associated with the critical legal studies movement appear, for example, in an excellent new casebook by Stephen B. Presser and Jamil S. Zainaldin, *Law and American History: Cases and Materials,*[22] and even more significantly in a strong series of books designed "to help

---

[16] See *id.* at 13-15, 85, 144.

[17] See *id.* at 20-21, 33-39.

[18] Judith A. Baer, *Equality under the Constitution: Reclaiming the Fourteenth Amendment* (1983).

[19] *Id.* at 13.

[20] *Id.* at 80.

[21] See *id.* at 36.

[22] Stephen B. Presser and Jamil S. Zainaldin, *Law and American History: Cases and Materials* (1980).

foster improved understanding among undergraduates of the role of law in society through the creation of a series of volumes in law and humanities."[23] The five legal history books in the series — *Early American Law and Society, Law in the New Republic, Law in Antebellum Society, Law and the Nation, 1865-1912,* and *Ordered Liberty*[24] — cover the whole of American legal history with thoughtful essays and a survey of basic source materials.

Given the critical legal studies orientation of some text authors together with the obligation of a text writer to present more than one viewpoint, it is not surprising that critical legal studies ideas should make an appearance in undergraduate texts. But, paradoxically, many undergraduates, whose goal in reading texts is not to understand academic debates but to amass factual knowledge, may misunderstand a book's intention, accept the critical position as truth, and later enter and perhaps retain through law school a strange, new received wisdom about the nature and history of law.

Critical legal studies perspectives also appear in a fine new survey of mid-nineteenth century constitutional development by Harold M. Hyman and William M. Wiecek, *Equal Justice Under Law: Constitutional Development, 1835-1875.*[25] Its sole chapter about common law doctrine accepts a main theme of critical legal studies history: that doctrinal changes in the law of torts, contract and property resulted from capitalist efforts to redistribute wealth and power from underclasses to the newly emerging rich.[26] This is surprising in a book that focuses, quite unlike critical legal studies history, on the American dream of "a biracial society, . . . a federal system of diverse states, a political democracy, and an economic capitalism, in which the races lived on legal terms other than that of master-slave"[27] and is replete with insights about the impact of the dream upon the structure of American government. It is not surprising, however, when one realizes that two erudite historians have little recent literature on mid-nineteenth century common law doctrine to which to turn other than that authored by scholars in the critical legal

---

[23] Jamil S. Zainaldin, *Law in Antebellum Society: Legal Change and Economic Expansion* iv (1983).

[24] The five books are Stephen Botein, *Early American Law and Society* (1983); George Dargo, *Law in the New Republic: Private Law and the Public Estate* (1983); Jamil S. Zainaldin, *Law in Antebellum Society: Legal Change and Economic Expansion* (1983); Jonathan Lurie, *Law and the Nation, 1865-1912* (1983); Gerald L. Fetner, *Ordered Liberty: Legal Reform in the Twentieth Century* (1983).

[25] Harold M. Hyman and William M. Wiecek, *Equal Justice Under Law: Constitutional Development, 1835-1875* (1982).

[26] See *id.* at 30.

[27] *Id.* at 255.

studies movement. To satisfy demands of comprehensiveness, Hyman and Wiecek must incorporate critical perspectives into their text, even though they are aware of the likelihood that some readers will give those ideas a credence which they themselves do not.

An incident that occurred as I was preparing this article is perhaps the best illustration of the paradoxical way in which the critical counter-culture is being transmuted into truth. The incident concerns Mark V. Tushnet's *The American Law of Slavery, 1810-1860.*[28] Tushnet's is an important critical legal studies contribution with a striking hypothesis: that the law of slavery reflected "a self-contradictory world" grounded, on the one hand, in "bourgeois social relations" whose main characteristics are the "exchange of labor power for a wage" and the development of "partial relations among people . . . restricted to concern for each other's place in the production system" and, on the other hand, in "the total relationships of slave society" whose primary qualities are the slave's total obligation to the master and the master's correspondingly total responsibility for the slave.[29] The incident arose out of my failure to find *The American Law of Slavery* in its appointed place in New York University's law library. I then turned to the public library system of which my local library is a part, and I was informed that I could find Tushnet's book, of all places, on a shelf of noncirculating *reference* books in another local library in a predominantly black neighborhood. I assume that some librarian who had not read the book had at one time placed it there for the benefit of high school students interested in learning basic facts about the American law of slavery. I wonder, though, whether the students who read the book appreciate that they are assimilating not the objective facts that the librarian believed it contained but a Marxist[30] interpretation of those facts.

The transmutation of critical legal studies history into truth requires that it, in turn, be critically evaluated. The legal history community as a whole can no longer simply welcome the critical perspective as a fresh new approach. Rather we must ask hard questions and systematically analyze whether critical legal studies history is preferable to traditional legal history.

II. *The Difficulties with Critical Legal Studies History*

Several recent articles focusing on some specific historical findings of critical legal studies scholars have begun this task of analysis. For

---

[28] Mark V. Tushnet, *The American Law of Slavery, 1810-1860* (1981).

[29] *Id.* at 32-33, 36.

[30] On Tushnet's self-proclaimed Marxism, see Mark V. Tushnet, *supra* note 28, at 9.

example, Tony Freyer has challanged the critical legal studies claim that early nineteenth-century law favored entreprenurial classes at the expense of the less privileged. To the contrary, Freyer suggests that "the law often was not as supportive of economic growth as some scholars have maintained" and that "*intra* -class rather than *inter* -class conflict most accurately describes the nature of debtor-creditor disputes prior to the Civil War."[31] Likewise, his study of the operation of eminent domain, "[f]ar from supporting the thesis of one-sided manipulation, . . . discloses complex interactions between landowner, local community, and transportation company."[32]

Gary T. Schwartz similarly rejects the critical legal studies assertion that the nineteenth-century negligence system favored industrial producers.[33] Rather he finds that the "system was applied with impressive sternness to major industries and that tort law exhibited a keen concern for victim welfare."[34] In the same vein, Thomas C. Grey finds that the appeal of Langdellian legal science was more complex than simply "the ideological support it provided for business."[35] Grey notes that classical legal thought "took only a moderately conservative stance in the political struggles of its time" and that its popularity rested largely on its "quasi-religious appeal" to intellectuals "seeking determinate answers in an increasingly incomprehensible world" and to the need of lawyers "to feel that they practiced a learned profession."[36] Finally, Bruce A. Campbell challanges notions that *Dartmouth College* v. *Woodward*[37] was a case designed by the Supreme Court to give corporate entrepreneurs immunity from state control. Rather he contends that they already enjoyed such immunity. Campbell further argues that the Supreme Court used a "popular consensus that business corporation charters were protected from arbitrary legislative amendment or repeal" to extend the same privilege "to private religious and educational corporations."[38] He thus sees *Dartmouth College* as the "first great civil liberties case," in which the Court extended "at least partial constitutional protection for religious,

[31] Tony Freyer, "Antebellum Commercial Law: Common Law Approaches to Secured Transactions," 70 *Kentucky L.J.* 593, 594 (1982).

[32] Tony Freyer, "Reassessing the Impact of Eminent Domain in Early American Economic Development," [1981] *Wis. L. Rev.* 1263-64, 1284 (1981).

[33] Gary T. Schwartz, "Tort Law and the Economy in Nineteenth-Century America: A Reinterpretation," 90 *Yale L.J.* 1717, 1773 (1981).

[34] *Id.* at 1720.

[35] Thomas C. Grey, "Langdell's Orthodoxy," 45 *U. Pitt. L. Rev.* 1, 33 (1983).

[36] *Id.* at 35-37.

[37] 17 U.S. (4 Wheat.) 518 (1819).

[38] Bruce A. Campbell, "*Dartmouth College* as a Civil Liberties Case: The Formation of Constitutional Policy," 70 *Kentucky L.J.* 643, 700-01 (1982).

quasi-religious and secular institutions from predatory majoritarian coalitions."[39]

The best of John Phillip Reid's new books, *Law for the Elephant,*[40] should also be understood as a sharp challenge to critical legal studies history. Reid questions "a theme currently fashionable among historians" — "that Americans are a violent people"[41] and that law was "imposed upon the people of nineteenth-century America by an elitist legal profession serving the greed of a corporate managerial class."[42] On the contrary, Reid shows that a random cross-section of Americans who journeyed west in 1849 and 1850 on the overland trail carried shared legal ideas with them, the most significant of which was an awareness of and respect for the property rights of others. Reid's conclusion speaks best for itself:

> Few emigrants traveling the overland trail to the Pacific coast could have explained the meaning of "words of purchase" or fee simple absolute, yet all understood and a vast majority respected the legal principles vesting in the individual exclusive enjoyment of property lawfully possessed. The overland travelers of 1849 and 1850 had been taught the lesson of the Good Samaritan and knew of Jesus' injunction to love their neighbors as they loved themselves. They might have interpreted the tenets of their faith to mean that no one should be allowed to hoard a surplus of provisions unless paid a high price to part voluntarily with what was not needed for survival. Instead, they respected the rights of property owners much as if still back in the east in the midst of plenty.[43]

Apart from these few essays and one book, however, there is virtually no criticism of critical legal studies history nor systemic discussion of whether scholars should write it in preference to traditional history. As Robert Gordon has observed, a "melancholy truth" is that the critical movement has not attracted "much relevant criticism from outside opponents."[44] I, for one, prefer traditional to critical history, and in the remainder of this section I will take up Gordon's challenge and attempt to offer the criticism he seeks.

Surely one preliminary difficulty with the critical genre is the style of language used by its practitioners. As Gordon puts it, critical legal studies authors "have for the most part not succeeded in communicating

---

[39] *Id.* at 706.

[40] John Phillip Reid, *Law for the Elephant: Property and Social Behavior on the Overland Trail* (1980).

[41] *Id.* at 3.

[42] *Id.* at 335.

[43] *Id.* at 339-340, 363-364.

[44] Robert W. Gordon, *supra* note 3, at 116.

their ideas clearly enough."[45] They have suffered from what A. E. Keir Nash labels "the linguistic peculiarities of Marxist writing."[46] But the addiction to Marxist jargon manifested by critical legal studies authors constitutes only a trivial objection.

A more substantial objection will emerge from an examination of lawyers' legal history, which I have defined previously as the genre of history that studies how the authors of statutes and constitutional provisions adopted in the past intended to resolve legal issues plaguing the present.[47] The consummate piece of recent lawyers' legal history is volume three of William W. Crosskey, *Politics and the Constitution in the History of the United States,* coauthored by William Jeffrey, Jr.[48] The book was written to bolster the claim made in earlier volumes that the framers of the Constitution intended to grant Congress broad power to regulate the national economy.[49] Unlike the first two volumes, however, volume three of *Politics and the Constitution* does not become mired in linguistic and doctrinal analysis, but instead traces the emergence of a "general consensus" by the time of the Constitutional Convention in favor of "a generally empowered government, whose legislature possessed, along with its many other powers, a complete power over the whole commerce of these United States."[50]

Another recent effort to use the past as precedent for resolving current issues is Peter C. Hoffer's and N.E.H. Hull's, *Impeachment in America, 1635-1805.*[51] Hoffer and Hull view impeachments as "the beginnings of court cases"[52] for which a law of impeachment, grounded in precedent, exists. The authors further argue that precedents point toward use of impeachment not as a political weapon, as it was used against Andrew Johnson and William O. Douglas, but as an instrument for curbing corruption and malfeasance in office.[53] The value of precedent

---

[45] *Ibid.*

[46] A.E. Kier Nash, "*In re* Radical Interpretations of American Law: The Relation of Law and History," 82 *Mich. L. Rev.* 274, 330 (1983).

[47] See Ch. 15 *supra,* n. 1.

[48] 3 William Winslow Crosskey and William Jeffrey, Jr., *Politics and the Constitution in the History of the United States* (1980).

[49] Indeed, Professor Jeffrey dedicated volume three "to the Congress of the United States in the hope that it may be led to claim and exercise for the common good of the country the powers justly belonging to it under the Constitution." *Id.* at v.

[50] *Id.* at 462.

[51] Peter Charles Hoffer and N.E.H. Hull, *Impeachment in America, 1635-1805* (1984).

[52] *Id.* at xii.

[53] *Id.* at 265

is also stressed in an article[54] about the 1872 case of *United States v. Klein*,[55] where the Supreme Court struck down an act of Congress directing it to reverse and then dismiss a case appealed to it from the Court of Claims. Its author, Gordon G. Young, argues that "*Klein* prohibits Congress from using its jurisdictional powers to manipulate federal courts so as to reach decisions which, if addressed in terms of substantive law, would be forbidden by the Constitution."[56]

Raymond Wolters' *The Burden of Brown: Thirty Years of School Desegregation*[57] presents a variant of lawyers' legal history. In examining school desegregation in the years since *Brown* in the five districts whose cases were incorporated in the 1954 litigation, Wolters contends that integration has failed in four of the five *Brown* school districts.[58] Like most lawyers' legal history, *The Burden of Brown* is concerned not with historical inquiry into why the past occurred as it did but with an existing line of decisions which, in the author's view, should be modified or overruled.

Similar in aim to Wolter's book is Hugh Rockoff's *Drastic Measures: A History of Wage and Price Controls in the United States*.[59] Rockoff finds that wage and price controls can "help in the fight against inflation:" in particular, that "a temporary application of controls can substantially reduce inflation at a reasonable cost." He nonetheless recognizes that controls are no panacea "for an ailing, inflationary economy "and thus concludes that "extremists on both sides of the debate over controls are wrong."[60]

Wolters' and Rockoff's books, in particular, illustrate the polemical, tract-like nature of history that is more concerned with achieving present political results than with dispassionate inquiry into the past. But why should this tract-like quality of lawyers' legal history — a quality that it shares with critical legal studies history — make it disturbing? Mark Tushnet suggests the obvious reason why liberals, if not critical legal studies radicals, should find tract-like history unsatisfying. Writers of lawyers' legal history, according to Tushnet, "are bad historians because

---

[54] See Gordon G. Young, "Congressional Regulation of Federal Courts' Jurisdiction and Processes: *United States v. Klein* Revisited," [1981] Wis. L. Rev. 1189 (1981).

[55] 80 U.S. (13 Wall.) 128 (1872).

[56] Gordon G. Young, *supra* note 54, at 1260.

[57] Raymond Wolters, *The Burden of Brown: Thirty Years of School Desegregation* (1984).

[58] *Id.* at 273.

[59] Hugh Rockoff, *Drastic Measures: A History of Wage and Price Controls in the United States* (1984).

[60] *Id.* at 234, 246.

they emphasize fragmentary evidence and minimize significant bodies of conflicting or complicating evidence in the service of their partisan goals."[61] Lawyers' legal history, whose function in a liberal political establishment is to resolve group conflict through recourse to a neutral past, is not neutral at all, as Tushnet gleefully observes, and hence fails to attain its end.[62]

Surely Tushnet is wrong, at least if one understands him to be asserting that historians can never portray any portion of the past neutrally. It is impossible within the scope of this essay to explain in detail why Tushnet is wrong, but one example may be illuminating.[63] The example is the willingess of all historians to accept as accurate the statement that Japanese warplanes bombed Pearl Harbor on December 7, 1941. Because all segments of the profession accept this statement as true, historians need not prefer values of one segment to those of another, and the statement's validity can be established neutrally — that is, independently of the conflicting values of the profession's different segments.[64]

Robert Gordon has offered a second reason for rejecting lawyers' legal history. He proposes "a kind of reverse Faustian bargain: our sacrifice of immediate influence in the councils of the great for a potentially enormous increase in understanding of our condition."[65] Gordon seems justified in recommending that some historians should strive to understand "our condition," but heeding his advice does not require that everyone relinquish "influence in the councils of the great." Lawrence G. Sager's 1980 Harvard Law Review Supreme Court Forward[66] will illustrate why. The essay, large segments of which are

---

[61] Mark V. Tushnet, "Following the Rules Laid Down: A Critique of Interpretivism and Neutral Principles," 96 *Harv. L. Rev.* 781, 793 (1983).

[62] See *id.* at 824-827.

[63] My forthcoming essay, William E. Nelson, "The Uses of History in Constitutional Adjudication," examines this question at length. The essay is currently on file at the *Annual Survey of American Law*.

[64] Even Tushnet seems to concede that a value supported by a societal consensus is neutral. See Mark V. Tushnet, *supra* note 61, at 825-826.

[65] See Robert W. Gordon, "Historicism in Legal Scholarship," 90 *Yale L. J.* 1017, 1056 (1981).

[66] Lawrence G. Sager, "The Supreme Court 1980 Term, Foreword: Constitutional Limitations on Congress' Authority to Regulate the Jurisdiction of the Federal Courts," 95 *Harv. L. Rev.* 17 (1981). For another essay on the same topic, see Leland E. Beck, "Constitution, Congress, and Court: On the Theory, Law and Politics of Appellate Jurisdiction of the United States Supreme Court," 9 *Hastings Constitutional L.Q.* 774 (1982). Many other articles also fit within the rubric of lawyers' legal history. See Stephen P. Halbrook, "The Jurispru-

straightforward lawyers' legal history,[67] influenced decisionmakers: it formed the basis of an American Bar Association memorandum sent to members of Congress in an effort to defeat legislation aimed at limiting the jurisdiction of federal courts over specific sorts of constitutional claims.[68] The essay may have even influenced some members of Congress to oppose the legislative proposals. Unless one favors a reduction of federal jurisdiction over constitutional matters, it is difficult to see how Sager's article had any but a salutary effect and even more difficult to see why we would have been better off if Sager had pondered "our condition" instead of writing his essay.

Thus, recourse to widely accepted understandings of our past, the core of lawyers' legal history, can sometimes be useful in resolving

---

dence of the Second and Fourteenth Amendments," 4 *George Mason U.L. Rev.* 1 (1981); David G. Adler, "The Framers and Treaty Termination: A Matter of Symmetry," [1981] *Ariz. St. L.J.* 891 (1981); Morris S. Arnold, "A Historical Inquiry into the Right to Trial by Jury in Complex Civil Litigation," 128 *U. Pa. L. Rev.* 829 (1980); Morris S. Arnold, "A Modest Reply to a Lengthy Discourse," 128 *U. Pa. L. Rev.* 986 (1980); Raoul Berger, "Incorporation of the Bill of Rights in the Fourteenth Amendment: A Nine-Lived Cat," 42 *Ohio St. L.J.* 435 (1981); Raoul Berger, "Incorporation of the Bill of Rights: A Reply to Michael Curtis' Response," 44 *Ohio St. L.J.* 1 (1983); James S. Campbell and Nicholas LePoidevin, "Complex Cases and Jury Trials: A Reply to Professor Arnold," 128 *U. Pa. L. Rev.* 965 (1980); Russell L. Caplan, "The History and Meaning of the Ninth Amendment," 69 *Va. L. Rev.* 223 (1983); Michael Kent Curtis, "The Bill of Rights as a Limitation on State Authority: A Reply to Professor Berger," 16 *Wake Forest L. Rev.* 45 (1980); Michael Kent Curtis, "Further Adventures of the Nine Lived Cat: A Response to Mr. Berger on Incorporation of the Bill of Rights," 43 *Ohio St. L.J.* 89 (1982); Don B. Kates, "Handgun Prohibition and the Original Meaning of the Second Amendment," 82 *Mich. L. Rev.* 204 (1983); William T. Mayton, "Seditious Libel and the Lost Guarantee of a Freedom of Expression," 84 *Colum. L. Rev.* 91 (1984); John V. Orth, "'Forever Separate and Distinct': Separation of Powers in North Carolina," 62 *N.C.L. Rev.* 1 (1984); Michael J. Phillips, "The Life and Times of the Contract Clause," 20 *Am. Bus. L.J.* 139 (1982); Robert E. Shalhope, "The Ideological Origins of the Second Amendment," 69 *J. Am. Hist.* 599 (1982); Martin S. Sheffer, "Did the Framers Intend their Intentions?: Civil Rights, the Fourteenth Amendment, and the Election Campaign of 1866," 12 *Capital U.L. Rev.* 45 (1982); Jonathan K. VanPatten, "In the End is the Beginning: An Inquiry into the Meaning of the Religion Clauses," 27 *St. Louis U.L.J.* 1 (1983); Stephen F. Williams, "'Liberty' in the Due Process Clauses of the Fifth and Fourteenth Amendments: The Framers' Intentions," 53 *U. Colo. L. Rev.* 117 (1981); Bradford Wilson, "The Origin and Development of the Federal Rule of Exclusion," 18 *Wake Forest L. Rev.* 1073 (1982).

[67] See Lawrence G. Sager, *supra* note 66, at 22-24, 34-35, 46-53.

[68] See Letter of David R. Brink, President, American Bar Center, to Members of Congress, May 28, 1982, on file at the *Annual Survey of American Law*.

divisive issues in a neutral way. For this purpose it is welcome. Nonetheless, as a historian, I share the critical scholars' residual discomfort with the tract-like nature of lawyers' legal history. My concern is that historians who write polemical tracts proving what they already know to be true will discover little new knowledge about the past. A fixation on current issues can blind a historian to anything in the past that undercuts his proposed solution to present problems and therefore to much of what the past can teach.

Raymond Wolters' *Burden of Brown*[69] provides an example. Despite Wolters' protestations about the objectivity of his scholarship,[70] I understand his book fundamentally to be a polemical argument that desegregation has generally failed. Wolters does concede that sometimes desegregation has succeeded, but his focus naturally is not on this concession. This failure to analyze the achievement of desegregation deprived Wolters of an opportunity for important historical insight. Wolters could have inquired into the reasons for the successes and failures of desegregation, which in turn, might have led to what is now totally missing from the book: badly needed, imaginative insight into American race relations and class structures.

When we return from our digression into lawyers' legal history, it will be apparent that critical legal studies is characterized by a comparable lack of imagination. Here William Chase's *The Rise of the American Law School*[71] will serve as the example. Chase, it will be recalled, argued that the American administrative process, to its detriment, had failed to develop a capacity for substantive review of legislation because law professors had a vested interest in Socratic class discussion that precluded their development of substantive standards of review. Some historians might criticize Chase for attributing undeserved power to the teaching and scholarship of law professors. But to me the flaw in his work is its failure to explore other reasons why the administrative process was left unchecked by law to develop into a handmaiden of special interests.[72]

---

[69] See Raymond Wolters, *supra* note 57.

[70] See *id*. at 273-75.

[71] See William C. Chase, *supra* note 15.

[72] I have suggested elsewhere that fundamental reasons, related to the law's capacity to protect individuals from government power, underlay such things as the late nineteenth century development of legal formalism, substantive due process, and the Socratic case method in law schools: for law to serve as the protector of individuals it first had to become an objective, scientific system of decisionmaking disconnected from the various political pressure groups that might impinge on individuals. See William E. Nelson, *The Roots of America Bureaucracy, 1830-1900*, at 133-55 (1982). Perhaps courts, in the formative years of the administrative process at the beginning of this century, declined to engage

It is crucial to explain precisely why critical legal studies history like lawyers' legal history tends to ignore novel questions. Its unimaginative character does not grow out of its precept that law is indeterminate and contradictory at its core.[73] Stanley Katz, one of the premier legal historians of our time, has written a fine essay about the nineteenth-century history of American family law which emphasizes indeterminacy and contradiction.[74] In the essay, Katz speaks of women's and children's rights as "expressions of a larger egalitarian trend," which he finds incompatible with the cherished American value of "family cohesion."[75] One may understand Katz to be repeating the standard critical legal studies dogma that law is filled with contradictions which render liberal law, at least, illegitimate, but I find Katz's message both more simple and more sophisticated: that life, not merely law, is replete with contradiction, that "[t]rue to human nature, we want it both ways."[76] By focusing on human nature rather than liberal legalism as the source of law's indeterminacy and contradictions, Katz distances himself from critical legal studies historians. He does not write a polemic against human nature as they would against liberal legalism. Instead of repeating the now familiar litany of liberal legalism's sins, Katz creatively brings to our attention the difficulty of maintaining enduring families in which one member does not dominate the others.

The problem with critical legal studies history lies, in short, in its commitment to polemical dissection of the indeterminacy and contradictions of liberal legalism. Before Roberto Unger wrote *Knowledge and Politics*[77] nearly a decade ago, the task of dissection required supreme creativity. But now the dissection has been completed, and application of Unger's analysis to the American legal past requires little imagination or insight. It is easy for critical legal studies scholars to elaborate the tensions with which nearly all our law is filled — far easier than it is to identify the dominant principles of the law or to analyze how and why they changed. Anyone can do such repetitive critical legal studies scholar-

---

in substantive review of administrative policy choices because they lacked the requisite neutral standards for doing so. Chase should have explored this interesting question and the paradoxical questions to which it leads about the relationship between the power of judges to protect individual liberties and the authority of the executive branch to make policy choices that ultimately impact upon those liberties.

[73] See note 6 *supra* and accompanying text.

[74] Stanley N. Katz, "Legal History and Family History: The Child, the Family, and the State," 21 *Boston College L. Rev.* 1025 (1980).

[75] *Id.* at 1035.

[76] *Ibid.*

[77] See generally Roberto M. Unger, *Knowledge and Politics* (1975).

ship, and other scholars can learn little, if anything new from it. Critical legal studies history simply has too narrow a focus.

As the dean of American legal historians, J. Willard Hurst, reminds us in his latest book,[78] legal historians must study not only conflict among interests, which Hurst has studied more than anyone else, but also how "politically effective sectors of the society have . . . shared ideas and feelings about themselves as a social whole,"[79] including the ideal that use of both private and public power "be consistent with humane regard for the worth and dignity of individuals living within the power system, and that the objective of using power be consistent with the same criterion of ultimate regard for the quality of individual life."[80] As Part III will show, many legal historians in the past five years fortunately have heeded Hurst's advice.

III. *The Advantages of Historians' Legal History*

In recent years, more legal historians than ever have undertaken scholarship unconstrained by either the critical legal studies paradigm or any other single doctrinal framework. Their varied work demonstrates how much can be learned from traditional historical research. Such work offers needed insights into questions that confront policymakers today. At all times history not bound to any one ideological position can provide interesting knowledge about the past.

A. *History Offering Policy Insight*

Several books on the history of criminal law provide insight into the relationship between crime and society that critical legal studies history could not provide. These books suggest that the amount and type of crime occurring in a society are largely determined by the society's structure and values. In this view reducing crime requires more than change in the police, criminal court, and prison systems. To change its criminals a society may also have to change itself.

In *Vengeance and Justice: Crime and Punishment in the 19th-Century South,*[81] Edward L. Ayers shows the superiority of traditional over critical legal studies history. Through his nondogmatic examination of the past, Ayers suggests how criminal violence stems from cultural

---

78 James Willard Hurst, *Law and Markets in United States History: Different Modes of Bargaining Among Interests* (1982).

79 *Id.* at 51.

80 *Id.* at 97.

81 Edward L. Ayers, *Vengeance and Justice: Crime and Punishment in the 19th-Century South* (1984).

glorification of violence. In examining crime statistics in the antebellum South, he observes that, since slave crime was punished almost entirely within the plantation system, most prosecutions were for serious crimes of violence committed by one native-born white against another.[82] These crimes were stimulated by the South's code of honor, which taught men that the failure to respond to insult was unmanly.[83] The same code of honor that produced violent assaults paradoxically explains why courts chose not to send violent convicts to jail. As a result, few people from rural counties went to prison in the antebellum South.[84]

The abolition of slavery transformed the South's criminal justice system by necessitating the system's extension to blacks. Black crime against whites, especially theft, preoccupied white courts,[85] and a new punishment system — the convict lease system — evolved to accommodate the large number of convicts that overburdened the South's prison capacity.[86] As before the war, Southern courts rarely punished white criminals severely for violent crimes committed against other whites.[87] Likewise, they treated crimes committed by blacks against other blacks as "*outside* the law."[88] Ayers continues:[89]

> The cleavage between honor and legality widened over time. . . . Manhood came to be equated with the extralegal defense of one's honor, a manhood made manifest in control of one's woman and in unquestioning respect from one's peers. The contempt antebellum whites felt for those who were so weak they had to go to the law for redress was amplified in the postbellum black community, for the law there represented not only an outside force, but the force of the oppressors.

Ayers sees this code of honor extended today to the cities of the North, where so many Southern migrants of both races have settled. And it remains dominant in the South, the region which, Ayers observes, "still leads the nation in homicide and assault rates, still holds the greatest

---

[82] See *id.* at 109-116.

[83] *Id.* at 13.

[84] See *id.* at 111. Ayers notes that prison was reserved for the lower class inhabitants of the South's cities; he observes that nearly all prisoners in the state penitentiary were recent immigrants who had been convicted of theft. See *id.* at 74-75.

[85] *Id.* at 179.

[86] See *id.* at 185-222.

[87] See *id.* at 179-181, 197.

[88] *Id.* at 234.

[89] *Id.* at 234-235.

number of men on death row, and still contains the largest number of handguns."[90]

Other work on criminal law is similarly valuable to present policy-makers. For example, Lawrence Friedman and Robert Percival find serious crime declining in the late nineteenth century both in the United States and throughout the Western world.[91] But they also find much petty crime in the late nineteenth-century.[92] Hundreds of petty criminals were arrested in order "to show that order and discipline were alive, were real — to show this both to those who made the rules and to those who broke them."[93] Elaborating on the work of Friedman and Percival, other historians have shown that arrest rates for public-disorder crimes have declined over the course of this century. They offer two explanations to account for this decline. One suggests that declining arrests result from the declining use of public space and from the increasing orderliness of America's cities.[94] The other attributes declining arrests to "a gradual shift from a social-control to a crime-fighting model of policing."[95] Both explanations, though, reinforce the policy insight of Ayers: that changing patterns of crime reflect fundamental social changes, such as in the use of public space, and that changes in police practices will most likely affect not the existence of crime, but only its manifestations.

---

[90] *Id.* at 275-276.

[91] See Lawrence M. Friedman and Robert V. Percival, *The Roots of Justice: Crime and Punishment in Alameda County, California, 1870-1910*, at 27 (1981).

[92] See *id.* at 311-13.

[93] *Id.* at 313.

[94] See Eric H. Monkkonen, "A Disorderly People? Urban Order in the Nineteenth and Twentieth Centuries," 68 *J. Am. Hist.* 539, 553 (1981).

[95] Eugene J. Watts, "Police Response to Crime and Disorder in Twentieth-Century St. Louis," 70 *J. Am. Hist.* 340, 342 (1983). Eric Monkkonen has also adopted this view. See Eric H. Monkkonen, *Police in Urban America, 1860-1920,* at 4 (1981). Two other articles focusing on the history of criminal law are also noteworthy. One, which examines the operation of military courts in the Reconstruction South, has found "that black defendants were not treated with even a semblance of equality" but received "much harsher sentences than whites," reflecting either "the common phenomenon of occupation forces adopting the attitudes of the conquered such as occurred in Germany and Japan after World War II" or "the racism that permeated northern communities." Thomas D. Morris, "Equality, 'Extraordinary Law,' and Criminal Justice: The South Carolina Experience, 1865-1866," 83 *S.C. Hist. Mag.* 15, 21, 32 (1982). The other examines how, paradoxically, the New Deal consciously increased the power of the FBI to lead a crusade against crime and then to investigate subversive activities including, ultimately, the New Deal itself. See Kenneth O'Reilly, "A New Deal for the FBI: The Roosevelt Administration, Crime Control, and National Security," 69 *J. Am. Hist.* 638 (1982).

Another area of historical writing with profound implications for today's policymakers concerns the women's movement.[96] The best work on women and the law was done by Norma Basch, who argues that reform of the common law marital property system resulted from (1) some incoherence in New York law following adoption of future interests legislation, (2) the need to protect family assets from creditors, (3) the egalitarian concern that poorer women have the same right to own property independently of their husbands that equity doctrine gave to wealthy women, and (4) demands by women for their rights.[97] In a later prize-winning essay, Basch compresses these concerns into two competing notions about the status of American women in the mid-nineteenth century — "the concept of equity," which "assumed that the property of a wife brought to marriage or inherited afterward . . . was hers," and "the concept of equality," which assumed in a more radical fashion that women should have the same legal and political rights as men.[98] The thrust of both pieces is that the presence of conservative notions of equity in early women's rights legislation provided more radical feminists "with a perfect bridge" which they and their more conservative sisters could later cross "to demand political rights for women not only in their capacities as wives and mothers, but as citizens of the state."[99]

---

[96] Two women's history articles, for example, document the gradual but persistent decline in the legal status of women in America over the course of the seventeenth and eighteenth centuries. See Joan R. Gundersen & Gwen Victor Gampel, "Married Women's Legal Status in Eighteenth-Century New York and Virginia," 39 *Wm. & Mary Q.* (3d ser.) 114, 133-134 (1982); C. Dallett Hemphill, "Women in Court: Sex-Role Differentiation in Salem, Massachusetts, 1636 to 1683," 39 *Wm. & Mary Q.* (3d ser.) 164, 175 (1982). These articles are obviously of importance to scholars seeking to understand how to prevent similar declines in the status of women in the future.

[97] See Norma Basch, *In the Eyes of the Law: Women, Marriage, and Property in Nineteenth-Century New York 113-135* (1982).

[98] Norma Basch, "Equity vs. Equality: Emerging Concepts of Women's Political Status in the Age of Jackson," 3 *J. Early Republic* 297, 299 (1983).

[99] Norma Basch, *supra* note 97, at 164, 199. Two other articles reaffirm Basch's view. Richard H. Chused agrees that "[t]he property reforms of the 1840's should not be perceived as an attack on coverture law. Though the seeds of later reforms were planted by the first wave of married women's property acts," Chused is clear that these acts were, in essence, "debtor protection measures." Only in very recent times, he concludes, "has the legal system taken seriously the notion that equality norms rather than special treatment norms should govern the outcomes of gender-based disputes." Richard H. Chused, "Married Women's Property Law: 1800-1850," 71 *Georgetown L.J.* 1359, 1361, 1424-25 (1983).

In an article about child custody, Michael Grossberg similarly notes that, while "the traditional superiority given paternal custody and guardianship

Several books on technical topics have also contributed to current policy analysis by focusing on issues other than the class struggle. One such book analyzes the history and theory of administrative law. *The Transformation of Wall Street*[100] by Joel Seligman, argues that the "'capture' theory," which holds "that the SEC has been a 'captive' of the industries it regulates" fails to explain "how any particular SEC decision was actually made."[101] Instead, Seligman divides the history of the SEC into two periods. First was the period prior to 1941, when reform of corporate law and corporate practices was a high priority for President Roosevelt and when the SEC, under the successive chairmanship of Joseph Kennedy, James Landis, William O. Douglas, and Jerome Frank, could pilot reform legislation through Congress and otherwise force the securities industry to reform itself. Second was the period since 1941, when presidents have either lacked interest in corporate reform or been distracted by other matters, especially international affairs.[102] Although he never makes the point explicitly, Seligman thus suggests that it is an

---

rights" had become "untenable" in mid-nineteenth century America, "[s]ignificantly . . . instead of granting mothers those powers directly and independently, the courts usurped the role formerly held by fathers and claimed the authority to determine which parent would be granted custody." Michael Grossberg, "Who Gets the Child? Custody, Guardianship, and the Rise of a Judicial Patriarchy in Nineteenth-Century America," 9 *Feminist Stud.* 235, 236 (1983). Grossberg then explains:

> Judges [thus] combined the traditional assumption that married women lacked economic and intellectual independence to act without male supervision (and thus needed special protection) with the new faith in separate and mutually exclusive sexual spheres so central to the organization of the modern family. The result was the double-edged character of married women's legal rights: judges remade the law to aid wives and mothers in performing their domestic chores while at the same time they used their powers to check radical alterations in the subordinate legal status of married women.

Id. at 237. By thus focuing on the conservatism of women's rights advocates in the nineteenth century and the slow and incomplete progress they made, these studies make an important point that the critical legal studies movement ignores — a point about the persistence of basic social values and social structures even in the face of just demands for reform.

Two other pieces that contain interesting insights about women's history are Charles C. Goetsch, *Essays on Simeon E. Baldwin* 186-290 (1981), and "Note: The White Slave Traffic Act: The Historical Impact of a Criminal Law Policy on Women," 72 *Georgetown L. J.* 1111, 1133 (1984).

100 Joel Seligman, *The Transformation of Wall Street: A History of the Securities and Exchange Commission and Modern Corporate Finance* (1982).

101 *Id.* at xi.

102 See *id.* at 212-214, 237-38, 349-355.

agency's political power that determines whether the agency actively directs the course of socio-economic change or serves as a buffer accommodating the competing interests of the groups it regulates and merely responds to basic socio-economic forces such as the market.

In another book about the pre-depression banking system, Eugene N. White argues that nineteenth-century legislation led to an industry composed of a large and growing number of very small unit banks. In the absence of a central bank capable of temporarily increasing bank liquidity, such a system, he observes, was vulnerable to financial crises. Although banking reforms have eliminated some specific weaknesses in the banking system, "[r]arely were attempts made to get at the root cause of many of the system's difficulties — the restrictive regulation that had produced the industry's structure and most of its problems."[103]

The historical scholarship examined here differs markedly from critical legal studies history in its lack of any overarching methodology or theme. Ayers, for instance, seems to have begun his work to determine why patterns of crime in the South differed from those in the North.[104] By contrast, the women's rights historians were probably motivated by their zeal for those rights.[105] Seligman seemed motivated simply to write "a comprehensive history" of the transformation of the nation's "system of corporate finance" during the past fifty years.[106] White, on the other hand, apparently wrote about banking history in an effort to influence contemporary banking policy.[107]

---

[103] See Eugene N. White, *The Regulation and Reform of the American Banking System, 1900-1929,* at 223-224 (1983). On the same subject see also Edward L. Symons, "The 'Business of Banking' in Historical Perspective," 51 *G. Wash. L. Rev.* 676 (1983). Another book on a technical subject is Robert A. Becker, *Revolution, Reform, and the Politics of American Taxation, 1763-1783* (1980), which studies the tax policies of the thirteen American colonies and states during the years in question. Becker's argument is that, during the decade preceding the Revolution, "tax policy was formulated in such a way as to benefit groups dominant in the various legislatures." *Id.* at 227. These policies could be maintained when taxes were low, but the War for Independence led to vastly increased taxes, to demands for tax relief, and ultimately to some tax reform. See *id.* at 225-229.

[104] I draw this inference about Ayers' aspiration from Edward L. Ayers, *supra* note 81, at 3-5.

[105] For insight into the motivation of many students of women's history, see the dedication of Norma Basch, *supra* note 97, "[t]o Carl E. Prince, Mentor, Scholar, Teacher, *Feminist*, and Friend," (emphasis added) and Richard H. Chused, *supra* note 99, at 1359 n.**.

[106] See Joel Seligman, *supra* note 100, at ix-x.

[107] See Eugene Nelson White, *supra* note 103, at 227.

It is precisely this variety of theme, objective, and method that gives the scholarship of these historians its power. No single thesis, not even one initially as illuminating as the critical legal studies focus on the inherent contradictions of liberal legalism, can provide so much insight on such diverse policy questions as how to reduce crime, protect women's rights and regulate industry. At least for those who seek insight into current policy issues, traditional history seems superior to the new critical legal studies variety.

B. *History Offering Knowledge of the Past*

Traditional history also constitutes a better instrument than critical legal studies history for simply learning about the past. The reason is the same: no one hypothesis can generate as much insight into the past as can the historian's basic conceptual tool, the examination of changes over time. Several recent books will demonstrate how much scholars can learn simply by examining processes of historical change.

Hendrik Hartog's fine book about the changing nature of government in eighteenth and nineteenth-century New York offers the first example. Hartog's book shows how nineteenth-century New York became unable to govern, as it had been accustomed, through using its personal, private estate to compel individuals to fulfill their obligations to the city and was forced to rely instead on public employees who could be "mobilized to do those tasks private residents of the city should not be expected to do."[108]

---

[108] See Hendrik Hartog, *Public Property and Private Power: The Corporation of the City of New York in American Law, 1730-1870* (1983). Hartog notes that the principal business of New York municipal government in the 18th century "was the management, care, and disposal of the real estate it owned." *Id.* at 40. It used this real estate — chiefly its lots along the waterfront — "to shift the burden of action to private individuals." *Id.* at 63. Hartog explains at length:

> [W]aterlot grants offered the possibility of achieving positive governmental goals — paving the streets, developing a harbor — at a time when there was no theory of direct government action. How do you get something done if you do not know how, or rather, if you cannot conceive of doing it yourself? . . . The promised reward of the waterlot (and its profits) gave the city the power to coerce grantees to do things that they were not obliged as citizens to do.

Id. at 68. In the nineteenth century, the city secured legislation from the Albany legislature to obtain new authority. See *id.* at 132. It thereby expanded state at the expense of city authority. *See id.* at 154, 262-63. Edwin A. Gere, "Dillon's Rule and the Cooley Doctrine: Reflections of the Political Culture," 8 *J. Urban Hist.* 271 (1982), further explains how state legislatures expanded their powers at the expense of localities as late nineteenth century courts adopted Dillon's Rule,

A book by Peter C. Hoffer and N.E.H. Hull, *Murdering Mothers,*[109] focuses on the Anglo-American law of infanticide from the sixteenth to the eighteenth century. The book documents the concerted effort of lawmakers and judges in the late sixteenth and early seventeenth centuries to put an end to infanticide. But then, "[o]ver the course of the next century, this severity turned into leniency," and child murderers frequently received either light punishment or none at all.[110] Surely this interesting book would not have been written had the critical legal studies focus on liberal legalism curbed the creativity of the authors.

Tony Freyer likewise focuses on change over time instead of the contradictions of liberal legalism in his study of the *Swift* and *Erie* cases in American federalism.[111] Freyer argues that Justice Story's opinion in *Swift v. Tyson*[112] was narrowly drafted to apply federal common law only in commercial cases.[113] But during the nineteenth century the narrow doctrine of *Swift* was transformed into an expansive federal common law.[114] Consequently dissatisfaction with *Swift* developed, and in 1938 the Court handed down *Erie R.R. v. Tompkins,* reversing the 96-year-old precedent.[116]

Also worthy of note is Paul Finkelman's *An Imperfect Union.*[117] Focusing on the doctrine of comity Finkelman argues that in the early part of the century both Northern and Southern courts deferred to each other and recognized the status, whether free or slave, which the other had conferred on blacks coming within its jurisdiction. He sees a harbinger of the civil war in the decline of comity and deference during

---

which limits municipal powers to those expressly granted in charters, in preference to the Cooley Doctrine, which credits municipalities with inherent rights. Gere attributes the preference for Dillon's rule to the "state and national moods of the . . . time, . . . when the evils of bossism, corruption in city hall, the spoils system, and machine politics pervaded the American urban landscape." *Id.* at 294.

[109] Peter C. Hoffer and N.E.H. Hull, *Murdering Mothers: Infanticide in England and New England, 1558-1803* (1981).

[110] *Id.* at ix-x.

[111] Tony Freyer, *Harmony & Dissonance: The* Swift & Erie *Cases in American Federalism* (1981).

[112] 41 U.S. (16 Pet.) 1 (1842).

[113] Tony Freyer, *supra* note 111, at 36-38.

[114] *Id.* at 45.

[115] 304 U.S. 64 (1938).

[116] See Tony Freyer, *supra* note 111, at 101.

[117] Paul Finkelman, *An Imperfect Union: Slavery, Federalism, and Comity* (1981).

the 1840s and 1850s when both North and South insisted on applying their own law in slave transit cases.[118]

Two final historians who focused in an interesting fashion on change were Bradley Chapin and Adam Hirsch. Chapin's book[119] argues that early colonial law often departed from English practice as the colonists adopted many of the law reforms being demanded at home. Detailed reception of the common law did not occur until after 1660, when "lawyers and the various English government boards charged with the oversight of colonial administration . . . moved in with all their gear and planted virtually all of the old seeds."[120] Adam Hirsch's study focuses on changes in the form of punishment in Massachusetts — from penalties like the stocks and pillory to imprisonment — in the years between 1785, when Massachusetts first experimented with a state prison, and 1805, when the first large, permanent prison was built.[121] As I have argued elsewhere, these were the very years when the cohesive communities of eighteenth-century Massachusetts were dissolving under pressures of economic growth and political and religious division,[122]and Hirsch, in fact, sees the demise of the old sanctions, which were effective only in tight-knit communities where residents needed each others' respect, as related to the breakdown of such communities.[123]

Not all traditional historians, of course, have searched for new insight. Some have strived merely to reaffirm existing knowledge. Thus, David G. Allen has reminded us that "New England communities continued the laws and customs of old England,"[124] while Charles M. Cook reasserts that early nineteenth century codification "was, by and large, a lawyer's reform designed to remedy ills that practitioners and

---

[118] See *id.* at 339-342. For another interesting piece by Finkelman on the clash between the law of slavery and freedom, see Paul Finkelman, "The Law of Slavery and Freedom in California 1848-1860," 17 *Cal. W. L. Rev.* 437 (1981).

[119] Bradley Chapin, *Criminal Justice in Colonial America, 1606-1660* (1983).

[120] *Id.* at 146-148.

[121] See Adam J. Hirsch, "From Pillory to Penitentiary: The Rise of Criminal Incarceration in Early Massachusetts," 80 *Mich. L. Rev.* 1179 (1982).

[122] See William E. Nelson, *Dispute and Conflict Resolution in Plymouth County, Massachusetts, 1725-1825,* at 133-152 (1981).

[123] Adam J. Hirsch, *supra* note 121, at 1240. Another student of crime in colonial New England, David H. Flaherty, also agrees that community cohesiveness was an important reason why "the incidence of serious criminal deviance in provincial Massachusetts was indeed of modest proportions." David H. Flaherty, "Crime and Social Control in Provincial Massachusetts," 14 *Hist. J.* 339, 343-345 (1981).

[124] David Grayson Allen, *In English Ways: The Movement of Societies and the Transferal of English Local Law and Custom to Massachusetts Bay in the Seventeenth Century* 4 (1981).

judges observed in the legal environment."[125] Samuel Walker's *Popular Justice*[126] is a useful compendium of existing knowledge about the history of American criminal justice, and Robert G. Dunbar's *Forging New Rights in Western Waters* retells how the western states adopted the doctrine of prior appropriation in water rights cases.[127]

Other scholars have tried to write comprehensive and definitive books on particular subject areas. The best book of this genre is Robert B. Stevens' *Law School: Legal Education in America from the 1850s to the 1980s,* an exhaustively researched and annotated summary of the available learning.[128] Another important body of work has been authored by Kermit L. Hall on the nineteenth century judiciary.[129] Other similar attempts to produce definitive monographs are Liva Baker, *Miranda: Crime, Law and Politics,*[130] a study of the *Miranda* case and of political

---

125 Charles M. Cook, *The American Codification Movement: A Study of Antebellum Legal Reform* 70 (1981).

126 Samuel Walker, *Popular Justice: A History of American Criminal Justice* (1980).

127 Robert G. Dunbar, *Forging New Rights in Western Waters* (1983). There were, of course, also many articles in the past five years that reaffirmed conventional wisdom. See Bruce Beezer, "North Carolina's Rationale for Mandating Separate Schools: A Legal History," 52 *J. Negro Educ.* 213 (1982); Kenneth W. Dam, "The Legal Tender Cases," [1981] *Sup. Ct. Rev.* 367 (1981); Calvin P. Jones, "Kentucky's Irascible Conservative: Supreme Court Justice James Clark McReynolds," 57 *Filson Club Hist. Q.* 20 (1983); Vukan Kuie, "John C. Calhoun's Theory of the 'Concurrent Majority,'" 69 *A.B.A.J.* 482 (1983); Joseph M. Lynch, "*Fletcher v. Peck:* The Nature of the Contract Clause," 13 *Seton Hall L. Rev.* 1 (1982); Paul L. Murphy, "*Near v. Minnesota* in the Context of Historical Developments," 66 *Minn. L. Rev.* 95 (1981); Joyce M. Ray & F.G. Gosling, "Historical Perspectives on the Treatment of Mental Illness in the United States," 10 *J. Psychiatry and L.* 135 (1982); Thomas J. Reed, "Training the American Aristocracy: An Historical Examination of American Legal Education Models," 6 *Texas S. L. Rev.* 317 (1979); Gilbert Ware, "*Hocutt:* Genesis of *Brown,*" 52 *J. Negro Educ.* 227 (1983).

128 Robert Stevens, *Law School: Legal Education in America from the 1850s to the 1980s* (1983).

129 See Kermit L. Hall, *The Politics of Justice: Lower Federal Judicial Selection and the Second American Party System, 1829-1861* (1979); Kermit L. Hall, "The Children of the Cabins: The Lower Federal Judiciary, Modernization, and the Political Culture, 1789-1899, 75 *Nw. U.L. Rev.* 423 (1980); Kermit L. Hall, "Mere Party and the Magic Mirror: California's First Lower Federal Judicial Appointments," 32 *Hastings L.J.* 819 (1981); Kermit L. Hall, "Hacks and Derelicts Revisited: American Territorial Judiciary, 1789-1959," 12 *W. Hist. Q.* 273 (1981); Kermit L. Hall, "The Judiciary on Trial: State Constitutional Reform and the Rise of an Elected Judiciary, 1846-1860," 45 *Historian 337* (1983).

130 Liva Baker, *Miranda: Crime, Law and Politics* (1983). For another book which is not as detailed as Baker's on a Supreme Court case, see Fred W.

and judicial reactions to it since its decision; Gordon M. Bakken, *The Development of Law on the Rocky Mountain Frontier;*[131] Catherine A. Barnes, *Journey from Jim Crow: The Desegregation of Southern Transit*[132] Joseph B. James, *The Ratification of the Fourteenth Amendment;*[133] and Ronald E. Seavoy, *The Origins of the American Business Corporation, 1784-1855.*[134]

Friendly, *Minnesota Rag: The Dramatic Story of the Landmark Supreme Court Case That Gave Meaning to Freedom of the Press* (1981).

[131] Gordon Morris Bakken, *The Development of Law on the Rocky Mountain Frontier: Civil Law and Society, 1850-1912* (1983).

[132] Catherine A. Barnes, *Journey from Jim Crow: The Desegregation of Southern Transit* (1983).

[133] Joseph B. James, *The Ratification of the Fourteenth Amendement* (1984).

[134] Ronald E. Seavoy, *The Origins of the American Business Corporation, 1784-1855: Broadening the Concept of Public Service During Industrialization* (1982). Many articles in the past five years also focused largely on the discovery and reporting of historical fact. See Morris S. Arnold, "An Early Opinion of an Arkansas Trial Court," 5 *U. Ark. L.J.* 397 (1982); Morris S. Arnold, "The Arkansas Colonial Legal System, 1686-1766," 6 *U. Ark. L.J.* 391 (1983); Hans W. Baade, "Law at Texas: The Roberts-Gould Era (1883-1893)," 36 *S.W. Hist. Q.*161 (1982); Hans W. Baade, "The Law of Slavery in Spanish Louisiana, 1769-1803," in Edward F. Haas ed., *Louisiana's Legal Heritage* 43 (1983); Gordon M. Bakken, "The Development of the Law of Mortgage in Frontier California, 1850-1890," 63 *S. Cal. Q.* 45, 137, 232 (1981); Warren M. Billings, "Pleading, Procedure, and Practice: The Meaning of Due Process of Law in Seventeenth-Century Virginia," 47 *J. So. Hist.* 569 (1981); David J. Bodenhamer, "The Democratic Impulse and Legal Change in the Age of Jackson: The Example of Criminal Juries in Antebellum Indiana," 45 *Historian* 206 (1983); John M. Bryan, "Robert Mills, Benjamin Henry Latrobe, Thomas Jefferson, and the South Carolina Penitentiary Project, 1806-1808," 85 *S.C. Hist. Mag.* 1 (1984); Keith Burgess-Jackson, "The Legal Status of Suicide in Early America: A Comparison with the English Experience," 29 *Wayne L. Rev.* 57 (1982); Frank L. Dewey, "The Waterson-Madison Episode: An Incident in Thomas Jefferson's Law Practice," 90 *Va. Mag. Hist. & Biog.* 165 (1982); Michael B. Dougan, "The Doctrine of Creative Destruction: Ferry and Bridge Law in Arkansas," 39 *Ark. Hist. Q.* 136 (1980); James C. Duram, "Thompson v. Auditor General: The Michigan Supreme Court and the Depression Emergency," 66 *Mich. Hist.* 12 (1982); Tony A. Freyer, "Politics and Law in the Little Rock Crisis, 1954-1957," 40 *Ark. Hist. Q.* 195 (1981); Russell W. Galloway, "The Roosevelt Court: The Liberals Conquer (1937-1941) and Divide (1941-1946)," 23 *Santa Clara L. Rev.* 491 (1983); Robert C. Hauhart, "The Origin and Development of the British and American Patent and Copyright Laws," 5 *Whittier L. Rev.* 539 (1983); Irving G. Hendrick, "Stare Decisis, Federalism, and Judicial Self-Restraint: Concepts Perpetuating the Separate But Equal Doctrine in Public Education, 1849-1954," 12 *J. L. & Educ.* 561 (1983); Shael Herman, "Llewellyn the Civilian: Speculations on the Contribution of Continental Experience to the Uniform Commercial Code," 56 *Tulane L. Rev.* 1125 (1982); Peter C. Hoffer, "Law and Liberty:

Examined together as a body of scholarly literature, the work of traditional legal historians over the past five years is simply of much greater interest and substance than the work of critical legal studies historians. Traditional legal historians are not constrained by their

---

In the Matter of Provost William Smith of Philadelphia, 1758," 38 *Wm. & Mary Q.* (3d ser.) 681 (1981); Michael W. Homer, "The Territorial Judiciary: An Overview of the Nebraska Experience, 1854-1867," 63 *Neb. Hist.* 349 (1982); R. Douglas Hurt, "The Populist Judiciary: Election Reform and Contested Offices," 4 *Kan. Hist.* 130 (1981); Yasuhide Kawashima, "Adoption in Early America," 20 *J. Fam. L.* 677 (1982); Richard Kilbourne, "Securing Commercial Transactions in the Antebellum Legal System of Louisiana," 70 *Ky. L.J.* 609 (1982); Robert B. Kirtland, "Keep Your Eye on the Bastards: Or Sobering Reflections on the 150-Year Record of Early Virginia's Attitude Toward Lawyers," 14 *Tol. L. Rev.* 685 (1983); J. Morgan Kousser, "Separate but *not* Equal: The Supreme Court's First Decision on Racial Discrimination in Schools," 46 *J. So. Hist.* 17 (1980); Cal Ledbetter, "The Constitution of 1836; A New Perspective," 41 *Ark. Hist. Q.* 215 (1982); Paul D. Marsella, "The Court of General Sessions of the Peace in the Eighteenth Century," 117 *Essex Inst. Hist. Coll.* 105 (1981); Joseph W. McKnight, "Protection of the Family Home from Seizure by Creditors: The Sources and Evolution of a Legal Principle," 86 *S.W. Hist. Q.* 369 (1983); Robert N. Peters, "The 'First' Oregon Code: Another Look at Deady's Role," 82 *Ore. Hist. Q.* 383 (1981); Garrett Power, "Apartheid Baltimore Style: The Residential Segregation Ordinances of 1910-1913," 42 *Md. L. Rev.* 289 (1983); Raphael J. Rabalais, "The Influence of Spanish Laws and Treatises on the Jurisprudence of Louisiana: 1762-1828," 42 *La. L. Rev.* 1485 (1982); Thomas J. Reed, "The Development of the Propensity Rule in Federal Criminal Causes 1840-1975," 51 *Cin. L. Rev.* 299 (1982); Steven A. Rosen, "Police Harassment of Homosexual Women and Men in New York City, 1960-1980," 12 *Colum. Hum. Rts. L. Rev.* 159 (1980); Marylynn Salmon, "Women and Property in South Carolina: The Evidence from Marriage Settlements, 1730 to 1830," 39 *Wm. & Mary Q.* (3d ser.) 655 (1982); Guadalupe SanMiguel, "The Struggle Against Separate and Unequal Schools: Middle Class Mexican Americans and the Desegregation Campaign in Texas, 1929-1957," 23 *Hist. Educ. Q.* 343 (1983); E. Lee Shepard, "Honor Among Lawyers: The Case of Charles Marshall Jones and Edward Sayre," 90 *Va. Mag. Hist. & Biog.* 325 (1982); E. Lee Shepard, "Breaking into the Profession: Establishing a Law Practice in Antebellum Virginia," 48 *J. So. Hist.* 393 (1982); Donna J. Spindel, "Law and Disorder: The North Carolina Stamp Act Crisis," 57 *N.C. Hist. Rev.* 1 (1980); Rebecca Wunder Thomson, "History of Territorial Federal Judges for the Territory of Wyoming: 1869-1890," 17 *Land & Water L. Rev.* 567 (1982); Jose M.C. Vasquez, "Reciprocal Influences between the Laws of Spain and Louisiana," 42 *La. L. Rev.* 1473 (1982); Christopher Waldrep, "Egalitarianism in the Oligarchy: The Grand Jury and Criminal Justice in Livingston County, 1799-1808," 55 *Filson Club Hist. Q.* 253 (1981); G. Edward White, "The Working Life of the Marshall Court, 1815-1835," 70 *Va. L. Rev.* 1 (1984); "Note: The Triangle Shirtwaist Company Fire of 1911: A Lesson in Legislative Manipulation," 62 *Tex. L. Rev.* 361 (1983); "Note: Commercial Arbitration in the Eighteenth Century: Searching for the Transformation of American Law," 93 *Yale L.J.* 135 (1983).

ideology to inquiries into only limited aspects of the past. Traditional legal historians can ask more questions than critical legal studies historians and, because they can ask more questions, they will inevitably accumulate more knowledge.

IV. *The Incompatability of Constitutionalism and Critical Legal Studies History*

The same characteristics that make traditional legal history preferable to critical legal studies history as an instrument for learning about the past also make traditional constitutional history superior. But a further reason also exists why the approach of the adherents of critical legal studies is inapposite to the study of American constitutional history.

The critical legal studies premise, as we have seen, is that law is indeterminate at its core. Indeed, law is simply politics, and decisions which courts make originate not in legal principles but in the political values of judges. Such a view of law, whatever its merits, will prove useless, however, to a polity that protects individual rights through constitutional law. Grounding law only in the self-interest or political values of judges provides a frail foundation for freedom. To insulate individual rights from political infringement, constitutional law must be perceived as a body of fixed principles beyond the reach of political forces. "Constitutional theory," as even critical legal studies thinkers have recognized, is thus "a concommitant of liberalism."[135] Constitutional history is similarly moored to the percepts of liberalism. Liberals who believe in individual freedom study constitutional history not merely to uncover interesting knowledge about the past, but to reveal the enduring constitutional values which determine the scope of individual rights. Critical legal studies precepts, on the other hand, are inconsistent with the protection of individual rights. Critical legal studies history that focuses on the work of the makers and interpreters of constitutional law is not constitutional history at all, but anti-constitutional history.

A number of books in recent years have added to legal historical knowledge through publication of source materials. See Michael R. Belknap ed., *American Political Trials* (1981); 1 and 2 Alfred S. Konefsky and Andrew J. King eds., *The Papers of Daniel Webster: Legal Papers* (1982-1983); John P. Reid ed., *The Briefs of the American Revolution* (1981). See also Michael S. Hindus, Theodore M. Hammett and Barbara M. Hobson, *The Files of the Massachusetts Superior Court, 1859-1959: An Analysis and A Plan for Action* (1980). Two other books have collected essays. See Herbert A. Johnson ed., *Essays on New York Colonial Legal History* (1981); Thomas K. McCraw, *Regulation in Perspective: Historical Essays* (1981).

[135] Mark V. Tushnet, *supra* note 61, at 783.

Liberal constitutional history must aspire to identify how determinate principles of constitutionalism can provide determinate answers to issues of constitutional law. Despite difficulties, the historical scholarship of recent years has moved in two ways. One body of scholarship has shown how the founding fathers' faith in the existence of fixed constitutional principles helped them to establish the institutions that have effectively, if not absolutely protected individual autonomy. A second body of scholarship has begun to elaborate some determinate principles upon which courts might base rights-sensitive constitutional doctrine.

A. *The Constitutional Faith of the Founding Fathers*

One important contribution to the constitutional history of the Revolutionary era is Herbert J. Storing's *What the Anti-Federlists Were For,*[136] the separately published introduction to a multi-volume set of Antifederalist papers.[137] Storing finds the Antifederalists' primary reason for opposing the Constitution[138] was their recognition thaι "a community of mere interest" provided an inadequate basis for freedom. The Antifederalists believed that the American polity had to be galvanized by a common moral purpose.[139] As Storing concludes, the need for a community of shared moral values — a need that members of the critical legal studies movement refuse to recognize — "is not less vital today than it was in the 1780s or the 1850s."[140]

Several historians have worked to elaborate the shared moral vision possessed by the founding fathers. Donald S. Lutz, for one, captures their vision in his new book on the political theory of the early state constitutions.[141] According to Lutz, America was dominated by a Whig political theory derived from seventeenth-century English Whig theory and grounded, in turn, in an assumption of homogeneity of interests.[142] Moreover, Lutz continues:[143]

> Homogeneity of interests was not only assumed, it was enforced. . . . Homogeneity was enforced in most communities through careful control of who could live there. . . . Political faction was looked

[136] Herbert J. Storing, *What the Anti-Federalists Were For: The Political Thought of the Opponents of the Constitution* (1981).

[137] Herbert J. Storing ed., *The Complete Anti-Federalist* (7 vols., 1981)

[138] See Herbert J. Storing, *supra* note 136, at 6.

[139] *Id.* at 76.

[140] *Ibid.*

[141] See Donald S. Lutz, *Popular Consent and Popular Control: Whig Political Theory in the Early State Constitutions* (1980).

[142] See *id.* at 214, 221.

[143] *Id.* at 224.

> upon as the greatest danger to these communities, and extraordinary means were taken to prevent it.

Willi Paul Adams, the author of *The First American Constitutions,*[144] one of the most notable books of the past several years, agrees that "the decisive element in founding the new nation" was not any Enlightenment ideology, but "the much more immediate Anglo-American constitutional tradition" that was at least as much institutional as ideological.[145] Because American Revolutionary thought had this institutional basis, "the founding situation of American political culture was not conducive to . . . simple-minded theory or to the establishment of neatly coordinated institutions,"[146] and, as a result, the American Revolution enjoyed an "undoctrinaire character."[147] Adams writes:[148]

> It was undoctrinaire in the sense that even guiding principles remained subject to the test of practicability. Where the test revealed irreconcilability with existing interests and institutions, . . . the ideal was —at least temporarily — abandoned. . . . [C]ontroversial issues were not resolved in one stroke by the disinterested application of the political norms professed in the founding situation. . . . The American leaders found support for this attitude in the revered model of the Glorious Revolution. In 1688, too, new political principles had been accommodated within traditional governmental forms.

In pursuit of this thesis Adams explains that the concept of equality, for example, grew out of the English constitutional tradition as the colonists put the tradition to work to undermine parliamentary supremacy.[149] He likewise notes that "the postulate of equality" was limited by the reality of slavery — an economic and political reality that "outweighed ideological considerations."[150] He finally observes that the structure of the federal government came not from some theoretical model but from patterns of localism and separation of powers which had existed in America since colonial times.[151]

---

[144] Willi Paul Adams, *The First American Constitutions: Republican Ideology and the Making of the State Constitutions in the Revolutionary Era* (1980).

[145] *Id.* at 24.

[146] *Id.* at 26.

[147] *Id.* at 118.

[148] *Ibid.*

[149] See *id.* at 164-169.

[150] *Id.* at 180.

[151] *Id.* at 290.

John Phillip Reid sees essentially the same pattern in another of his books, *In Defiance of the Law,*[152] where he addresses the standing army controversy to illuminate the dichotomy between the imperial view of constitutional law as the command of the sovereign (today, the critical legal studies view) and the colonial view of the constitution (which remains a sensible basis for contemporary constitutionalism) as grounded in Whiggish customary rights carried over to America from seventeenth century England.[153] A.G. Roeber also attends to the ideology of the pre-Revolutionary era, with its division between court and country, to show how the legal profession, which at least in Virginia began as an interest associated with the court, exploited widely shared concerns with inefficiency in the administration of justice to realign itself by the outbreak of the Revolution with the country party.[154] Finally, the constitutional ideology of the Revolutionary era is the subject of *A Constitutional*

---

[152] John Phillip Reid, *In Defiance of the Law: The Standing-Army Controversy, The Two Constitutions, and the Coming of the American Revolution* (1981).

[153] See *id.* at 3-4. See also John Phillip Reid, "In the Taught Tradition —The Meaning of Law in Massachusetts Bay Two-Hundred Years Ago, 14 *Suffolk U.L. Rev.* 931 (1980).

[154] See A.G. Roeber, *Faithful Magistrates and Republican Lawyers: Creators of Virginia Legal Culture, 1680-1810,* at 126-145 (1981). For a further elaboration of some of Roeber's points, see A.G. Roeber, "'The Scrutiny of the Ill Natured Ignorant Vulgar': Lawyers and Print Culture in Virginia, 1716 to 1774," 91 *Va. Mag. Hist. & Biog.* 387 (1983). Three other essays dealing with constitutional history also merit note. In the first, Michael Conant makes the persuasive argument that one of the rights which the ninth amendment was intended to protect was freedom from government-supported monopolies — a right violated today by numerous regulatory statutes. See Michael Conant, "The Antimonopoly Tradition under the Ninth and Fourteenth Amendments: *Slaughter-House Cases* Re-Examined," 31 *Emory L.J.* 785 (1982). In the second, Michael Belknap observes that many proponents of the New Deal argued that the Congressional power to deal with emergencies rather than the commerce power provided the constitutional basis for its activities. He then proceeds to explain why the Supreme Court rejected the emergency powers doctrine in favor of a broad reading of the commerce clause. See Michael R. Belknap, "Historical Observation: The New Deal and the Emergency Powers Doctrine," 62 *Tex. L. Rev.* 67 (1983). In the third essay, James L. Kainan argues that, in the early nineteenth century, the Marshall Court protected vested rights, which he defines as traditional rights in land duly sanctioned by state legislatures, but by the end of the century, Kainen maintains, the Court was protecting substantive rights, by which he means rights sanctioned by some vision of a higher law whether or not the right had received any legislative sanction. James L. Kainan, "Nineteenth Century Interpretations of the Federal Contract Clause: The Transformation from Vested to Substantive Rights against the State," 31 *Buffalo L. Rev.* 381 (1983).

History of Habeas Corpus.[155] There William F. Duker argues that the federal constitution was intended to prevent congressional suspension of state habeas corpus issued to prisoners in federal custody, not to provide a federal writ on behalf of federal and state prisoners.[156] Duker's main point reinforces Willi Paul Adams' perception that the Constitution grew chiefly from existing institutional practices and not from any elaborate ideology.

George L. Haskins and Herbert A. Johnson have also written on the formative era of American constitutionalism in *Foundations of Power: John Marshall, 1801-15,*[157] the best book yet to appear in the Holmes Devise history of the Supreme Court. Their findings are quite consistent with other work that sees a consensus growing out of institutional practice as the basis of American constitutionalism.[158] Haskins and Johnson show specifically how Marshall transformed the Court from a "relatively feeble institution during the 1790's" into a powerful one.[159] According to the authors, Marshall succeeded because he understood what scholars in the critical legal studies movement fail to perceive: that courts can play a useful social role in a liberal polity only when they serve as "bulwark[s] of an identifiable rule of law as distinct from the accommodations of politics."[160]

B. *Elaborating Determinate Principles of Constitutional Rights*

The primary argument of critical legal studies theorists, however, is that the rule of law is a concept without meaning. In response, the most crucial contribution of constitutional historians in the past several years has been to put specific content into the rule of law by elaborating determinate principles that must underlie any constitutional jurisprudence devoted to protecting individual autonomy. While no one piece of scholarship self-consciously strives to elaborate these principles, several pieces, read in conjunction, constitute a step toward the effort.

We must begin consideration of this literature with an important book — Jean V. Matthews, *Rufus Choate: The Law and Civic Virtue.*[161] Through the medium of a biography of Choate, this book examines the

---

[155] William F. Duker, *A Constitutional History of Habeas Corpus* (1980).

[156] See *id.* at 126.

[157] George L. Haskins and Herbert A. Johnson, *Foundations of Power: John Marshall, 1801-15* (1981).

[158] See William E. Nelson, "The Eighteenth Century Background of John Marshall's Constitutional Jurisprudence," 76 *Mich. L. Rev.* 893 (1978).

[159] See George L. Haskins and Herbert A. Johnson, *supra* note 157, at 7.

[160] *Ibid.* The same view is also presented in George L. Haskins, "Law versus Politics in the Early Years of the Marshall Court," 130 *U. Pa. L. Rev.* 1 (1981).

[161] Jean V. Matthews, *Rufus Choate: The Law and Civic Virtue* (1980).

significance of the rule of law as a stabilizing force in American society since the early nineteenth century. Matthews commences with a statement of the problem which constitutional theorists have confronted since that time: that

> economic development and diversification . . . [had] differentiated the ideas and interests of the individual from those of others and offered him unprecedented opportunities to maximize his own personal satisfactions, . . . to prefer private to public good, or merely to retire into a private world and renounce any obligation or responsibility for the larger whole.[162]

As a result, people in the nineteenth century experienced a "poignant sense of loss: loss experienced as separation — from God, from the self, in particular from the community of fellow men. . . . [T]raditional pieties, deference and notions of civility" collapsed, and people became "acutely aware of living in an age of disassociation and disaffiliation, of being poised always on the edge of dissolution."[163] The rule of law served to recreate "the conviction that society had a certain organic unity and that government had an obligation to act for the common good,"[164] and nineteenth century Americans came "to see their existence as a society as depending upon the bounds and restraints provided by law."[165]

The mid-nineteenth-century faith of Choate and others that law encapsulated public virtue became institutionalized through the efforts of nineteenth century judges. The first important case in the institutionalization process was *Commonwealth v. Alger,*[166] the focus of a recent essay by Harry N. Scheiber.[167] Scheiber argues that "the concept of 'public rights,'" which was first adumbrated in *Alger,* rested not only on policy grounds, but also on a principled belief that rights of the public were different from rights of individuals.[168]

---

[162] *Id.* at 83.

[163] *Id.* at 83-84.

[164] *Id.* at 74.

[165] *Id.* at 191.

[166] 61 Mass. (7 Cush.) 53 (1851).

[167] Harry N. Scheiber, "Public Rights and the Rule of Law in American Legal History," 72 *Calif. L. Rev.* 217 (1984).

[168] See *id.* at 217-220. This distinction between public and private rights has considerable analytic importance in American constitutional law. For example, it underlies an interesting argument by Daniel J. Gifford that the *Schechter, Butler,* and *Carter Coal* cases, despite what they said, forebade not all unstructured delegations to administrative agencies but only delegations that established cartel-type production controls under effective administration by and for the probable benefit of private industry. See Daniel J. Gifford, "The New Deal Regulatory Model: A History of Criticisms and Refinements," 68 *Minn. L. Rev.* 299, 308-309 (1983). These 1935 delegation cases can thus be read as mere

The rule of law and the promotion of the general good remained dominant judicial concerns during the half century between the 1870s and 1920s, a period conventionally viewed as conservative. But, as I have argued elsewhere,[169] the conventional view that judges of the period were promoting the private interests of a narrow elite is misleading. The judges who then dominated the bench were not seeking to oppress the poor; rather they were seeking to restore older moral and communitarian values guaranteeing justice to all. In his history of the Third Circuit,[170] Stephen B. Presser agrees. Presser concludes that the "predominantly pejorative view of the period following the Civil War in American jurisprudence seems ripe for revision."[171] In a chapter about New Jersey's postwar District Judge, John Thompson Nixon, Presser shows that Nixon was not an unimaginative formalist who favored "an entrenched plutocracy" but instead decided cases "on the basis of [a] personal morality"[172] derived from the pre-Civil War era that sought "to redress . . . economic imbalances."[173] Similarly, in his final two chapters, Presser shows how many, though not all, late nineteenth century judges "believed that part of their role was to make sure that traditional democratic ideals were not slighted" by the managers of newly emerging giant corporations.[174] In another biography of a late nineteenth century judge, Simeon E. Baldiwn, Charles Goetsch maintains that judges of the period were not seeking to promote particular class interests or specific social changes, such as economic growth, but to resolve issues by "first deciding who was 'in the right' and then turning to principles for justifiction."[175] Likewise

---

substantive due process cases prohibiting the use of public power to protect private as distinct from public rights.

169 See William E. Nelson, *The Roots of American Bureaucracy, 1830-1900,* at 160-161 (1982).

170 Stephen B. Presser, *Studies in the History of the United States Courts of the Third Circuit* (1982).

171 *Id.* at 70.

172 *Id.* at 115.

173 *Id.* at 83.

174 *Id.* at 131.

175 Charles C. Goetsch, *Essays on Simeon E. Baldwin* 53 (1981). See also William E. Nelson, *supra* note 169, at 133-148. The notion of law as a reflection of objective principles rather than political expediency had important by-products. In an essay on the role of Populist judges in the 1890's, R. Douglas Hurt reports that "no Populist-endorsed justice was prepared to enter the game of partisan politics while serving on the bench"; rather "the judges concerned themselves with interpreting the law on sound legal principles." As a result, law derived from principle "served as a necessary stabilizing force in a volatile area where political passions were strong and opponents were viewed as enemies." R. Douglas Hurt, "The Populist Judiciary: Election Reform and Contested Offices," 4 *Kansas Hist.* 130, 141 (1981). Another by-product of the depoliticization of

John W. Johnson finds the impulse for early twentieth century legal reform not in class conflict but in "a seemingly ubiquitous concern for finding, fashioning, and using new sources of information."[176]

Through the efforts of such judges as Shaw and Baldwin, law unified American society. According to the conclusion of a cliometric study by Robert A. Silverman,[177] diverse people coming to America "from many cultures . . . participated in the judicial process as plaintiffs and defendants regardless of their ethnic antecedents" and thereby developed "homogenized . . . notions of law, if not of justice."[178] From the earliest arrivals at Jamestown and Plymouth to the most recent immigrants from places like the Mediterranean, all Americans have participated, through legal institutions, in the liberal ideal that law promotes a public good transcending their private advantage. Historians who have recognized the link between the promotion of public welfare and faith in the rule of law have thus given the latter concept important content.

But the most notable contributions toward putting content into the rule of law come from Robert M. Cover and Benno C. Schmidt, each currently at work on the Holmes Devise history of the Supreme Court. In an article that puts important theoretical content into the key constitutional concept of minority rights,[179] Cover explains how the modern concept of a minority as a small, politically isolated ethnic group replaced the earlier concept of a minority as a political faction out of power. Cover's thesis is that the breakup of the Austro-Hungarian, Russian and Ottoman empires at Versailles, in response to the ideal of national self-determination, forced Western thinkers to confront the problem of protecting the rights of small ethnic groups left resident in a

---

law in the late ninteenth century, according to Richard D. Friedman, was that "opposition" to judicial selections "on parochial and political grounds" came to "appear illegitimate" and "political interference in the selection process" came to be "scorned." Richard D. Friedman, "The Transformation in Senate Response to Supreme Court Nominations: From Reconstruction to the Taft Administration and Beyond," 5 *Cardozo L. Rev.* 1, 4-5 (1983).

[176] See John W. Johnson, *American Legal Culture, 1908-1940,* at 4 (1981). Another valuable contribution is Stephen A. Siegel, "John Chipman Gray, Legal Formalism, and the Transformation of Perpetuities Law," 56 *U. Miami L. Rev.* 1439 (1982), which shows how John Chipman Gray, through his classic treatise *The Rule against Perpetuities* (1st ed. 1886), transformed perpetuities law from a pragmatic, instrumental and disconnected set of policy prescriptions into a coherent, formal body of apolitical doctrine.

[177] Robert A. Silverman, *Law and Urban Growth: Civil Litigation in the Boston Trial Courts, 1880-1900* (1981).

[178] *Id.* at 146.

[179] Robert M. Cover, "The Origins of Judicial Activism in the Protection of Minorities," 91 *Yale L.J.* 1287 (1982).

nation dominated by a different group. Answers to this European problem rapidly crossed over to America,[180] where, as a series of articles authored by Benno C. Schmidt suggests,[181] the courts were still struggling with the Reconstruction promise of freedom for blacks.

In the wake of *Plessy v. Ferguson,* the Supreme Court according to Schmidt, did not abandon the cause of equal protection for blacks, but rather struck down various racist efforts to hold blacks in peonage, to exclude them from residential neighborhoods, and to keep them from voting and serving on juries. Efforts for black equality failed, Schmidt maintains, not because the Supreme Court lacked commitment but because the federal courts were "without troops, . . . without executive reinforcement, . . . [and were] operating against a complex system of rampant terror, political exclusion, and pervasive legal discrimination in race relations."[182] The best the Supreme Court could do was to proclaim the principle of equality in race relations while blindly ignoring the realities of an emerging American apartheid. Safe "at appellate remove," the Court served as "a distant keeper of the Ark of the (paper) Convenant, unembarrassed by hands-on confrontations with the frustration of federal guarantees."[183]

Illustrating the concern of judges for the protection of black rights and the emergence of new concepts of minority rights during the erroneously labelled conservative era of 1870-1930[184] Schmidt and Cover offer

---

[180] *Id.* at 1297-99.

[181] Benno C. Schmidt, "Principle and Prejudice: The Supreme Court and Race in the Progressive Era (pts. 1-3)," 82 *Colum. L. Rev.* 444, 646, 835 (1982); Benno C. Schmidt, "Juries, Jurisdiction, and Race Discrimination: The Lost Promise of *Strauder v. West Virginia,*" 61 *Tex. L. Rev.* 1401, 1414 (1983).

[182] *Id.* at 1486. Consistent with Schmidt's interpretation of the Court's late nineteenth century race relations cases is John V. Orth's interpretation of its eleventh amendment cases. In "The Interpretation of the Eleventh Amendment, 1798-1908: A Case Study of Judicial Power," [1983] *U. Ill. L. Rev.* 423 (1983), Orth argues that at most times in American history, the amendment has been no more than a pleading rule which requires a plaintiff to name as defendant a particular state officer rather than a state itself. But for a period of time in the late nineteenth century, the amendment did in fact bar creditors from collecting debts against certain, though not all Southern states — a bar that Orth explains as grounded in the Court's awareness that, once Reconstruction had ended, it could not enforce orders compelling certain Southern states to pay debts. Orth notes, however, that the Court continued to issue orders compelling state officials to act in instances in which they believed the orders could be enforced.

[183] Benno C. Schmidt, *supra* note 181, at 1486.

[184] Even the *Schenck, Frohwerk,* and *Debs* cases, which upheld espionage convictions during World War I against first amendment challenges, should perhaps be understood as libertarian decisions; indeed, according to David S. Bogen, they should be viewed as the cases in which Justice Holmes first elaborated the modern pro-speech framework of constitutional law. See David

contemporaty constitutional law several clusters of values upon which to build rights-oriented, individualist doctrine. At its base, constitutionalists might install the value in Schmidt's work that courts not permit practical concerns about the enforceability of individual rights to dilute their definition and proclamation of those rights. A second value that might emerge from study of the "conservative" era, as suggested by an essay of William F. Duker,[185] is that the federal courts have a long-term duty to enhance their jurisdiction so that they will ultimately possess the power required to enforce the principles they proclaim.

Two further values are suggested by the writing of Robert Cover. One, already noted, is the protection of racial, ethnic, and religious minorities. Another, suggested by Cover in a second essay, is a commitment "to order, to public civility, and to the elimination of private organized violence."[186] Cover finds that this commitment was an essential element in the work of the Taft Court, which was used both against labor on the left, and against groups like the Ku Klux Klan on the right.[187]

No one, of course, would suggest that these constitutional principles ought to constitute the entire corpus of American constitutionalism. Traditional forms of constitutional history can not generate an entire corpus of constitutional law. But, whereas traditional forms of historical study promise to contribute to an understanding of the neutral principles of constitutional law, critical legal studies history can only undermine whatever principles might exist.

Nor would anyone suggest that ultimate elaboration of a determinate body of constitutional principle will put an end to all injustice in American life. The effort of late nineteenth century judges to govern on the basis of neutral, objective legal principles did not end oppression. As

---

S. Bogen, "The Free Speech Metamorphosis of Mr. Justice Holmes," 11 *Hofstra L. Rev.* 97, 150-189 (1982).

185 See William F. Duker, "Mr. Justice Rufus Peckham and the Case of *Ex Parte Young:* Lochnerizing *Munn v. Illinois,*" 3 *B.Y.U.L. Rev.* 539 (1980).

186 Robert M. Cover, "The Left, the Right and the First Amendment: 1918-1928," 40 *Md. L. Rev.* 349, 354 (1981). Some readers may be troubled, perhaps, by the thought that civility is an important or worthwhile constitutional principle. But surely, if all other things are equal, civility is better than incivility and violence. Without descending into detailed argument that would not be completed in less than a full-length monograph, it may be suggested that civility, also known as respect for the rights of others, is at the heart of first amendment rights and of dissatisfaction with the death penalty; the principle of civility may also constitute a basis for the lines of authority emerging out of the cases of *Griswold v. Connecticut,* 381 U.S. 479 (1965), and *Roe v. Wade,* 410 U.S. 113 (1973). It might also be noted that the incivility of some scholars in the critical legal studies group is related, perhaps, to their rejection of the liberal value of respect for the rights of others.

187 See Robert M. Cover, *supra* note 207, at 354-356.

John R. Wunder has documented, Chinese on the Pacific Coast suffered oppression in the courts, especially after the Chinese Exclusion Act of 1883.[188] And oppression of West Coast Asian-Americans culminated in one of the darkest moments in our constitutional history, the internment of Japanese-Americans during World War II.[189]

But even during Japanese internment, American respect for individual rights and the rule of law was not irrelevant. It was relevant first because internment occurred only after two months of opposition by lawyers within the Roosevelt administration who were committed to human rights and the rule of law.[190] Under more favorable political circumstances, these lawyers might have won. Second, American respect for law and for rights arguably led, in G. Edward White's view, to Japanese-Americans receiving better treatment in the internment camps than they would have received in analogous institutions in most other societies.[191] Finally, that respect has been vital in the ultimate moral and social, if not full legal vindication of the Japanese-Americans since World War II.[192]

Commitment to the rule of law and respect for individual rights cannot always insure that law will be enforced and rights respected. Rights were not respected in what Stanley I. Kutler has labelled "the American inquisition,"[193] the era of Senator Joseph McCarthy's reign of lawlessness in the middle of the present century. Yet, as Kutler concludes, "the very autonomy of the law thwarted any total inversion of the system. There *were* limits to repression and abuse of the norms, as the guardians and executors of the law ultimately found themselves bound to the Rule of Law."[194] Individual rights, it seems, will be more secure in a polity that values law and rights than in one that does not.

C. *Biographies of the Justices*

Before concluding this survey of recent writing in constitutional history, note should be taken of the unusually large number of recent biographies of twentieth century Supreme Court justices.

---

[188] See John R. Wunder, "The Chinese and the Courts in the Pacific Northwest: Justice Denied?," 52 *Pac. Hist. Rev.* 191 (1983).

[189] See generally Peter Irons, *Justice at War: The Story of the Japanese American Internment Cases* (1983).

[190] See *id.* at 1-64.

[191] See G. Edward White, *Earl Warren: A Public Life* 73 (1982).

[192] See Peter Irons, *supra* note 189, at viii.

[193] See Stanley I. Kutler, *The American Inquisition: Justice and Injustice in the Cold War* (1982).

[194] *Id.* at 245.

Two excellent studies of Chief Justice Earl Warren appeared during the past two years. *Superchief*, by Bernard Schwartz,[195] relies on previously unexamined internal court papers and on interviews with people who had close relationships with Warren to investigate how the Warren Court reached its more significant decisions. *Superchief* will, for years to come, serve as a valuable reference work for students of constitutional law who are searching for information about the Court's decisionmaking process.

But Schwartz's book devotes little attention to Warren's pre-Court career, nor does it strive to present an interpretation of Warren as a political figure. This gap is filled by G. Edward White's *Earl Warren: A Public Life.*[196] In an effort to unearth the roots of the attitudes that marked Warren's tenure as Chief Justice, nearly half of the work reports on Warren's early life and career. White argues that Warren underwent no radical, philosophical change after becoming a Supreme Court Justice. Rather, White contends, "the surface contradictions in his thought can be seen as manifestations of a deep commitment to a general set of principles that were consistent in themselves."[197] Those principles, White explains, included a "strong commitment to family responsibilities, . . . 'personal forbearance' in his habits," and an "abiding belief in education."[198] Warren also adhered to the fundamental progressive values of "honesty and openness in government" and of "affirmative governmental action in the 'public interest,' as opposed to 'special' economic or class interests."[199] According to White, these "ethical imperatives" guided Warren as a justice. "It was inconceivable to Warren that these values would not be embodied in constitutional principles, since he believed that they formed the essence of American democracy," and indeed, Warren felt bound as a judge to forego orthodox doctrinal consistency for the sake of his "ethical imperatives".[200]

Felix Frankfurter has also been the subject of several biographical works. The best is Michael E. Parrish's *Felix Frankfurter and His Times: The Reform Years*[201] which portrays Frankfurter as an intellectual

---

[195] Bernard Schwartz, *Super Chief: Earl Warren and his Supreme Court —A Judicial Biography* (1983).

[196] G. Edward White, *supra* note 191.

[197] *Id.* at 4. For a contrary view, see Edward R. Long, "Earl Warren and the Politics of Anti-Communism," 51 *Pac. Hist. Rev.* 51 (1981).

[198] G. Edward White, *supra* note 191, at 13.

[199] *Id.* at 18.

[200] *Id.* at 218.

[201] Michael E. Parrish, *Felix Frankfurter and His Times: The Reform Years* (1982). For another book on Frankfurter, see H.N. Hirsh, *The Enigma of Felix Frankfurter* (1981).

progressive, "who believed that under wise and enlightened stewardship," such as his own, "America would experience an upward spiral of human rationality and welfare."[202] As Frankfurter himself wrote to Learned Hand, "I can't help believing it's the one assurance we've got — to peg away, genially and generously, along the road of reason."[203] Mark Silverstein's *Constitutional Faiths: Felix Frankfurter, Hugo Black, and the Process of Judicial Decisionmaking*[204] compares Frankfurter's approach to constitutional adjudication with that practiced by his contemporary Hugo Black. Silverstein argues that, while both Frankfurter and Black believed in restrained judicial protection of fundamental constitutional norms, they broke over whether those norms should be found in "immutable principles, fundamental to American democracy"[205] or in the literal text of the Constitution.[206]

Two new books deal with the interconnected careers of Justices Louis D. Brandeis and Felix Frankfurter. While both works are based upon exhaustive research primarily in the Frankfurter papers, they reach opposite conclusions. Bruce Allen Murphy's *The Brandeis/Frankfurter Connection,*[207] contends that neither Brandeis nor Frankfurter, upon ascending the bench, entered upon a monastic retirement from politics. Both men remained close to the presidents, namely Wilson and Roosevelt, who appointed them, and both men worked hard to influence the policies of those administrations. Murphy's evidence is overwhelming, and his book will serve to rebut claims that justices should insulate themselves from politics. As Murphy concludes, both Brandeis and Frankfurter "were forces for good on the American political scene, and were good Supreme Court justices."[208] But Murphy overestimates their influence. One example is his suggestion that Frankfurter was the architect of Franklin Roosevelt's bipartisan appointment of Henry L. Stimson as Secretary of War in 1940.[209] In this regard Nelson L. Dawson's *Louis D. Brandeis, Felix Frankfurter, and the New Deal,*[210] is a useful corrective, for its thesis is that, while Brandeis and Frankfurter

---

[202] *Id.* at 4.

[203] Quoted in *id.* at 128.

[204] Mark Silverstein, *Constitutional Faiths: Felix Frankfurter, Hugo Black, and the Process of Judical Decision Making* (1984).

[205] *Id.* at 88.

[206] For an essay critical of Black, see David F. Shores, "Justice Black and the Antitrust Laws," [1982] *Antitrust Bull.* 389 (1982).

[207] Bruce Allen Murphy, *The Brandeis/Frankfurter Connection: The Secret Political Activities of Two Supreme Court Justices* (1982).

[208] *Id.* at 342-343.

[209] See *id.* at 196-200.

[210] Nelson L. Dawson, *Louis D. Brandeis, Felix Frankfurter, and the New Deal* (1980).

tried hard to influence presidential policies, the impact they had was relatively slight.

Brandeis himself has been the subject of two new biographies. Philippa Strum's *Louis D. Brandeis: Justice for the People* [211] is a thoroughly researched and documented account written from the perspective of a New Deal progressive. It portrays Brandeis as a man of extraordinary ability who believed "in democracy, in education, in the ability of the people to choose wisely, in liberty and equality, [and] in the development of a society that would enhance the possibilities and potential of human beings."[212] A similar portrait is painted in Lewis J. Paper's *Brandeis,*[213] in which the Justice's life is characterized as "extraordinary" and grounded in "optimism."[214] Paper calls Brandeis "a complex figure of unusual talents" who was always "working for his vision of what society should be — a place where people could control their environments and maximize the chances of fulfilling their potential."[215]

Not to be outdone, Justice Oliver Wendell Holmes, found himself the subject of a symposium celebrating the 100th anniversary of publication of *The Common Law*. One of the writers finds Holmes' legacy to lie in the "mysterious power" of his "language,"[216] while another finds *The Common Law* of interest because it contained "multiple and contradictory strands of thought," as Holmes tried to resolve "the tension between his continually increased recognition of the political role of judges and his desire to maintain their status as disinterested scientists."[217] Only G. Edward White finds "integrity" in "Holmes' jurisprudence"[218] by seeing Holmes as an activist legal reformer seeking coherence in the law at the time he authored *The Common Law,* who learned the limitations of judicial rationality through his years of experience on the bench.[219]

---

[211] Philippa Strum, *Louis D. Brandeis: Justice for the People* (1984).

[212] *Id.* at 416.

[213] Lewis J. Paper, *Brandeis* (1983).

[214] *Id.* at 395.

[215] *Id.* at 4-5.

[216] Saul Touster, "Holmes a Hundred Years Ago: *The Common Law* and Legal Theory," 10 *Hofstra L. Rev.* 673, 679 (1982).

[217] Robert W. Gordon, "Holmes' *Common Law* as Legal and Social Science," 10 *Hofstra L. Rev.* 712, 720, 745 (1982).

[218] G. Edward White, "The Integrity of Holmes' Jurisprudence," 10 *Hofstra L. Rev.* 633 (1982).

[219] Other biographical articles about modern justices which are worthy of note are Stephen M. Dane, "'Ordered Liberty' and Self-Restraint: The Judicial Philosophy of the Second Justice Harlan," 51 *U. Cin. L. Rev.* 545 (1982); Dorothy Glancy, "Getting Government off the Backs of People: The Right of Privacy and Freedom of Expression in the Opinions of Justice William O. Douglas," 21 *Santa Clara L. Rev.* 1047 (1981). There is also a series of articles criticizing John Marshall for opinions containing "rhetorical flourish, bare

V. *Conclusion*

In this survey I have argued that traditional approaches to legal history are superior to the new critical legal studies approach. I have offered two reasons in support of my argument. The first reason is that traditional legal and constitutional history will more likely lead the historian to imaginative insight about and useful knowledge of both past and present. The second is that traditional forms of constitutional history can help give determinate meaning to constitutional principles. Critical legal studies history, on the other hand, undermines constitutionalism.

But now I must offer a concession that will vouchsafe my much greater affinity to the critical legal studies movement than to many of the readers who have accepted my analysis so far. The critical legal studies movement does have one lesson to teach. It is an old lesson first taught by the legal realists, but its age and pedigree do not diminish its importance. The lesson is that "LAW IS POLITICS, pure and simple."[220] No argument about law, therefore, is self-evidently correct; the soundness of any argument depends upon the political judgments that underlie it.

What are the political judgments that underlie my arguments? Paradoxically, underlying my first argument — that traditional history will lead to great insight and knowledge — is my willingness to make the "kind of reverse Faustian bargain" suggested by Robert W. Gordon: to sacrifice "immediate influence in the councils of the great for a potentially enormous increase in understanding of our condition."[221] Connected to this willingness is a skepticism about whether, in light of our present shadowy "understanding of our condition," we can be confident that any single ideology will lead to deeper understanding. Ignorant today of the knowledge we shall need tommorrow, I feel more confident placing my faith in the pluralistic endeavors of many different historians than in singleminded pursuit of any one idea.

---

assertion, plentiful dicta, multiple holdings, inattention to favorable precedent, and emphasis on the undesirable consequences of an interpretation at variance with his own." David P. Currie, "The Constitution in the Supreme Court: The Powers of the Federal Courts, 1801-1835," 49 *U. Chi. L. Rev.* 646, 723-24 (1982). Accord, David P. Curie, "The Constitution in the Supreme Court: State and Congressional Powers, 1801-1835," 49 *U. Chi. L. Rev.* 887 (1982). See also David P. Currie, "The Constitution in the Supreme Court: 1789-1801," 48 *U. Chi. L. Rev.* 819 (1981); David P. Currie, "The Constitution in the Supreme Court: Contracts and Commerce, 1836-1864," [1983] *Duke L.J.* 471 (1983); David P. Currie, "The Constitution in the Supreme Court: Article IV and Federal Powers, 1836-1864," [1983] *Duke L.J.* 695 (1983).

220 John Henry Schlegal, *supra* note 1, at 411 (emphasis in original).

221 Robert W. Gordon, *supra* note 65, at 1056.

But, as I argued earlier, Gordon's "Faustian bargain" did not make sense for all legal history scholars. Some scholars, I suggested, may be inclined to pursue influence rather than seek understanding.[222] My skepticism about whether I can know what is best for other scholars or can induce them to do it leads me to think that some should seek understanding while others pursue influence. Some might strive for both.

If one makes the judgment that he or she wants to seek knowledge, then it seems clear that traditional legal history is the better path to follow. But, if one wants influence, then the decision whether to engage in traditional forms of legal and constitutional history or to become a critical legal studies historian depends upon a further judgment: Whether one wants to preserve the existing American political order designed to enhance individual autonomy and freedom or to participate in imposing some new collective vision of the good on the polity.

There should be no doubt: to join the critical legal studies movement is to join an advance phalanx of a new collective polity. There should also be no doubt that scholars who retain a "fundamental liberal commitment to the separate life of the individual" can coherently practice traditional, liberal forms of history in the pursuit of either influence or understanding.[223] Many legal historians have done that in the past five years. Others, I trust, will continue.

---

[222] See notes 65-68 and accompanying text.

[223] Frank I. Michelman, "Politics as Medicine: On Misdiagnosing Legal Scholarship," 90 *Yale L.J.* 1224, 1227 (1981).

Chapter Seventeen

CONCLUSION: STANDARDS OF CRITICISM

William E. Nelson

As the foregoing chapters have shown, the character of scholarship in the discipline of American legal history has undergone a fundamental change during the past several decades. A half century ago, the understanding of practitioners of the discipline was that legal historians undertook research in order to obtain data that would provide answers to or at least insight into legal questions that had come or were likely to come before the courts. About two decades ago, the relationship between legal development and social change became the central concern of most scholars working in the field. Today, as the most recent essays suggest, significant work is being done by scholars who are pursuing each of these approaches as well as some others.

The change in the character of legal history scholarship has occurred for a variety of reasons over which those who work in the field of legal history have little control. Although I do not wish to suggest that the change is either a good one or an irreversible one, it is a deep, structural one. As such, the change in the character of legal history scholarship ought to affect the way in which we think about the field and criticize each others' scholarship. I am convinced that most of us continue, however, to apply critical standards to each others' work that were appropriate two or more decades ago and hope that an essay raising questions about the critical standards we ought to be applying will stimulate new thought on the subject.

I plan to begin by analyzing why the discipline of American legal history has changed in recent decades from one in which nearly all scholars in the field shared a common sense of purpose to a field in which different scholars pursue quite different ends. I shall begin here because I think that an understanding of why the field has changed is essential to understanding how work in the field ought to be evaluated. In the past, when legal historians shared an understanding of the purpose of research and writing in the field, they could evaluate work by examining how well it accomplished that purpose. It is my thesis that today, on the other hand, legal historians who do not agree about the goals of their discipline must carefully distinguish between critical standards by which all scholarship can be judged and their own more personal aesthetic and ideological values, which can give meaning to their own scholarly careers but which ought not be forced upon others from positions of academic power. The soundness of this thesis depends, however, upon whether differences of approach among legal historians are so deep that a new consensus about the purpose of legal history research is unlikely soon to emerge, and an appreciation of the depth of those differences, in turn, depends on understanding why the differences arose.

A. *The Diversification of Legal History: Some Underlying Factors*

Why did legal historians in the years immediately preceding and immediately following 1960 lose their collective sense that the purpose of research in the field was to obtain data that would help solve pending legal problems? I cannot offer a definitive answer to this question, but I can point to several factors that have contributed to the transformation of scholarship in the field.

1. *The Burgeoning Academic Community.* — One factor contributing to the breakdown of the shared sense of purpose has been the growth of the American academic world in general,[1] and of the field of legal history, in particular. Fifty years ago, fewer than ten scholars were engaged in or had recently completed major research projects in American legal history. I would estimate that approximately fifty scholars were actively engaged in research in the field by the second half of the 1960's. Today — little more than a decade later — the number of active scholars in American legal history exceeds one hundred. The same pattern of growth can be observed by examining the quantity of published material in the field. It appears, for example, that more work was published in the two year period 1979-1980 than in all the years prior to 1960.[2] Most of the pre-1960 work, moreover, was published during the 1950's. In some years prior to the 1950's, no significant scholarly work was published.[3] By the 1960's, in contrast, some significant work was appearing every year.[4]

---

[1] For a description of the expansion of the academy between 1950 and 1970, see Patrick J. McCarthy, "Higher Education: Expansion without Growth," 104 *Daedalus* 78-82 (1975).

[2] This estimate results from a comparison of the work discussed in chapter 15 above with the work discussed in chapter 1 above.

[3] For surveys of the literature in years in which little was written, see, e.g., Warren Dean, "Legal History," 1947 *Ann. Survey Am. L.* 1009; Warren Dean, "Legal History," 1948 *Ann. Survey Am. L.* 927; Warren Dean, "Legal History," 1949 *Ann. Survey Am. L.* 1031.

[4] See, e.g., chapter 2 above.

As the number of people working in a field grows, it becomes more difficult for all or nearly all of them to agree about the purpose of their work. A half century ago, research in legal history was quite tightly centered in two universities, Columbia and Harvard. The dominant assumption at both universities was that research in legal history would be directed toward the solution of current legal issues. To have been an established legal historian at that time was difficult without some association with one of these schools and hence with their dominant assumption. Today graduate students are being trained in legal history in at least ten universities, and significant research is being carried on at a host of others. Scholars at these institutions have not even begun to approach agreement on the ends toward which legal history research should be directed, and nurture can be found somewhere for almost any view that a scholar might adopt about the purposes of his research. This rapid growth in the discipline of American legal history will not, I believe, be reversed in the decades to come. As long as the number of scholars in the field remains as large as it is now, I think it unlikely that a consensus about the purposes of legal history research will emerge.

2. *The Growing Irrelevance of History.* — The growth in legal history explains much about why the discipline now lacks and probably will continue to lack consensus about purposes and ends. But that growth does not explain why the consensus that had been maintained into the 1950's collapsed at the time that it did: in the years around 1960.

Events outside the field contributed to the timing of the old consensus' breakdown. The maintenance of that consensus had required, I think, some tangible evidence that scholarly research into the past helped judges decide the cases before them. Evidence of the sort required was provided by such events as Justice Brandeis' citation in *Erie Railroad v. Tompkins*[5] of Charles Warren's history of the Judiciary Act of 1789.[6] Three events of the late 1940's and the early 1950's, however, served as evidence to the contrary — evidence that scholarly research into the past could not assist judges in the decisionmaking process.

The first event was the decision in *Adamson v. California*[7] and its aftermath. In this 1947 case, Justice Black used historical material generated by his own extensive research to support his contention that the Fourteenth Amendment incorporated the Bill of Rights and made it applicable to the states.[8] Justice Black's history was promptly rebutted,

---

[5] 304 U.S. 64, 72-73 (1938).

[6] Charles Warren, "New Light on the History of the Federal Judiciary Act of 1789," 37 *Harv. L. Rev.* 49 (1923).

[7] 332 U.S. 46 (1947).

[8] Id. at 68 (Black, J., dissenting).

however, by an even more extensive historical analysis by Charles Fairman, entitled "Does the Fourteenth Amendment Incorporate the Bill of Rights?: The Original Understanding."[9] The scholarly debate that has raged on the issue ever since has had little impact on the Supreme Court: in the 1960's, a time when Fairman's view probably seemed more persuasive to observers of the debate, the Court adopted the substance of Black's position.

The second event was *Brown v. Board of Education,*[10] in which the Court asked lawyers for both sides to undertake research into the question of what light history shed on the constitutionality of public school segregation.[11] The lawyers enlisted leading historical scholars to assist in the research. But the Court concluded from their efforts that, while the historical "sources cast some light," they were ultimately "inconclusive." The light they cast was "not enough to resolve the problem with which we are faced."[12]

The third event which showed that historical research had little impact on the direction of constitutional doctrine was the publication of William W. Crosskey's *Politics and the Constitution in the History of the United States* in 1953.[13] Crosskey's book, which was the product of years of painstaking research, met with severe criticism from such leading scholars as Ernest Brown, Julius Goebel, Henry M. Hart, and Arthur E. Sutherland.[14] A disturbing message emerged from the various reviews of Crosskey's book: historical research had not only failed to provide answers to pending questions, such as the propriety and scope of judicial review in constitutional cases; it had led to an escalation of the level of controversy. But the most telling evidence that Crosskey's historical research would have little impact on judicial decisionmaking came from the courts themselves. Judges simply ignored Crosskey's work, citing it only four times in the first ten years after its publication and only six times in the next ten years.[15]

---

[9] 2 *Stan. L. Rev.* 5 (1949).

[10] 347 U.S. 483 (1954).

[11] Id. at 488 n.3.

[12] Id. at 489.

[13] 1,2 William W. Crosskey, *Politics and the Constitution in the History of the United States* (1953).

[14] See, e.g. Ernest Brown, "Book Review," 67 *Harv. L. Rev.* 1439 (1954); Henry M. Hart, "Book Review," 67 *Harv. L. Rev.* 1456 (1954); Julius Goebel, "Book Review," 54 *Colum. L. Rev.* 450 (1954); Arthur Sutherland, "Book Review," 39 *Cornell L.Q.* 160 (1953).

[15] The number of citations was obtained by conducting a Lexis search for combinations of the following words, "Crosskey, Politics and the Constitution."

These three occasions on which history failed to provide answers for pending legal questions were symptomatic of a more general trend in which the past simply decreased in importance. The late 1950's and especially the 1960's were perceived by contemporaries as a time of great social upheaval, and there was little support for the idea that legal or other values derived from the past could or should stand in the path of social change. Legal thinkers in the 1960's did not wish to learn how to govern society with law discovered through historical study. They sought to determine whether and how law could channel, respond to, and otherwise relate to more basic social forces. The study of the relationship between law and society became an organized academic concern with the founding of the Center for the Study of Law and Society at Berkeley in 1961 and the publication of the first volume of the *Law and Society Review* in 1965.

After 1960 legal historians also focused their attention on how legal development was related to social change. As Chapter 1 suggested, the important work of George Haskins and J. Willard Hurst in the years around 1960 addressed this issue, as did the work of other scholars. I recall well my own view in the mid-1960s — a view reflected in the 1966 essay on Constitutional History[16] — that efforts to address current legal issues through history were fruitless and that the study of legal and social change was the proper task for legal historians to pursue. My own expectation during the 1960's — an expectation in which most others then working in American legal history joined — was that a new consensus about the purpose of legal history research was emerging to replace the old consensus that had dominated the field until the 1950's.

3. *Factors Preventing the Development of Consensus.* — My hoped for new consensus has never quite emerged. There continues to be scholarship, such as Charles Warren's essay on the Judiciary Act of 1789,[17] Robert Cover's book about judicial responses to moral claims advanced by abolitionist lawyers,[18] and Robert Gordon's essay urging that legal history should play a larger role in legal scholarship and ultimately in legal reasoning,[19] that addresses in a quite useful manner issues of current concern to the courts. "Lawyers' legal history"[20] refuses

[16] See chapter 7 above.

[17] Charles Warren, supra note 6.

[18] Robert M. Cover, *Justice Accused: Antislavery and the Judicial Process* (1975).

[19] Robert W. Gordon, "Historicism in Legal Scholarship," 90 *Yale L.J.* 1017 (1981).

[20] The term was coined in Morton J. Horwitz, "The Conservative Tradition in the Writing of American Legal History," 17 *Am. J. Legal Hist.* 275, 276

to die. Meanwhile a new genre of neo-Marxist legal history also has emerged. As a result, the discipline of American legal history is today farther from a consensus about its purposes than it has ever been.

The old consensus has broken down, and a new one has failed to emerge, largely as a result of institutional and intellectual forces impinging upon the field of legal history from the outside. But accidents of personality have also contributed to the present lack of consensus. Almost any consensus will need to be imposed on recalcitrant individuals through instrumentalities of power. Leading legal historians in the pre-1960 era, especially Julius Goebel, did not hesitate to use biting criticism — the chief weapon that an academic possesses — to attack the occasional maverick, like Richard Morris, who saw the field of legal history differently than they did. Although I have no documentation, I suspect that criticism from the discipline's leading figures preserved and strengthened their view that research in legal history should be directed toward the resolution of current legal problems and retarded the emergence of opposing views.

When a new approach — one that understood the relation between law and social change to be the proper subject of legal history — finally did emerge around 1960, its two leading figures adopted a very different attitude. Both George Haskins and Willard Hurst have consistently refused to criticize scholars who have a conception of the discipline of legal history different from their own. Instead, both men have assisted the careers of other scholars committed to other approaches. I suspect that this openness on the part of leading scholars has contributed to the diversity of approach which currently characterizes scholarship in American legal history.

Both structural factors and accidents of personality will continue to determine the character of the field, and both point to a continued diversity of approach. The most important personality factor likely to affect the future of American legal history is the existence of a generation of legal historians who have entered the discipline since 1960 and who now hold tenured professorships at most of the nation's major universities. Since these legal historians are generally quite young, they are likely to remain among the leaders of the discipline for the next two or three decades. And since they are sharply divided about what ought to be the purpose of legal history research, no consensus about purpose is likely to emerge while they remain leaders.[21]

(1973). I use the term slightly differently than did Horwitz to apply only to work addressing current legal questions and not to work examining the origins of modern rules.

[21] The improbability that a consensus about purpose will soon emerge is illustrated by Robert Gordon's recent essay, supra note 19, which is the most

The structural forces that will affect the direction of American legal history in the future are more difficult to anticipate, but I will take note of a few. I am prepared to predict, for instance, that Marxism is not about to disappear as an attractive ideology or as a powerful political force in the world, and hence I expect neo-Marxist legal history to continue to flourish. Rapid social change also seems likely to continue in much of the world in the decades to come, together with attempts to use law to further and to channel that change. Hence I expect historical study of the relationship between legal development and social change to continue. Finally, I expect a revival of the use of historical materials to help solve current legal problems. Two structural forces point toward such a revival.

One is the increasing dissatisfaction of various groups in America with the direction of social change — a dissatisfaction that may induce many people, both progressive and reactionary, to look backward to find traditional values with which to advance their causes. The other is the growing economic squeeze on American universities, which will compel them and their constituent schools to focus on their central educational missions and to eliminate apparent frills. This will require legal historians to focus more attention on how historical study can help address the current legal issues that are the core concern of law faculties. Otherwise

---

articulate statement yet to appear of the scholarly agenda of the critical legal studies movement. In the essay Gordon argues that "basic conceptual limitations in modern liberal political thought," id. at 1050, have "restricted thinking about law to minor changes in its present forms, thereby preventing us . . . from imagining that law might be other than the way it is." Id. at 1056. Although he is not explicit, Gordon apparently would urge legal historians to abandon their liberal preconceptions and thereby "move legal scholarship beyond its long practiced modes of response." Ibid.

I believe, on the other hand, that legal historians should continue writing classical liberal history, analyzing what Gordon, in reference to my work, calls the reconciliation of the conflicting "claims of atomized individuals and interest groups." Id. at 1049. I continue to find this paradigmatic liberal enterprise important because the United States remains today, more perhaps than at any time in its history, a richly diverse society that can be justly governed only if the conflicting interests of its many social groups can be reconciled.

I am aware, of course, that contradictions exist in classical liberal thought. But contradictions also exist in the vision of the critical legal studies movement, especially in regard to the question how a humanitarian with a utopian vision should treat dissent that prevents fulfillment of his vision. Legal historians like myself, who are more concerned with how dissenters are treated than with moving scholarship beyond its long practiced modes, will continue striving to resolve the contraditions of liberalism while other historians like Gordon develop new research paradigms. Given such cross purposes, no new consensus about the purpose of legal history research is likely to emerge in the forseeable future.

the discipline may not continue to receive from the law schools the nurture that has been so central to its recent growth. Economic pressures on law faculties may not induce all legal historians to devote all their energy to writing lawyers' legal history, but I do believe that legal historians will and should devote more of their attention to the difficult and important questions that the discipline has tended to slight during the past two decades.

In short, legal historians are unlikely to develop a single, monolithic consensus about the ends and purposes of their research in the coming decades. They will probably remain as divided as they are today about where the field is and should be going. I am convinced that the diverse character of legal history scholarship ought to lead us to alter our old standards for evaluating our own and other scholars' work and to abandon the discipline's traditional critical stance.

B. *The Failings of the Traditional Critical Stance*

What I label the traditional critical stance came into being in conjunction with the assumption that the purpose of research into legal history was to provide judges with objective data that would help them decide cases. But that assumption was never expressly incorporated into the traditional canons of criticism. Instead, the traditional stance has been marked by two other characteristics. One is the use of words of evaluation, especially adjectives of evaluation, which in essence rank scholarship along a continuum ranging from excellent, through good and indifferent, to unsatisfactory. The other is the oft-advanced claim that a scholar whose work is under examination has failed to consider and discuss relevant evidence, with the result that his work is alleged to misstate important facts. The traditional critical stance never became linked expressly with its underlying assumption about the use in law of objective historical knowledge, and as a result it survived the collapse of that assumption.

Karl Llewellyn's review[22] of Richard B. Morris' *Studies in the History of American Law,* exemplified the traditional stance.[23] It declared Morris' book to be factually inaccurate and questioned the trustworthiness of his judgment. We have seen that Llewellyn's criticisms, which seem both unfair and erroneous, make sense only if they are understood to reflect the fundamental methodological disagreement that Llewellyn

---

[22] Karl N. Llewellyn, "Book Review," 31 *Colum. L. Rev.* 729 (1931).

[23] Richard B. Morris, *Studies in the History of American Law, with Special Reference to the Seventeenth and Eighteenth Centuries* (1930).

had with Morris' work. Llewellyn, like most other legal scholars of his time, believed that historical research should be undertaken to obtain data that would provide answers or at least insight into legal questions that were likely to come before the courts. The breadth and generality of Morris' research did not provide data on which a lawyer could rely concerning, for instance, some particular point of New York procedure at a particular point in time. Llewellyn would have been correct if he had said that Morris' book could not be used by a lawyer or a court in the same way that Charles Warren's study was relied upon by Justice Brandeis in *Erie Railroad v. Tompkins.*[24] He was wrong, however, in saying that *Studies in the History of American Law* could not be trusted, because the book could be trusted by historians seeking to understand colonial society or to engage in further research in colonial law.

Unfair and vituperative reviews like Llewellyn's have unfortunately been the most common type of criticism in the literature of American legal history. Ernest Brown's review of William W. Crosskey's *Politics and the Constitution in the History of the United States* followed the same pattern.[25] Brown used adjectives like "imperious," "breath-taking," and "disquieting" in referring to Crosskey's methods and conclusions; in another passage he referred sardonically to "Mr. Crosskey's saltatory method of reaching conclusions."[26] Llywellyn's attack on Morris was echoed in Brown's condemnation of Crosskey for mishandling evidence. Brown was especially critical of Crosskey's discounting of *The Federalist* as significant contemporary evidence of the meaning of the Constitution. He rejected Crosskey's claim that *The Federalist* was not received with respect by contemporaries, pointing to evidence ignored by Crosskey and then commenting:

> Can thirteen years of research have left Mr. Crosskey uninformed of these contemporaneous opinions, of the evidence of respect and reception? If not, can he, on even the lowest level of scholarship, fail to mention them? Can he, on the Crosskey ipse dixit, dismiss from consideration the classic exposition of the Constitution?[27]

Brown contended that Crosskey's treatment of *The Federalist* was symptomatic of the book's flaws. He observed that "[a]lmost every page calls for some question regarding completeness of statement, some remark concerning twisted dialectic or excess of venom. . . ."[28] Brown concluded:

---

[24] 304 U.S. 64, 72-73 (1938).
[25] Ernest Brown, supra note 14.
[26] Id. at 1443-46.
[27] Id. at 1446.
[28] Id. at 1455.

> It is unfortunate that Mr. Crosskey's years of research should have produced a book so incomplete in the evidence it presents, so curious in its reasoning processes, so bitter in its address to unwelcome ideas and to the men identified with them. To critical judgment it must quickly become apparent that this is a work of advocacy; not the advocacy of balanced appraisal, but the insistent advocacy of the *idee fixe,* which must either mold to its purpose, or simply reject, all that it touches.[29]

I am about as unsympathetic as anyone to Crosskey's style of linguistic argumentation, and many of his conclusions do violence to what I have always understood to be the correct historical meaning of the Constitution. Yet I suspect it is mistaken to see in Crosskey's "work the insistent advocacy of the *idee fixe.*" Rather, I believe Crosskey should be viewed as an early member of a school of constitutional theorists, of which Herbert Storing and his students are more recent members, that approaches the subject with methods and premises radically different from my own. The fact that I and most other scholars of American law and history neither appreciate nor even understand those methods and premises does not justify our labelling the scholarly work to which they have led unsatisfactory on a unilinear scale of quality. Instead, those of us who find Crosskey's work unsettling should strive to understand his methods and premises, to identify how they differ from our own, and to articulate in a more philosophical manner the ends and purposes for which our premises are preferable.

The pages of the law reviews, at least, continue to contain scholarly criticism like that of Brown and Llewellyn, in which evaluative language substitutes for analysis of how the reviewer's methodological or philosophical assumptions differ from those of the author whose work is being reviewed. Consider, for example, A.W.B. Simpson's 1979 attack on on Morton Horwitz in "The Horwitz Thesis and the History of Contracts."[30] At one point in his critique, Simpson charged Horwitz with having a "romanticized view" of eighteenth century English law, while in another place he wrote that "Horwitz tends here to perpetuate a myth that scholars have long attempted to put to rest."[31] He also claimed that Horwitz' "vague references" were supported by "very weak" evidence.[32] Simpson found Horwitz' argument "hard to test against the evidence — partly because it is so general and partly because Horwitz, with true rhetorical mastery, interweaves evidence from England and America,

---

[29] Id. at 1456.

[30] 46 *U. Chi. L. Rev.* 533 (1979).

[31] Id. at 536.

[32] Ibid.

from different periods of time, and from different types of cases."[33] Simpson concluded that Horwitz had "[t]hrough an unsatisfactory and loose use of evidence . . . made a complex, confused story fall into a preordained pattern."[34] Simpson was convinced that "Horwitz allowed himself to be misled by his striking and seductive thesis into a general and systematic misinterpretation of the evidence, and that his thesis, once tested in detail, [was] quite misconceived."[35]

Note how Simpson's critique was written in the evaluative language of Brown and Llewellyn, even though it appeared only six years ago. Note in particular Simpson's recurrent use of adjectives that bear a great deal of the weight of his argument. Note also his claim that Horwitz, who spent nearly a decade accumulating an impressive quantity of new historical data, somehow failed to find the evidence that he should have found.

What I find most striking about Simpson's critique of Horwitz, however, is Simpson's own selective use of evidence. An example of this occurs in the discussion of whether a promisee had to perform part of his promise before he could bring suit on an executory contract. Simpson found Horwitz' "sparse evidence" that part performance was required in eighteenth-century America "unconvincing."[36] Simpson then examined some of the evidence in support of Horwitz' view, but he himself neglected to consider an extensive body of data from Massachusetts reported in my own book, *Americanization of the Common Law.*[37] The data from Massachusetts is not unimportant, since it comes from the only jurisdiction whose manuscript records have been systematically studied, it strongly supports Horwitz,[38] and Simpson was well aware of it.[39]

My conclusion is that, if Horwitz misused or misselected evidence and thereby reached unwarranted conclusions about what happened in the past, so too did Simpson. If a reader accepts Simpson's indictment of Horwitz, then he must indict Simpson for similar failings. I, however, would indict neither Horwitz nor Simpson as a poor historian. I think that they reached different conclusions about the history of contract largely because they began their research and writing with fundamentally different jurisprudential views that necessarily and properly guided them

33 Id. at 534-35.

34 Id. at 600.

35 Id. at 542.

36 Id. at 546.

37 William E. Nelson, *Americanization of the Common Law: The Impact of Legal Change on Massachusetts Society, 1760-1830* (1975).

38 See id. at 57-58.

39 See A.W.B. Simpson, supra note 30, at 544 n.58.

to focus on certain evidence, to treat other evidence as irrelevant, and to interpret ambiguous evidence in particular ways.

Simpson appears to have had a lawyer's perspective on legal history, which led him to view contract law as essentially a body of rules and principles that have not changed since they were first imported into English law in the late sixteenth and early seventeenth centuries. He thus read ambiguous eighteenth century contract cases — and most contract cases from that time are quite ambiguous — as reflective of the same principles as those governing contract law in the nineteenth century and today. His legalistic approach also led him to focus on crafted appellate opinions as the best source of evidence and to place little weight on pleadings drawn from manuscript cases culminating in default judgments, since those pleadings are not true precedents for future cases. Hence the evidence reported in *Americanization of the Common Law,* which consists principally of such pleadings, had little relevance for him.

Horwitz, on the other hand, brought to his research the social historian's assumption that contract law, like all law, responds to social and economic change. He interpreted ambiguous eighteenth century materials to show how contract law responded to the nation's shift from a pre-capitalist, agrarian economy to a bourgeois, industrialist one. His assumptions also led him to place more weight on the many pleadings that culminated in default judgments than on a single crafted appellate opinion. Hence the evidence from Massachusetts, for example, was more important to him than it was to Simpson.

What is regrettable about Simpson's critique is that he never examined how his assumptions differed from Horwitz', but instead simply explained how on the basis of Simpson's own assumptions Horwitz wrote a weak book. Simpson erroneously assumed that his standards were those of the whole discipline, and he unquestioningly based his judgment of Horwitz' work on them. His use of evaluative language disguised, perhaps even to himself, his philosophical differences with Horwitz.

A final outstanding monograph that was the subject of unfair criticism was Lawrence M. Friedman's *Contract Law in America.*[40] One reviewer declared "Mr. Friedman's language . . . so pejorative, and his view of contract so irrelevant, as to leave one in doubt on many points. . ."[41] Like Llewellyn, Brown, and Simpson, this reviewer, Robert Childres, rested the weight of his argument on adjectives. Thus, he found that Friedman's "model of 'abstraction' . . . [was] objectionable."[42] "The

---

[40] (1965).

[41] Robert Childres, "Book Review," 13 *J. Legal Education* 478, 479 (1966).

[42] Id. at 479.

model," he added, ultimately "decline[d] into incomprehensible metaphysics."[43]

The failing of all four reviewers is that they did not comprehend the books they were reading. Childres admitted as much when he commented that Freidman's discussion of various subjects, such as insurance contracts, construction contracts, government contracts and brokerage contracts, which "define[d] these into irrelevance, while devoting much of its energy to discussing them, puzzles one, and makes one wonder why we are conducting the exercise."[44] But failure to appreciate an approach to a subject radically different from one's own should not be a basis for castigating a book; such a failure reveals at least as much about the reviewer as it does about the book.

Nothing I have said about the criticism of Brown, Llewellyn, Simpson, and Childres should be understood as an objection to well-reasoned criticism, however negative it may be. The field of American legal history, like all scholarly fields, needs evaluative standards. Those of us who work in the field must be able to recognize the difference between good work and bad work and between outstanding scholarship and that which is simply good. Criticism is the only way in which criteria and standards can be elaborated and maintained. In the remainder of this chapter, I will suggest some criteria and standards on which criticism can be based.

C. *New Standards of Criticism*

More than a century ago a professor at Princeton who reviewed a book adumbrating Darwin's theory of evolution criticized it as "atheistic in its essential character" and thought that his criticism constituted "an ample refutation" of the book.[45] Few professors at American colleges and universities today would agree. The twentieth century has known no unitary set of standards brooding in the sky above us all. Contemporary standards for evaluating the quality of scholarly work cannot come from God, but only from the knowledge, values and preferences of individual scholars in the academic community.

But, if scholarly standards must ultimately be a product of the intellects of individual scholars, how can it be possible to have standards that transcend the volition of the many diverse scholars who comprise the academy today? How can a single set of scholarly standards exist in a

---

[43] Id. at 480.

[44] Id. at 482.

[45] 7 *Biblical Repertory and Princeton Review* 505-57, quoted in Thomas Jefferson Wertenbaker, *Princeton, 1746-1896,* at 233 (1946).

world in which every individual is entitled to choose his own values and standards? This question seems especially troublesome at a time when disciplines like legal history are as fragmented as they now appear to be. But neither the question nor possible answers to it are new.

Those who a century ago transformed religiously oriented American colleges like those of the professor who condemned evolution into modern universities serving a pluralistic, secular world have left us with a legacy with which to address the question. The creators of the modern university assumed that knowledge, meaning and standards of scholarship could emerge from the joint enterprise of individual scholars working together in scholarly communities. They put their assumption into practice by creating institutions such as academic departments, professional assocations and professional journals that would facilitate the establishment of a scholarly consensus.[46] This institutional legacy remains with us today.

At a theoretical level, the assumption that scholarly standards can emerge out of a consensus of individual scholars with quite different ideological and aesthetic preferences retains respectability today. Two of the leading philosophers of this century, Ludwig Wittgenstein and Jurgen Habermas, have argued that people who engage in an activity together do so on the basis of shared, common values even when they proclaim their values are different. People cannot engage in a common activity unless they agree at least implicitly upon rules for conducting it and share a common language with which they can communicate.[47] Two people, moreover, probably will not engage in the same activity unless they believe the activity has value, perhaps the same value for both of them.

Scholars who label themselves legal historians do, in fact, read and review each others' work and otherwise engage in discourse in a common language. They also share at least some assumptions about subjects that are and are not worth investigating: no one who calls himself an historian of American law would deem the law of slavery outside the pale of professional study, and no one would deem study of Beethoven's nine symphonies within the pale. Many American legal historians may also share common assumptions about the value of devoting their professional lives to study of the law's past; few, if any, have entered the discipline for pecuniary profit.

---

[46] See William E. Nelson, *The Roots of American Bureaucracy, 1830-1900,* at 87-95, 105-112 (1982).

[47] See Jurgen Habermas, *Legitimation Crisis* 10-11, 43-44, 109-110 (T. McCarthy trans. 1975); Ludwig Wittgenstein, *Philosophical Investigations* secs. 198-208, 239-242 (3d ed. G. Anscombe trans. 1958). See also Robert J. Fogelin, *Wittgenstein* 144-49 (1976).

Thus, however much legal historians may proclaim that their scholarship is tied to differing aesthetic and ideological values, they do, in fact, continue to engage in a common enterprise that entails acceptance of a common language, some common rules and perhaps some common value assumptions. The remainder of this chapter will suggest tentatively how some of the common rules and values accepted by most legal historians might be perceived as critical standards transcending the aesthetic and ideological preferences of individuals — standards for separating good work from bad and outstanding work from what is merely good.

1. *Standards of Minimal Scholarly Competency.* — Let me suggest two possible standards for distinguishing good legal history scholarship from bad. First, judgments can be made about the comprehensibility of a scholarly work. Second, judgments can be made about the factual accuracy of a work. Let us consider and analyze each sort of judgment in turn.

a. Comprehensibility. — I trust I can begin an analysis of the need for comprehensibility with the premise that scholars, at least in the field of legal history, normally have an obligation to write prose that others can understand. The ability to communicate with words is a prerequisite for entry at a minimal level into the disciplines of both history and law: a person who cannot communicate with others cannot engage in the descriptive and persuasive activities that are at the core of the two disciplines. This emphasis on the ability to communicate does not involve a judgment about which anyone is likely to disagree. Even if it were possible to imagine an historian or lawyer carrying on his profession without language, all historians and lawyers in fact communicate with language of some sort. It is thus sound to conclude that a legal historian whose prose cannot be comprehended is simply a poor legal historian.

In practice, however, most judgments about comprehensibility are not so simple. Difficulty arises because lack of skill on the part of a scholar attempting to communicate is not the only obstacle to effective communication. An author may be a very skillful writer, but a particular critic may lack sufficient intelligence or reading ability to understand what the author is saying. Communication will also fail when an author and his reader are using different languages. Before a reviewer can justly accuse an author of failing to communicate effectively, he should be certain that he and the author are using the same language and that the failure to communicate is attributable to the author's inability to write clearly rather than the reviewer's own inability to read effectively.

I suspect that most failures of communication arise neither from lack of writing skill on the part of the author[48] nor from lack of reading skill by the critic. Although I cannot confirm my suspicion with statistical documentation, its soundness is suggested by the extensive training in verbal skills which almost all American scholars receive before anything they write is published and by the daily activities of most scholars in the highly verbal academic world. An occasional scholar may be unable to write or read well enough to communicate effectively; hence a reviewer who is confident of his own skills and cannot understand an author's work must consider whether that author is simply unable to write. But the critic should recognize that most failures of communication occur not because anyone lacks basic verbal skills but because two scholars are using English so differently that they are, in a sense, using two different languages.

Thus, the ultimate question that a critic must address is when it is appropriate for an author to use language differently than he, the critic, does. That is an immensely difficult and complex question which cannot be addressed definitively in this brief chapter. Two reasons probably account for most disparate language usage in the discipline of American legal history. One is the hybrid nature of the discipline, which results in some scholars using the language of history and some using the language of law.[49] The other is that some scholars will decide that the standard language of legal and historical scholarship is for aesthetic or ideological reasons inadequate, and they will accordingly invent new language.[50]

---

[48] Although occasional sentences or paragraphs may fall below a minimally acceptable standard, most published writing in legal history is sufficiently well written to be readily comprehended by its readers. Perhaps a reviewer could evaluate a scholarly work by counting the number of times on which it lapses briefly from the minimal standard, but most of us, I suspect, would find such an evaluation trivial.

[49] Compare Douglas Greenberg, *Crime and Law Enforcement in the Colony of New York, 1691-1776* (1976), with Julius Goebel and T.R. Naughton, *Law Enforcement in Colonial New York: A Study in Criminal Procedure* (1664-1776) (1944). The issue of whether legal history should be written by lawyers or historians goes back at least to 1885, when Maitland argued that only lawyers could be legal historians. See Frederic W. Maitland, "Why the History of English Law Is Not Written," in 1 *The Collected Papers of Frederic William Maitland* 480, 493-94 (H. Fisher ed. 1911). For criticism of work by a nonlawyer for failing to appreciate legal subtleties, see "Book Note," 71 *Harv. L. Rev.* 1395 (1958).

[50] Consider, for example, the following sentence of Willard Hurst: "Three stories show law's relation to inertia, social function, and deliberated decision in social growth." J. Willard Hurst, *Law and Social Process in United States History* xiv (1960). The only explanation one can have for this sentence is that

I am convinced that good legal history can be written either in the language of history or in the language of law. It is not self-evident that historians must learn to write in the traditional jargon of law before they can be eligible to do legal history. Indeed, a legal historian might want to replace technical jargon with ordinary English whenever possible in order to reach a lay audience that cannot comprehend technical vocabulary. At other times, he might want to use technical vocabularly to bring greater precision to his prose. For example, an historian who tells of replevying a cow rather than of getting a cow back will inform a knowledgeable reader that the legal system was used to regain the cow. Depending upon the context of the word "replevin" and upon the reader's knowledge, the author may provide even more information. On the other hand, a reader who does not know the meaning of the word "replevin" will not understand what happened to the cow. In deciding whether to use the word "replevy" or the words "get back" to describe what happened to the cow, the legal historian must make carefully balanced judgments about the audience he is seeking to reach. Whatever he decides, his decision will be neither plainly wrong nor plainly right. A reviewer may perform a useful service by analyzing the judgment that the author of a book did make, but he ought neither lightly praise nor easily condemn an author for choosing either the same language or different language from the one he would have chosen. A reviewer who ignores the complexity involved in an author's decision is either ignorant of that complexity or somewhat dishonest in accusing the author of making a simplistic decision.

The complexities that arise when a reviewer seeks to second-guess an author's decision to use historical or legal language are trivial, however, compared to those facing a critic who is seeking to examine a language choice made on ideological grounds. The critic's task is equally difficult whether he speaks favorably or unfavorably of an author's ideological values. Consider, for example, whether the Lawrences and the Lowells of early nineteenth century Massachusetts should be labeled "builders of America," "mill owners," "entrepreneurs," "capitalists," or "pigs"? I know of no right way to make that decision, although I am quite certain that in making it, an author will reveal a great deal about his ideological values. I am also quite sure that an author's decision will attract and repel different segments of his audience, and that he will make his decision with some awareness of its impact. Because our pluralistic political order treats all ideological choices as equal and leaves individuals free to make the choices they prefer, an author's decision about how,

---

Hurst, an accomplished stylist, found ordinary language unsuitable to his needs and so invented new language, which he carefully defined elsewhere, to accomplish his rhetorical objective.

for instance, to characterize the Lawrences and the Lowells is properly his, and I can find no basis for a reviewer's approval or disapproval other than his own personal preference.

What is true about ideological judgments is also true about aesthetic ones. Aesthetic judgments commonly take the form of praise rather than condemnation: reviewers frequently comment on the pleasing style of an historian.[51] What is pleasing to some, however, will be a matter of indifference or even displeasure to others, and in a pluralistic order it is important that individual aesthetic preferences not be imposed on others. While I do not want to discourage reviewers from expressing aesthetic preferences, I do want them to make clear that those preferences are merely personal and must not be confused with widely shared judgments about quality that transcend personal preference.

There are a few writers whose inability to write English may interfere with comprehension of their work by anyone in the discipline of American legal history. In such cases, comprehensibility becomes a standard of quality transcending the personal aesthetic and ideological preferences of the individual critic and should be expressed as such. But only rarely will anyone be called upon to enforce this standard of quality in reference to published scholarly work. Normally, we enforce the standard not in our roles as scholars reviewing the work of other scholars, but in our roles as teachers examining the progress of our students. Most questions of comprehensibility that arise in reference to published work will turn on aesthetic and ideological preferences and on difficult judgments about the prospective audience for a scholarly work. Reviewers should be encouraged to analyze the preferences and judgments of authors and to specify how and why their own preferences and judgments might differ. But they should always keep in mind that their own preferences and judgments are merely personal and, as such, are entitled to no greater weight than the preferences and judgments of others.

b. Factual Accuracy. — Just as comprehensibility is a standard of quality that rarely should be applied negatively to published scholarship, factual inaccuracy is also an allegation that the critic should make only occasionally and with great care. Karl Llewellyn, it will be recalled, was quite convinced that Richard Morris was wrong about important facts, but in the hindsight of a half century Llewellyn's charges have not been

---

[51] See, e.g., William H. Dunham, "Book Review," 67 *Yale L.J.* 763 (1958), where Maitland is described as a "poet in his skill to pick and place the *mot juste,* and designer of epigram and paradox." Id. at 763.

substantiated and Morris has, in large part, been vindicated.[52] Llewellyn should not have accused Morris of factual inaccuracy, but instead should have recognized that Morris was examining facts from a different perspective than he and hence was perceiving them differently.

Important studies on the psychology of human understanding, which have been synthesized in books such as E.S.Gombrich's *Art and Illusion*[53] and Thomas S. Kuhn's *The Structure of Scientific Revolutions,*[54] indicate that the human mind can often interpret a single sense datum in more than one way and that the interpretation given to the datum depends on preexisting expectations in the mind. Consider, for example, the following black marks on white paper:[55]

[52] Llewellyn had three specific substantive disagreements with Morris. (1) Morris thought that there were some matters as to which thirteen American colonies shared a common legal culture; Llewellyn did not. (2) Morris thought that the common law was an important segment of English law with which colonial law could be usefully compared; Llewellyn thought that local English law was more important, especially in the lives of the people who settled in America. (3) Morris attributed some American departures from the common law to frontier-like conditions in the American colonies; Llewellyn attributed them to "the background of the particular colonists." Llewellyn, supra note 22, at 731. In regard to all three substantive disagreements, Llewellyn's views are not self-evidently correct. Furthermore, during the past half century considerable scholarship has appeared agreeing with Morris' position that the legal systems of the thirteen colonies were in significant respects similar, see, e.g., Lawrence M. Friedman, *A History of American Law* 32, 49 (1973); William E. Nelson, "The Eighteenth-Century Background of John Marshall's Constitutional Jurisprudence," 76 *Mich. L. Rev.* 893, 902-17 (1978); that the common law was an important element in those legal systems, see, e.g., "Editor's Introduction: A Guide to the Use of the Plymouth Court Records," in 1 David T. Konig ed., *Plymouth Court Records, 1686-1859,* at 139, 149-74 (1978); and that frontier-like conditions had some impact on colonial law. See, e.g., J. Goebel & T.R. Naughton, supra note 44; David T. Konig, *Law and Society in Puritan Massachusetts, Essex County, 1629-1692,* at 36-46, 60-63. (1979).

[53] Ernst Gombrich, *Art and Illusion* (1960).

[54] Thomas S. Kuhn, *The Structure of Scientific Revolutions* (2d ed. 1970).

[55] "Rabbit or duck?" *Die Fliegenden Blatter,* reprinted in E. Gombrich,

Some readers will see those marks as a picture of a duck; others, as a picture of a rabbit; and still others, who are familiar with the body of literature on which I am here drawing, as the duck-rabbit. What a reader sees will depend on what he expects to see and his expectations, in turn, will be conditioned by other sense data in conjunction with which these black marks on paper are being examined.

These studies of the psychology of human understanding are important in explaining how legal historians should and often do organize their data. They can help explain, for instance, why two highly competent historians like Morton Horwitz and A.W.B. Simpson can interpret eighteenth century contract law so differently. As anyone who has studied contract law is aware, many of the cases are quite ambiguous and can be read and synthesized with other cases in a number of divergent ways. The way in which a particular legal historian reads the many ambiguous cases will depend, I am convinced, on the other cases that he has in mind and on the purposes for which he is studying the cases. If, like Horwitz, he is seeking to explain legal development in the Northeastern United States and has the pattern of legal and social change that occurred in New England in mind as a model for his explanation, he will read the ambiguous cases differently than if, like Simpson, he is seeking to explain the history of English contract law against a background of modern doctrine. Neither Horwitz nor Simpson was guilty of factual inaccuracy, and it was wrong for Simpson so to accuse Horwitz. Each was merely making the interpretative judgments that must be made if ambiguous black marks on yellowing paper, which have no single correct meaning in themselves, are to be synthesized into a pattern that does have meaning.

This is not the place to evaluate the epistemological position advanced in books like Gombrich's and Kuhn's. But I want to argue that, unless a critic of legal history scholarship can be certain that the Gombrich-Kuhn position is wrong, he must hesitate before accusing another legal historian of committing factual error. A critic should search instead for a model of explanation that could have induced the author to interpret the source materials as he did, recognizing that in a pluralistic academic order the author is privileged to select his own model rather than the critic's. Although it might be helpful for a critic to explain why he finds his explanatory model superior to the author's, he should not accuse the author of making a factual error unless he is certain that no perspective

---

supra note 53 (Copyright (c) 1960 by the Trustees of the National Gallery of Art. Reprinted by courtesy of Princeton University Press).

exists that permits the author's interpretion of ambiguous sources. A critic must distinguish between plain errors of fact and factual interpretations derived from differing perspectives, one of which the critic might prefer but none of which is in any ultimate sense superior to the others. If critics carefully keep in mind this distinction between factual errors and differing factual interpretations, they will, I believe, rarely find plain errors in published scholarly work. Judgments of plain error may often be made of student work, but the training that professional scholars in legal history have undergone, together with the processes of reading and editing to which their work has been subjected, should insure that few errors appear in print.

2. *Standards for Identifying Outstanding Scholarship.* — The two standards of quality on which I hope all scholars in the discipline of legal history can agree — the requirements of comprehensibility and factual accuracy — set a floor that properly distinguishes scholarship which is genuinely competent and hence merits publication from that which is not. Only on rare occasions, however, can published work properly be criticized on the basis of these minimal standards. Most published legal history is entitled to recognition as scholarship that meets basic standards of professional competence. Of course, everyone will prefer some pieces of competent scholarship over others. Are there any principled bases for these preferences? Is it possible to distinguish between scholarship that is truly outstanding and scholarship that is merely competent?

Scholarship must be at least somewhat unconventional in order to be outstanding; indeed, to Maitland, "an orthodox history seem[ed] . . . a contradiction in terms."[56] There are two reasons why unconventionality is important. The first is definitional: work that adheres to widely shared conventions will not stand out from other work that adheres to the same conventions. In the absence of distinctiveness — perhaps a better word would be distinction — a scholarly work will be ordinary and commonplace, not outstanding.

The second reason work cannot be outstanding unless it is unconventional relates to the processes by which knowledge grows and to the definition of scholarship as that which contributes to knowledge's growth. Most of the time knowledge grows incrementally: a scholar who is pursuing the conventional thought modes of his discipline uncovers new facts that lend support to a commonly accepted perspective or pattern of analysis. Occasionally, however, knowledge takes a large step forward. In

[56] Frederic W. Maitland, supra note 49, at 491.

science, those large steps are associated with names like Copernicus, Newton, and Einstein; in legal history, with names like Maitland and Hurst. All five of these scholars broke out of conventional modes of thought and pushed the frontiers of knowledge well forward by creating new conventions of thought. They stood out because they were extra ordinary; and they were extra ordinary because they rejected many of the scholarly conventions of their time, did not ask commonplace questions, and did not ground their work on widely held perspectives and analytical forms.

Unconventionality is thus a prerequisite for outstanding scholarly work. Conventional work can expand knowledge only at the margins —only by increments. Only unconventional scholarship can enable knowledge to leap forward. Not all unconventional work, however, moves knowledge forward: much of it — perhaps most of it — does not contribute to the growth of knowledge at all. Knowledge ultimately is a possession of the community of scholars, not of the idiosyncratic individual; an unconventional idea appreciated only by its creator will die with him. For a work of legal history to advance knowledge, its unconventional ideas must be addressed to problems of concern to others and must influence the way in which others think about those problems. A great legal historian not only must break with the conventions of his predecessors but also must create new conventions for his successors. He must be influential as well as original.

No one doubts the greatness of Frederic William Maitland. His and Sir Frederick Pollock's *The History of English Law before the Time of Edward I*[57] is a true masterpiece. S.F.C. Milsom has called it "one of the greatest works of English history," containing a portrait of the past that was largely Maitland's "own creation."[58] But The History of English Law was not only original; it was also influential. As Milsom has said, the book not only remains "useful to scholars"; "it is still their starting-point."[59] Maitland showed that English law and the English Constitution were not, as Whig historians in essence had assumed, immemorial, but that they had beginnings. He showed that English law and the English constitution were human creations and were subject to human change. Maitland thereby enabled us to conceive of Anglo-American legal history as a process by which rules develop in response to political and social

---

[57] Frederick Pollock & Frederic W. Maitland, *The History of English Law before the Time of Edward* I (2d ed. 1968) (orig. ed. 1898).

[58] S.F.C. Milson, "Introduction," to 1 Frederick Pollock & Frederic W. Maitland, *The History of English Law Before the Time of Edward I,* at xxv (2d ed. 1968).

[59] Id. at xiii.

decisions, instead of a process in which professional analysts work out the implications of timeless principles.

Maitland's work had a unique impact: it has influenced at their core our conceptions of law and legal history. Like all processes of influence, however, Maitland's was a product both of his intellectual effort and of his audience's receptivity to that effort. His creative intelligence perceived a new mode of thinking about early English law, and his painstaking research uncovered evidence in support of his creative insights. His work would have come to naught, however, had not his audience, for reasons of its own, been searching for an insight such as his. His audience was ready to find his new historical analysis and the evidence supporting it persuasive.

J. Willard Hurst's *Law and the Conditions of Freedom in the Nineteenth Century United States,*[60] and his follow-up, *Law and Economic Growth: The Legal History of the Lumber Industry in Wisconsin, 1836-1915,*[61] stand out for the same reasons. Prior to these two books, the common law in America typically had been studied as an elite, intellectual force, disconnected from economic growth and social practice. Hurst broke with this convention and demonstrated how the common law had both responded to and caused economic and social change at several levels of American society. His unconventional approach has borne fruit: his work has influenced many subsequent legal historians to study the relationship between law and economic and social change.[62]

No other American legal historian has been as creatively unconventional and as influential as Willard Hurst. Hurst identified economic and social forces and forces of drift and inertia that previous legal historians had ignored.[63] Few scholars will be able to make a similar contribution in the future, since the major forces affecting American legal development — legal principle, precedent, shared moral values, economic compulsion, technological change and social needs — already have been identified. But other forms of unconventionality do exist, and note must be taken of them, as well as of other forms of influence, in order for us to be as explicit as possible about how these two qualities can be used to distinguish between outstanding and merely competent legal history.

---

[60] J. Willard Hurst, *Law and the Conditions of Freedom in the Nineteenth Century United States* (1956).

[61] J. Willard Hurst, *Law and Economic Growth: The Legal History of the Lumber Industry in Wisconsin, 1836-1915* (1964).

[62] See, e.g., Lawrence M. Friedman, supra note 52; Harry N. Scheiber, "Federalism and the American Economic Order, 1789-1910," 10 *L. & Soc'y Rev.* 57 (1975).

[63] See J. Willard Hurst, supra note 50, at 28-92.

Two forms of unconventionality are illustrated by Robert M. Cover's *Justice Accused: Antislavery and the Judicial Process.*[64] One form of unconventionality is Cover's interdisciplinary approach: Cover turns to what he calls "the 'theory' of cognitive dissonance"[65] for an understanding of how judges react to pressures from formal legal rules that are inconsistent with their moral values. The insights available to American legal history from disciplines other than law and history are numerous, waiting to be exploited by scholars seeking to organize data in ways other than the commonplace and conventional.

The second form of unconventionality appearing in *Justice Accused* is Cover's explicit analysis of his personal, idiosyncratic reasons for writing the book. As Cover explained, "the determination" to write *Justice Accused* arose out of "a short polemic [written in 1968] against . . . judicial complicity in the crimes of Vietnam," which Cover compared "with judicial acquiescence in the injustices of Negro slavery."[66] *Justice Accused* inquired how judges could participate in such injustice. The important fact about this inquiry is that it was not framed conventionally as a neutral and objective investigation of slavery cases: Cover did not repress a highly personal sense of injustice to achieve what might be called scholarly objectivity. Rather, he used his personal values to launch an unconventional and creative inquiry into a subject others had earlier studied. Other scholars can also avoid conventionality and make creative contributions to knowledge if they heed instead of repress their idiosyncratic responses to events both past and current.

A third way for a legal historian to be unconventional is to exploit source materials in novel ways, as John P. Reid did in his *Law for the Elephant: Property and Social Behavior on the Overland Trail.*[67] Reid used diaries of lay travelers on the overland trail as records of legal decisionmaking on the trail, thereby gaining an insight into life on the trail that had eluded earlier historians. Other source materials could be used in similarly unconventional and hence creative ways.

A fourth form of unconventionality is illustrated by Morton Horwitz' treatment of negligence law in his *Transformation of American Law.*[68] Horwitz achieved a breakthrough in our understanding of the concept of

---

[64] Robert M. Cover, *Justice Accused: Antislavery and the Judicial Process* 227 (1975).

[65] Id. at 227.

[66] Id at xi.

[67] John P. Reid, *Law for the Elephant: Property and Social Behavior on the Overland Trail* (1980).

[68] See Morton J. Horwitz, *The Transformation of American Law,* 1780-1860 (1977).

negligence initially by engaging in linguistic analysis of the concept, demonstrating that in the eighteenth century negligence did not mean that a defendant had been at fault but only that he had neglected to perform a duty. He then expanded the breakthrough by showing how the newly defined linguistic concept, when applied to certain fact situations, ineluctably was transformed into the concept of negligence as fault liability. Horwitz's book illustrates well how linguistic analysis of legal concepts, and application of those concepts with their different meanings to varied fact patterns, has an immense capacity to produce unconventional insight into the structure of legal doctrine.

The examples given above do not constitute the only forms that unconventionality in legal history scholarship can assume. Unconventionality can take as many forms as the ingenuity of scholars can conceive. But I hope the examples above can assist critics and scholars in identifying unconventionality — an essential ingredient of outstanding scholarship.

The other ingredient of outstanding scholarship is the influence that it attains. The work of Maitland and Hurst typifies one substantial way in which scholarship can have influence. Both have had disciples who have investigated the questions posed by their mentors' methodological and sociological assumptions. Roscoe Pound's work was influential in a different way. His *The Formative Era of American Law*[69] has been one of the most widely read books in American legal history, due in part to the international repute and large network of friends that Pound possessed when he published it. Although Pound has not had disciples, his wide influence has resulted in other scholars addressing the same questions that he did, if for no other reason than to prove Pound wrong.

What is common to the work of Maitland, Hurst and Pound — and what is at the core of the concept of influence used in this chapter — is that an audience thought that their work set the parameters of the field of legal history and determined the questions to be asked. It must be emphasized that, while an author can decide whether to make his work conventional or unconventional, only his audience can decide how much influence it will have. The audience, moreover, will make its determination over a period of time. As a result, a critic can never be certain at the time of a work's publication whether it is outstanding; all he can do is predict whether the work will become influential and outstanding.

What, then, can one assert about the quality of a work of legal history? First, a critic can determine whether a work is minimally competent: whether it is comprehensible, factually accurate, and makes a contribution to knowledge. Second, he can make a judgment about a

---

[69] Roscoe Pound, *The Formative Era of American Law* (1938).

work's conventionality — a judgment that will indicate whether the work has the potential to be outstanding. Third, he can predict whether an unconventional work is likely to become influential — a prediction of the work's potential to be outstanding rather than merely competent.

3. *Judgments Based on Aesthetic and Ideological Preference.*— In addition to making judgments about quality reflecting a consensus of values shared by most practitioners of legal history, critics can also express a judgment on the basis of their personal aesthetic and ideological preferences. Many aesthetic and ideological critiques are possible. A consensus historian, for example, might criticize a neo-Marxist for focusing upon American legal history with a paradigm that fails to take into account unique characteristics of American social life and thought. A neo-Marxist, on the other hand, might criticize a consensus historian for failing to recognize how those very characteristics have been used by elites to deprive other groups of a share in the nation's wealth. Ideological criticism can also occur when a reviewer, who shares an ideology with an author, accuses the author of failing to interpret or apply the ideology properly.[70] The range of ideological criticism is, indeed, as extensive as the range of ideologies that exist in the nation's pluralistic political culture.

Aesthetic criticism can be equally diverse. A reviewer could, for example, comment upon the turgid, as distinguished from the incomprehensible style of a book. Or a reviewer might state why he would have preferred an author to organize his book differently. No doubt the number of writing styles, tones, and organizational structures approaches the number of critics.

What is important about aesthetic and ideological criticism is that it be expressed openly and honestly, not disguised as a comment upon the scholarly quality of work. The importance of open expression lies in the pluralist nature of our political and academic order. That pluralism, as I have already suggested, rests on our awareness that transcendent ideological and aesthetic values either do not exist or cannot be apprehended with certainty by any individual. In either event, a critic can claim to know better than an author only what pleases him ideologically or aesthetically, not what is ultimately superior.

Thus, when the critic claims that a scholarly work is simply inferior, I think he is guilty of one of three things. First, he may have failed to understand the differences between his own and the author's values. This was, I suspect, Llewellyn's failure in his review of Morris' *Studies in the*

---

[70] For an example of such a review see Eugene Genovese, "Book Review," 91 *Harv. L. Rev.* 726 (1978).

History of American Law:[71] Llewellyn never saw that Morris had a different conception than he of the ends and purposes of legal history scholarship; he could see only that Morris had failed to pursue his — Llewellyn's — conception effectively. Such criticism must be seen as what it is: a failure of insight and analysis on the critic's part. Second, a reviewer may recognize that an author's work rests on a set of values different from his own, and may even recognize that those values are as worthy as his own, but he may nevertheless proceed to criticize the author for failing to follow his, the critic's, value system. I would find such a failure to disclose, with its possible detriment to another, dishonest. Third, the critic may not be committed to a pluralist vision, but instead may be prepared to use the power of his pen to impose his views on others. It is not illogical for someone who has no doubt of his premises to try to sweep away all opposition and to impose what he sees as the truth on others,[72] but those pluralists among us who do not believe in ultimate truths should be aware of the schemes of those who do.

In arguing that aesthetic and ideological judgments should not be disguised by a reviewer as judgments about quality, I do not wish to be misunderstood. I am not contending that it is impossible for a critic to make judgments about the quality of a scholarly work. On the contrary, as I have already suggested, such judgments can and should be made. But judgments about quality should reflect what a critic honestly knows to be the standards and values of the discipline of legal history as a whole. When a critic bases judgments on standards and values that never have commanded or no longer continue to command broad assent, he shows himself to be either dishonest or not initiated into the standards of the field.

D. *Conclusion*

The discipline of American legal history will benefit if critics carefully distinguish critical standards shared by all legal historians from their own personal aesthetic and ideological values. If critics adhere to standards at all similar to those I have outlined above, they will find little published work that can be labeled incompetent. Moreover, they will have only a limited capacity to predict whether the scholarship they are reviewing will become influential and hence outstanding. If they adhere to standards like those I have outlined, critics will be compelled to eschew false standards of quality and to discuss openly the personal values and the

[71] Karl Llewellyn, supra note 22.

[72] Cf. Abrams v. United States, 250 U.S. 616, 630 (1919) (Holmes, J., dissenting).

perspectives on the past that cause them to like or dislike a work under review.

Critics who engage in such open discussion can be honest and fair to those they criticize. They will also be able to rescue the book review genre from its present sterile state, in which reviewers anachronistically proclaim unilinear standards of quality that few scholars any longer accept and then apply those standards to work written from entirely different perspectives. Critics sensitive to the current fragmented state of the discipline can transform book reviews into genuinely philosophic discussions about the ends and methods of legal history research.

Explicit discussion of the values, preferences and perspectives that affect our judgment of the scholarly work of others will instruct all of us in the premises underlying our work and in the variety of ways in which we can structure our own intellectual and moral lives. Such discussion will make us aware of the alternative ways in which we can study and write about the past; such an awareness, in turn, will compel us to consider thoughtfully many of the steps that we now take unconsciously as we do our research and writing. I expect that better criticism will in the end produce better scholarship.

INDEX

This index consists of several sections: (1) an author index, (2) a table of cases, (3) an index of personal names,(4) a geographical index, (5) a chronological index, and (6)a subject index. A reader seeking references to an individual such as James Willard Hurst should search in the author index for references to scholarship written by Hurst and in the personal name index for references to scholarship about Hurst. A reader seeking references to work written about a specific jurisdiction or about a specific region, such as the frontier, should use the geographical index. A reader seeking references to work about a specific period, such as 1760-1790, should use the chronological index. A reader seeking references to a specific subject, such as the Supreme Court, should use the subject index.

AUTHOR INDEX

TABLE OF CASES

PERSONAL NAME INDEX

GEOGRAPHICAL INDEX

CHRONOLOGICAL INDEX

1600-1689

1689-1760

1760-1789

1789-1860

1860-1932

1932-1980

SUBJECT INDEX

www.ingramcontent.com/pod-product-compliance
Ingram Content Group UK Ltd.
Pitfield, Milton Keynes, MK11 3LW, UK
UKHW041646011026
15471UKWH00018B/70

9 781587 982804